THE
ANCIENT
CELTS

THE ANCIENT CELTS

BARRY CUNLIFFE

Oxford   New York

OXFORD UNIVERSITY PRESS

1997

…ord University Press, Great Clarendon Street, Oxford OX2 6DP

Oxford New York

Athens Auckland Bangkok Bogota Bombay
Buenos Aires Calcutta Cape Town Dar es Salaam
Delhi Florence Hong Kong Istanbul Karachi
Kuala Lumpur Madras Madrid Melbourne
Mexico City Nairobi Paris Singapore
Taipei Tokyo Toronto Warsaw

and associated companies in
Berlin Ibadan

Oxford is a trade mark of Oxford University Press

Published in the United States
by Oxford University Press Inc., New York

British Library Cataloguing in Publication Data
Data available

Library of Congress Cataloging in Publication Data
Data available
ISBN 0–19–815010–5

1 3 5 7 9 10 8 6 4 2

Typeset by Hope Services (Abingdon) Ltd.
Printed in Great Britain
on acid-free paper by
Butler & Tanner Ltd., Frome

Preface

FOR two and a half thousand years the Celts have continued to fascinate those who have come into contact with them. For the Greeks and Romans the fascination was tinged with fear tempered with a degree of respect for Celtic prowess in battle. Later generations, further removed from the reality of the barbarian Celts of the first millennium BC, generated their own myths and stereotypes about the past, recreating Celtic ancestors for themselves in the image of the day designed to explain their own attitudes and aspirations and to provide a legitimacy for actions. The study of the Celts and of our changing visions of them offer an incomparable insight into the human need to establish an identity—and of the difficulties which this poses to archaeologists, who, by their best endeavours, attempt to remain objective.

It could be argued that biased historical anecdotes, ill-understood patterns of early language development, and hard archaeological 'facts'—the artefacts, ecofacts, and structures of the past recovered through excavation—should not, and indeed cannot, be brought together to create a coherent picture of the past. The position is firmly taken by some and energetically argued; it is not one with which I have much sympathy. Given an array of disparate evidence, we would, I believe, be failing if we were to fight shy of the challenges posed by using every available scrap in our attempt to construct a European protohistory. In doing so we will, inevitably, be drawn into simplification and generalization, laying ourselves open to criticism from the purists, but better the attempt to create a whole, however imperfect, than to be satisfied with the minute examination of only a part.

In writing this book, within the entirely reasonable constraints suggested by the publishers, I have found it impossible to go into areas of detail which I would like to have covered, while at the same time being drawn into the wider themes of European pre- and protohistory. Rather than adhere to the preconceptions of my original plan, I have allowed myself to be led by the subject. What emerges is much less an 'archaeology' than it might have been.

My other indulgence is to have written the text during a sabbatical term living in a house on the north coast of Brittany, overlooking a narrow bay to the headland of Le Yaudet beyond. In the Late Iron Age, the promontory was defended by a massive rampart, and it is quite conceivable, though yet unproven, that it was one of the communities attacked by Caesar in 56 BC. Living here in Brittany has provided a constant reminder of the Celtic world. In the nearby church at Loguivy-lès-Lannion we attended a musical celebration for the pardon of St Ivy. The long address of welcome was in Breton.

Then followed music and singing dominated by bagpipes and bombardes identical to those played by the shepherds in the Adoration depicted on the seventeenth-century altarpiece above. Two months later, in July, the local *fête folkloric* was held within the promontory fort of Le Yaudet. The event is an entirely new creation only some ten years old, but it is fast becoming a focus for the community. The displays of old farm machinery and ancient crafts are as fascinating to the local population as they are to the tourists, and in the evening, as dinner in the open air proceeds, old and young alike join in the singing of Breton songs and the dancing, and listen to the telling of stories. It is, of course, a conscious recreation of a past, but a past not long gone and one which offers a much-needed sense of identity and continuity in a fast changing world.

The archaeology of Le Yaudet, the Breton language still spoken, and the underlying sense of a Celtic ethnicity are aspects of the phenomenon of the Celts: in their coherence and disparity they provide a leitmotiv for the book to follow.

Finally a few acknowledgements: to the editorial and design departments of Oxford University Press for their help and advice throughout; to the many individuals and institutions who provided photographs; to Alison Wilkins for producing a new series of line drawings; to Lynda Smithson for preparing the text; and to my family for their forbearance and understanding with my mild obsession.

Pont Roux   B. W. C.
January 1996

Contents

List of Colour Plates

List of Maps

1
Visions of the Celts

WITHOUT the descriptions and speculations of Greek and Roman writers, our understanding of the Iron Age communities of central and western Europe—the traditional homeland of the Celts—would be very different. Alone, the mute archaeological evidence would allow us to sketch a warrior society focused in west central Europe whose aristocracy demonstrated its prowess through elaborately equipped burials. Over the period from the eighth to the fifth centuries different ways of displaying status were introduced. We would be able to recognize growing links with classical cultures of the west Mediterranean, reaching a new intensity in the period from the mid-sixth century to the mid-fifth BC, after which local schools of fine metalwork, using concepts and techniques learned from the Mediterranean world, developed to serve the élite.

The archaeological evidence would amply demonstrate the emergence of a more warlike society by the fourth century whose values and technology, represented largely in the material culture recovered from cemeteries, spread across much of Europe, from northern France to Romania and from Poland to the Po Valley. Without the classical sources as a guide, there would be much learned speculation about the meaning of this phenomenon. Towards the end of the second century and throughout the first, in the decades preceding the Roman Conquest, we would observe an intensification in production and exchange over much of the central area, focusing on large nucleated settlements, many of them defended, which were beginning to appear at this time.

If we stood back and took a broader geographical perspective, it would become immediately clear that at any one time there was considerable cultural variation from one area to another: we would be able to identify core zones of innovation and intensification, and peripheries in which these developments were reflected with decreasing clarity as distance from the core grew.

What we would *not* be able to appreciate with any degree of certainty is the long period of conflict between the Celtic communities of the Po Valley and the Roman world; and we would be entirely ignorant of the violent raids of the Celts deep into Greece in the third century and of the large-scale migrations of communities from the Middle Danube into the heart of Asia Minor which followed. Nor would we have in our minds visions of white robed Druids cutting mistletoe with golden sickles when the moon was just at the right stage of its cycle, or of harsh-voiced warrior queens with waist-length golden hair, or of feasting warriors slurping their wine through drooping moustaches while boasting outrageously of their prowess. The classical sources provide a storyline and colour. They offer us a range of characters, with a large supporting cast. There is a real excitement in following their achievements and their failures.

Whilst the purist archaeologist might argue that one should study the Iron Age communities of Europe only through the archaeological data, since the classical sources by their inherent partiality and deliberate manipulation distort our understanding, to reject such a rich vein of anecdote would be defeatist: it would admit to an inability to treat the sources critically.

The Greek and Roman authors have provided us with their own vision of the Celts—a vision born of contemporary or near contemporary experience. That vision has pervaded Celtic studies for 2,000 years and cannot be ignored.

The Graeco-Roman Vision

The peoples who we may now recognize collectively as the Continental Celts are referred to by a variety of names in the classical sources. The Roman historians writing of the migrations from north of the Alps to the Po Valley and beyond called them *Galli*, and this tradition was followed by Polybius, to whom they were *Galatae*, a name also commonly used in other Greek sources. Most of the first-century BC writers, however, realized that these names were interchangeable with the Greek *Keltoi* and Latin *Celtae*. Indeed Caesar, writing of the inhabitants of central Gaul, specifically says: 'we call [them] Gauls, though in their own language they are called Celts.' The second-century AD Greek writer Pausanius also stresses that *Keltoi* is a more long-established term than *Galli*. The simplest way to explain this apparent confusion would be to accept that *Celtae/Keltoi* was the general name by which the broad sweep of peoples stretching from north of the Alps to Iberia were known to the classical world, and knew themselves, and that *Galli/Galatae* was a specific term applied to those tribes who chose to migrate to the south and south-east. Caesar's phrase 'we call them Gauls' may be thought to take with it the implication that the term had a Mediterranean origin. One possibility is that it comes from an Indo-European word meaning 'stranger' or 'enemy', in which case it can hardly be an ethnonym.

Knowledge of the Celts grew slowly before the fourth century BC. One of the earliest references, which may contain material going back to the sixth century, is provided in the rather florid and style-conscious poem *Ora Maritima* written by Rufus Festus Avienus at the end of the fourth century AD in which the poet sets out to display his considerable learning by quoting from authors, many of whose texts no longer exist. Among them was an early sailing manual referred to most conveniently as the *Massilliot Periplus*. On internal evidence this lost work is thought to date to about 600 BC. The importance of the source is the information it gives about the Atlantic sea-ways and the tin-producing regions. Avienus makes only one direct reference to the Celts when he mentions that beyond the tin-producing Oestrymnides was a land now occupied by the Celts, who took it from the Ligurians. The vague nature of the reference and the lack of geographical or chronological precision rob it of much significance except the existence of the name at a supposedly early date. Rather more interest attaches to his naming of Britain as *Albion* and of Ireland as *Iernè* (whence Old Irish *Érin* and modern *Éire*). Both names are widely accepted to be in an early form of Celtic.

The geographer Hecataeus of Miletus, who wrote at the end of the sixth century BC, also had access to some knowledge of the Celts. He was aware that the Greek colony of Massalia, founded about 600 BC, lay in the land of the Ligurians, which was near the territory of the Celts, and that the settlement at Narbo (Narbonne) was Celtic. Elsewhere he mentions *Nyrax* as a Celtic city. No certain identification can be offered, but Noreia in Austria has been favoured by some commentators. Hecataeus, then, firmly establishes the presence of Celts in southern Gaul in the late sixth century.

Herodotus of Halicarnassus, writing in the early fifth century BC, makes reference to Celts in his *Histories*, though he admits that his information about the west is imperfect. He provides three geographical 'facts': that the source of the Danube is in the land of the Celts; that it rises near the Celtic city of Pyrene; and that the Celts lived west of the 'Pillars of Hercules' (Straits of Gibraltar) next to the Cynetoi, who were the westernmost peoples of Europe. Thus Herodotus' informants seem to have provided him with information about Celts living in south-west Iberia and central Europe. The mention of Pyrene being near the source of the Danube does, however, present some difficulty if it is assumed to be related geographically to the Pyrenees and much scholarly effort has been spent in trying to explain this insoluble confusion.

By the fourth century the Greeks had come to accept that the Celts occupied a large swath of western Europe from Iberia to the Upper Danube. Ephorus (*c.*405–330), in regarding them as one of the four great barbarian peoples of the world, along with the Scythians, Persians, and Libyans, was reflecting the broad general model which helped the Greeks to explain the nature of the periphery beyond the civilized Mediterranean core.

It was during the fourth century that information about the Celtic peoples began to accumulate, when Celtic bands became involved in the politics and military affairs of the Mediterranean as settlers, raiders, and mercenaries. Knowledge of the large-scale migration of Celts from north of the Alps to the Po Valley *c.*400, and their subsequent raids southwards against Rome and beyond beginning in c.390, soon reached the Greek world, which gained first-hand experience of Celtic warriors, who, along with Iberians, were employed as mercenary troops in the war between the Spartans and Thebes in 367 BC. Thus, when Plato (429–347) in his *Laws* describes the Celts as warlike and hard-drinking, he may have been doing so on a basis of fact rather than repeating a stereotype of 'barbarians'.

Aristotle (384–322) clearly had access to a number of sources on which to base his generalized comments about Celtic peoples and he was certainly aware of the attack on Rome. For him the Celts were a hardy northern people: they exposed their children to their harsh climate with little clothing to toughen them, and excessive obesity among men was punished. They were warlike and ferocious and fearless to the point of irrationality, they took little notice of their women and rather preferred male company, and they had strict rules of hospitality especially to strangers. A lost text, *Magicus*, sometimes ascribed to Aristotle, is said to mention the existence of Druids and holy men among the Celts and Galatae. The Aristotelian stereotype is a compound of anecdotal scraps presented within a vision of how barbarians ought to be. The balance of fact and prejudice is difficult to assess, but the range of information available from first-hand observation had greatly increased during the fourth century and it would be surprising if Aristotle had not used it with some judgement and discretion.

While the intrusion of Celtic peoples into the Mediterranean world increased familiarity of them, expeditions, like that undertaken by Pytheas of Massalia, c.320–10, will have broadened the knowledge base still further. Pytheas sailed extensively along the Atlantic sea-ways in a voyage of discovery, no doubt underpinned by sound economic motives, exploring the tin-producing peninsulas of the west, and the south and east coasts of Britain, and even venturing still further north. For him the British Isles lay north of the land of the Celts and were known as the *Pretanic* islands. There is no suggestion in the surviving quotations about his voyage that he regarded the Pretani as Celtic.

In parallel with the scientific discoveries of men like Pytheas and the philosophical considerations of Aristotle, Greek mythology expanded to take account of the Celts. According to Timaeus, they were descended either from the union of Polyphemus and Galatea or from the giant Keltos. Another version sees the Galatians as the descendants of Galatos, the son of Cyclops and Galatea. A different tradition assigns the fatherhood of Galatos or Keltos to Heracles, who, during his wanderings in the west, was seduced by Keltine, the beautiful daughter of King Bretannos. Unable to resist her charms, and her refusal to retrieve the cattle of Geryon, he felt impelled to sleep with her.

The Celts were brought into much sharper focus for the Romans and the Greeks during the fourth and third centuries BC, as hordes of warriors, sometimes accompanied by migrating communities, thrust into Italy, Greece, and Asia Minor. For Rome the dangerous conflict lasted from the initial advance southwards towards Rome soon after 400 BC to the decisive battle of Telamon in

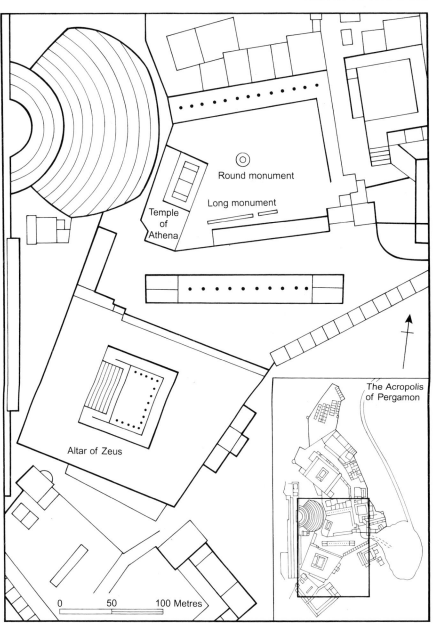

Round monument

Long monument

Temple
of
Athena

Altar of Zeus

The Acropolis
of Pergamon

0   50   100 Metres

1 The acropolis of Pergamum in western Turkey was the focus of Pergamene power in the third and second centuries BC. The two religious precincts, the temple of Athena and the altar of Zeus, were focal points for the display of sculptural compositions celebrating Pergamene victories over the Celtic raiders. Through these monuments the kings of Pergamum were laying claims to be the saviours of Hellenism.

225. The Greek confrontation was shorter lived, focusing around the invasion of 280–78, which culminated in an attack on Delphi. In Asia Minor the Hellenistic and Roman armies were to confront Galatians throughout the century or so after the initial migration from Europe in the aftermath of their Greek expedition.

It was during these two centuries that the Celtic stereotype was to acquire its familiar form. They were wild fearless warriors, irrationally brave in the first onslaught but prone to wild despair when the battle turned against them.

Unpredictable and unreliable as allies, who could be too drunk or too paralysed by superstitious fear to fight, they were a people otherwise easily aroused to battle fury. And above all they were barbarians—people of alien behaviour, cruel, and prone to such savagery as human sacrifice and even cannibalism. It is easy to see in this broad sketch—a sketch which any Greek or Roman schoolboy might have been expected to turn out—a standard, almost timeless, description of 'the enemy from without', and yet beneath its simplistic exaggeration lie some elements of the truth learned by the bitter experience of two centuries of confrontation and conflict.

The historians of Greece and Rome, writers like Polybius (*c.*204–*c.*122 BC), Livy (59 BC–AD 17), and Pausanias (late second century AD), were all attempting to project particular images of history. Their individual presentations of the Celt were necessarily conditioned by this, but the common thread which all wished to communicate was of their own systems triumphing over forces from without—the rational, civilized order of state control contrasted with the wild, savage, chaos of the primitive barbarians. It is, therefore, the antitheses to the ideals of Graeco-Roman civilization that were emphasized in the classical accounts of the Celts. To point up the classical achievement, however, the enemy had also to be presented as a worthy opponent, fearless in battle and with a savage nobility that made his defeat the more remarkable.

These attitudes come together in the dramatic visual reality of contemporary sculpture. The savagery and chaos of the Gauls looting a temple are brilliantly portrayed in a sculptured frieze of the second century BC from Civitalba,

2 The Dying Gaul. The marble statue, now in the Capitoline Museum, Rome, is the image *par excellence* of Celtic nobility in battle. The naked warrior, with tousled hair and drooping moustache and wearing a neck torc, reclines bleeding on his shield, his discarded sword nearby. The statue is generally considered to be a copy of an original which adorned the monument erected in Pergamum by Attalus I after 228 BC and is thus a reliable representation of the Celts of Asia Minor in the late third century BC.

6

Ancona (Pl. I*b*), but the power and nobility of the Celt is nowhere better captured than on the victory monuments erected by the Attalid kings at Pergamum and at Athens in the third and second centuries BC. The acropolis monument at Pergamum, commissioned by Attalus I in the 220s, is known to us only from later Roman marble copies, including the famous Dying Gaul, the Gaulish warrior with his dead wife committing suicide (Pl. II), and the head of a bearded Gaul. Together they convey the vision of an enemy one would have been proud to have defeated.

The theme of the Pergamene kingdom as the saviour of Hellenism was displayed in an even more dramatic form in a victory monument erected on the acropolis of Athens after the final defeat of the Gauls between 168 and 166 BC. Here, according to Pausanius, the Pergamene defeat of the Gauls in Asia Minor was presented in parallel with the Greek victory over the Persians at Marathon and both were balanced with mythological battles, the Greeks against the Amazons and, by implication, the ancestors of the Pergamenes against the Giants. The claim of the Attalids is, thus, blatant: they, like the Greeks, have throughout time been the saviours of civilization against the external forces of chaos and destruction. The allusion was already there in the *Hymn to Delos*, written by Callimachus, who lived at the time of the Celtic attack on Delphi, in which the Celts are likened to 'Latter-day Titans'.

3 Marble relief from the sanctuary of Athena Nikephoros at Pergamum, now in the Pergamon-museum, Berlin. The relief gives an accurate impression of Celtic armour of the late third century BC showing a tunic of chain mail, shields, a spear, and an animal-headed carnyx (war trumpet).

A similar message was conveyed in a great frieze around the altar at Pergamum in which Zeus and Athena defeat the Giants while the Attalids defeat the Gauls. Of the many Gauls who would have been depicted, five survive in Roman marble copies (one in the Louvre in Paris, one in Naples, and three in Venice), all caught at their moment of defeat cowed by the might of their conquerors.

In these remarkable survivals the classical vision of the Celts, as it was perceived by those with the power to purvey their own version of history and its messages, stands out in sharp focus. Once created it has remained in the consciousness of all subsequent observers.

As the threat of the Celts as a force for destruction receded in the second century, a somewhat different metaphor of them began to develop. The most informative source, from the modern viewpoint, is the work of Poseidonius, a Syrian Greek from Apamaea (*c*.135–*c*.50 BC). Poseidonius wrote a series of *Histories* in fifty-two books beginning in the mid-second century to follow on from the *Histories* of Polybius. Book 23 contained an ethnographical introduction about the Celts as a background to the Roman conquest of Transalpina completed in 121 BC. For this he had access to a variety of earlier sources augmented by travels of his own in Gaul. The information at his disposal, then, comprised much

ΒΑΣΙΛΕΥΣΑΤΤΑΛΟΣΝΙΚΗΣΑΣΜΑΧΗΙΡΟΛΙΣΤο

4 The 'round monument', only the base of which remains in the sanctuary of Athena at Pergamum, is thought by some scholars to have been the focus for the display of statues of the defeated Celts. Marble copies of these works were taken to Italy, where several have survived. This imaginative reconstruction by A. Schober was published in 1952.

anecdotal material reflecting earlier times, which he was able to present against his own more systematic observations. The *Histories* are no longer extant but were extensively used, sometimes with direct acknowledgement, by three later writers, Strabo (*c*.64 BC–AD 21), Diodorus Siculus (who wrote *c*.60–30 BC), and Athenaeus (*c*. AD 200), and may also have been used by Julius Caesar as a source for the ethnographic descriptions in his *Commentaries* in Book VI of the *Gallic War*. Poseidonius was a Stoic philosopher, and, as Athenaeus tells us, in describing the many customs of many peoples he composed his work 'in accordance with his philosophical convictions'. In essence Poseidonius believed that contemporary barbarian peoples reflected a condition closer to the Golden Age than civilized societies, and that in that Golden Age society was ruled by the wise. To this extent his account of the Celts has something of a rosy glow about it. Thus he approves of their bravery and of their honouring of the brave, and comments favourably upon their hospitality to strangers. He excuses their fondness for war and their impetuous nature by saying that they were a straightforward people and not of evil character: he even came to terms with the idea of Celtic headhunting. They were, in fact, only like boisterous schoolchildren. 'To the frankness and high-spiritedness of their temperament must be added the traits of childish boastfulness and love of decoration.' But they were ruled by wisdom because among those specially honoured and given authority were the Druids, who were the natural and moral philosophers and men of science. 'They are believed to be the most just of men.' In his Celtic ethnography Poseidonius can fairly be accused, as modern commentators have suggested, of being a 'soft primitivist' who shielded himself and his readers from the realities

8

of Celtic societies. This same attitude is evident in the works of the Alexandrian school from the first century AD onwards which, using written sources rather than field observation, present Celtic religion and Druidism as on a par with Pythagorean systems.

A new sense of reality was instilled, from the middle of the first century BC, by writers such as Caesar, Lucan, and Tacitus, who reported on the conquest of the Gauls and the Britons. Although there was some recourse to the old stereotypes for the standard ethnographic introductions, much of the sense of the political turmoil among the Celtic peoples comes over. Thus Caesar: 'In Gaul there are factions not only in every state and village and party but practically even in individual households'; and Tacitus: 'Once they owed obedience to kings: now they are distracted between the warring factions of rival chiefs.' Implicit in comments of this kind is the justification for conquest, for not only could Rome not tolerate such instability on her borders but conquest and romanization brought peace to the barbarians. The point is explicitly made in a set-piece speech which Tacitus attributes to Petilius Cerialis in AD 69, though in all probability it is the historian speaking:

Throughout the whole of Gaul there were always despots and wars until you passed under our control. We ourselves, despite many provocations, imposed upon you by right of conquest only such additional burdens as were necessary for preserving peace. Stability between nations cannot be maintained without armies, nor armies without pay, nor pay without taxation. Everything else is shared equally between us. (*Hist.* 4.73)

Tacitus takes a rather more realistic view when he puts into the mouth of the British war leader Calgacus, facing the Roman army in northern Scotland in AD 84, a damning indictment of Rome: 'Pillagers of the world, they have exhausted the land by their indiscriminate plunder . . . to robbery, butchery, and rapine, they give the lying name of "government"; they create a desolation and call it peace' (*Agricola* 30).

While Caesar has a specific political agenda to achieve through his presentation of the Gauls, Tacitus uses the Britons and Germans as part of a general tirade against his perception of the shortcomings of the Roman leadership. Modern decadence and indiscipline and the loss of individual liberty are his themes, and the Britons and Germans provide convenient characters through which to purvey these views. The Celts are no longer a serious threat to Rome; it is the danger from within that is more insidious. For Tacitus, then, the Celts provide the allegory.

From the end of the first century AD barbarians other than the Celts provided the raw material for invective and polemic, and attitudes began to mellow as second- and third-generation Gauls and Britons became creative and influential citizens of the empire. Martial, born at Bilbilis in AD 40, several times proclaimed his pride in his Celtiberian origins—'we who are descended from Celts and Iberians'—and both Iberia and Gaul produced men of real literary talent. Only in occasional disparaging references to the northern Britons—such as

Ausonius' epigram, that 'matus' (drunk) rather than 'bonus' (good) is a more appropriate description for a Briton—can we see the old Celtic stereotype recurring.

Oblivion and Awakening: *c*.1500–1700

From the fourth century until the sixteenth century AD the world cared little for Celts. The classical texts were largely forgotten and lost, and the universal appeal of Christianity, with its own texts, mythologies, and stereotypes, provided all the models that were required to order behaviour and to invent origin myths and protohistories. Yet it was Christianity that kept alive a knowledge of the Celts in the manuscript copies of the classical sources preserved in monastic libraries.

In the sixteenth century many of these texts began to become more widely available in printed form. The manuscript of Tacitus' *Agricola* reached Rome about 1470 and was published in Milan five to ten years later, while Caesar's *Gallic War* was published in Venice in 1511. By the beginning of the seventeenth century most of the major texts were available in their original languages and in translation. This coincided with a general awakening in western Europe of the need to create national prehistories based on fact rather than myth. In Britain scholars like John Leland (1503–52) began avidly to collect data, while at the end of the century William Camden (1551–1623) produced the first serious attempt at explaining the early origins of Britain in his *Britannia*, first published in 1586. In France the Celts were beginning to come to the fore in such works as Jean Le Fèvre's *Les Fleurs et antiquites des Gaules*, published in 1532, and particular attention was beginning to be paid to the practices and philosophy of the Druids throughout the sixteenth and seventeenth centuries.

The discovery of the New World with its startling range of 'primitive peoples' each living in their own distinctive ethnographic present, and the beginning of the exploration of Africa and the East, provided ample comparative material for those writing about the prehistory of European society. Samuel Daniel could liken the tribal warfare of pre-Roman Britain to that of the American Indians, while John White could

5 A seventeenth-century vision of an Ancient Briton: a woodcut from John Speed's *Historie*, published in 1611. The ultimate source seems to be a watercolour drawing by John White dating to about 1588. Nakedness, body-painting, long hair, neck torcs, and head-hunting are all characteristics of the generalized 'Celt' derived from classical sources, which were becoming available in printed form at about this time.

6 Raphael Holinshed's vision of Queen Boudica (Boadiccea as she was then known), queen of the British tribe, the Iceni, who in AD 60 led a rebellion against the Romans. Illustrated in his *Chronicles* (1578). The similarity to Queen Elizabeth I reviewing her troops is unmistakable.

use his field drawings of Virginian Indians as models for Picts and Britons. What was beginning to emerge throughout the sixteenth and seventeenth centuries was the concept of the Celts, Gauls, and Britons as Noble Savages, not unlike the soft-primitivist approach of Poseidonius, though frequently they were displayed in contemporary dress. It was a trend which was to develop still further in the eighteenth century after an awareness of the islanders of the South Seas enlivened the European consciousness.

Celtomania and Nationalism: *c.*1700–1870

By the beginning of the eighteenth century the antiquarians concerned with early Europe had access to the principal classical texts, a varied array of ethnological analogies, and a growing knowledge of the prehistoric monuments and artefacts of their countries. The three elements were combined, particularly in France and Britain, to create a vision of the past peopled by Celts and Druids. In Britain the movement was led by William Stukeley (1687–1765), who began, in 1723, to write a *History of the Ancient Celts* in four parts. The work was never completed, but his two volumes on Stonehenge and Avebury, published in 1740 and 1743, ascribed both monuments to the 'British Druids'. In the wake of Stukeley's energetic proselytizing, virtually all the megalithic monuments of Britain—tombs, circles, and alignments—were considered to be the preserve of Druids, while the hill forts were seen as 'Ancient British' strongholds or as the camps of Caesar built during his expeditions in 55 and 54 BC.

In France the same enthusiasms prevailed. In 1703 Paul-Yves Pezron published his *L'Antiquité de la nation et la langue des Celtes, autrement appelez Gaulois.* By the end of the century the belief that the megaliths were Celtic was

7 A Druid seen through the vivid imagination of William Stukeley. From his volume *Stonehenge*, published in 1740. The axe in the belt is of Bronze Age type, but such details were unappreciated in Stukeley's time.

9 Queen Boudica (*far right*) as she appears resplendent in her chariot on the Thames Embankment facing the Houses of Parliament. The statue, erected in 1902, shows the British queen as in the model of late Victorian regal nobility.

firmly entrenched in such works as Malo Corret de la Tour-d'Auvergne's *Origines gauloises* (1796) and Jacques Cambry's *Monuments celtiques* (1805), which assigned all the Breton megaliths to the Celts.

Another pursuit of those caught up in the romance of Celtomania was to 'discover' Celtic literary traditions still extant in the folk memory of peasants living in remote areas. The most blatant case of invention came from Scotland, where James Macpherson created single-handed the poems of Ossian, which he published between 1760 and 1763. They were to have a profound effect throughout Europe in the fight for national identity: Ossian features large in the freedom poetry of the Hungarian Sandor Petofi (1823–49). In Brittany similar 'discoveries' were being made by Vicomte Hersart de la Villemarqué, whose *Barzaz-Breiz* (Songs of Brittany) was first published in 1838, at the time when the French government was attempting to wipe out Breton culture and language. Nor were the Welsh free from romantic invention. In 1792 the ceremony of *Maen Gorsedd* was created. It was held on the autumn equinox and involved Welsh bards in an extended performance of pompous ritual heavy with symbolism, requiring for its props an altar and a circle of stones. The entire pastiche of an 'ancient tradition' was the invention of Welsh stonemason Edward Williams, who preferred to be known by his bardic name Iolo Morganwy. By managing to have the Gorsedd attached to the more ancient and respectable ceremony of the Welsh Eisteddfod in 1819, Williams ensured the survival of his nonsensical Celtic creation.

The Celtomania of the eighteenth and early nineteenth centuries, with its mixture of facts and fantasies, has its place in the history of scholarship. It was a stage through which west European antiquarianism, almost inevitably, had to pass, since it provided the first faltering attempts in bringing together classical sources, the study of antiquities, oral traditions, and language to create a European past. What is more surprising is that much of the romantic nonsense of this phase still persists.

The French archaeologist Salomon Reinach, looking back over the outpourings of *Les Celtomanes*, could characterize their beliefs somewhat wryly:

The Celts are the oldest people in the world; their language is preserved practically intact in Bas-Breton; they were profound philosophers whose inspired doctrines have been handed down by the Welsh Bardic Schools; dolmens are their altars, where their priests the Druids offered human sacrifice; stone alignments were their astronomical observatories.

He could afford to be scathingly dismissive, for after 1870 the results of archaeological activity throughout western Europe were casting an entirely new light on the culture of the Iron Age (see Chapter 2).

Beneath the romantic Celtism of the eighteenth century lay an undercurrent of nationalism which intensified and became more explicit in the nineteenth century. The classical sources provided a galaxy of national heroes—Boudica in Britain, Vercingetorix in France, Ambiorix in Belgium, Viriathus in Iberia—all of whom could be used as symbols of national identity and freedom when required. The statue of Vercingetorix erected at Alesia in 1865, that of Boudica set up on the Thames Embankment in London in 1902, and Ambiorix depicted in heroic guise at Tongres in Belgium were there to provide much-needed inspiration of nationhood in the tumultuous century between the end of the Napoleonic War and the outbreak of the First World War.

In much of this, France took the lead. The famous statue of the Dying Gaul, bought at great expense by the French monarchy in 1737, was eventually transferred to France by Napoleon Bonaparte, on whom the potency of the image will not have been lost. Bonaparte established the Académie Celtique in Paris in 1805, but it was left to Napoleon's nephew, Louis Napoleon, to initiate what must surely be the earliest planned research programme in Iron Age archaeology. Returning to France after a period in exile, he was elected President of the Second Republic in 1848, seizing further power four years later to become Emperor, thereafter styling himself Napoleon III. France had been through a long period of upheaval and was facing the threat of increasing Prussian militarism. Napoleon was a scholar as well as being a politician and skilfully combined his personal academic inclination with the need to boost French morale by sponsoring a spectacular campaign of fieldwork and excavation to provide archaeological data for his projected work, the *Histoire de Jules César*. The

8 Statue of Vercingetorix, the Gaulish resistance leader who confronted Caesar at Alesia in 52 BC. The statue, which dominates the plateau of Alesia, was erected at the instigation of the Emperor Napoleon III in 1865. Napoleon organized a detailed field study of Caesar's campaigns. There is a certain stylized resemblance between the emperor and the statue.

fieldwork was undertaken between 1860 and 1865 by Colonel E. Stoffel with the aid of up to 300 assistants and labourers. The colonel's task was to research the topography of Caesar's campaigns and to identify the battlefields, an assignment completed with varying degrees of success, the highlight being the excavation of the siege works and a battleground of Alesia, where the war leader Vercingetorix made his last heroic stand against Rome. To provide further Celtic background to these events, Napoleon initiated the large-scale excavation of the principal *oppidum* of the Aedui at Bibracte (Mont Beuvray)—a task which he entrusted to J. G. Bulliot. Of the three projected volumes of the *Histoire*, two were published, in 1865 and 1866. The foundation of La Musée des Antiquités

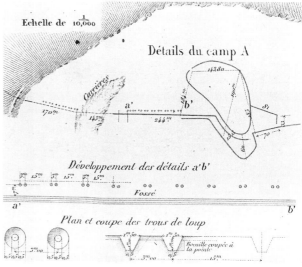

11 Colonel Stoffel, in his quest to discover details of Caesar's military installations, cut trial trenches to test the existence and form of buried ditches and pits. This careful work enabled him to produce plans of Caesar's forts and associated defensive works. The illustration, taken from Napoleon III's *Histoire de Jules César* (1865), is the plan of one of Caesar's camps on the outer circumvallation designed to restrain the army of Vercingetorix at Alesia.

10 Napoleon III, emperor of France from 1852 until 1870, when he was defeated and captured by the Germans at Sedan. During the Second Empire, largely as a result of Napoleon's scholarly interests, the archaeology of Iron Age Gaul flourished.

Nationales in Paris in 1863 ensured that his growing collection of Celtic antiquities, complete with models and reconstructions, would become readily accessible to the general public.

There can be little doubt that in intensifying, and possibly even creating, public awareness of the Gauls and of their heroic resistance to the outside aggressor, Rome, Napoleon III was deliberately setting out to inculcate a national spirit. His attitude to Caesar was ambivalent. Caesar confronted Gaulish opposition, but he did so, he claimed, because otherwise the country would have been overrun by Germans—the parallels would not have needed stressing to the French public in the 1860s. The conquest also had the advantage of unifying Gaul in a long period of peace in a way never before or after achieved. When in 1870 Napoleon rode out at Sedan to lead the French army in disastrous defeat at the hands of the Germans, one wonders whether it was Vercingetorix or Caesar that provided his role model.

The Romantic movement which had gripped Europe in the eighteenth and early nineteenth centuries provided a major stimulus to Celtomania in those regions which could claim to be Celtic. The 'discovery' of poetic traditions like the Ossian epic invented by Macpherson and La Villemarqué's *Barzaz-Breiz* (recently shown to be based on genuine folk traditions) and the nonsenses which sprang from the fertile imagination of Iolo Morganwy should not detract from more serious work, such as Evan Evans's *Some Specimens from the Poetry of the Ancient Welsh Bards* published in 1764, or, for that matter, the literary

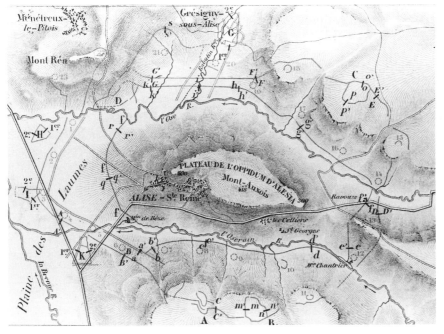

12 Plan of the *oppidum* of Alesia showing the siege works constructed by Julius Caesar in 52 BC. The plan, based on fieldwork and excavation undertaken by Colonel Stoffel, who led the research team set up by Napoleon III, was published in Napoleon's *Histoire de Jules César* in 1865.

genius of Sir Walter Scott, whose novels and poems gave a new nobility to the Highlander at the moment when all things Celtic were being proscribed in Scotland. Out of this ferment of literary and folkloric outpourings more solid structures began to crystallize: the foundation of the Society of Cymmrodorion in 1751 and the Cambrian Archaeological Association in 1848 provided a sound academic framework for Wales, while in Scotland the Society of Antiquaries of Scotland was instituted in 1780. The Royal Institution of Cornwall emerged in 1818 and in Ireland the Royal Irish Academy came into being in 1785.

13 A model of Caesar's circumvallation of Alesia based on descriptions in his Commentaries and excavations undertaken by Colonel Stoffel in the 1860s.

For the most part these organizations provided structured fora where the like-minded could research and celebrate their past, but inevitably such societies provided, often unwittingly, an underpinning for nationalist sentiments, and the perceived shared 'Celtic' ancestry offered a degree of unity. This was particularly developed in Brittany, where, in 1867, La Villemarqué set up the first of a series of Interceltic Congresses to which were invited 'kith and kin' from Wales, 'brothers' from Cornwall, and 'cousins' from Ireland and Scotland. It was from these roots that the Breton separatist movement *Breiz Atao* ('Brittany for Ever') was to grow in the interwar years. Pan-Celticism provided strength, it also offered an identity of otherness: *we* the Celts as opposed to *them* the French and English. It is a powerful metaphor which is still very much alive.

The Contribution of Archaeology: 1870–1970

The growing awareness of the material culture of the pre-Roman Iron Age in the middle of the nineteenth century began to instil a new sense of realism into the study of late prehistoric Europe, but it was not until 1871, with the recognition that the cultural assemblages found in the graves of the Champagne and the lake-side site of La Tène in Switzerland were closely matched by those associated with a series of burials inserted into the ruins of the Etruscan town of Marzabotto, that the historic Celts could confidently be identified (see Chapter 2). Thereafter the belief that the movements of people could be traced in the archaeological record gained wide acceptance, and the invasionist model became central to much archaeological writing.

Material of La Tène type found throughout central and eastern Europe was directly related to the historic expansion of the Celts, though the extreme paucity of La Tène material in Greece and Asia Minor, where the Celts were known to have been active, was a salutary warning of the adage that absence of evidence is not evidence of absence.

In the west the situation was more complex. The study of ancient European languages had shown that forms of Celtic were spoken over much of the Iberian Peninsula, the British Isles, and Ireland, and yet there was no historical record of Celtic migrations into these areas. It was, therefore, left to archaeologists and linguists to construct models of invasion from their two disparate viewpoints. Since each relied heavily on the other, a considerable degree of circularity developed in the arguments. In Iberia the classical sources indicated a Celtic presence by the sixth century BC, and this was supported by linguistic arguments that suggested that the Celtic spoken in the Peninsula was more ancient than that recorded in Gaul. Thus it was incumbent on archaeologists to 'discover' evidence for the Celtic migration from west central Europe through the Pyrenees in the material culture of the Late Bronze Age. This approach was most influentially propounded by P. Bosch-Gimpera in his famous paper 'Two Celtic Waves in Spain' published in 1939 in the *Proceedings of the British Academy*. In Britain and Ireland invasionist theories were summed up in the elegant formulation of Christopher Hawkes, presented in a paper entitled 'Hillforts' published in the journal *Antiquity* in 1931, in which a series of migratory waves were envisaged.

Simple invasionist theories of this kind were in common use until the 1960s and are still found from time to time in the more popular literature. Their modelling was based partly on the classical accounts of Celtic movements, but also derived inspiration from an awareness of the migrations of the late Roman and early medieval periods. Behind it all lay the knowledge, gleaned from recent history, of the dramatic cultural changes, linguistic and material, that had been brought about by west European imperial expansion. This strengthened the implicit belief that cultural change was most simply to be explained as the result of folk movement.

The 'Celts' that emerged during this period still retained the image of the warrior intent upon feasting and raiding—in other words the classical vision—but, in a century dominated by recurring war, much of it resulting from German militarism, a new image began to develop in which the 'Celt' was given a more homely, creative appearance in contrast to other barbarians, in particular the 'warlike Germans': in other words the 'Celt' was becoming domesticated. This was subtly, and perhaps unconsciously, done by putting increased emphasis on artistic and technical achievements and on the 'hearth-and-home' aspects of the archaeological record. Such an approach was particularly well developed in Britain, where the creative originality of Celtic art had long been

14 Celtic domesticity as imagined by A. Forestier in his illustration of 1911, based on the excavated evidence derived from the examination of the lake village of Glastonbury, Somerset.

recognized, largely because the extreme paucity of cemeteries producing warrior equipment forced archaeological activity to focus on settlement sites and on the productive systems which maintained them.

The first recognizable ordering of the British agrarian landscape became known as 'Celtic field systems', and the term was readily, if inappropriately, adopted in the Low Countries and Denmark, where isolated Celtic elements of material culture have tended to be given particular emphasis in contrast to the Germanic.

The Celt of the period 1870–1970 is, therefore, a complex creation. In the image of the nineteenth-century imperialists, he was prepared to fight his way into new territories, taking his women and children with him, but there to settle down to till the soil while the womenfolk spun, weaved, and ground the corn. His love of art was well developed and he was served by craftsmen of great originality and skill. Even his wife could add to the artistic ambience of the home by making pleasantly decorated pots. He was not unduly aggressive but would fiercely protect his family and home if danger threatened. The discovery of a 'war cemetery' at the gate of the hill fort of Maiden Castle, in Dorset, attributed to the gallant Celts defending their settlement against Roman invaders, provided a potent image which caught the grim public mood in the late 1930s, and, by the time that the excavation report was finally published in the depths of the Second World War, the 'war-mad' Celt of the Poseidonian tradition had become *celticus domesticus*!

In France, too, opportunity for allegory was not lost. In the aftermath of the war, in 1949, a monument was erected on the plain of Les Laumes below Alesia. It records that

On this plain 2,000 years ago Gaul saved her honour pitting, at Vercingetorix' call, her peoples against Caesar's legions. After her reversal upon the battlefield, reconciled with the victor, united, defended against the invasions of the Germans, open to the enlightenment of Greece and Rome, she knew three centuries of peace.

Celts at the End of the Millennium

Since 1970 there has been a subtle change in the vision of the Celt, with an increasing emphasis on the economic systems which underpinned society and the use of 'world-systems' models. The development of coinage and the emergence of *oppida*, which are widely believed to be of urban character, are areas upon which much research has recently focused. These developments are, in part, the result of a more widespread interest in economic structures among archaeologists, which can be related to a much broader awareness of economics among the public at large. This, in some considerable measure, is a reflection of modern European politics, with its concern for the development of the more unified European Community. The pan-European image of the Celts is highly appropriate to this political imperative.

The mounting of the spectacular exhibition 'The Celts, the Origins of Europe' in Venice in 1991, under the auspices of Palazzo Grassi and sponsored by the multinational Fiat company, is an example of the current use to which the Celts are being put. The point was explicitly made by the President of Palazzo Grassi in his introduction to the exhibition catalogue *The Celts*:

This exhibition is a tribute both to the new Europe which cannot come into fruition without a comprehensive awareness of its unity, and to the fact that, in addition to its Roman and Christian sources, today's Europe traces its roots from the Celtic heritage, which is there for all to see.

It is in the light of this vision that one can best understand the initiative of President Mitterrand in providing lavish funds from the French state to support a new programme of multinational excavations at the Aeduian capital of Bibracte. In doing so he was echoing the gesture of Napoleon III, though for rather different political motives.

Jacquetta Hawkes summed it all up in the memorable thought that each generation gets the archaeology it deserves. Put another way, it is difficult, indeed impossible, to study the past without our understanding being encumbered and perverted by the impediment of the social mores in which we live and the transient values of the moment. At best, by attempting to understand the distortions of the past, we can be more on guard against introducing distortions of our own and accepting those forced on us by our political leaders.

There are currently two extreme perceptions of the Celts: the New Celtomania, which provides a vision of a European past to comfort us at a time when ethnic divisions are becoming a painful and disturbing reality, and a politically correct view, which argues that the term is so abused as to be useless except to those who wish to increase the sales of their books. Both views contain some threads of value but in their extremity they are sterile. There were, in Europe and beyond, peoples who were known as Celts, whose movements and behaviour are reflected in contemporary sources. They spoke a language which spread over a huge area, versions of which are still spoken and taught today in the western fringes of the former territory. Some of these ancient Celtic communities developed a unique art and a distinctive material culture, which spread throughout Europe, and in the remote west, in Ireland, echoes of their society come down to us through the written versions of a long-extinct oral tradition. These threads are real and are worthy of our attention.

2
The Reality of the Celts

THE concept of the Celts has many realities born of different disciplines. The earliest awareness to break upon the academic world was the vision provided by the Greek and Roman authors, a vision which, as we have seen, was moulded through closely circumscribed historical traditions to produce a range of familiar metaphors. These were translated into visual form through Hellenistic statuary, which in turn became widely known through Roman copies. Together these sources produced a 'classical reality', the great and lasting advantage of which is that it gives the Celts a place in history endowing them with motives, passions, names, and a fearsome alien character. Through the eyes of the classical world, the Celts, though familiar in some ways, were sufficiently foreign to send a *frisson* of fear down the spine whenever their name arose.

This clearly sculpted model began to take on a more complex character in the eighteenth and nineteenth centuries through a growing understanding of the intricacies of the Celtic language, further to be enlivened by the great vernacular literature of the Insular Celts of Ireland and Wales, which offered a quite different insight into the 'Celtic character'. The crisply defined Celts of Roman sculptors and Greek and Roman historians became worryingly distorted by the unreality of magic and shape-shifting.

Archaeological advances in the nineteenth and twentieth centuries provided a new reality through the discovery first of the weapons and artefacts used by Celtic peoples and later of the settlements in which they had lived and the detritus of the economies which had sustained them. Finally, in the 1930s and 1940s, the art of the Celts came to be recognized as a subject worthy of study, making it possible to bridge the gap between the classical vision, the vernacular mystery, and the harsh, if somewhat mundane, archaeological reality. The excitement of the subject is that it can be approached from these very different directions, all of which have a validity within their own academic parameters, and yet what emerges presents an altogether different set of images.

I*a Left*: Statue of a warrior embossed from bronze sheets. The eyes are inset with glass paste. The swept-back hair and long drooping moustache are characteristic of Gaulish representations of Celtic warrior deities. Probably first century BC. From Saint-Maur-en-Chausée (Oise), France. Musée Départemental de l'Oise, Beauvais.

I*b Below*: Fragment of a stone frieze from Civitalba (Marches), Italy. The partial scene shows two fleeing Celts dropping spoils of war. Both are long haired and naked apart from belts and cloaks, as the classical stereotype of the Celtic barbarian requires. The shields are typical of Celtic armour. Museo Nazionale Archeologico della Marche, Ancona, Italy.

In the previous chapter we considered the classical model and its evolution in broad outline. Here it is necessary to explore in more detail the main classes of evidence which help to expand and modify that model.

The Celtic Language

Celtic belongs to the family of Indo-European languages. It is closest to the Italic languages, to such an extent that some linguists have postulated a common Italo-Celtic origin for both. This hypothetical group is believed to be broadly equivalent to two other European families, one from which the Baltic, Slav, and Germanic languages were to evolve and the other ancestral to Greek. The point at which Celtic began to be distinguished is much debated. On one extreme it has been suggested that the main Celtic-speaking groups were in place using their distinctive tongue as early as 3000 BC, but the more conventional view accepts that Italic and Celtic separated and developed in the regions in which they were to flourish during the period 1300–800 BC, before outward migration of the Celts and the Latins.

Celtic languages are spoken now only in the extreme Atlantic periphery of Europe, but originally they extended in a broad swath from south-western Iberia, through Gaul and the Alpine region, into the Middle Danube, and one group of settlers, the Galatians, introduced Celtic into central Asia Minor, where, according to St Jerome, it was still recognizable in the fourth century AD.

The different types of recorded Celtic may be divided into two broad groups: Continental and Insular. Continental Celtic is known from the evidence of place names and personal names recorded by classical historians, on coins, and from a comparatively small number of inscriptions. Using this evidence it is possible to distinguish three, possibly four, Continental Celtic languages. In Iberia, Celtiberian was spoken over much of the centre, west, and north of the Peninsula. The earliest inscriptions date to the third century BC, but, as we have seen, the Greek writers show that Celts were to be identified in the region at least two centuries earlier. In Gaul, the Gaulish language was spoken extensively in the first century BC and is well represented in a hundred or so inscriptions. South of the Alps in the northwestern part of the Po Valley a distinctive form of Celtic known as Lepontic has been identified in about seventy inscriptions. That the earliest of these date back to the sixth century BC raises a number of important questions which will be introduced later (see p. 70). Finally, in the Middle Danube Valley place names and personal names indicate that the Celtic spoken here differed from the western Celtic languages, but little is known of its structure or date except that many of the names are no later than the first century BC.

II *Facing:* A Celtic warrior committing suicide in defeat by the body of his dead wife. The group, now in the Museo Nazionale delle Terme, Rome, is probably a marble copy of an original which once adorned the Temple of Athena Nikephoros at Pergamum commissioned by Attalus I at the end of the third century BC.

15 Stone slab from Vaison-la-Romaine, Vaucluse, France, inscribed in Graeco-Gaulish. It probably dates to the middle of the first century BC and records the gift of land to the goddess Belesma by Segomaros, son of Villonos, citizen of Nemauso (Nimes). Musée Calvet, Avignon.

16 A bilingual inscription in Latin and Celtic from Todi, Italy, dating to the second century BC. Museo Gregoriano Vaticano, Rome.

The Insular Celtic languages were spoken in Great Britain, Ireland, and Brittany. It is conventional to divide them into two groups: Q-Celtic, or Goidelic, spoken in Ireland, the Isle of Man, and western Scotland, and P-Celtic, or Brythonic, which forms the basis of modern Welsh, Cornish, and Breton. The long-established belief has been that Q-Celtic was the older form and was adopted by the Atlantic communities at an early date but was overtaken in Great Britain by the more recently evolved P-Celtic, which was the basis of Gaulish. It was further believed that Q-Celtic was reintroduced in Scotland and the Isle of Man by invaders from Ireland in the third and fourth centuries AD and that P-Celtic was reintroduced to Brittany by settlers from south-west Britain arriving in the fifth century AD. Recent work has, however, suggested that this model is probably a considerable oversimplification. It has been noted that P-Celtic place names are recorded in Ireland, though they may be transliterations of Q-Celtic names by P-Celtic speakers reporting them to the geographers of the classical world. The introduction of the Breton language poses more problems and it is probably more in keeping with reality to interpret it as native Armorican P-Celtic, surviving beneath an overlay of Latin, reinvigorated by the similar language of the British settlers. A further factor to bear in mind is that the division between the two types of Celtic may be less significant than was originally believed.

Awareness of the character of the Insular Celtic languages emerged in the late seventeenth and early eighteenth centuries, inspired by the researches of the Oxford scholar Edward Lhuyd, Assistant Keeper at the Ashmolean Museum from 1687 and its Keeper from 1691 until his death in 1709. As a true polymath, Lhuyd had many interests and skills, but it was in the field of comparative Celtic linguistics that he made his most lasting contribution. In 1695 he presented a prospectus for an ambitious publication to be entitled *Archaeologia Britannica*, which was to contain a comparison of Welsh with other European languages, especially Greek, Latin, Irish, Cornish, and Armorican. After extensive travel in the Celtic West, he retired to Oxford in 1701 to begin writing. The first volume of *Archaeologia* contains grammars and vocabularies of Irish, Breton, and Cornish, with supporting discussions and etymologies. He noted the close relationship between Gaulish, Irish, and British, and the similarities between Welsh, Cornish, and Breton, but he did not systematize it as a Q/P distinction.

In the Welsh preface to *Archaeologia*, as well as in correspondence, he used his linguistic studies to put forward a scheme to explain the 'colonization' of Britain, suggesting that the Irish Britons were a colonial movement from Gaul settling first in the British Isles. They were pushed out into the north of Britain and to Ireland by a second wave of Gaulish settlers. In attempting to relate language, through the careful study of etymology, to people and migrations, Lhuyd was opening up a huge area of study which has occupied many scholars ever since.

Lhuyd was working in one corner of the web of European languages. Already, a century before, Joseph Scaliger (1540–1609) had divided the European languages into four groups (characterized by their word for God). Subsequently various attempts were made to trace the European and related languages back to a common ancestor. In 1796 Sir William Jones, Chief Justice of India, suggested, in a lecture, that language groups as disparate as Celtic, Gothic, Sanskrit, and Old Persian might belong to the same family, and it was from this stream of scholarship that the concept of a common Indo-European language began to develop, to be systematized, in the middle of the nineteenth century, by Augustus Schleicher (1821–68). Schleicher developed the notion of the tree-like growth of languages. Beginning with a primeval Indo-European language, groups diverged until seven 'fundamentals' emerged, one of which was Celtic; this in turn split still further, giving rise to the individual branches of Celtic such as Cornish, Welsh, and so on. The model was a convenient way of ordering the data then available and formed a significant stage in the development of Indo-European studies.

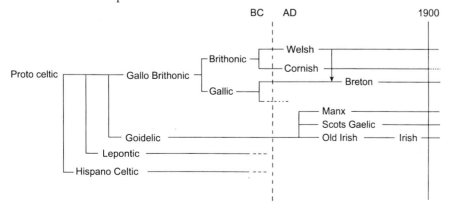

17 Diagram to illustrate the possible development of the Celtic language group.

23

As the broad study of the Indo-European languages advanced, so too did the analysis of the Celtic languages. Theories about Insular Celtic centred around the questions of folk movement. The most influential work in this field was published by Sir John Rhŷs, holder of the Chair of Celtic at Oxford University, in a wide-ranging book *Early Britain: Celtic Britain* published in 1882. In it he developed Lhuyd's ideas by putting forward the view that the Goidelic Celts from the Continent first overcame southern Britain and thence spread to Ireland. Thereafter there was an invasion of Brythonic Celtic speakers, also from the European mainland, who forced the Goidelic settlers into western areas of Britain, some taking ship to join their distant relations in Ireland. This simple hypothesis provided a convenient basis around which linguists and archaeologists have built and argued ever since.

Continental Celtic poses a rather different array of questions, since the languages nowhere survive in spoken form (with the possible exception of Breton) and are known only from comparatively few texts, augmented by a scattering of place names and proper names.

In Iberia, Celtic language studies were given a major boost by the decipherment of a long text inscribed on a bronze tablet found at Botorrita, near Saragossa, announced in 1971. This, together with the work of Antonio Tovar and others, has greatly advanced our understanding of the languages of the Peninsula. Indigenous non-Indo-European languages survived into classical times in the south-east, as Iberian, and possibly in Tartessus, while in the north Basque is also the remnant of a separate and once more-extensive non-Indo-European group. On this basis it is argued that Celtiberian was intrusive, arriving some time before the earliest mention of Celts in Iberia in the sixth century. The primary focus of Celtic lay in the north-eastern central zone, whence the language spread to the north, west, and south-west. The mechanisms by which Celtic was introduced into Iberia and the processes by which it expanded are subjects of much current debate.

It has long been recognized that Lepontic, focused around the lakes of Lombardy, was a Celtic language and that a distinctive Lepontic alphabet was used in the second and first centuries BC, but the demonstration that the Lepontic language dates back to the sixth century BC and possibly a century earlier raises a most interesting range of questions, since these early examples significantly pre-date the migration of Celts from north of the Alps in the early fourth century BC.

Gaulish Celtic has benefited from a long and distinguished tradition of scholarly study based on the hundred or so inscriptions and the wealth of place and proper name evidence. Major sur-

18 Part of a stone relief from Bormio, Sondrio, Italy, dating to the fifth century BC. The warriors appear to be equipped with Celtic-style arms. Recent work on the Lepontic language of this area suggests that Celtic was spoken here as early as the sixth–fifth centuries BC, before the historic migrations began. Museo Civico Arqueologico Giovio, Como.

veys by David Ellis Evans (1967) and Joshua Whatmough (1970) have provided full catalogues and discussions, the overriding view being that beneath a variety of dialects Gaulish is broadly Brythonic, though some doubt has been placed on the classificatory value of the term.

Standing back from the complex and highly incomplete picture created from these linguistic scraps, one may distinguish a central Celtic linguistic zone comprising Gaul, the British Isles, and possibly the eastern Celtic province, beyond which, in Ireland, Iberia, and the Lepontic region, was a periphery where somewhat different versions of the Celtic language were spoken. Two of these 'peripheral' areas were Celtic-speaking by the sixth century BC, and there is a strong possibility that the third, Ireland, was as well. The importance of linguistic studies for an understanding of Celtic culture is considerable, especially if it is accepted that a Celt was one who spoke Celtic. At its very simplest, it enables the uncoupling of 'Celt' from the archaeologically defined La Tène culture, by demonstrating that the Celtic language was spoken considerably earlier than the development of La Tène culture and over a more extensive area.

The Insular Tradition of Vernacular Literature

It is reasonable to assume that the warrior aristocracy of the Celts, like other warrior aristocracies throughout the pre-modern world, created and transmitted in ever-changing form a rich oral history in cycles of epic narrative. In suitable gatherings these epics would be recounted by storytellers to an audience keen to hear the deeds of their ancestors unfold and the nature of their gods familiarized through stories of them interfering in the lives of ordinary mortals. Such traditions were important in giving the community its roots and providing models of behaviour: above all they created a sense of identity.

The survival of such epics, if they survive at all, is a matter of chance. From continental Europe and Britain little remains of what must have been a rich and vivid corpus of tradition, except for obscure and partial allusions in Celtic art, difficult now for us to interpret. But in Ireland, where Celtic culture survived untouched by the heavy hand of romanization, a selection of this narrative tradition was committed to writing and in this form has been transmitted to us across the ages.

The most extensive of the vernacular sources is the Ulster Cycle, comprising about eighty individual stories of which the most complete and by far the longest is the Cattle Raid of Cooley (*Táin Bó Cuailnge*). The rest of the corpus is made up of stories which set the scene for the central drama or expand upon the lives of the main characters.

The entire corpus is contained in ten separate manuscripts, overlapping in content. The oldest extant version of the *Táin*, known as Recension I, survives in two separate manuscripts each providing part of the story, *The Book of the Dun Cow*, dating to the eleventh century, and *The Yellow Book of Lecan*, compiled in the fourteenth century. A fuller and more coherent version, Recension

II, occurs in the late-twelfth-century *Book of Leinster*. Recension I is probably based on two lost ninth-century manuscripts, and it is possible that even earlier versions, going back to the seventh century, once existed.

The *Táin* must be read to be appreciated, but the essential action focuses around a cattle raid mounted by the people of Connacht against the people of Ulster at the urging of Queen Medb—a strong-willed, promiscuous woman who is part mortal and part a goddess of the land and therefore prone to test the virility of male heroes. The army of Connacht is opposed by a company of aristocratic warriors, the young and vital Cú Chulainn, the more mature and experienced Ferghus mai Roich and Conall Cernach, the wise Sencha mai Ailella, and the two-faced scheming Bricriu the 'Poison-tongue', who sets men against each other to advance his own interests. As the story unfolds, we are introduced to many scenes and actions reflecting behaviour familiar through the ethnographic works of Poseidonius and Caesar: feasting and the hero's portion, chariot warfare, single combat, severed heads, joint dowries of husbands and wives, fosterage, and above all the ethics and motivations of a warrior aristocracy for whom raiding was a commonplace.

The similarities have long been recognized and commented upon. The most influential work has been Kenneth Jackson's *The Oldest Irish Tradition: A Window on the Iron Age*, published in 1964, in which he argued that the Ulster tales reflected an Irish ethnographic present of the fourth century AD, which in turn gave direct access to an earlier Celtic society. The situation is, however, more complex. The Ulster Cycle undoubtedly contains elements of an ancient folk tradition, but it was composed in its final form by Christian monks with a considerable knowledge of Greek and Roman literature as well as the Scriptures and other Christian writings. Thus, while it might be tempting to argue that similarities to the Homeric epics reflect a common European origin, it may be more reasonable to suppose that the Homeric allusions were inserted by the highly educated medieval redactors. There are, therefore, real dangers of being led astray by false archaisms.

A detailed study of the 'material culture' represented in the Ulster Cycle has led James Mallory to the indisputable conclusions that the constant reference to silver among the prestigious items depicted must be a reflection of the broader world experience of Ireland in the sixth to ninth centuries AD and has no bearing at all on the culture of the La Tène period. In his words, 'The material culture of the Ulster Cycle is essentially a "Window on the Dark Ages".'

Given, then, that the medieval Christian redactors were responsible for creating the text which comes down to us, by presenting an epic tradition in the light of their own scholarly erudition and a desire to preserve a memory of the splendours of their more recent past, how much of the pre-Christian tradition survives? It is tempting to take the easy way out and to argue that the basic material that was moulded, redecorated, and to some extent repackaged by the succession of saga tellers and saga writers throughout the first millennium AD does belong to the European Celtic tradition of the first millennium BC—the same tradition that is visible in dismembered scraps in the surviving writings of the classical historians and geographers.

There is, however, a slightly unnerving disparity between the archaeological record in Ireland and aspects of warfare which must be regarded as central to the action of the epic. Two items in particular stand out: the sword and the chariot. In the Ulster Cycle the heroes use massive slashing swords and are driven to battle on light war chariots; cavalry is not mentioned at all. All of this would be quite acceptable in parts of continental Europe in the fourth or third century BC, but the archaeological record of Ireland has produced no large slashing sword of this type, and no chariot fittings, such as terret rings, strap fasteners, linch pins, hub rings, and iron tires, of the types which commonly recur in Britain and the Continent. The word constantly employed for the vehicle used in the hero tales is *carpat*, which elsewhere is used to describe transport or travelling vehicles with two wooden seats, one for the driver, the other for the passenger. From brief textual references it would seem that this was an indigenous vehicle totally different from the war chariot of Britain and Gaul. It remains, therefore, a strong possibility that the core of the epics, deeply embedded within the Ulster Cycle, lies in a Continental European tradition which was transmitted at some stage to Ireland, there to be woven into a network of indigenous folk tales in a local geographical and technological setting to which was added a sprinkling of real history. Thereafter, the tales were constantly modified, in each retelling taking on some new aspect, material or oral, gleaned from the contemporary world, until their final editing for Christian consumption in the medieval period.

This said, the Ulster Cycle is a remarkable survival providing a tantalizing glimpse of the rich epic tradition of Celtic Europe which would otherwise be totally inaccessible.

Another source of considerable interest are the Old Irish law texts, the majority of which originate in the seventh and eighth centuries AD and come down to us in varying states of corruption or incompleteness in documents of late medieval date. From these it is possible to gain an intimate insight into the working of society—rank, kin groupings, personal relationships, property, offences and punishment, contracts and pledges, and the teaching and maintenance of the law itself. No doubt, embedded within all this, are rules of behaviour which date back to the time of the earlier Celtic populations of Ireland, but to tease out these early threads is an uncertain, perhaps impossible, task. At best the law tracts may be enjoyed as a distant and distorted echo of a past era.

Archaeology

The contribution of archaeology to the study of the Celts has been considerable. From the sixteenth century large numbers of antiquities have been published and variously ascribed as 'British', 'Gaulish', or 'Celtic'. Many were indeed of Iron Age date, but at first correct designations were achieved more by luck than through knowledge. Systematization began early in the nineteenth century with the work of the Danish archaeologist C. J. Thomsen (1788–1865), who is credited with the creation of the Three Age model through his arrangement of the collections of the Danish National Museum into items of Stone, Bronze, and Iron, which he presented as three developmental stages applicable to the prehistory of the whole of Europe. Thomsen's work was further elaborated by his assistant J. J. A. Worsaae (1821–85), who, by stratigraphical excavations, was able to demonstrate its general validity. By the 1840s it was possible to make a broad correlation between the material culture of the Iron Age and that of the Celts in those areas of Europe where the classical sources indicated the Celts to have lived. Thus, when Johann Georg Ramsauer began to excavate an extensive cemetery at Hallstatt in Austria in 1846 (Pl. IIIa), he was simply following convention by calling the graves he found 'Celtic'. Excavations at Hallstatt continued until 1863, by which time about 1,000 graves had been opened and meticulously recorded in a series of fine watercolour sketches drawn by the excavator. For the most part the graves, both cremations and inhumations, were well furnished with artefacts, including an array of weapons, bronze and ceramic vessels, and personal equipment and jewellery. This enormous collection, together with well-preserved organic material, such as clothing and wooden tools, recovered from the neighbouring salt mines, provided the archaeological world with a detailed insight into the material culture of the central European Iron Age. Most of the Hallstatt graves belonged to the period

19 *Above*: Georg Ramsauer, a government director of mining, who, in 1846, discovered the Iron Age cemetery at Hallstatt in Austria and continued excavating it until 1863.

20 *Right*: The location of the settlement and salt mines of Hallstatt, Austria.

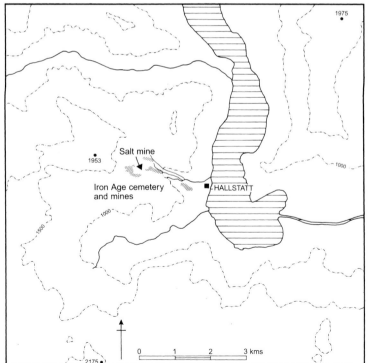

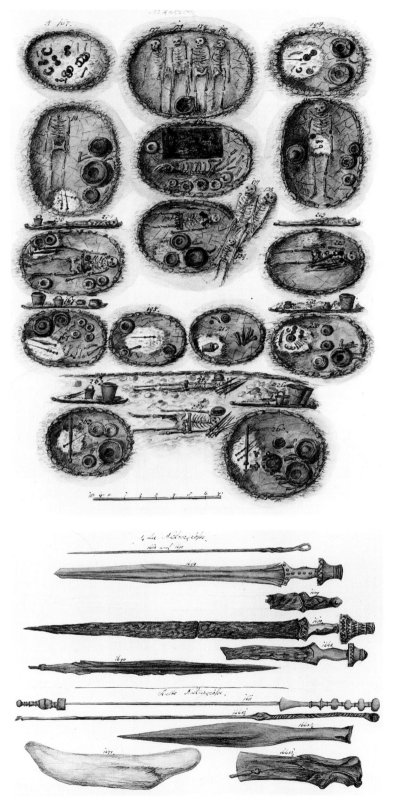

21 *Left*: Georg Ramsauer conducted the excavations at the cemetery at Hallstatt with some skill, recording each individual burial complete with grave goods in meticulously detailed watercolours, of which this is one page. Library of the Society of Antiquaries, London.

22 *Above*: A rucksack made from leather over a wooden frame preserved in the salt mines at Hallstatt, Austria, dating to the sixth century. The sack was probably used by a miner to carry rock salt. Naturhistorisches Museum, Vienna.

23 The location of the site of La Tène on Lake Neuchâtel, Switzerland. This is Paul Vouga's plan published in 1923.

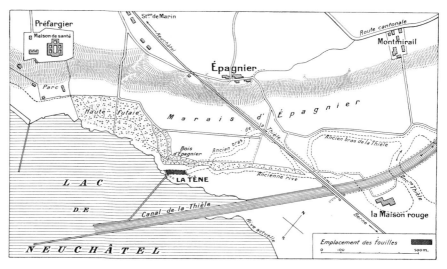

24 Excavations at La Tène, Neuchâtel, Switzerland, in the early twentieth century, showing the timbers of a bridge, named after the excavator as Le Pont Vouga.

spanning the seventh and sixth centuries BC with a few continuing into the early fifth. Thereafter the importance of Hallstatt declined rapidly, as the salt deposits at Dürrnberg began to be developed.

In 1857, at the north-western corner of Lake Neuchâtel in Switzerland, a local collector Hansli Kopp discovered a series of wooden piles and in groping in the mud between them located about forty iron weapons. Thus began the exploration of the famous site of La Tène, which continued sporadically until 1917 (Pl. III*b*). La Tène is a puzzling site which has variously been interpreted as a pile dwelling, a fortified *oppidum*, a bridge overwhelmed in a catastrophe, and a platform from which ritual depositions were made. Its fame lies in the extremely large collection of artefacts which have accumulated as a result of the various excavations. The assemblage is particularly rich in weapons—swords, spears, and shields—but also includes a number of smaller personal items, such as fibulae, belt clasps, and razors, as well as bronze vessels, iron ingots, and parts of vehicles. The finds became widely known in the 1860s, largely as a result of

25 Plan of the timber structure and votive deposits unearthed at La Tène. Based on part of Paul Vouga's original excavation plan, published in 1923.

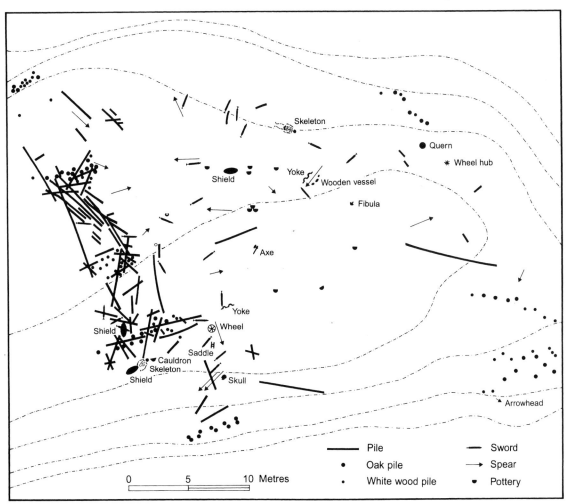

31

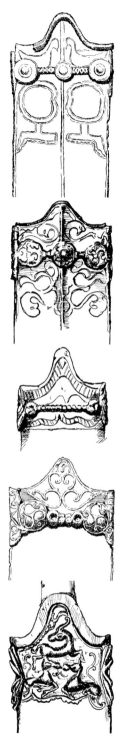

Ferdinand Keller's publication, in which he presented La Tène as a lake village of the Celtic period. It was soon realized that they differed markedly in form and therefore age from the material which had been recovered on the other side of the Alps at Hallstatt, but were similar to other finds coming to light in cemetery excavations in northern France.

In 1871 the International Congress of Prehistoric Anthropology and Archaeology was held at Bologna. Among the delegates were Gabriel de Mortillet from France and Émile Desor from Switzerland; both had a detailed knowledge of Iron Age material, de Mortillet having worked with finds from cemeteries in Champagne and Desor at Neuchâtel. During the congress they were able to view material recovered from a cemetery recently excavated towards the edge of the Etruscan city of Marzabotto. The finds were closely similar to those with which they were familiar and left the two men in no doubt that the Marzabotto burials were of Celts who had crossed the Alps to settle in the Po Valley, just as Livy and Polybius had described. The recognition meant that, from then on, archaeological finds of La Tène type came to be regarded as the material culture of the Celts. Moreover, the correlation provided a convenient dating horizon, assuming the chronology of the classical sources to be correct.

In 1872, the year following the Bologna conference, the Swedish archaeologist Hans Hildebrant proposed systematizing the Iron Age by dividing it into two parts, the earlier characterized by the finds from the Hallstatt cemetery, and the later by those from La Tène. Henceforth the concepts of a Hallstatt culture and a La Tène culture came widely into use, with the La Tène culture being regarded as the archaeological expression of the Celts.

Subsequently the scheme was modified by subdivision. In 1881 Otto Tischler divided the Hallstatt period into two phases, Early and Late, and then turned his attention to the La Tène material, in 1885 proposing a threefold division into Early, Middle, and Late, or I, II, and III, following the discovery of the votive deposit at Duchcov in 1882. The Early phase was characterized by fibulae whose recurved feet simply touched the bow; the contemporary swords were short with the scabbard chapes perforated. In the Middle phase the fibulae had developed so that the foot wrapped around the bow, while the sword sheaths now had unperforated chapes. The Late phase was characterized by fibulae with solid catch plates often perforated. The contemporary swords were much longer with rounded ends.

Tischler's system was widely used, and by the turn of the century firm dates were being proposed. Thus, for France, Oscar Montelius suggested the La Tène I should be dated 400–250, II, 250–150, and III, 150–1 BC. Joseph Déchelette argued that a period IV should be added to contain the later British material. In Switzerland the careful excavation of the cemetery at Münsingen and elsewhere allowed further subdivisions to be made by David Viollier in 1916; La Tène I was thereafter divided into a, b, and c and La Tène II into a and b.

While the Tischler scheme worked well for the Champagne, Switzerland, and Bohemia, the material from Bavaria posed problems, because here an early

26 A selection of the decorated sword scabbards discovered at La Tène and illustrated in the excavation report, *La Tène*, by Paul Vouga, published in 1923.

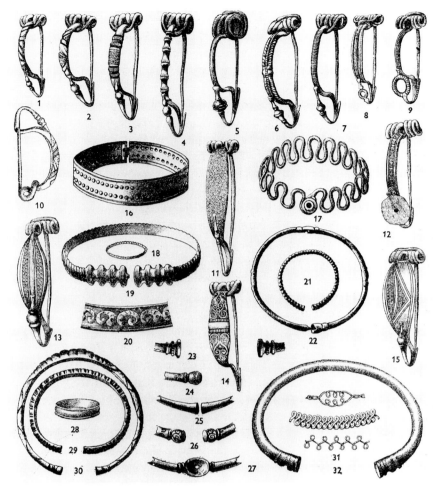

27 Early La Tène metalwork from the hoard found at Duchcov in Bohemia in 1882 from the original publication.

phase of burials, usually under tumuli, was identified. To contain these, in 1902 Paul Reinecke proposed that this assemblage, dating to the fifth century BC, should be recognized as a distinct phase known as La Tène A. Thereafter his La Tène B, C, and D approximately equated with Tischler's Early, Middle, and Late. This was a significant amendment in that it gave recognition to the formative phase of the La Tène culture, pre-dating the period of the migration. Reinecke also subdivided the Hallstatt culture, giving specific recognition to its Bronze Age origins (his Hallstatt A and B), allowing C and D to represent the two stages of the Early Iron Age. In Britain, throughout the late nineteenth and early twentieth centuries, Iron Age material was simply designated 'Late Keltic' or 'Early British' without subdivision, following the suggestion of Augustus Franks in 1863, though in the first decade of this century some attempts were made to link the Insular finds to the Continental scheme. It is the Reinecke system of 1902, with many subdivisions, regional variants, and chronological adjustments, that has underpinned Iron Age studies this century.

The systematizing of the European Iron Age in the late nineteenth century was, to a large extent, driven by the flood of new material deriving from the excavation of cemeteries, which provided a favourite focus of activity for collectors and archaeologists. In France a lead was provided by Louis Napoleon (1808–73), who became President of the Second Republic in 1852, assuming the title of Napoleon III after a *coup d'état* established the Second Empire a year later. Napoleon's scholarly concern with the campaigns of Julius Caesar led him to take an active interest in the casual discoveries that were being made in the Champagne when, each summer, he spent time at the military base at Châlons. From material given to him and bought from the local peasants, and obtained from excavations which he ordered, he built up a large collection which was to form the basis of the Musée des Antiquités Nationales.

Among the other collectors inspired by the emperor's example were Frédéric Moreau (1798–1898) and Léon Morel (1828–1909). Moreau carried out extensive excavations in the Aisne and Marne region from 1873 to 1893, and the large collection of La Tène material which he accumulated, and in part published, was given to the National Museum in 1899. Morel's interest in archaeology began in 1863, when he became involved in a La Tène cemetery at Somsois, near Vitry-le-François. Thereafter he continued to excavate in Champagne until his death, except for a brief period (1879–88) when his work took him to Provence. The collection which Morel amassed, and published in *La Champagne souterraine* in 1898, was second in quality only to that of The National Museum at Saint-Germain-en-Laye. When eventually it was put up for sale in 1901, it was considered to be too expensive by the French government and was eventually purchased by the British Museum. Among the most important assemblages is that from the fifth-century chieftain's burial at Somme-Bionne.

The frenetic activity in the Marne, Aisne, and Ardenne regions between 1865 and 1914, most of it carried out by peasants on behalf of local collectors, brought to light many thousands of graves from hundreds of cemeteries. This corpus of material inevitably contributed significantly to the understanding of the Celts, particularly of their burial practices. Comparable, though less intensive, work was underway at this time in

28 Plan of the chieftain's burial found at Somme-Bionne, Marne, France, and dating to the late fifth century BC. The chieftain was laid on a two-wheeled vehicle and was accompanied by his weapons, feasting gear, and horse trappings. It was excavated in 1873.

29 The Grand Duchess of Mecklenburg was an enthusiastic archaeologist. She was born in Carniola (now Slovenia) in 1856. Between 1905 and 1914 she spent a considerable part of her fortune conducting excavations on Iron Age cemeteries at Hallstatt and Stična, Magdalenska gora, Vinica, and elsewhere, amassing a collection of some 20,000 artefacts.

other parts of Europe. In Slovenia, for example, in the decade before the First World War, the Grand Duchess of Mecklenburg was instrumental in encouraging the excavation of cemeteries at Magdalenska gora, Stična, and Vinica, uncovering more than 870 graves, and also at Hallstatt itself in 1907. The Mecklenburg collection, which was eventually acquired by the Peabody Museum in Harvard, is among one of the most important for understanding the development of Iron Age societies in the eastern Alps.

Much of the archaeological activity of the last half of the nineteenth century was directed towards the examination of cemeteries. These were, after all, the sites that produced collectable artefacts with a market value, but some attention was also being given to settlement sites, in particular to the large *oppida*. Of these, Stradonice, in Bohemia, provides one of the most notorious examples. During the last quarter of the nineteenth century it was dug over at the instigation of antique dealers, the artefacts being dispersed throughout Europe while the local peasants found a ready market for the animal bone refuse recovered, selling it for the production of bonemeal. The discovery of a hoard of gold coins in 1877 increased interest still further. In all it is estimated that between 80,000 and 100,000 items were recovered, mostly belonging to the late second and first centuries BC. Some flavour of the importance of the collection began to dawn on the academic world following the publication of some of the material by J. L. Pić in 1903.

Interest in *oppida* in France was initiated by Napoleon III, whose study in the campaigns of Julius Caesar naturally led him to select for attention Bibracte, the capital of the Aedui, situated on Mont Beuvray near Autun. In 1867 he appointed Gabriel Bulliot to direct the work, which was eventually published as *Fouilles de Mont Beuvray 1867 à 1895* in 1899. Bulliot was succeeded by his nephew Joseph Déchelette, who was to become one of Europe's most influential scholars of the Iron Age before his death in the First World War at the age of 53. By that time Déchelette had published the two Iron Age volumes of his *Manuel*, a work of synthesis which summed up the advances of the great period of discovery 1860–1910 and presented the culture of the *oppida*, visible through the work at Stradonice and Mont Beuvray, in its proper context as the culmination of the Celtic achievement.

The publication of *Le Second Age du fer*—the third part of the second volume of Déchelette's *Manuel d'archéologie*—in 1914 marks the end of the pioneering phase of Celtic archaeology. Twenty years before, S. Reinach and M. Bertrand had presented an array of material in their *Les Celtes et les Gaulois dans la vallée du Po et du Danube* (1894), but the *Manuel* provided the first European-wide synthesis of La Tène material culture, demonstrating the remarkable similarities which could be detected from one side of Europe to the other. It was now possible for scholars to begin to integrate the textual and archaeological data, providing pan-European syntheses of which the two volumes of Henri Hubert, *Les Celtes et l'expansion celtique jusqu'à l'époque de La Tène* and *Les Celtes depuis l'époque de La Tène et la civilization celtique* (both 1932), were among the most ambitious.

Celtic Art

In some ways it is surprising that the awareness of the importance of Celtic art did not develop further during this formative period, but this may, at least in part, have been due to the dismissive attitudes of art historians, whose sense of values was narrowly constrained by the products of the Graeco-Roman world. The first real appreciation of the distinctive identity of Celtic art appeared in 1863, when Augustus Woolaston Franks (1826–97), who became Keeper of the Department of British and Medieval Antiquities at the British Museum (1866–96) after joining the staff in 1851, published a collection of British masterpieces in John Kemble's *Horae Ferales*. These he described as 'Late Keltic', offering a consideration of them in their European context. In doing this he was far in advance of the thinking of his continental contemporaries, most of whom would have subscribed to the belief that barbarians were incapable of producing significant works of art.

There was, however, a developing awareness of the part played by the classical world in introducing artistic concepts to the Celtic barbarians north of the Alps. The importance of the Rhône route, via Massalia, was generally accepted, and in 1875 Hermann Genthe published a work stressing the significance of the Alpine passes for the transport of Etruscan goods and ideas to the north. Five years earlier Ernst Werth had identified Etruscan inspiration in the 'Gaulish'

metalwork found in the aristocratic burial at Waldalgesheim and in 1889 the classical archaeologist Adolf Furtwängler offered an analysis of the Celtic art represented in rich grave finds from Schwarzenbach, preferring to see the exotic items as Massilliot products designed for the barbarian market. This view was still adhered to by Paul Reinecke in his publication of 1902. It followed the reasoning of art historians working on material around the Black Sea interface, who believed that many of the Scythian masterpieces had been produced in Greek workshops located in the coastal colonial settlements, specifically for the Scythian aristocracy.

Meanwhile, in Britain an alternative view was developing which saw Celtic art not as a pale, ill-mannered, reflection of classical art but as an original creation. These ideas were elegantly summarized by Sir Arthur Evans in *The Origins of Celtic Art* based on a series of lectures given in 1895. Evans's view was that Celtic art emerged from the interaction of a number of cultural influences. He acknowledged the contribution of Etruscan and Greek ideas but argued that Hallstatt elements from the eastern Alpine area as well as Scythian motifs from further east were also integral to what eventually emerged.

Evans's thesis formed the starting-point of the monumental survey undertaken by Paul Jacobsthal, Professor of Classical Archaeology at Marburg University (1912–35) and thereafter a scholar at Oxford University. Jacobsthal began his study of Celtic art in 1921 and published his seminal *Early Celtic Art*, the first volume of what he planned to be a three-volume work, in 1944. In it he recognized three principal continental styles. His 'Early Style' was an aristocratic art confined to the high status burials of the fifth and early fourth centuries BC. Here he detected native Hallstatt elements as well as the influence of an eastern nomadic or 'orientalizing' trend adding to the more obvious classical input. His second style, named after the Waldalgesheim burial, used classical floral patterns as the basis, from which was developed an original treatment of plant motifs. In the early third century the third style emerged, divided into two sub-styles, a 'Plastic Style', in which motifs were used in an essentially three-dimensional mode, and a 'Sword Style', involving inscribing and some embossing to create two-dimensional patterns.

The importance of Jacobsthal's work was that it established Celtic art as one of the great artistic achievements of Europe, with an originality and vitality which owed little to the formulaic inspiration which the Celtic masters undoubtedly received from the classical world.

We are told that the Gauls were valiant, quarrelsome, cruel, superstitious, and had the gift of pointed speech: their art also is full of contrasts. It is attractive and repellent; it is far from primitiveness and simplicity, is refined in thought and technique; elaborate and clever; full of paradoxes, restless, puzzlingly ambiguous; rational and irrational; dark and uncanny—far from the lovable humanity and transparency of Greek art. Yet, it is a real style, the first great contribution by the barbarians to European arts, the first great chapter in the everlasting mutual stock-taking of Southern, Northern and Eastern forces in the life of Europe.

IV*a* *Facing*: Helmet made in iron partially cased in repoussé decorated bronze inlaid with coral: from Canosa di Puglia, Bari, Italy. The decoration is typical of Celtic art of the Vegetal Style. Second half of fourth century BC. Staatliche Museen Antikensammlung Preussischer Kulturbesitz, Berlin.

IV*b* *Inset, left*: A gold stater of Verica who ruled the Atrebates in central southern Britain in the years leading up to the Roman invasion in AD 43. The reverse of the coin shows a mounted warrior armed with a large shield and a spear and wearing a helmet.

IV*c* *Inset, right*: A gold stater of Tasciovanus, ruler of the Catuvellauni in eastern Britain about 10 BC. The horse rider holds aloft a carnyx, or war trumpet.

Although his 'Styles' still provide a convenient general model, they are classificatory rather than explanatory. With a greatly enlarged corpus from which to work and a deepening understanding of the nature of artistic expression in pre-modern society, the study of Celtic art promises to become one of the more lively areas of debate.

Celtic Culture

The publication of *Early Celtic Art* in 1944 can be regarded as the point at which the broad range of Celtic studies at last came of age—when the uniqueness of the Celts was firmly and finally established. The second half of the twentieth century has seen major advances in all fields but none more than in archaeology. It would be impossible to fully review the achievements of this remarkable period of activity. The sheer quantity of material recovered has increased the database many hundredfold, but what is more important is the far greater attention which has been placed on context—the nature of the site itself whether it be a cemetery or a settlement. There has also been, at least in some parts of Europe, a concern to see the site as an element in a landscape and to use this larger geographical concept as the unit of study. Human communities are only one of the elements of the biome, and to understand these the entire system must be studied.

In parallel with all this there is a growing willingness, as the discipline moves away from its traditional nineteenth-century artefact-based focus, to see the values and approaches of anthropology as being of relevance to archaeology. The archaeologist's concern now lies with attempting to model and to understand the different systems which make up a society, and by examining the interactions of these systems to approach the fascinating dynamic of social change. Increasingly the archaeologist, like the anthropologist, is being drawn into considerations of communication through symbols, art, language, and oral traditions. In this way the disparate threads which make up our understanding of the Celtic peoples—defined through the disciplines of archaeology, art history, linguistics, and history—are now, at last, being drawn together in a single study. It remains to see what will emerge.

3
Barbarian Europe and the Mediterranean

1300–400 BC

To take the broad perspective of European development, it can be said that the period 1300–1100 BC was a time of major reformation. It marked the end of an early cycle of food-producing economies (traditionally the Neolithic to the end of the Middle Bronze Age), which had culminated in the emergence of the Aegean-centred Mycenaean–Minoan 'civilization', and the beginning of a new cycle which was to see the rise and fall of the broader, Mediterranean-centred, civilization of the Graeco-Roman world. At its maximum extent, in the third century AD, the culminating Roman Empire was to stretch from the desert fringes of Africa in the south to the forests of the North European Plain and from the eastern deserts to the Atlantic. The collapse of that system in the fourth and fifth centuries AD created a turmoil from which western European civilization was to emerge to become, for a brief interlude from the late fifteenth to early twentieth centuries, the centre of a world system.

It is within this 'middle cycle'—1300 BC–AD 400—that the communities speaking a Celtic language and known to contemporary writers as an ethnically distinctive people called 'Celts' or 'Gauls' emerged and made their dramatic and lasting impact on the consciousness of their literate neighbours. To understand the origins of the Celts we must begin by considering the world they were to inhabit.

The Aegean World: 1300–1000 BC

Europe's first civilization, focused on the island of Crete, began its spectacular development about 3000 BC, reaching its peak of energy and influence by the middle of the second millennium BC, by which time the island had become a centre for a widely flung exchange network linking the Aegean coasts of Asia Minor with the mainland of Greece. It was here, centred largely on the Peloponnese, that a peripheral zone developed whose archaeological manifestation is known as Mycenaean and whose society is dimly reflected in the epic tradition codified by Homer. By the middle of the second millennium BC Mycenaean power had developed to such an extent that over the next two centuries its influence was to spread not only to the Minoan homeland of Crete but to the Asia Minor coast and the island of Rhodes in the east and to southern Italy and Sicily in the west, some of its distinctive pottery reaching as far west as Andalucía.

The Mycenaean–Minoan civilization created a centralizing focus in the Aegean, which lay at the core of a complex network of exchange contacts drawing commodities from Egypt in the south, most notably ivory, and from central, western, and northern Europe, whence came such desirable raw materials as tin, copper, gold, amber, and probably furs. The relative stability of the system over the period 1600–1200 BC gave time for the networks of exchange to become consolidated, and those barbarian communities commanding rare resources or trade routes began to benefit in a variety of ways from these long-distance exchanges.

During this time, in the heart of Anatolia, the Hittites were reaching a peak of their development. One of their particular achievements was a knowledge of iron production, a skill at this stage unknown in the Mediterranean and Europe. Iron was at first a rare and highly valued commodity which appears to have been used principally for aristocratic gift exchanges. The iron-bladed dagger in the tomb of Tutankhamun (1352 BC) was precisely such a gift. One of the Hittite texts dating to the thirteenth century gives a fascinating insight into exchanges at this time. It is a letter from the Hittite king Hattusilis III to the king of Assyria, responding to a request for iron. He says that no good iron is being made at the moment, but as soon as some is produced he will send it, meanwhile 'Today I am dispatching an iron dagger blade to you.'

The stability of the late-second-millennium world was shaken and eventually fell apart in a series of convulsions in the twelfth and eleventh centuries BC—the period known as the Greek Dark Ages. Many reasons have been suggested for this complex and ill-understood event—folk movement from the barbarian north, overpopulation, and plague. Whether there were indeed significant prime causes or simply a systems-collapse brought about by a number of interacting or self-intensifying factors is difficult to say from the ill-focused archaeological evidence. What is clear is that it was a period of folk mobility during which much of the old order disappeared. Surviving texts refer to the raids of the 'Sea People' who impinged upon coastal Egypt. There were major population replacements in Cyprus and the Levant and the Hittite empire collapsed. In the Peloponnese—the focus of Mycenaean culture—the aristocratic power centres all but disappeared and a major decline in population is evident.

It is possible that the ripples of these momentous events were felt in the western Mediterranean. The settlement of the Shardana in Sardinia is thought to be one such event. If so, the new settlers were simply following long-established maritime trading routes to the west.

The impact of the Aegean systems-collapse on the European hinterland was considerable. Existing exchange systems broke down or were transformed. Some communities, once part of European-wide networks, found themselves isolated and new configurations emerged.

The Re-Formation: 1000–800 BC

The first two centuries of the first millennium BC was a crucial period in the formation of Europe. During this time the principal social and economic groupings that were to dominate the scene for over a millennium began to crystallize out.

In the Aegean, complex movements of Greek-speaking communities led to a repopulation of some areas of Greece and a reinvigoration of others, whilst from here some groups moved eastwards across the Aegean, settling the islands and eventually carving out for themselves a foothold on the peninsulas and sheltered havens of the Aegean coast of Asia Minor, where three broad configurations were to emerge—Aeolians in the north, Ionians in the centre, and Dorians in the south. No doubt many of these early immigrant communities mixed with the local populations—the Lycians, the Legians, and the Carians—to absorb new genes and new cultures. For many, particularly the Ionians, it was a time of experiment and energy from which emerged the earliest and most vital manifestations of Greek culture. Significantly, according to tradition, it was in one of the Ionian cities, either Smyrna or Chios, that the epics with which we associate the name of Homer were first written down.

The Greek enclaves on the coast of Asia Minor provided an interface between the Aegean and the rising power of the Persians in the east, buffered for a while by powerful inland states such as the Lydians. They were thus able to benefit from the culture of their eastern land-locked neighbours, while at the same time becoming part of the maritime world of the Mediterranean.

The Levantine coast (now Syria, Lebanon, and Israel) also developed a culturally distinctive maritime interface—peopled by communities collectively known as Phoenicians whose cities, Byblos, Tyre, and Sidon, became famous in trading ventures reaching to the Atlantic. To the east of them lay the demanding empires of the Assyrians and Babylonians, who provided the motivation behind much of the Phoenician commercial enterprise.

Both the eastern Greeks and the Phoenicians were to have a significant impact on barbarian Europe, and the subjugation, in the sixth century BC, of both coastal interfaces, Greek Asia Minor by the Persians and Phoenicia by the Babylonians, was further to influence the course of barbarian development.

It was during this period that new cultural configurations were developing on the Pontic Steppe along the northern shores of the Black Sea. The area had long been settled by communities who depended upon the horse and horse-drawn vehicles to enable them to maintain a degree of nomadic mobility over the huge tracts of steppe which they inhabited. Archaeologically these communities are known, after their favoured burial mode, as the Catacomb culture.

In the eastern hinterland, roughly centred on the middle stretches of the Volga River, another semi-nomadic group developed, adopting a different burial rite, a wooden cabin-like grave set in a pit beneath a barrow mound. These burials typified the Timber Grave culture. The archaeological evidence suggests that the Timber Grave culture expanded westwards during the early centuries of the first millennium, eventually taking over much of the Pontic Steppe region previously occupied by the Catacomb culture. The *Histories* of Herodotus written in the early fifth century BC describe a group known as the Cimmerians who originally occupied the northern shores of the Black Sea and were ousted by Scythians coming from the east. It is tempting to relate the Cimmerians with the archaeologically defined Catacomb culture and the Scythians with the Timber Grave culture, though the exact chronology of the events, or whether it was as simple as the literary account suggests, remains unclear. Some additional support for the turbulent nature of the times is given in Assyrian tablets which refer to both the Cimmerians and Scythians as hordes of warlike horsemen serving as mercenaries in the conflicts played out in Asia Minor in the eighth and seventh centuries.

From the point of view of our present concerns, what is of particular interest is that there should be evidence of unrest and folk movement among the horse riders of the Pontic Steppe, building to a peak in the eighth century when some moved south-east into Asia Minor. Given the geography of the region and the fact that the western shores of the Black Sea, including the Lower Danube region, are really an extension of the Pontic Steppe, it is not unreasonable to suggest, as many archaeologists have done, that there was a parallel movement of Cimmerians eastwards along the Danube into central Europe. It is a suggestion to which we shall return.

The western fringe of Europe, facing the Atlantic, was altogether different. Here in a broad arc, stretching from Scotland to south-western Iberia, the maritime communities were linked in a complex of exchange networks probably stretching back in time at least to the Neolithic period. By the Bronze Age metals were among the more important commodities shipped, copper from Ireland, Wales, and western Iberia, tin from Cornwall, Brittany, and Galicia, and gold from Ireland, Wales, and north-western Iberia. This metal-rich arc will have provided much of the bronze and gold circulating in western Europe, and the enhanced consumption of metal in the Aegean may well have provided a market eager for gold and tin from the Atlantic zone. With the collapse of the Mycenaean–Minoan centre, demand would have slackened, but there is ample evidence for a still-vigorous zone of contact along the sea-ways. In so far as the archaeological evidence allows us to estimate, there seems to have been an intensification of activity in the eighth century, occasioned, as we will suggest, by developing Phoenician interests in the south-west of Iberia.

In the heart of Europe, stretching from eastern France to Hungary and from northern Italy to Poland, in the period from about 1300 to 700 BC, there developed a considerable degree of cultural uniformity indicative of convergent development. The period is called the Urnfield period and the broadly defined culture which it represents shares the name (Map 1). The characteristic which serves to give the impression of uniformity is the burial rite, which, as the cultural name implies, involves the burial of the cremated remains of the dead in cinerary urns in well-defined cemeteries. In addition to this the varied array of cast and beaten bronze-work, normally personal ornaments, tools, and weapons, shares considerable stylistic similarities over large areas.

Within the broad zone exhibiting these generalized characteristics it is possible to define regional groupings, and within each subregions can be recognized, usually on the basis of decorative styles of pottery. Many of the groupings which first appear at this time retain a degree of identity throughout the Urnfield period and into the Hallstatt Iron Age which follows. In other words, the social and economic processes which can first be detected in the period 1300–1000 BC over much of central Europe create a structure which is largely maintained over the next half millennium or so, by which time Greek historians have identified 'Celts' as living within this region.

The origin and development of the Urnfield cultural continuum is a much debated issue. It is probably best to see within the Transalpine core zone an initial phase of development in the period 1300–1150 BC, responding to the dislocations and reorderings occasioned by the decline and collapse of the Mycenaean–Minoan world. To what extent the communities of the eastern part of this zone, centred in what is now the territory of Hungary, played an active role in the events across the Balkan mountains to the south is an important but still ill-focused issue. Some similar weapon and armour types are found in both regions, while alien pottery forms from Bulgaria and the Troad are highly reminiscent of vessels more normally found further north. Another observation of some significance is that the long-established tell settlements in the Middle and Lower Danube region were widely abandoned during this formative period when an entirely new settlement pattern emerged. The evidence as it comes down to us in its fragmentary form suggests a phase of disruption and upheaval in the Middle and Lower Danube which must, in some way, be related to events in the Aegean. To what extent folk movement was involved, and in what direction populations may have moved, are questions at present beyond the limits of reasonable conjecture.

Urnfield developments in the Hungarian region preceded those in the Alpine zone to the west and may indeed have helped to exacerbate changes among indigenous groups already set in train as a result of the breakdown of the older trade routes which had developed to serve the consumer needs of the Aegean. In this zone there is no direct evidence of major disruption but rather an internal development linked to an intensification of contact southwards through the Alps to the Po Valley and beyond, across the Apennines, deep into peninsular Italy. By 1000 BC Italy, the Alps, and Transalpine Europe from east-

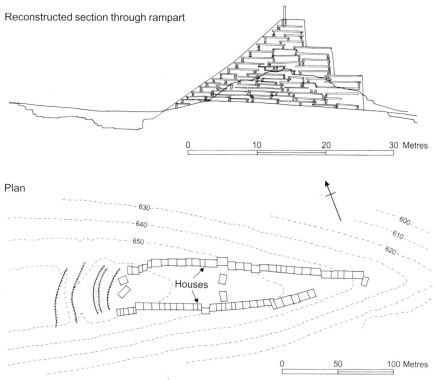

Reconstructed section through rampart

0   10   20   30 Metres

Plan

630
640
650
600
610
620

Houses

0   50   100 Metres

30 The Late Bronze Age
fortified settlement of
Wittnauer Horn, Aargau,
Switzerland. The site occupied a ridge-end protected
by a massive rampart. The
houses inside were arranged
in a regular fashion around a
central open area.

ern France to Slovakia were closely interlinked, as similarities in material culture vividly demonstrate.

Within the Alpine and Transalpine zone of the Urnfield culture the evidence suggests a degree of social and economic stability. In such conditions it is possible to understand something of the changes which begin to take place. In several areas there appears to have been a marked rise in population, with the appearance of new settlements closely spaced in an increasingly farmed landscape. In parallel with this, copper production intensified, particularly in the eastern Alpine metal-rich zone. Hill forts, quite often spurs cut off by massive timber-laced ramparts, were constructed in some number, indicating that the coercive power of some sector of the population was now able to command surplus labour to aggrandize or protect a chosen settlement. That this power may have been that of a leading individual or lineage is suggested by the occurrence of certain burials more elaborately furnished than others and, in particular, by the appearance of horse trappings representing the riding horse or horse-drawn vehicle of the warrior or aristocrat.

The Foundation of the New Order: 800–650 BC

The eighth century BC was a formative period in the history of Europe: in the Mediterranean it saw the beginnings of the Greek colonial adventure and the development of the far-flung Phoenician trading system, while in barbarian

44

Europe the infiltration of Pontic Steppe communities into the Great Hungarian Plain made the horse even more readily available to the emerging Hallstatt aristocracy of central and western Europe. These various threads need to be explored, for together they provide the essential basis for developments throughout the rest of the millennium.

Towards the beginning of the century the two Ionian city-states of Chalcis and Eretria on the island of Euboea, at first together and later separately, began to sail through the Straits of Messina to explore the resources of the coasts of the Tyrrhenian Sea between the Italian peninsula and the islands of Corsica and Sardinia (Map 6). In doing so they were echoing journeys made centuries before by travellers from the Mycenaean world. Among the attractions they discovered were the rich metal resources of Etruria and the adjacent island of Elba. By about 770 BC they had founded a colonial settlement at Pithecusae on the island of Iscia in the Bay of Naples, admirably sited as a forward post to trade with the Etruscan metal producers. A little later a new establishment was set up on the nearby mainland coast at Cumae.

From these early beginnings followed the rapid colonization of Mezzogiorno and Sicily. Zancle (Messina) was founded on the north-eastern extremity of Sicily, with Rhegion (Reggio) on the opposite Italian coast. Naxos was established further down the coast. Soon other Greek city-states joined in. Rhodes may have been early on the scene, while Megara founded an establishment at Megara Hyblaea in the mid-eighth century south of Naxos. The primary colonization of the east coast of Sicily was completed by the Corinthian foundation of Syracuse, traditionally in 733 BC. In the following two centuries many more Greek colonies claimed intervening territories, until the region could justify its name of Magna Graecia.

The establishment of a Greek presence just beyond the southern fringe of Etruscan territory provided a significant stimulus to the development of Etruscan culture, but it would be wrong to assume that the colonists were the sole contact. A more likely scenario is that the foundation of the Greek colonies encouraged maritime trade to develop rapidly, providing a framework of safe havens to allow sailors and merchants from many countries to explore and to trade. In this way Corinth was able to play a significant part in introducing Greek culture to the Etruscan aristocracy, and in the seventh century, according to Pliny, Corinthian artists were well established in Etruria. Along with the Greek merchants would have come others, including Phoenicians, bringing a range of exotic goods and ideas from the east Mediterranean in return for iron, copper, and silver from Elba and the Colline Metallifere just north of Populonia and Vetulonia.

The appearance of a range of luxury goods added a stimulus to social development in the late Villanovan culture of Etruria. Cities began to grow, providing an opportunity for the aristocracy to manipulate the newly available prestige goods and thus to consolidate and enhance the status of themselves and their lineages. Towards the end of the eighth century BC these 'orientalizing' influences were well underway in Etruria. The coastal cities, growing commercially stronger every minute, began to develop maritime interests of their own, which, in the seventh century, were to expand through the Tyrrhenian Sea and westwards to the coasts of Gaul and Iberia.

In parallel with the expansion of Greek influence in the western Mediterranean and the rising power of the Etruscans, the Phoenicians of the Levant were rapidly establishing their own trading enclaves as far west as the Atlantic (Map 7). Traditionally Phoenicians had already founded a port-of-trade on the Atlantic island of Cádiz, just off the coast of Andalucía, in 1104 BC. Another intermediate port was established at Utica on the northern coast of Tunisia at about the same time and served as a primary port of call until Carthage was settled nearby in 814–13. If these traditional dates are to be believed, little time elapsed between the end of Mycenaean involvement in the west and the beginning of Phoenician. There are, however, uncertainties about the historical dates, since there is as yet little reliable archaeological evidence to suggest a Phoenician presence much before the eighth century, though an early Phoenician inscription found at Nora on Sardinia has been dated to the mid-ninth century by some authorities. Lack of archaeological evidence cannot, of course, be taken as proof of the absence of early Phoenician enterprise in these regions.

Whatever the origin of Phoenician penetration in the west, it is abundantly clear that the eighth century saw a consolidation of the sea routes, via Tunisia, western Sicily, and Sardinia to southern Andalucía and Cádiz (Phoenician Gadir) and a dramatic intensification of trade with the west. The main attraction appears to have been metals and in particular silver produced in huge quantity from the metal-rich pyrite zone of the Rio Tinto and Sierra Morena. This region—the kingdom of Tartessos—developed close links with the Phoenicians at Cádiz, and the amount of silver exported from there became legendary. In return, eastern goods and craft skills became available to the Tartessian aristocracy, and Tartessian culture, like that of Etruria, experienced a rapid phase of 'orientalization', most readily apparent in the luxury goods found in the graves of the local aristocracy in the eighth and seventh centuries.

While the port at Cádiz was admirably sited to exploit Tartessian resources, by virtue of its Atlantic position it was also able to tap into long-established Atlantic trade routes along which gold, copper, and, most important, tin were transported. Phoenician exploitation of these sea-ways, northwards along the Iberian coast and southwards along the Atlantic shores of Morocco, was to develop in later centuries, but by building the trading node at Cádiz in the eighth century the Phoenicians created a new interface between the Mediterranean and Atlantic systems. The effect was to intensify activity along the Atlantic sea-ways in the final stages of the indigenous Bronze Age.

Turning now to the eastern approaches to Europe, we saw how the semi-nomadic communities of the Pontic Steppe—known to classical writers as the Cimmerians—were undergoing a phase of turbulence and disruption resulting in folk movement. The Cimmerian penetration of eastern Europe is a complex issue which has been much debated in the past. The principal argument for the presence of a 'Pontic' element rests on sets of bronze horse gear—bits, side pieces, and phalarae from the harness found extensively distributed over much of the territory of Hungary, often in contexts with local material of the eighth and seventh centuries. The eastern (Pontic) inspiration, if not the production, of this material is clear. Other 'eastern' items, found less frequently, are short bronze daggers and bird-headed rattles from the tops of ceremonial staffs. Recent work at Mezöcsat and nearby, in the north of the Great Hungarian Plain, has identified a series of cemeteries which may well belong to immigrant groups, while similar enclaves in the south of the Plain suggest that settlement may have been widespread.

Interpretation of this kind of archaeological evidence is not straightforward, but the simplest explanation would be to see groups of people moving from the turbulent areas of the Pontic Steppe westwards along the Danube Valley into the Great Hungarian Plain, an area geographically similar to their homeland, bringing with them their breeding stock of horses superior in speed and strength to the west European type. Once established to the east of the Danube, and maintaining their links with their ancestral homelands, these new neighbours to the Urnfield cultures of central and western Europe would have been well placed to trade superior horses and their gear to the Hallstatt aristocracies, introducing at the same time new concepts of horse-riding. Although, as we have seen, the horse was already a symbol of status among the Urnfield communities, the folk movements of the eighth century established the culture of the horse and a ready supply of beasts, close to the eastern frontier.

Within the old Urnfield zone of western central Europe, bounded on the west by the communities of the Atlantic arc, on the east by the 'Pontic' communities of the Great Hungarian Plain, and on the south by the Alps, significant changes can be detected after the middle of the eighth century BC. This period, dating from *c*.750–600 BC, is referred to as the Hallstatt C culture—a generalized term which reflects a broad cultural continuum shared by a variety of distinctive regional groupings. It is at the aristocratic level that the culture is at its most universal, being reflected in the widespread distribution of warrior gear, in particular the Hallstatt long sword of iron or bronze (Maps 3 and 4), a distinctive array of chapes with which the sword sheath terminated, and the trappings for horses both as cavalry beasts and yoked in pairs for pulling vehicles. The distribution of these various artefacts demonstrates a core area stretching in a broad zone from central France to Bohemia and Hungary, but with a number of more isolated finds beyond indicating the huge peripheral territory linked by systems of exchange to the core.

Within the Hallstatt C cemeteries it is possible to distinguish different sets of grave goods. Warriors might be accompanied only by a sword and other personal gear, while a mounted warrior might also have been provided with his horse's tackle. The highest social level was probably that represented by vehicle burials, which, in this period, were restricted to a zone stretching from the

Middle Rhine to Bohemia (Map 5). The vehicles involved were four-wheeled and comparatively heavy and unwieldy, as would befit a ceremonial or funerary cart. Their spoked wheels, strengthened by iron tires shrunk on and nailed to the composite wooden felloe, represent a high level of technical achievement. In some burials, like the Bohemian graves of Hradenin and Lovosice, wooden yokes studded with decorative bronze nails survive.

The long slashing sword suitable as a cavalry weapon, horses, ceremonial vehicles, the rite of inhumation, and the widespread use of iron for weapons mark a distinct break with traditional Urnfield culture. None of these characteristics (except for abundant iron (Map 2)) was entirely unknown earlier, but taken together they demonstrate a significant change. The élite was now attempting to distinguish itself by employing exotic modes of burial adopted from beyond their homeland. The horses and the style of trappings are essentially eastern in origin. The inspiration for the vehicle is more difficult to determine. Vehicle burial was widespread among Pontic communities, but the technology of the Hallstatt carts with their spoked wheels and composite felloe is more likely to have been transmitted from the east via the Mediterranean. Similar vehicle burials have been discovered at Salamis in Cyprus dating to the late seventh century BC and one likely possibility is that knowledge of the technology spread via Etruria to the Transalpine communities. A similar route is possible for the introduction of iron technology, though iron trinkets are also known in the early Pontic-style graves of the Great Hungarian Plain.

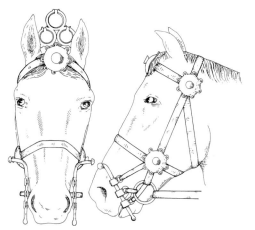

31 Reconstruction of the way in which horse trappings of the seventh and sixth centuries BC were probably arranged, based on evidence from graves in southern Germany.

Perhaps a simpler way to view the emergence to archaeological visibility of the Hallstatt C aristocracy is to see it as an élite eagerly absorbing cultural influences from the east via the mid-Danube, and from the south, through the east Alpine passes, and adapting the ideas and technologies to its own social needs. It was a time of energy and innovation. The fine iron sword and the iron-tired wheels can reasonably be regarded as Hallstatt C developments of some originality. This readiness to adopt new exotic ideas as a means of displaying élite status was to intensify still further in the sixth and early fifth centuries, as contact with the Mediterranean systems developed.

The Western Mediterranean: 650–450 BC

Greek and Phoenician interest in the trading potential of the western Mediterranean was well underway by the seventh century BC, as spheres of commercial activity began to crystallize. At this stage Etruria seems to have played a leading role in the trans-shipment of goods around the northern part of the west Mediterranean and some way down the coast of Italy, but in the second half of the seventh century certain of the eastern Greeks, from the coasts of

Asia Minor, began to explore more widely. One of these adventurers, Kolaios of Samos, is reputed to have travelled to Tartessos about 630 BC, finding the market 'untouched'—untouched, that is, by Greeks. That he was said by Herodotus to have been sailing south for Africa when he was blown off course is not particularly convincing but may hide a different reality. At the trading station of Naucratis in the Nile delta, where eastern Greeks as well as Phoenicians regularly met, the Samians may well have learned of the lucrative Phoenician contacts with Tartessos and decided to explore for themselves.

Soon to follow were the Phocaeans from the Aeolian coast. According to Herodotus, they set sail in their pentekonters (warships), exploring the Adriatic region, Etruria, Iberia, and Tartessos, establishing friendly relations with the Tartessian king. Their route almost certainly took them along the north shores of the west Mediterranean, where they would have become aware of the Etruscan entrepôts along the littoral of Provence and Languedoc, possibly to the port of Rhode in north-west Spain, which may have been established as early as the eighth century. Years of seasonal sailing in these waters would have familiarized them with the best harbours and landfalls, and in c.600 BC the first Phocaean colony was founded at Massalia (Marseilles). Others followed: Emporion and Agde in the fifth century and Tauroention, Olbia, and Nice in the fourth. In this way the Greek presence began to impose itself within the traditional preserve of the Etruscan cities.

The attractions of Massalia were many. Not only was it an excellent well-protected anchorage in the heart of a comparatively productive territory, but it also

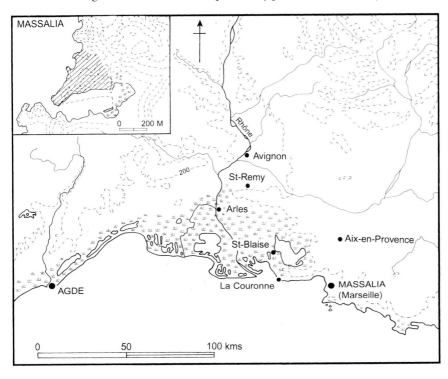

32 The Greek port of Massalia (Marseilles) was founded on the southern coast of Gaul about 600 BC by colonists from Phocaea. An easily defended promontory was chosen, overlooking a large almost land-locked harbour. Massalia was well sited to control trade along the Rhône: it lay conveniently close to the Rhône mouth but clear of the marshy delta.

lay close to the mouth of the Rhône, which provided access into the barbarian hinterland, from which a variety of commodities could be obtained. More significant, at least in the first decades of the colony's existence, was its convenient location in the centre of the long coastal route linking the productive Spanish Levant with Etruria and Magna Graecia. The quantity of Etruscan pottery found in early deposits in the city are impressive indications of the importance of Etruscan-dominated exchanges at this time (Map 8).

Before looking at the impact of the colonization on the Hallstatt communities of the hinterland, we must continue to consider in outline the history of the western Mediterranean in so far as it is likely to have had an impact on temperate Europe.

Towards the middle of the sixth century BC major political events in the east were to send shock waves throughout the west Mediterranean. In 574 BC the great trading cities of Phoenicia were overrun and incorporated into the expanding Babylonian empire. The effect was to sever long-established links between the mother cities of Tyre and Sidon and their overseas trading systems. Henceforth, with the umbilical cord cut, Carthage became the leading power in the Phoenician, now Punic, west Mediterranean. A few years later, in 545, Persia expanded its influence westwards to the Aegean, absorbing into its state system the eastern Greek cities of the coastal zone. The opposition of the Greek states encouraged the Persians to undertake a further westward advance to the Greek mainland, where, at Salamis in 480 and Plataea in 479, the Persian forces were soundly beaten.

Many of the eastern Greek cities accepted Persian sovereignty, but the Phocaeans, agreeing that subservience was intolerable, decided to migrate *en masse* to the west Mediterranean to build upon their maritime enterprises already well rooted in the colony at Massalia. The site chosen for the migrant population to settle was Alalia on the eastern coast of Corsica. Such a move was perceived by the Etruscans to be a direct threat to Etruscan trading enterprises, and the opposition, led by the city of Caere, amassed a fleet of sixty Etruscan and sixty Carthaginian vessels to oppose the Phocaeans. The ensuing battle, in the Sardinian Sea, probably between Sardinia and Corsica, was a Phocaean victory, but such was the cost that the Phocaeans decided to abandon Alalia, eventually founding their colony on the Italian mainland at Velia in the territory of Posidonia.

The Battle of the Sardinian Sea, which took place about 540 BC, was a major event in west Mediterranean history, in that it significantly changed the political geography of the region, isolating Massalia and throwing her far more on her own resources, leading to the establishment of further colonies along the southern French coast. The greatly strengthened Etruscan–Carthaginian coalition now began to pose a serious threat to the commercial interests of the Greek cities of Magna Graecia. The establishment at the Etruscan port of Pyri of a place sacred to the Phoenician goddess Astarte by the 'king' of Caere (recorded on gold plaques in a bilingual text) is an indication of the close relations which existed between Carthage and Etruria, a point further emphasized by large volumes of Etruscan goods found at Carthage.

However, the growing power of Magna Graecia began to tell. An Etruscan expedition against the Greek enclave at Cumae in 525 BC failed, thus preventing Etruscan expansion southwards. The pressure continued, but fifty years later the destruction of an Etruscan fleet off Cumae in 474 marked the end of Etruscan expansionist policies in the south.

Increasing pressure on the Etruscan thalassocracy in the Tyrrhenian Sea throughout the sixth century was a significant factor in the landward expansion of Etruscan interests northwards through the Apennines into the southern reaches of the Po Valley. New cities like Marzabotto and Felsina (Bologna) were established on the major routes, and there was a significant Etruscan involvement in the development of the two Adriatic ports of Spina and Adria. By the middle of the fifth century the northern frontier of Etruscan settlement had extended to the north bank of the Po and the ports were providing outlets of growing importance to the Adriatic shipping lanes. In parallel, Etruscan influence in the Tyrrhenian Sea declined. The Syracusan-led offensive against coastal Etruria in 454 and 453, though inconclusive, was symptomatic of the pressures besetting the once-flourishing maritime cities.

The developing Etruscan interests in the Po Valley in the century c.550–450 BC brought them into increasingly close contact with native communities occupying the territory from the Po to the Alps, where two archaeologically defined cultures can be identified (Map 17): the Este culture in the east, occupying a broad zone from the sea to Lake Garda in the valley of the Adige, and the Golasecca culture, the main focus of which lay around Lakes Como, Lugano, and Maggiore. Both groups were deeply rooted in the indigenous cultures of the Late Bronze Age and by virtue of their geographical location dominated the routes through the Alps which linked the Etruscan south with the Hallstatt north. The development of an urban agglomeration at Como in the fifth century, extending to some 150 hectares, must, in part at least, be due to the intensity of commercial activity and the model of urbanism derived from the Etruscan zone. As we will see, the Golasecca culture formed a significant bridge between the Mediterranean states and the changing Hallstatt world.

The Hallstatt World: 650–450 BC

In order to discuss the rapidly developing social, economic, and political systems of the west central Hallstatt zone in this crucial period it is necessary to introduce the chronological framework that will be adopted. A great deal has been written on the subject and there are still areas of debate, but the following is now widely accepted as a serviceable scheme:

Hallstatt C	c.750–c.600 BC	Hallstatt D2–3	c.530/520–c.450/440 BC
Hallstatt D1	c.600–c.530/520 BC	La Tène A	c.450/440–c.370/350 BC

33 *Right*: The burial mound of Hohmichele, near Heuneburg, dating to the late sixth century BC, is shown here under excavation in 1937–8. The style of digging, in arbitrary horizontal spits, was typical of German excavations at the time.

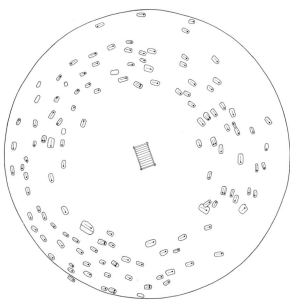

The scheme usefully correlates with the principal events in western Mediterranean history, with Hallstatt D1 beginning at the time of the foundation of Massalia and the beginning of Hallstatt D2–3 coinciding with the turmoil following the Battle of the Sardinian Sea and running parallel with a major phase of Etruscan expansion northwards.

We have already seen how in the Hallstatt C period the zone of élite burials, represented by wagons and horse gear, or harness and yokes without wagons, extended in a broad, and discontinuous, zone from Bohemia to southern Germany, apart from rare exceptions seldom spreading west of the Rhine (Map 5). At this time the principal concentration lay in southern Germany (Baden-Württemberg and Bavaria), where more than ninety élite burials have been identified. In addition to vehicle and horse-related accoutrements, élite lifestyle was frequently represented by pottery and bronze vessels of various kinds related to feasting accompanying the dead to the grave. Élite burials continued to be found in southern Germany

34 *Above, left*: The great burial mound of Magdalenenberg bei Villingen, Schwarzwald-Baar-Kreis, Germany, contained a central burial in a log-built chamber dating to the mid-sixth century BC. A number of other burials were inserted into the mound over the next two centuries.

35 *Left*: The barrow of Magdalenenberg, in Germany, covered a well-preserved timber chamber protected beneath a cairn of stones.

during Hallstatt D1, but no longer appear in Bohemia. Some of them, like the barrow burials of Hohmichele near Hundersingen and Magdalenenberg near Villingen, were colossal structures requiring much effort in the interests of monumentalizing the lineage of the dead aristocrats, and the Chinese silk used to embroider the dress of the woman buried at Hohmichele indicates the ability of the élite to acquire rare trade goods.

To what extent the foundation of Massalia about 600 BC influenced the growing power of the west Hallstatt chieftains is difficult to say. Certainly some exotic products, such as the hydria found at Grächwil, 'Rhodian' flagons (Map 9), and bead-edged bronze basins from Magna Graecia, were becoming available as grave goods, and these may well have been transported via Massalia and the Rhône corridor to add a touch of the exotic to the Hallstatt feast enhanced by Massilliot wine (Map 10).

That Greek ideas were being readily accepted is vividly demonstrated by the hill fort of

36 The Greek bronze hydria, found in a burial at Grächwil, Switzerland, was imported from the Mediterranean in the sixth century BC. It may have been a diplomatic gift to a local chieftain. Historisches Museum, Berne.

Heuneburg overlooking the Danube. The earliest Hallstatt rampart was constructed in the middle of the seventh century, and the site continued in use for some 200 years. During Hallstatt D1 the defences were completely remodelled in a style unique in Transalpine Europe: stone wall footings were laid with hollow, forward projecting bastions regularly spaced along its west side. Above the foundations the wall was built of carefully squared mudbricks of regular size and shape. This alien structure, so clearly the concept of a Greek mind, and presumably overseen by a Greek architect, is a striking example of the willingness (and ability) of the local Hallstatt élite to adopt totally foreign modes of expression in the interests of displaying status and power.

That the colony of Massalia was now contributing to the aristocratic culture of the west Hallstatt zone is clear, but the intensity or duration of this contribution is not. All that can safely be said is that there is no evidence to suggest that, at this stage, the Rhône corridor saw a massive movement of goods and commodities. Massalia was still part of an extensive Mediterranean network and there would have been little impetus actively to seek markets in the hinterland.

A major change came about at the beginning of Hallstatt D2–3, that is about 530–520 BC. In the west Hallstatt zone this can best be characterized as a 'concentration of power' in fewer centres. The phenomenon can be recognized in two ways: by the increasing exclusivity of the élite burial rite and by the abandonment of a number of hill forts, leaving fewer sites to develop as strong cen-

37 The hilltop settlement of Heuneburg, Baden-Württemberg, Germany, showing the situation in the late sixth century BC (Period IVb), when the walls were built in Greek style of mud-brick on a stone-rubble foundation. The barrows nearby lay above an earlier settlement.

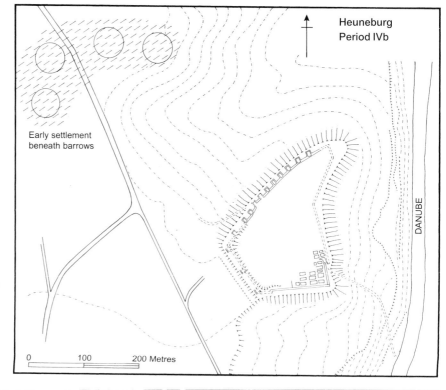

Early settlement beneath barrows

Heuneburg Period IVb

DANUBE

0   100   200 Metres

38 Aerial view of the hill fort of Heuneburg overlooking the River Danube. The site was used and fortified inter-mittently from the Late Bronze Age and in the late sixth century became a centre of princely power.

39 *Above*: For one brief period in the late sixth century the defensive wall of the Heuneburg was built of mudbrick on a stone foundation in a style closely reminiscent of Greek defensive building. Such a project, deep in barbarian Europe, would imply the intervention of a Greek architect.

40 *Right*: The north-facing wall of the Heuneburg was, during the phase when it was constructed in Greek style, provided with close-spaced rectangular bastions designed more for grandiose effect than for defensive necessity.

41 *Below*: Excavations inside the south-east corner of Heuneburg. The archaeological stratigraphy was well preserved. Here, a succession of close-spaced timber buildings was recovered dating to the second half of the sixth century BC.

42 *Below, right*: Excavations in the south-east corner of the hill fort of Heuneburg, showing the archaelogical traces of the timber buildings.

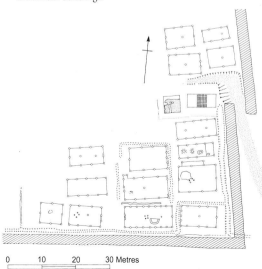

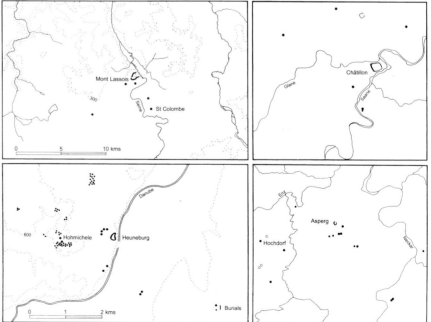

43 *Above*: The hill fort of Ipf, Bopfingen, Germany, dominates the surrounding countryside. In all probability it served as a centre of princely power in the late sixth century BC.

44 *Right*: The location of four of the 'princely centres' of the late sixth century BC. The focus of each is a fortified hilltop often commanding a major river route. Rich burials cluster nearby.

Mont Lassois

300

Saône

St Colombe

0   5   10 kms

Glane

Châtillon

Saône

Danube

600

Hohmichele

Heuneburg

0   1   2 kms

Burials

Enz

Asperg

Hochdorf

Neckar

tral foci. In southern Germany, for example, the core of aristocratic power, the number of known burials with wagons or harness decreases from forty-six to twenty, and in some areas of the Swabian Alps élite burials disappear altogether after the end of Hallstatt D1. In the region of Breisgau, of the twelve hill forts occupied in Hallstatt D1, only one continued in use in the subsequent period.

The archaeological data imply a rapid social change, but one which would be entirely understandable within the context of indigenous development. In parallel with the emergence of fewer, richer centres of power in the core area of southern Germany, there was a marked expansion of the system westwards from the Rhine into northern and eastern France. A glance at Map 5 will show that the focus of power now occupied a swath of territory to the north of the Alps linking the river systems of the Rhône/Saône, Seine, Rhine, and Danube. It could fairly be said that the nexus of west central European communications was now dominated by a single cultural and social system, and the amount of gold found in the burials (Map 15) is an indication of its productive capacity.

The élite systems of Hallstatt D2–3 are characterized by the appearance of comparatively large quantities of Mediterranean imports found in both the major hill forts and the princely burials (Maps 10–12). That the range of goods is limited to wine-drinking equipment appropriate to the Greek *symposion* strongly suggests that it was the *idea* of the symposion that was accepted and adopted by the élite, as an extension, no doubt, of their long-established feasting rites. The rich female burial at Vix neatly exemplifies the range of imports with its huge krater for wine-mixing, jug for pouring, basins, and Attic cups for drinking. The discovery of numerous fragments of Attic cups in the nearby hill fort of Mont Lassois is an indication of the princely residence. A similar array of Attic pottery from Heuneburg III, found together with the Massilliot amphorae in which the wine was transported, shows that after the rebuilding which followed the violent destruction of the mudbrick defences of Heuneburg IV in about 530/520 BC, contact with the Mediterranean world developed even more strongly. It is to this period that the rich chieftain burial of Hochdorf near the hill fort of Hohenasperg belongs.

While it could reasonably be argued that this late phase of Hallstatt development was little more than an intensification of social trends deeply rooted in the indigenous Urnfield culture of the region, it would be perverse to say that the economic impetus of the Greek littoral, after the traumas of the 540–530s BC, had nothing to do with the sudden appearance of Mediterranean trade goods in the barbarian hinterland. The most satisfactory explanation would be to accept that both societies had needs—the Greeks to develop new trading partners, the Hallstatt élite to find new modes of expression consistent with their aristocratic systems. For a brief period, 530–450, these needs coincided and the Rhône corridor provided the principal axis of communication between the two zones. How the exchanges were articulated is uncertain, but the identification of a major trading centre at Bragny-sur-Saône, close to the confluence of the Saône, Doubs, and Dheune, dating to this crucial period, is of considerable interest.

45 The princely burial found beneath a substantial barrow at Vix, Chatillon-sur-Seine, France, was contained in a wood-lined chamber. The female burial was accompanied by personal ornaments, a set of imported Mediterranean wine-drinking gear, and a dismantled funerary vehicle. The burial dates to the end of the sixth century BC.

Here, in the earliest phase (late sixth and early fifth century), Massilliot amphorae and other Mediterranean-produced pottery together with Attic imports and polychrome glass vessels were found in some quantity. Bragny, situated on the interface between the Hallstatt north and the southern Mediterranean sphere, is very well sited to have been the principal port-of-trade through which exchanges could have been articulated. In the ready accessibility of luxury goods from the south may lie the reason for the westward extension of the Hallstatt élite zone after c.530.

The rich burials of the Late Hallstatt zone have been characterized as

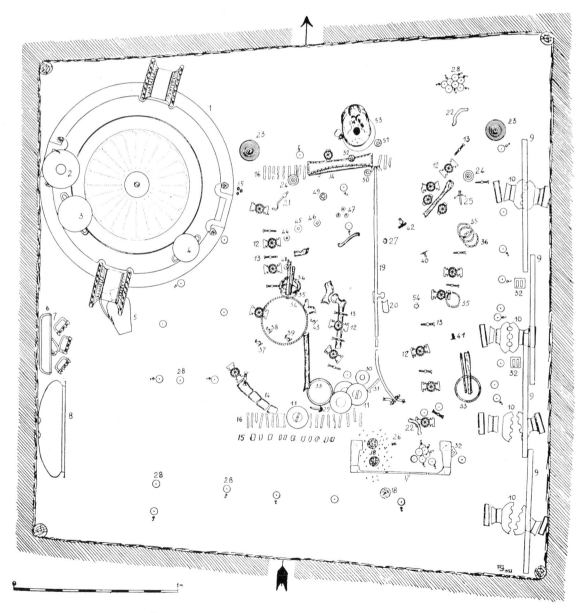

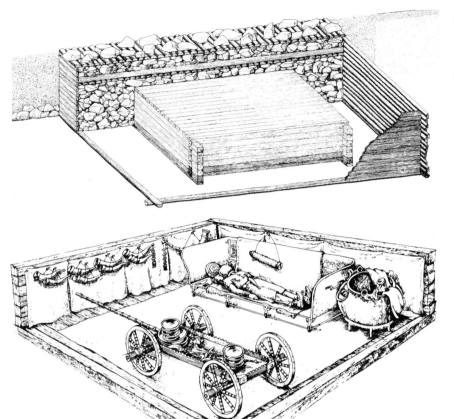

46 The chieftain's grave at Hochdorf, Stuttgart, Germany, dates to the second half of the sixth century BC. After the roof had been added, the inner grave chamber was surrounded by stone rubble laced with horizontal timbers to hinder grave-robbing, and buried beneath a large barrow.

47 Reconstruction of the interior of the timber-built grave chamber of the chieftain's burial at Hochdorf.

48 *Below*: Funerary wagon from the princely tomb of Hochdorf. The wooden structure was cased in iron sheeting. Württemberg-isches Landesmuseum, Stuttgart.

49 Bronze couch from the burial at Hochdorf upon which the dead chieftain was laid. The castors allow the couch to be easily moved. The decorative panel illustrates four-wheeled vehicles pulled by paired horses and warriors in single combat: both may be scenes from funerary rituals. Württembergisches Landesmuseum, Stuttgart.

50 Greek bronze cauldron from the princely burial of Hochdorf. One of the decorative lions is a replacement made in inferior style. The cauldron probably contained mead when buried. Württembergisches Landesmuseum, Stuttgart.

reflecting a *prestige goods economy*—that is, a socio-economic system in which élite status was maintained by the manipulation of rare and valuable commodities available only to the paramount chieftains (Map 16). They would retain their power by making gifts of lesser value to those below them in the social hierarchy in return for goods and services. So long as the supply of exotics was kept up and the paramounts held the monopoly, the system would remain relatively stable. Such a theoretical scheme provides a useful model for understanding Late Hallstatt society. It gains support from the graded status differences which can be recognized in the burial record, and from the evidence for the manufacture of lower value personal ornaments, such as brooches and bracelets, useful in gift exchange, in the princely hill forts of Mont Lassois and Heuneburg.

So far we have assumed that the Mediterranean wine-drinking gear which was imported into the Hallstatt sphere at this time all came via Massalia. This may well be, but a significant number of items were of Etruscan manufacture, vessels such as the stamnos from Gurgy, the griffon-headed cauldron and tripod from Sainte-Colombe, the beaked flagons and dishes from Vix, and the amphora from Conliège. The list is impressive, but there is nothing inherently unlikely in supposing that those entrepreneurs seeking to trade with the interior should have put together sets of wine-drinking gear deriving from a variety of sources. The most reasonable explanation for these exotic Etruscan bronzes of the period 540/530–480/470 BC, therefore, is that they were, indeed, channelled through the Greek port of Massalia. This should not, however, be confused with the direct Etruscan trade which developed at the very end of the Hallstatt period, 480/470–450/440, as a direct result of the consolidation of Etruscan commercial interests in the Po Valley. In this development, the Golasecca communities, commanding the Italian lakes and the central and west Alpine passes, served as the middlemen.

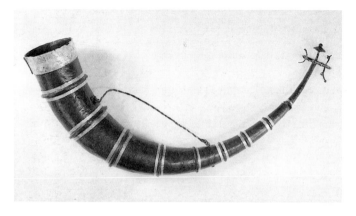

An assessment of the nature of the contacts through the Alps depends entirely upon archaeological evidence. Links between the Transalpine communities and the Golasecca culture (Map 17) were long established and are most dramatically exemplified by the four-wheeled funerary wagons of the seventh and sixth centuries BC found at Sesto Calende and Ca'Morta as well as a number of broadly contemporary sword types which have Transalpine origins or antecedents. A similar pattern of contact continuing into the middle of the fifth century is reflected in the second four-wheeled vehicle from Ca'Morta, which shares a number of structural details with the somewhat earlier vehicle found in the Late Hallstatt burial of Vix. Whether the persistence of the use of funerary vehicles at Ca'Morta and Sesto Calende was the result of diplomatic gifts from the north or the adoption of alien burial rites by the Golaseccan élite is impossible to say, but at the very least the vehicles must reflect constant cultural contact over a long period. These long established systems of communication and exchange facilitated Etruscan trade in the period after c.480/470. It is in this period that the settlement at Como developed rapidly into an extensive proto-urban agglomeration, probably as a direct response to an intensification in commerce.

The settlement at Bragny-sur-Saône was re-established at this time following a phase of destruction. Numerous items of north Italic origin were recovered, together with Golasecca-type pottery, thus demonstrating the continued use of an established port-of-trade. The presence of Massilliot amphorae in the same layers, however, shows that the Rhône corridor continued to function.

Among the most prolific of the Etruscan exports of the period 480–420 BC was the beaked flagon used as a wine-pouring vessel (Map 14) sometimes accompanied by bronze stamnoi (Map 13). Made in Etruscan cities such as Vulci and exported through the Golaseccan middlemen, they travelled far into barbarian territory. A particularly dense concentration in the élite graves of the Middle Rhine dating to the latter half of the fifth century—the La Tène A period—suggests a very deliberate and well-focused axis of exchange which no doubt contributed to the emergence of a discrete zone of power on the northern fringe of the old west Hallstatt cultural zone. The impression given by this

51 One of the nine drinking horns from the Hochdorf burial bound with bronze and gold. Württembergisches Landesmuseum, Stuttgart.

52 *Facing*: The stone statue found at Hirschlanden, Baden-Württemberg, Germany, probably once stood on top of the burial mound excavated nearby. It dates to the second half of the sixth century BC and compares in style to statues from northern Italy. The nakedness of the warrior, wearing only a sword belt and neck torc, was to become a characteristic of the Celts in battle in the fifth century and after. The conical hat which the figure wears is very similar to the birch bark hat worn by the Chieftain buried at Hochdorf. Württembergisches Landesmuseum, Stuttgart.

startling phenomenon is that Etruscan trade through the Alpine passes rather than being directed by the producers was, by this stage, being drawn by newly emerging élites in the north. The southern link is further demonstrated by the stone statue found near the barrow at Hirschlanden in Baden-Württemberg, which has very close stylistic similarities to north Italian statues.

New Centres of Power: The La Tène Élite, 450/440–380/370 BC

In the middle of the fifth century the political geography of barbarian Europe changed dramatically. While the processes and precise chronology of these changes are not easy to define, the broad picture stands out with clarity, and it is from this point that the discussion is best begun. Simply stated, over much of the west central Hallstatt élite burial zone rich burials ceased and the hill forts occupied by the aristocracy came to an end, in the case of Heuneburg with a catastrophic fire. Meanwhile, in a broad zone to the north stretching from the Marne to Bohemia there developed in the course of the La Tène A period a warrior aristocracy which frequently buried its dead with their spears and swords. It was in this zone that the highly distinctive Celtic art style developed (Map 19).

One of the difficulties of studying this change is the imprecision of our chronologies. Did the La Tène period begin immediately after the end of the Hallstatt in c.450, as some would argue, or was there an overlap of a generation or so, with the earliest La Tène beginning c.480? On balance, a period of overlap seems more likely.

Early La Tène culture differed in many significant ways from that of the old Hallstatt chiefdoms; the geographical focus of the two barely overlapped. In the La Tène burials fighting weapons were frequent, in contrast to the Late Hallstatt élite, whose only weapons were for hunting or display; moreover, the La Tène aristocracy favoured the two-wheeled vehicle as a funerary cart in contrast to the traditional four-wheeled vehicle. The one important similarity was that both had a system of élite burial employing the funerary cart together with sets of wine-drinking equipment derived from, or inspired by, the accoutrements of the Mediterranean symposion.

A plausible explanation for the evidence, so far discussed, is that towards the middle of the fifth century BC centres of power and innovation shifted from the old west central Hallstatt core to its immediate northern periphery. Why this should be is a matter to which we shall return.

That there was a significant degree of continuity between the Late Hallstatt and Early La Tène social systems is evident. This is particularly true of the Middle Rhineland. In the Late Hallstatt period the focus of power was in the valley of the Neckar between Stuttgart and Heilbronn, centred on the hill fort of Hohenasperg, around which there clustered a remarkable group of élite burials including Hochdorf, Grafenbühl and Römerhügel, all dated to the Hallstatt D2–3 phase. Little is known of the chronology of the Hohenasperg settlement, but the possibility that it continued in occupation into Early La Tène times is suggested by the date range of the élite burials in the area. Both Grafenbühl and Römerhügel were later used for La Tène burials. Similarly at Kleinaspergle the barrow mound contained a grave chamber with a burial accompanied by gold-mounted drinking horns, four bronze vessels including an Etruscan stamnos, and two Attic cups, dating to the La Tène A period. The continuity of power in this area throughout the fifth century is impressive.

Another focus of power lay some 150 kilometres north-west in the valley of the Moselle close to its confluence with the Rhine. Here several élite burials of the Late Hallstatt period have been discovered, including the well-known vehicle burial of Bell. During the fifth century the number of rich graves in the region increases dramatically. Many of the tombs contain bronze vessels imported from Etruscan workshops at Vulci and elsewhere. These include the characteristic beaked flagons, stamnoi, amphorae, and bowls. The number and density of these exotics vividly demonstrate the close links between the Rhineland and Etruria at this time (Maps 13 and 14). Even more impressive are the array of locally manufactured gold-work and the inventiveness of local craftsmen in adopting and adapting Etruscan motifs in a highly selective manner to create an entirely new art form.

If we take the Middle Rhine as a single region, we can suggest that in the early fifth century BC there were probably two centres of power, one in the Neckar valley and one (possibly) in the Moselle, with the Neckar region being the more prominent. By the end of the century a distinct shift had taken place, with the Moselle region now being not only rich but vibrant and innovative. Throughout, economic links were maintained with the Etruscan world to the south,

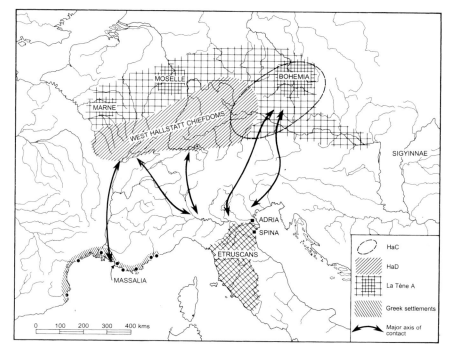

53 Map showing the shift of centres of power from *c*.700 to *c*.400 BC. The rich 'horsy' burials of the Hallstatt C period focused on the region from Bohemia to the Upper Danube. Hallstatt D power represented by the west Hallstatt chiefdom zone developed further west in the sixth century. Early La Tène aristocratic cultures emerged in three zones—the Marne, Moselle, and Bohemia—on the northern periphery.

though whether the impetus for trade came directly from the Etruscan cities or was instigated by entrepreneurs in the now-thriving Golasecca centres is a debatable point.

The second major centre of innovation in the Early La Tène period was the valley of the Marne lying some 150 kilometres north of the Late Hallstatt centre focused on Vix. Already in this period occupation was intense and the rite of vehicle burial is known from a tomb containing a four-wheeled cart at Les Jogasses. The number of burials increased dramatically throughout the fifth century, and élite burial became more common (though rare compared with the Moselle region). Characteristically, the dead aristocrat was buried in a pit accompanied by a two-wheeled vehicle, a range of harness trappings, and a drinking set. Etruscan bronze vessels have been recovered from burials at Somme-Bionne, Somme-Tourbe, and Sept-Saulx, while Somme Bionne also contained a red-figured Attic cup dated to *c.*420. If the archaeological evidence is a fair reflection of the actual percentage of élite burials in the region, then it was significantly poorer than the Moselle and evidently had less access to luxury goods from the south. In spite of this, Marnian culture displays a high degree of stability during the fifth century and its craftsmen play a significant part in the development of a distinctive style of Celtic art.

The relationship between the Moselle and Marne groups in the later part of the fifth century raises a number of questions. Both shared a common warrior-dominated social system and at some levels a common material culture based on patterns of exchange, but by any standards the Marnians were the poor relations and may indeed have depended for their Mediterranean prestige goods on reciprocal exchanges with the Moselle communities whose access to the south was direct. It is interesting to speculate what commodities the Marne may have been able to contribute. One possibility is that its links with the Seine provided a means of tapping into Atlantic systems producing the much-desired tin. Another is that the warrior society was able to supply a flow of slaves, useful in exchanges with the south. Direct evidence is, however, lacking.

A subsidiary focus of power in the fifth century lay in western France, at Bourges, at the confluence of the Auron and the Yèvres, tributary of the Cher. Settlement levels have produced quantities of Massilliot amphorae together with a range of Attic black- and red-figured wares spanning the fifth century. Contemporary technological innovations included the local adoption of the potter's wheel. A range of élite burials has also been found containing imported vessels. Judging by the date range of the imported pottery recovered, it is clear that Bourges was established as a significant trading centre in the Late Hallstatt period but continued to function throughout the Early La Tène. It is well sited to control the movement of goods from the Atlantic corridor.

The fifth century also sees the development of an axis of communication extending from the Po Valley through the territory of the Veneti and along the eastern fringes of the Alps to the valley of the Vltava and the North European Plain beyond. This long established route saw the transport of Baltic amber southwards to the Adriatic. From about 1000 BC, salt, mined at Hallstatt, would have contributed to the flow of commodities passing along the east Alpine corridor. About 600 BC the rich salt deposits at Dürrnberg (near Salzburg) began to be worked in parallel with the Hallstatt mines, both ceasing about 400 BC.

The community at Dürrnberg began to increase in size and prosperity at the beginning of the fifth century and a cemetery of several hundred burials was established. Among them were two élite burials, each with a two-wheeled funerary vehicle. One produced a locally made bronze beaked flagon inspired by Etruscan prototypes; the other a range of elaborate locally made wine-drinking equipment together with a pottery Attic kylix made in about 470. The occupant, a male, was also provided with his warrior equipment including a bronze helmet, an iron sword, three spears and bows and arrows. The Dürrnberg finds are particularly interesting in that, like those of the Moselle and Marne, they demonstrate trade links to the Po Valley providing goods and inspiration for highly inventive local craftsmen. The difference, however, is that some of the concepts incorporated by the craftsmen were learned from the already well-developed bronze-working skills of the Venetic community to the south.

To the north of Dürrnberg the amber route leads through the valley of the Vltava and the territory of Bohemia. Here, one of the principal sites was the settlement of Zavist, south of Prague. It was established in the Hallstatt period and developed throughout the fifth century as a major cult centre. That a number of Bohemian cemeteries also show continuity throughout the sixth and fifth centuries indicates a degree of social and economic stability. It was during the latter part of the fifth century that élite burials began to appear, characterized by Etruscan wine-drinking equipment. Some of the graves also produced items of gold and silver. Although the exact form of the Bohemian graves is not known in detail, their number (eight at present) and the range of imports indicate a distinctive enclave with close contacts via the Dürrnberg region to the Adriatic.

Standing back from the evidence, briefly summarized here, we can see that during the course of the fifth century there arose two zones of power and innovation: a Marne–Moselle zone in the west with trading links to the Po Valley via the central Alpine passes and the Golasecca culture, and a Bohemian zone in the east with separate links to the Adriatic via the eastern Alpine routes and the Venetic culture. Both zones, and their constituent regions, had already begun to develop as significant foci of power towards the end of the Late Hallstatt phase, but what stands out as particularly dramatic is that most of the core of the west Hallstatt élite zone, so dominant in the late sixth and early fifth centuries, was now a cultural backwater. In other words, as the centre decayed, its northern periphery flourished—in much the same way as a mushroom ring grows.

To offer explanations for the phenomenon is not easy. On the one hand, it could be argued that readjustments in trading pressures from the Mediterranean states caused social dislocation north of the Alps upsetting the delicate balance of the prestige goods economy. Perhaps the interests of the Greek cities of the Golfe du Lion turned more to the west as the lucrative Iberian market developed leaving the northern markets open to exclusive Etruscan manipulation. It could also be that internal social dynamics in Transalpine Europe were the prime cause. The peripheral zone, so long producing the supplies of raw materials such as furs, amber, iron, gold, and slaves for the core, may have developed a penchant for southern luxuries. Given the warrior nature of peripheral society, reflecting no doubt the practice of raiding, then aggressive moves against the west Hallstatt core may have destabilized and destroyed the old system. Perhaps it was a combination of all these factors which brought about the dramatic changes of the fifth century. At any event, by about 400 BC the scene was set for a new act in the story of Europe—the Celtic migrations.

4
The Migrations
400–200 BC

ON 18 July 390 BC the army of Rome was soundly defeated by a horde of Celts on the banks of the River Allia not far from the city. It was a devastating moment for the Romans, as they saw their city ransacked by these little-known northern barbarians. According to tradition, the Consul M. Popillius Laenas had told the citizens before the event: 'These are not civilized people who will become your ally when you have taken their city but wild beasts whose blood we must shed or spill our own.' The attack remained a vivid folk memory in Rome's collective consciousness, and stories about the Celtic migrations from beyond the Alps would have been told to every schoolchild. It is appropriate, therefore, to begin a consideration of the migrations by exploring how they were viewed by Greek and Roman historians writing well after the event.

The Graeco-Roman Tradition

The classic Roman view of the Celtic migrations is provided by Livy writing towards the end of the first century BC and deserves to be quoted in full.

The Celts, who make up one of the three divisions of Gaul, were under the domination of the Bituriges and this tribe supplied the Celtic nation with a king. Ambigatus was then the man and his talents . . . had brought him great distinction; for Gaul under his sway grew so rich in corn and so populous, that it seemed hardly possible to govern so great a multitude. The king, now old, wishing to relieve his kingdom of a burdensome throng, announced that he meant to send Bellovesus and Segovesus, his sister's two sons, two enterprising young men, to find such homes as the gods might assign to them by augury; and promised them that they should head as large a number of emigrants as they themselves desired, so that no tribe might be able to prevent their settlement. Whereupon to Segovesus were by lot assigned the Hercynian highlands [the Black Forest and Bohemia], but to Bellovesus the gods proposed a far pleasanter road, into Italy. Taking

68

with him the surplus population—Bituriges, Arverni, Senones, Aedui, Ambarri, Carnutes, Aulerci—he set out with a vast host, some mounted, some on foot.   (*Hist.* 5. 34)

He goes on to describe how they passed through the Alps by the passes of Taurine and Duria and defeated the Etruscans near the River Ticinus. Thereafter they established a settlement at Mediolanum (Milan).

Pompeius Trogus, a native of southern Gaul who composed his histories at the time of the Emperor Augustus, adds that, in addition to Mediolanum, the first Celtic settlements included Como, Brescia, Verona, Bergamo, Trento, and Vicenza. His understanding of the initial stages of the migrations was similar to that of Livy in that he believed overpopulation to have been the reason for the Gauls sending '300,000 men to seek new territories'. 'Some', he said, 'settled in Italy . . . some were led by birds, spread through the head of the Adriatic and settled in Pannonia.'

Livy dates these events to the reign of the Roman king Tarquinius Priscus, which would place the migrations in the period about 600 BC. The Greek historian Polybius, who wrote in the early second century BC, firmly believed them to have taken place some 200 years later. Livy was clearly aware of this discrepancy when he went on to say:

it was two hundred years before the attack on Clusium and the capture of Rome that the Gauls first crossed over into Italy: neither were the Clusini the first of the Etruscans with whom they fought: but long before that the Gallic armies had often given battle to those who dwelt between the Apennines and the Alps.

Livy's remarks raise questions which will be considered again below when the archaeological evidence is examined.

While it is generally agreed by the ancient authors that overpopulation in the Celtic homeland was the initial prime cause of the migrations, the reason for the movement to Italy was seen to be the lure of the products of the south. The point is explicitly made by Pliny:

The Gauls, imprisoned as they were by the Alps . . . first found a motive for overflowing into Italy from the circumstance of a Gallic citizen from Switzerland named Helico who had lived in Rome because of his skill as a craftsman, [and] brought with him, when he came back, some dried figs and grapes and some samples of oil and wine: consequently we may excuse them for having sought to obtain these things even by means of war. (*Nat. Hist.* 12. 2. 5)

Much the same point is made by Livy—that it was the attraction of 'delicious fruits and especially wine' that drew the Celts south. He adds the unlikely anecdote that the Celts were deliberately enticed by an Etruscan, Arruns, from Clusium, in order to bring retribution on those who had seduced his wife (*Hist.* 5. 34).

As one might expect, the historical tradition has a degree of cohesion. Against this we may now consider the archaeological evidence.

A Prelude to the Migration of 400 BC?

Livy's considered view, that there was a Celtic penetration of the Po Valley in the two centuries before the main migration in c.400 BC, is not, on the face of it, unreasonable. A foreknowledge, based on raid and trade, is usually a precursor to migration and settlement. The obvious place to look for evidence is the Golasecca culture of the Upper Po Valley.

The language spoken in the region covered archaeologically by the Golasecca culture was 'Lepontic'—an Indo-European tongue closely related to 'Celtic' which can be traced back, by means of inscriptions, to as early as the sixth century BC. Here, at least superficially, is evidence which might be used in support of earlier Celtic folk movements, but, since no break in culture can be recognized at this time, it is generally assumed that the 'Lepontic' language dates back much earlier, perhaps to the time of the genesis of the culture as defined archaeologically in the late second millennium. The similarity of the languages on both sides of the Alps would, however, have facilitated intercourse between the two zones over a long period.

That active contact was, indeed, maintained is abundantly clear from the archaeological evidence. Vehicles found in the burials at Ca'Morta and Sesto Calende are vivid demonstrations of an exchange of ideas and possibly even of goods at an aristocratic level. Weapons too, in particular the short swords and daggers of the Golasecca region, have close affinities to those found in the region from Burgundy to southern Germany in the period from the seventh to the fifth centuries BC. Many similarities can also be recognized among pottery types. Reciprocal influences can be claimed based on the distribution, in the Transalpine area, of small trinkets such as bronze pendants common in the Golaseccan cultural zone and we have already referred to the range of Golaseccan material found at the trading port of Bragny-sur-Saône in the fifth century. Taken together, the evidence suggests that close links between the two zones existed for at least three centuries before 400 BC. One might even go so far as to argue that the Golasecca culture underwent a degree of 'Celticization' during this period.

The point at issue is to what extent Celtic peoples from the north moved south to establish enclaves of their own among the Golaseccan communities or, more likely, beyond their southern border in land disputed by the advancing

54 Stone funerary stela found at Bologna dating to the fifth century BC. The lowest panel shows a mounted Etruscan attacking a naked Celtic foot soldier. Museo Civico Arqueologico, Bologna.

Etruscans. Some evidence for such groups has been claimed on the basis of weapon types found with burials at Casola Valsenio near Bologna and at San Martino further to the south-east, both cemeteries being dated by Attic pottery to within the fifth century. Also of late fifth-century date are the famous grave stelae from Bologna depicting Celtic-style warriors in battle. The evidence is not extensive but is sufficient to suggest the presence of warriors, adopting Transalpine weapon types and fighting methods, in the Po Valley in the fifth century.

A closer reading of the classical texts may provide a further insight to the problem. Polybius (*Hist.* 2. 17), in a somewhat enigmatic sentence, speaks of Celts as neighbours to the Etruscans. Envying the beauty of the Etruscan territory they 'gathered a great host and expelled the Etruscans from the valley of the Padus'. This might suggest a phase of Celtic settlement preceding the main migration. In another passage Livy (*Hist.* 5. 34) mentions that the invading Celts, 'having learnt that they were in what was known as the territory of the Insubres, the same name as one of the cantons of the Aedui, took it as a favourable omen and founded the town of Mediolanum'. A *possible* implication of this is that the Insubres, who occupied the territory south of the Golasecca culture just north of the Po at the time of the main migration, may have been a Celtic community long established in the region.

The whole question of a pre-400 BC Celtic settlement in the Po Valley is impossible to resolve with certainty, though, on balance, the evidence would allow there to have been an early settlement of Celtic warrior groups in the

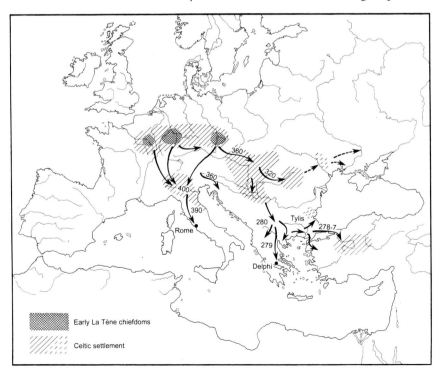

55 The principal movements of the Celts, 400–270 BC.

Early La Tène chiefdoms

Celtic settlement

frontier zone between the Golaseccan domain and the Etruscans. Such enclaves, perhaps encouraged to come initially as mercenaries by the Golaseccan communities, may have been sufficiently numerous to have retained a degree of ethnic identity sufficient to have impressed the sources upon which Livy based his *History*. Their presence and links with the homeland would have provided the context for the massive influx which began about 400 BC.

The Initial Settlement: *c.*400 BC

Polybius provides an outline of the course of the migration. The lands near the Po were occupied by the Laevi and Lebecii, then came the Insubres, and, to the east of them, on the north bank of the river, settled the Cenomani. Further penetration eastwards was halted by the Veneti, a long established indigenous tribe. South of the Po, in the west, close to the Apennines, the Ananes established themselves, with the Boii to the east and the Lingones along the Adriatic coast. To the south of them, along the littoral, the Senones appropriated territory. At a later date Polybius mentions that the two largest tribes, the Insubres and the Boii, sent messages to tribes living 'about the Alps and on the Rhône' calling for additional forces. These mercenary bands, called Gaesatae, arrived in formidable numbers 'furnished with a variety of armour'.

Polybius (*Hist.* 2. 17) then goes on to provide a sketch of the life of the Celtic communities. They occupied open villages and lived simple lives following

56 The Celtic tribes of the Po Valley and the migration routes by which they arrived. The Ligurians and the Veneti were indigenous peoples.

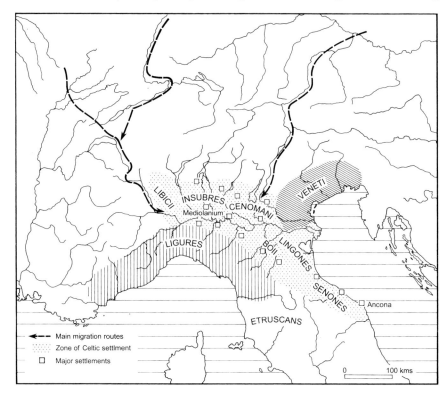

72

'no pursuit other than war and agriculture'. Wealth was measured in gold and cattle which could be easily transported when 'they wandered from place to place and changed their dwelling as their fancy directed'. Hospitality was important and a man's status was gauged by the size of his entourage of clients or 'companions in his wanderings'. This characteristic is one which persists in the works of classical writers whenever Celts are described.

Archaeological evidence for the Celtic settlement of the Po Valley is already considerable and is growing rapidly, and it is now possible to identify cultural differences reflecting the different tribal groups. One notable characteristic—the prevalence of cremation among the Boii—serves both to distinguish them from other Celtic communities in the Po Valley and to link them to the Bohemian homeland from which they came. The Boian inhumation burials also generally lacked ankle rings and torcs, while their arm rings were often arranged in a distinctive asymmetric way. These, too, are characteristics of contemporary communities in Bohemia. The burials of the Senones and Cenomani, on the other hand, reflect more closely styles already apparent in the Marne region. Distinctive belt hooks were found in both regions, females often wore torcs, and arm rings were symmetrically arranged. Taken together the evidence emerging for regional patterns and their Transalpine parallels is beginning to offer a striking confirmation of the traditional account of the settlement.

In their new homeland the Celtic communities came into close contact with Graeco-Etruscan culture, and inevitably there was a degree of assimilation. This was most noticeable in the artistic field, where Celtic craftsmen began to incorporate new motifs into their decorative creations. The dissemination of Celtic items made in Italy, and quite possibly the migration of craftsmen, to the Transalpine homelands introduced a new vitality to the now flourishing workshops of temperate Europe. Thus, albeit through a different social mechanism, the Graeco-Etruscan world continued to influence the Transalpine communities.

The Celtic Homeland at the Time of the Migrations

It is reasonably clear from a variety of archaeological evidence that in the fourth century two principal axes of communication existed between the Transalpine regions and the Po Valley, a western route funnelling from the Seine, Marne, and Rhine, through the Great St Bernard Pass, to the upper reaches of the valley and an eastern route from the Upper Danube, and Bohemia beyond, via the River Inn and the eastern Alpine passes, to the lower reaches of the plain. It is along these traditional routes that migrating bands are likely to have passed, filtering off surplus population from the Marne, Moselle, and Bohemian regions, where, as we have seen, the principal innovatory centres were developing at this time.

Of the two reasons given by the classical writers for the folk movement—

overpopulation and the lure of southern luxuries—the first is more likely to have been the prime cause. An increase in population, especially in societies which had created warrior systems as an essential part of the social structure, would inevitably have led to instability, which could best have been alleviated by the thinning-down of population by migration. But the situation may have been more complicated. The warrior élites, represented in the archaeology of the three core Early La Tène territories—the Marne, the Moselle, and Bohemia—probably maintained themselves by acts of prowess and their ability to command sizeable entourages at times of social display. One structure within which this could be done was the raid, which, if successful, would reward both the leader and his followers. This is the kind of system which Polybius recorded among the Cisalpine Celts. We have already seen that, within the northern 'peripheral' zone, raiding may have developed as an economic necessity to provide resources for the prestige goods system of the 'core' to distribute. Once established, it may have become embedded in the social system of the Early La Tène periphery, generating a momentum of its own, particularly after the collapse of the west Hallstatt chiefdoms. In this way, one of the defining characteristics of early Celtic society was created.

In such a situation, the problem of a growing population could be dealt with in several ways. At its simplest, a small entourage under a leader could move out from the homeland to find a new ecological niche to occupy. A process such as this would have led to the establishment of enclaves of élite warriors, distant from the homeland, who might, at least for a generation or two, have retained their identity in an archaeologically-visible form. It is possible that the clusters of Early La Tène vehicle burials along the Lower Seine, in the Ardennes and the Haine, and even the group who emerged in Yorkshire, may have owed their origin to this kind of small-scale warrior exodus.

At the other end of the scale, larger bands of roaming warriors having no particular territorial base may have come together under one or more charismatic leader. It is quite possible that the Gaesatae—warriors who, according to Polybius, were 'available for hire' and were decked out in 'a variety of armour' and were to be found 'about the Alps and on the Rhône'—were itinerant fighters of this kind. Growing population and rigid social constraints in the homelands could well have swelled their numbers. In such a turbulent and unstable situation, it would need only the decision on the part of one leader to take his entourage to the rich pickings of the south for the news to spread and others to follow, swelling the numbers to a migration and creating a momentum which drew in the ambitious young from the home regions. A rapidly escalating social upheaval of this kind could explain the apparently rapid movement of Celtic populations into the Po Valley: it might also be expected to have left traces in the home territories.

The most convincing evidence for an exodus of population comes from the Marne region. A study of the rich burial data shows that during the fifth century a large stable population occupied the region, its élite buried in state with their two-wheeled vehicles and wine-drinking equipment. But some time about 400 BC the population suddenly declines. Thereafter, only one major focus developed, in the Reims area, while much of the rest of the Champagne region appears to have been deserted. Taken at face value, the evidence strongly suggests that a very high proportion of the population must have moved out, leaving only one lineage to maintain a single power centre.

Much the same kind of evidence can be seen in the Rhineland. Although there was a marked degree of continuity between the distribution and range of burials from the fifth to the fourth centuries, a sharp reduction in the actual number of burials is recorded, particularly of warrior burials normally accompanied by swords. The evidence from Bohemia is rather less clear-cut, but a number of cemeteries came to an end at the end of the fifth century and élite burials disappeared. The archaeological data are therefore consistent with there having been a major social change in Transalpine Europe at the time of the early migrations.

From what has been said it is reasonable to suppose that the three most developed centres of Early La Tène culture—the Marne, the Moselle, and Bohemia—contributed to populations which made their way through the Alpine passes about 400 BC to set themselves up in the lush lands of the Po Valley. But the Celtic tribes mentioned by name by Livy as taking part were numerous. The names of many still appeared on the political map of Gaul, sketched by Julius Caesar in the middle of the first century BC, occurring within the broad territory stretching from the Marne south to the Massif Central and from the Rhône to the Middle Loire Valley—the core of Caesar's Celtic zone of Gaul. While it might at first sight be tempting to suggest that it was from this huge territory that the migrating tribes came, tribal mobility in subsequent centuries is likely to have confused the picture. Indeed, it may be that many of the tribes encountered by Caesar in central Gaul arrived in their traditional territories at the time of the initial migrations as sectional groups from diffuse migratory bands. The situation is likely to have been confused and the archaeological evidence is too ill focused yet to throw much light on it.

The Celts in Italy: 400–180 BC

The initial Celtic settlement of the Po Valley at the end of the fifth century brought the invaders hard up against the barrier of the Apennines—a barrier permeated by well-trodden routes linking the Etruscan-dominated north to the Etruscan homeland backing onto the Tyrrhenian Sea. Inevitably Celtic war bands were drawn southwards into the heart of Etruria. This occurred at the moment when Rome, expanding her power northwards, was taking over the old Etruscan cities one by one. The clash that followed is recorded in some detail by Polybius and by Livy, though with slightly differing chronologies.

The first stage of the southern thrust brought the Celts to the Etruscan town of Clusium in 391 BC, where their principal demand was to be assigned land to settle. Roman ambassadors were sent to act on behalf of the city, but negotiations broke down and in the ensuing battle the ambassadors, in breach of accepted custom, joined in the mêlée, one of them killing a Celtic warlord. The Celts' demand for recompense was ignored by the Roman authorities, thus hastening the next stage of the Celtic advance—the march on Rome.

In July 390 (Livy's date; Polybius says 386), at the Tiber tributary, the Allia, the Roman army was destroyed and the city, all except the defended Capitol, fell. The sack of Rome was followed by months of uncertainty, with the Celtic warriors camped around growing increasingly restive as they suffered waves of disease. Eventually a compromise was reached and the Celts departed with 1,000 pounds of gold given by the thankful Roman authorities. It is possible that news of aggressive moves by the Veneti on the eastern border of the Po Valley settlements may have encouraged their departure. A more likely explanation is that the rapid advance of 391–90 was little more than a series of exploratory raids from the home base north of the Apennines, and, with honour, curiosity, and the desire for spoils assuaged, the warring bands could return satisfied.

The devastating blow to Rome's power and authority was in part responsible for the unrest which gripped central Italy throughout the next half century or so, during which time Celtic raids and Celtic mercenary forces made intermittent appearances. The raids can best be understood in the context of the Celtic social system, which employed the raid as a way of maintaining and enhancing prestige. Expeditions of this kind may have been constantly mounted by the tribes settled on the Apennine flank. Those raids, which were more ambitious and deep thrusting than others, brought the Celts into episodic contact with Roman forces.

The presence of Celtic mercenary forces was an altogether different matter. Bands of warriors willing to fight were available for employment and were seen as useful complements to the fighting force by aspiring tyrants. One such man was Dionysius of Syracuse, who, having gained control of the Etruscan port of Adria, established a colony further down the coast, at Ancona, in the territory occupied by the Senones. Ancona provided a convenient base from which to enlist Celtic mercenaries. An alliance was struck in 385, and one band of mercenaries, returning from service in southern Italy, joined Dionysius' naval expedition in a joint attack on the Etruscan port of Pyrgi in 384–3. Thereafter Ancona continued to provide Dionysius and his son with mercenaries for thirty years. For the most part they served in Italy, but one force was transported to Greece in 367 to take part in the conflict between Sparta and her allies against Thebes. Livy specifically mentions the presence of Celtic armies in Apulia, one of which moved against Rome in 367. The fact that another attack came from the same area in 149 might suggest that there may have been a long-established Celtic enclave in the area, but there is little archaeological evidence for this, except for the rich grave of Canosa di Puglia with its extremely fine Celtic helmet dated to the late fourth century BC.

By the 330s Rome had recovered sufficiently to begin a new expansionist drive, and, to secure its northern frontier, a peace treaty was negotiated with the Senones in 334. The peace was short-lived and Celtic attacks became more frequent and serious, but the situation was temporarily stabilized when, following a defeat of the Senones in 283, Rome founded a colony at Sena Gallica at the estuary of the River Misa on the Umbrian coast. The Boii reacted by joining with the Etruscans in a move on Rome, but were defeated and cut to pieces near Lake Vadimone. The peace treaty which the Boii were persuaded to sign with Rome was to last for forty-five years.

After the First Punic War (264–41 BC) Rome's attention turned once more to the north, and in 232 the territory of the Senones was confiscated and made over to Italian settlement. Further Roman activity in the western Apennines alarmed the neighbouring Boii. Strengthened by a large force of Gaesatae—mercenary Celts from beyond the Alps—the Boii, the Insubres, and the Taurisci began a long march on Rome through Etruria. In 225 at Telamon on the Tyrrhenian coast they were caught between two Roman forces. Polybius' account of the battle (*Hist.* 2. 28–3. 10) provides a vivid impression of Celtic warfare. He describes how the Celtic army drew up its ranks to face the attacks coming from two directions, with the wagons and war chariots on both wings and their booty stacked on a nearby hill well protected. The Insubres and Boii wore their breeches and light cloaks, but the Gaesatae fought naked. The Romans were

terrified by the fine order of the Celtic host and the dreadful din for there were innumerable trumpeters and horn-blowers and . . . the whole army were shouting their war cries at the same time. Very frightening too were the appearance and gestures of the

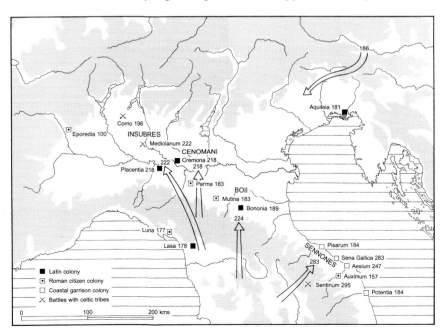

57 Northern Italy in the second century BC, at the time when the Celts were coming under pressure from the advancing Romans.

naked warriors in front, all in the prime of life and finely built men, and all the leading companies richly adorned with gold torcs and armlets.

The Romans, impressed by the sight of the gold, took courage and battle commenced. Eventually Roman might prevailed and the Celtic force was destroyed. Estimates of numbers taking part in ancient battles are notoriously unreliable, but Polybius records that the Celtic force comprised 50,000 infantry and 20,000 horse and chariots. Of these about 40,000 were slain and 10,000 taken prisoner. It was a defeat on a grand scale: thereafter Celtic attacks from the north were much reduced.

The Roman triumph was quickly followed up with campaigns in Boian territory in 224 BC and among the Insubres in 222. The foundation of two Roman colonies, in 218, among the friendly Cenomani who had taken no part in Telamon, marks a tightening of the Roman hold on the Celtic Cisalpine homeland.

After the Second Punic War, in which Celts had been employed by Hannibal as somewhat ineffective mercenaries, the Roman armies moved quickly to subjugate the Po Valley. The Cenomani made their peace in 197 BC, Como was taken in 196, and in 189 a colony was founded at Bononia (Bologna). As a result of these campaigns, many of the Boii decided to migrate northwards, back into Transalpine Europe. But Celtic migrations *from* the Transalpine region were not entirely at an end, for in 186 a Celtic horde including 12,000 fighting men moved through the Carnic Alps intent to plunder and settle. The Roman army, which marched against them in 183, forced those who survived to return home. While not a major event in itself, it was a reminder to the Romans that history might repeat itself and that the only sure defence was the thorough italianization of Cisalpine Gaul.

The Danube Corridor in the Fifth and Fourth Centuries

The valley of the River Danube provided the principal corridor of communication between west central Europe and the east. At two points the valley is constricted by the proximity of mountain ranges. In the west, in the vicinity of modern Bratislava, the western Carpathians on the north and the Alpine Burgenland on the south create a comparatively narrow gap but east of this the landscape opens up into the Carpathian Basin roughly equivalent to present-day Hungary and parts of Serbia with the hilly countryside of Transdanubia to the west of the river and the flatter Great Hungarian Plain to the east. The eastern extremity of this huge and desirable territory is marked by the narrowing of the valley once more when the eastern Carpathian mountains come close to the Balkan range at the Iron Gates, now on the border between Serbia and Romania. Culturally the region divides into two: the western zone from the Danube to the eastern fringes of the Alps was occupied by indigenous communities sharing in the generalized Hallstatt culture, while to the east, in the Great Hungarian Plain, the distinctive Vekerzug group, closely related to the horse-riding communities of the east, may be regarded as part of the extensive 'Thracian' culture which, in the sixth century, occupied much of eastern Europe.

The ancient authors, writing about the Celtic expansion, were broadly agreed that some part of the migration of *c.*400 BC moved eastwards (Fig. 55). Geography dictates that the principal route used would have been along the Danube corridor into Moravia, Slovakia, and Hungary. Certainly, by 335 BC, Celtic groups are historically attested in the Balkans and it is simplest to interpret them as settlers or raiders who had moved through the Middle Danube region, though an alternative view—that they were an offshoot of Celts moving eastwards via the Po Valley—should not be too readily rejected.

The nature of the celticization of the Carpathian Basin can be approached only through archaeological evidence—primarily the evidence of cemeteries. It is convenient to divide the material culture of the period into two horizons, the Vorduchcov (*c.*400–370/360 BC) and the Duchcov–Münsingen (*c.*370/360–300 BC), the latter being typified by distinctive brooch types found in a votive deposit at Duchcov in Bohemia and at a prolific cemetery at Münsingen near Berne.

It needs to be stressed at the outset that the movements of Celtic peoples throughout the Transalpine region in the fourth century are likely to have been highly complex, varying from large-scale folk migrations, on the one extreme, to the simple exchange of wives and warriors, on the other. Similarly we must allow that some of the changes recognizable in the archaeological record need be nothing more than the adoption of new styles and new behaviour patterns by indigenous communities. An attempt to give historical meaning to these shades of cultural variation is a hazardous procedure. Having said this, certain broad interpretations seem valid.

In Bohemia, for example, following the phase of migration, there are indications of new cultural infiltrations in the first part of the fourth century affecting north-western, central, and eastern areas. A little later, at the end of the Vorduchcov phase, a more significant cultural change is apparent. It is at this time that the hilltop settlement of Zavist was destroyed and flat-grave cemeteries, with a new range of grave goods, make a comparatively sudden appearance. Cultural similarities with material found in western Switzerland and Baden-Württemberg is generally taken to imply an immigrant warrior population moving in from the west to take up lands previously vacated by the move of the original Bohemian population to the south. In the Rhineland during the fourth century there is a noticeable reduction in the number of settlements and cemeteries. Some of these populations presumably travelled south into the Po Valley, but others may well have joined a general movement to the east to Bohemia and beyond.

The fourth century sees the development of Celtic communities across a substantial and diverse territory comprising Moravia, Lower Austria, western Hungary, and south-west Slovakia. The earliest settlements date to the first half of the fourth century, but a second phase, in the latter part of the century, can be distinguished, typified by the flat-grave cemeteries, and characterized by a material culture closely similar to that found in the Bohemia–Bavarian region but with elements reflecting contacts further west in Switzerland and the Middle Rhine and the Marne. This complex spread of Celtic culture, presumably reflecting successive movements of people, filled up the northern part of Transdanubia and extended to the northern fringes of the Great Hungarian Plain during the fourth century. There is some evidence to suggest that some Celtic settlers reached Transylvania, in the heart of modern Romania.

Standing back from the dimly perceptible eastward 'movement' of Celts, the general situation developing during the fourth century can be appreciated from Map 20 showing the European-wide spread of various Early La Tène groups dominated by the burial of warriors. It demonstrates, with great clarity, a degree of cultural uniformity brought about in this century of migration, stretching from the Marne to Transylvania. Though there are distinct regional variations, it is reasonable to regard this uniformity as a cultural continuum through which ideas and people moved freely.

The Celts in the Balkans and Greece in the Fourth and Third Centuries

Celtic war parties had penetrated the mountains of Illyria by the early fourth century BC and were in conflict with the Ardiaioi of southern Dalmatia in 380. It was, however, the expansion of Macedonian power under Alexander the Great that occasioned the first recorded contacts between the Celtic and Macedonian leaders when, in 335 BC, Celtic emissaries from the Adriatic region visited the court of Alexander to negotiate a treaty of 'friendship and hospitality'. Strabo's famous description of the event is worth repeating in full:

The king received them kindly and asked them, when drinking, what it was that they most feared, thinking that they would say himself, but they replied they feared nothing except that the sky might fall on them, although indeed, they added, they put above everything else the friendship of such a man as he.   (*Geog.* 7. 3. 8)

The record of a second embassy is recorded by the Greek historian Arrian in 323, when a group of Celtic leaders visited Alexander, who was then in Babylon. It may well have been on this journey that the wealth of Asia Minor was noted for future reference.

Little is heard of the Celts in Illyria for the next fifty years or so, but the breakdown of Alexander's empire after his death, and the dissipation of the energy of the Macedonians in the political turmoil which followed, so weakened Macedonia and its Greek outpost that the south-east Balkans must have begun to look like an attractive prospect to the more energetic of the Celtic leaders based in Illyria and southern Pannonia. In 298 BC a force had been led into Macedonia and Thrace under the war leader Cimbaules, but it met substantial resistance. In 280 another attempt was made, this time by Bolgius leading a Celtic and Thracian force: the leader of the Macedonians was killed and his head paraded on a Celtic spear.

Whether or not these were exploratory expeditions designed to pave the way for the massive folk movement which was to follow or were skirmishes caused by a build-up of population in the Celtic homeland in southern Pannonia is impossible to judge. One further possibility which has to be borne in mind is that the Romans were at this time moving against the Senones on the Adriatic coast of Italy, winning two decisive battles in 295 and 283. The disruption caused by the Roman aggression may well have encouraged groups of Celts from the Po Valley to move eastwards through Slovenia to seek new land, swelling the numbers of dislocated warriors.

Matters seem to have come to a head in 279 BC. In the previous year, while Bolgius was involved in Macedonia, some Celtic groups, led by Kérethrios, had been operating in Thrace and others under Brennus and Achichorius were in Peonia. Bolgius' victory over the Macedonian army opened the way for a more concerted thrust to the south-east.

The onslaught was headed by Brennus moving southwards from central Bulgaria. An account of what followed was provided by Pausanius, a second-century AD writer who seems to have made use of an earlier, now lost, history compiled by Hieronymus of Cardia. Allowing for the potential inaccuracies and bias of the sources, the main events are tolerably clear. The lure, says Pausanius, was the 'wealth of the Greek states and the even greater wealth in the sanctuaries including votive offerings and coined silver and gold'. This is not an unreasonable assumption, but his estimate of the size of the Celtic force—152,000 infantry and 20,400 horse—is likely to be an exaggeration.

At an early stage in the advance there was discord, and, according to Livy, some 20,000 men led by Leonorios and Lutorios moved off on their own, eventually settling in Asia Minor. The remainder under Brennus and Achichorius first suffered heavy losses against a Macedonian force before continuing southwards to enter Greece through the pass of Thermopylae. Thermopylae was well defended by the Greeks, but, by splitting forces in an outflanking movement, the Celts overcame the opposition, though not without considerable losses. Not pausing for the troops commanded by Achichorius to join him, or even to bury his own dead, Brennus pushed on towards Delphi. What ensued is not immediately clear. One tradition records that the sanctuary was pillaged, some of the treasure obtained eventually ending up in the sacred enclosures of the Volcae Tectosages at Tolosa (Toulouse), where it was appropriated by the Roman commander Caepio in 106 BC. According to the Greek tradition, on the other hand, the presiding deity, Apollo, came to the defence of the sanctuary. Thunder and lightning accompanied by earthquakes caused rocks to roll down from the heights onto the discouraged Celts, while the Phocians, used to the stark and sudden nature of the countryside, employed guerrilla tactics in attacking the Celtic rear. It may have been these events, combined perhaps with news that a large part of the force led by Achichorius had been left to guard baggage and spoil at Heraclea, while the remainder had been attacked by the Aetolians and Phocaeans, who had captured their supplies, that disheartened the forces of Brennus. In the event, the retreat began after the wounded had been put to death. In the night of panic which followed fighting broke out among the Celts and the next day constant Phocaean sniping prevented the forage parties from collecting the necessary food.

Eventually the two Celtic armies were reunited but such was the effectiveness of the growing Greek opposition that Brennus, who had been wounded, succumbed to the despair of a failed leader and committed suicide, either by drinking undiluted wine or by some other means when drunk (depending upon the source). The remaining force retreated through Spercheius, where Thessalians and Malians were waiting to fall on them in retribution for the brutalities which the Celts had inflicted on the local population on their way south to Delphi. The depletion of the Celtic force must have been considerable, but it was surely an exaggeration of Pausanius to say that hardly one escaped safely from Greece.

The thrust into Greece and the subsequent retreat probably took place within the single year 279 BC. It seems to have been no more than a raid designed to obtain treasure. What distinguishes the attack on Delphi is that the Celts had chosen to move against a literate people who could record events and present them according to their own concepts of history. Thus it survives as one of the great stories of brutality and heroism. While a notable event in the history of the Celtic expansion, it may have been no more significant than many such events for which no written records exist. It is a sobering fact that, had we had to rely entirely on the archaeological evidence, no trace of the events of 279 would have been suspected (Map 21).

Whatever the effectiveness or otherwise of the raid in gaining spoils, the event was celebrated at Delphi by a regular four-yearly festival of salvation—the *Soteria*.

In the immediate aftermath some part of the Celtic force seems to have moved back northwards to the Middle Danube Valley, contributing to the large tribal complex which jelled there to become the Scordisci. Some, according to Polybius, moved eastwards through Thrace and carved out for themselves a territory around Tyle (Tylis), which became the capital. Here they were conveniently sited to demand, and receive, regular protection money from Byzantium until the enclave was annihilated by the Thracians c.212 BC. Another band under Kérethrios was defeated by Antigonus Gonatus in 278–7 at Lysimacheia. Of the rest, many will have stayed in Greece and Macedonia to serve as mercenaries, where there was ample employment to be had. Some were active in the army of Antigonus in 274, and their shields were among the trophies of victory, dedicated in the temple of Athena Itomia near Larissa following Antigonus' defeat by Pyrrhus. Another, very considerable, force was invited to cross the Hellespont into Asia Minor to fight in the army of Nicomedes of Bithynia in 278. Their passage opens up a new chapter in Celtic history.

The Celts in Asia Minor, Third Century BC to Fourth Century AD

The Celts who crossed the narrow strip of water between Europe and Asia were a varied group comprising three separate tribes, the Tolistobogii, the Tectosages, and the Trocmi. They had separated from the main force which attacked Delphi and were led by Leonorios and Lutorios. What is particularly interesting is that half their total number of 20,000 were non-combatants—the women, the children, and the aged. This suggests that, unlike the warriors who chose to follow Brennus on his raid, the groups who stayed with Leonorios and Lutorios were migrant populations in search of new land to settle.

In Asia Minor the various Celtic groups were referred to collectively as Galatians and their history was recorded in the lost books of Demetrios of Byzantium, which probably served as the source used by Polybius and for Livy. Nicomedes employed them in his conflict with Antiochus I, settling them in disputed territory between his own kingdom of Bithynia and that ruled by Antiochus. The period of instability which followed culminated in the defeat of the Celts in 275–4 BC in the famous 'Elephant Battle'. Thereafter the Celts were moved to a barren highland area flanking the Halys. From here, for the next

58 The Celts in Asia Minor, showing the principal areas of settlement and the sites of the major conflicts.

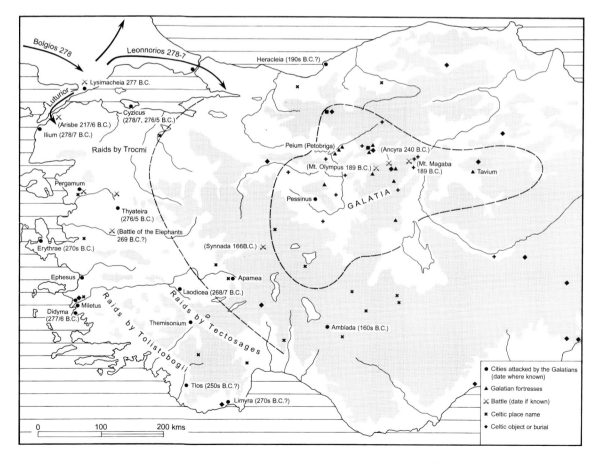

83

forty-five years or so they became a scourge to the surrounding cities, organizing frequent raids from their home base particularly against the rich hellenized cities, where plunder or bribes could easily be had. According to Livy, each of the three Galatian tribes had their own territory to raid: the Tolistobogii raided Aeolis, the Trocmi focused on the Hellespont, while the Tectosages regarded inland Asia Minor as their sphere of activity. Eventually an alliance with Mithridates I of Pontus encouraged them to move to a new land around Ancyra.

From the middle of the third century the Celtic raids against the cities of the Aegean coastal area began to intensify, and Eumenes I of Pergamum (263–41), now the prime power in the west, decided to buy them off. His successor, Attalus I (241–197), however, chose instead to stand his ground, eventually winning a decisive battle at the Springs of Kaikos in about 233 BC. It was to celebrate this victory that a monument was erected on the acropolis of Pergamum, some statues of which survive in Roman copies, the most famous being the 'Dying Gaul'.

In the later part of the third century Celts were used extensively as mercenaries in the armies of the Seleucid and Ptolemaic rulers, though from the fragmentary accounts that survive they appear to have been unruly and somewhat unreliable. One group who became demoralized at an eclipse of the moon had to be returned with their wives and children to the Hellespont in case they had decided to change sides. The incident is interesting, because it shows that some at least of the Celtic mercenaries may have been arriving in fresh groups from Europe. It was during this period that Celtic warriors were in action as far afield as Egypt. In 218 Attalus II employed a European tribe, the Aigosages, to take part in his campaigns in Aeolis and Phrygia and afterwards gave them land on the borders of Phrygia, from where, under their own initiative, they began to carry out extensive raids until the entire Celtic population was slaughtered by Prusias of Bithynia.

In 191 BC the Romans were drawn into the political turmoil of Asia Minor as allies of Pergamum against the Seleucid king Antiochus III. At Magnesia, in 190, the Seleucid army, together with its Galatian mercenaries, were soundly defeated by a combined Roman and Pergamene force, and in the next year the new Roman commander Cn. Manlius Vulso set out for central Anatolia to deal with the Galatians in their home territory. In preparation for the onslaught the Tolistobogii and the fighting men of the Trocmi rallied at Mount Olympos, three days' travel west of Ancyra, while the Tectosages and the families of the Trocmi made for Mount Magaba just east of Ancyra. In a lightning strike Manlius defeated first the Tolistobogii and the Trocmi, selling 40,000 men, women, and children as slaves, and then moved quickly on to defeat the Tectosages. In the peace which was concluded, the Galatians agreed to stop all raids in the western parts of Asia Minor. Apart from an abortive attempt by Ortiagon, the Tolistobogian chief, to unite Galatia and in doing so to make war on Pergamum, comparative peace prevailed, the Romans ensuring that the Galatians

GUERRIER GAULOIS
Époque Gallo-romaine
Mondragon (V.-se). Acquis en 1834.

remained free from Pergamene control. However, in 167 the Galatian attacks began again and Eumenes II was forced to engage in vigorous campaigns against them. Two years later a new peace treaty was agreed.

The Pergamene victory was widely celebrated. At Pergamum a great sculptured frieze was added to the altar of Zeus, while on the Athenian acropolis a victory monument was dedicated by the Pergamenes proclaiming, in sculptured allegory, that the rulers of Pergamum, like the Greeks, were the saviours of the civilized world (see p. 7).

Thereafter the raid, so necessary for the maintenance of Celtic society, was deflected away from the territory controlled by the western powers towards other states. Cappadocia was first to suffer and later Pontus, but gradually the Celtic communities—known universally as the Galatians—absorbed the ways of Greece and Rome and of their Asiatic neighbours. When, in the middle of the first century AD, the Christian apostle Paul wrote his letter to the Galatians, he treated them no differently from any other community in the now Roman world.

In the formative century following the first incursion of Celts into Asia Minor in 278 BC, the Celtic tribes, fed by new bands arriving from time to time from Europe, maintained a distinctive lifestyle in which the raid, and its more extreme form, mercenary activity, remained an essential part of the social system.

The maintenance of a Celtic social structure, and indeed a sense of ethnic identity implied by the widespread use of the name 'Galatian', are a remarkable reflection of the deep-rooted strength of the Celtic tradition. An even more impressive reminder of this is the persistence of their language. When, in the fourth century AD, St Jerome offered the observation that the language used by the Galatians around Ancyra was similar to that he had heard among the Treveri at Trier, he was recognizing, though perhaps with the hindsight of a historian, the Celtic ancestry of both people.

The North Pontic Regions in the Fourth and Third Centuries

The north Pontic region, lying both east and west of the Sea of Azov in the basin of the Kuban River, has produced an array of artefacts which can be regarded as Celtic. Celtic-style weapons, such as shields and anthropomorphic-hilted swords, are also depicted on coins minted in the Bosporus in the second half of the third century (Map 22). Equally significant is a group of Etruscan helmets, found in Sarmatian graves, the manufacture of which can be dated to before the middle of the third century. Other finds include a La Tène iron sword from Neapolis, a Celtic helmet from Boiko-Ponura in the Krasnodar region, which has close similarities to helmets from Slovenia, and horse gear of Bohemian type from a grave at Marjevka.

To suggest a historical context for these finds presents some difficulties. One possibility is that some were introduced by Celtic mercenaries from Asia Minor

VIIIa *Facing, above*: Stone head of a Celtic deity found close to a rectangular ditched sanctuary at Mšecké Šehrovice, Bohemia, Czech Republic. Note the characteristic swept-back hair, drooping moustache, and neck torc. Second or first century BC? Národni Muzeum, Prague.

VIIIb *Below*: Celtic helmets sometimes had attachments on the crest either to signify lineage or status or, more likely, as religious symbols to protect the wearer. These two small boars may well have been used in such a way. They were found at Hounslow in Middlesex, England and may possibly have been part of a votive offering. The boar was a frequently used image suggesting that it was endowed with particular potency.

who are recorded to have served in the campaigns of Mithridates VI around the northern shores of the Black Sea in 63 BC, but many of the finds are significantly earlier and require a different explanation. It is possible, therefore, that they reflect a separate incursion from the Balkans or from Transylvania.

European Celts in the Third and Second Centuries

In the aftermath of the Celtic expulsion from Greece there appears to have been a period of some turmoil among the Celtic communities roaming south-eastern Europe. Historical sources are few and vague. One thread which can be distinguished suggests that one of the returning groups, led by Bathanatos, finally settled in the Middle Danube region at the confluence of the Sava, Drava, and Danube, whence they had originally come, creating an extensive confederation thereafter known as the Scordisci, forming the southernmost extremity of what can be regarded as the settled core of Celtic Europe. Over succeeding centuries the Scordisci were responsible for intermittent raiding against neighbouring Macedonia and Greece.

To the north of the Scordisci, in Transdanubia and the Great Hungarian Plain, the third century BC saw a steady increase in the number and density of La Tène settlements and cemeteries resulting from movements of Celts from the north as well as groups returning from the south-east. It is tempting to see

the Greek bronze kantharos found at Szob in Hungary, which has its closest parallels at Galaxidi near Delphi, as a trophy brought back from the campaigns. The tribal configuration is not clear but much of Transdanubia was in the hands of the Taurisci. The Volcae Tectosages are also mentioned and it is possible that the Boii were establishing some enclaves in the north.

In the Great Hungarian Plain the burials of the native Siginni continued until the mid-third century, but thereafter La Tène influence became more apparent, possibly as a result of the

59 Greek bronze kantharos of the late fourth century BC found at Szob, Pest, Hungary. It is very similar to vessels found in the vicinity of Delphi and may possibly have been among the spoils from the attack on the sanctuary. Magyar Nemzeti Múzeum, Budapest.

settlement of infiltrating Celtic groups, and it is in this period that some of the La Tène cemeteries extending from the Hungarian border into Transylvania begin to develop. Taken together, the archaeological evidence suggests that the broad swath of territory stretching from the eastern fringes of the Alps to Transylvania was rapidly becoming celticized. It was in this zone that the classic La Tène styles and the artistic concepts of indigenous peoples rooted in an eastern tradition of animal art interacted to create an eastern La Tène art distinguishable from that developing in the west.

86

The distribution of La Tène material extends northward of the Suddetin Mountains into southern Poland. Finds have been made in sufficient quantity to suggest that migrant populations may have moved northwards from north-ern Bohemia in the late fourth and early third centuries to settle in Lower Sile-sia in the present region of Wrocław, Okawa, and Strzelin, where cemeteries, presumably indicating the distribution of settlements, are found to occupy the most fertile lands. In Upper Silesia, in the valleys of the Rivers Cyna and Troja, the initial La Tène settlement is a little later, dating to the second half of the third century, and may have originated as the result of the movement of peoples from Moravia. Both communities were ideally located to command trade in desirable commodities, such as amber, furs, wax, salt, and graphite, acquired from the north European zone for exchange with the communities of the south, where such materials were avidly sought.

The possibility that Celtic groups from the Balkans may have moved west-wards through Europe and settled in the west is suggested by archaeological and literary evidence. In the Marne region, for example, a new range of warrior burials accompanied by well-furnished female graves makes a sudden appear-ance towards the middle of the third century. New cemeteries were established and old burial sites reused. It is now that areas long abandoned are reoccupied. The implication is that new Celtic groups had moved into the Champagne region to augment the thinly scattered indigenous Celtic population. That these new settlers may have come from the Carpathian Basin is suggested by similarities in dress between the two areas, in particular the use of anklets by women, and by the prevalence of small funerary enclo-sures which now appear.

In southern Gaul there is also evidence sug-gestive of an influx of new people from the Danube region. The southern Gaulish histo-rian Pompeius Trogus, quoted by Justinus, records that a number of the Tectosages, who were involved in the retreat from Greece, moved west eventually to settle in the vicinity of Toulouse, bringing with them treasure from the sack of Delphi which they deposited

in sacred lakes. When, in 106 BC, Caepio was sent in charge of a Roman force to put down a revolt among the Volcae and Tectosages, he had the lakes drained and the treasure seized with the intention of keeping it for himself. The later disasters which befell him were believed by Strabo and Justinus to have been the result of Apollo's wrath, angered that the sacred treasures of Delphi were again disturbed.

Some potential archaeological confirmation for this suggested influx is to be found in the sudden appearance of La Tène material in the Languedoc region and in the Garonne Valley. At the hilltop settlement of Ensérune, near Béziers,

60 Gold torc from Fenouil-let, Haute-Garonne, France. Third century BC. The elaborate style of decora-tion, typical of torcs from south-western France, may have been introduced from the Middle Danube region, perhaps by migrating bands. Musée de Saint-Raymond, Toulouse.

61 Gold torc from Gajič, Vojvodina, former Yugoslavia. Third century BC. The style is very similar to those found in south-western France. Magyar Nemzeti Múzeum, Budapest.

from the early third century, a high percentage of the burials contain Celtic warrior gear, including swords, spears, chain mail, and shields. Although some La Tène material is found in earlier contexts, this sudden appearance of warrior panoply may indicate more than just trade. Further west in the Garonne Valley, in the general region of Toulouse, highly decorated gold torcs and armlets made their appearance in the third century, many being deposited in hoards such as those at Fenouillet and Lasgraïsses. Stylistically they can be compared to items found in the Danube region. Although the density of the distribution suggests local manufacture, the strong possibility is that they were made by migrant craftsmen coming from the east.

The third century was evidently a time of great mobility in Celtic Europe when coherent groups of people moved vast distances and were frequently able to maintain their ethnic identity. The extent of flux and ferment is only dimly recognizable in the works of the ancient historians, while the archaeological evidence, as is so often the case, is ambiguous and open to a variety of interpretations. Yet the huge sweeps of territory over which a distinctive La Tène culture spread in the third century, and the similarity of artistic style and behaviour represented in grave goods and burial practice, are a dramatic demonstration of a fluidity of ideas caused in some considerable part by an equal flux of population.

The Mechanisms of Movement

To understand the nature of the motivation behind this remarkable phase of migration, it is necessary to return to the phenomenon of 'the raid'. For a Celt to enhance his status, it was necessary to engage in acts of prowess—to demonstrate ability to lead, to provide the context for acts of valour, and to acquire booty for distribution in displays of largess. We have seen above how the socio-economic system at the end of the Hallstatt period created a situation in which the raid could develop, but in all probability it was endemic throughout Europe over a long period, rising to prominence from time to time as conditions demanded. Late Bronze Age Greece, manifest in Mycenaean culture and reflected in the Homeric literature, provides one such example.

Once the raid had become an established part of the status system, there was an inbuilt imperative to intensify. A successful raid with spoils to distribute provided enhanced status for the leader so that on the next occasion he would attract more followers and there would be increased expectations. Younger men, wishing to aspire to greatness, would feel compelled to compete, and so the cycle would feed itself, growing all the while. In such a situation it is easy to see how the limited raid on neighbours would need to give way to more adventurous expeditions, and how, for some sectors of the community, raiding could have become a full-time occupation. In this context the long-distance raid, requiring the absence from home for many months, becomes readily understandable: mercenary activity, notionally in the employ of others, is simply a further extension. It is against this background that the long periods of raiding—from Cisalpine Gaul into Italy, from the Middle Danube into Macedonia and Greece, and from central Anatolia to the Aegean coasts—must be seen. The imperative to raid was the central focus of Celtic society.

The social 'transhumance' embodied in the system created the context for entire populations to move when the territory became too constricted either for the population to grow or to provide suitable marcher zones around for small-scale military activity. The situation is vividly demonstrated in one of the last and most fully documented migrations—that of the Helvetii in 59 and 58 BC. Although we see the situation develop only in the words which Julius Caesar chooses to provide for us (*De Bello Gallico* 1), his account contains a ring of truth.

The Helvetii lived in Switzerland hemmed in by mountains and the Rhine.

These geographical features meant that they could not range over a wide area and had greater difficulty in making war on neighbouring tribes. Since the Helvetii enjoyed fighting, they bitterly resented the restrictions. They considered that the territory they had did not match the size of their population or its reputation for bravery in war: it was too small . . .

Caesar goes on to describe the preparations for migration, the buying of draught animals and wagons, the sowing of as much land as possible to provide food for the march, and the establishment of diplomatic relations with neighbours through whose territories they wished to travel. 'They thought two years would be enough for completing their preparations and passed a law declaring that they would set out on the third . . .' When they were ready to start the migration, they set fire to their twelve *oppida* and 400 villages as well as the surplus grain to prevent any possibility of return and, with several like-minded neighbouring tribes, they set off for a new territory on the Atlantic coast of Gaul.

Their march was intercepted by Caesar, who with massive force stopped the advance and drove the remnants to return, except for the Boii, who were invited to settle in the territory of the Aedui. Caesar claims to have

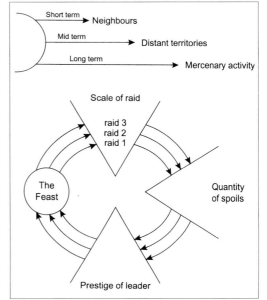

62 The raid. A diagram to illustrate the dynamics of the raid as an integral part of the Celtic social system. Competitive emulation among aspiring leaders will have created a situation in which raiding might escalate. Mercenary activity and migration are extreme manifestations of the same system.

found documents in the Helvetian camp listing, in Greek, the migrants, distinguishing them by tribe and by gender and age. In total there were 368,000: 263,000 Helvetii, 36,000 Tulingi, 14,000 Latovici, 23,000 Raurici, and 32,000 Boii. Of these 92,000 were armed. After the battle those forced to return numbered only 110,000. How reliable these figures are will remain unknown, but at the very least Caesar's account gives some idea of the reasons, magnitude, and organization of a Celtic folk movement.

5
Warfare and Society

THE Graeco-Roman world had many opportunities to observe Celtic armies in action. Their viewpoint was usually, though not invariably, that of opponents, and those who recorded the confrontations did so to communicate more than just ethnographic observations and the facts of history. The writing of Greek and Roman history was formulaic. Pausanius would write of the Celtic attack on Greece in the third century BC using the same structure and balance as did Herodotus when writing of the Persian Wars two centuries earlier. This equation of Celts with Persians—two enemies of the civilized world—is found in a fragment of poetry preserved on a papyrus of the third century and again recurs in sculptured form on the great victory monument erected by the Pergamene king Attalus I in Athens in the second century. The message is the same: the enemy from without is fierce and brutal but can be overcome by the Greek peoples working together for the common good. Pausanius was writing in the second century AD and was therefore using a variety of earlier sources, among them Hieronymus of Cardia, who served the Pergamene king Eumenes in the late fourth century BC, and Timaeus, who was in Athens during the Celtic raids, as well as other writers, including, perhaps, Menodotus of Perinthus and Agatharchides of Cnidus. The range of information available to him was varied, but the constraints of his selection and presentation were rigidly circumscribed.

One of the key figures in the Roman historical tradition was Polybius, a citizen of the Greek town of Megalopolis who was deported to Rome in 168 BC. Polybius' intention was to present the Celts as a formative influence on the development of Roman military power. In his view the initial invasion in the early fourth century and the continuous threat created by the Celtic settlement in the Po Valley were instrumental in the honing of Rome's military competence. For him the Celts are to be presented as a contrast to the calm efficiency of the Roman army. While the Romans are steadfast, level-headed, well-led, and achieve victory by dogged determination, the Celts are volatile and unpredictable and, though fierce in the initial onslaught, can easily lose heart and panic. It is, therefore, their antithetical qualities to the Romans that he gives most attention to. Polybius' writings provide one of the prime sources used by Livy (59 BC–AD 17) for his *History*, and, while it is evident that Livy had other sources of information on the Celts, the influence of Polybius' thesis is evident. Once more the Celts are presented as impulsive barbarians with an inability to plan rationally.

The narrative history of Polybius was continued by Poseidonius for the period 145–82 BC. The importance of Poseidonius (135–51 BC) is that he travelled widely in the Alps, Gaul, Spain, and possibly also Britain, observing for himself different Celtic societies in different states of development. His description of the Celts has survived only in the works of other writers, notably Strabo, Diodorus Siculus, Athenaeus, and Caesar, but when these are taken together it is clear that Poseidonius was a keen observer with the eye of an anthropologist and that he was well aware of the changes that were taking place. From his viewpoint as a Stoic he may be critical of many of the more irrational and exuberant aspects of Celtic society and tend to overemphasize them, but what he offers has a ring of truthful reporting. His approach is to present the Celt as a Noble Savage—a natural man untouched by civilization—but in pointing up the contrast to the civilized world he was prone to overemphasis.

Julius Caesar probably used Poseidonius as a source, but he also had the unique opportunity of observing a variety of Celtic tribes from close hand during his eight years of campaigning. His war *Commentaries* are, by their very nature, biased sources. Caesar is at pains to present the Celts in a way that would have been familiar to his audience, playing on old prejudices, not least by emphasizing the fierceness and unreliability of the enemy, thereby enhancing his own achievements and providing a justification for his action. While his descriptions of Celtic society in Gaul and his picture of Britain and the Britons may be selective interpolations, culled from the sources available to him, there is much in his general accounts of military and political matters that is highly informative about the Celtic communities he was confronting.

Of the later sources, Tacitus offers new insights particularly about the Britons. Once more there is a reliance on stock stereotypes and the bias inherent in using the concept of the Noble Savage to point up the iniquities of the times, but behind the selection and the rhetoric there are many useful insights into native customs and social and political organization.

Clearly all the historical sources available to us are biased in one way or another—such is the nature of historical sources—but it should not prevent us from using them in an attempt to characterize Celtic society and warfare. The greatest difficulties concern chronological and regional variation. To imply that any generalized description has universal application is evident nonsense. Most of our sources concern Celtic groups in the fourth to second centuries living in, and raiding from, those parts of Europe that were in proximity to the

Mediterranean world. Within these parameters we may legitimately attempt to reconstruct a generalized picture of classic Celtic culture. Of the more remote Celtic regions, all that can be said is that some of them may have shared aspects of the classical model at some time in their history. There are, however, real difficulties in extending the model. Thus, while the troops led by Calgacus against Agricola in northern Scotland in AD 84 appeared to have behaved in many ways like Celtic armies in Italy in the fourth and third centuries BC, it is not easy to decide whether these apparent similarities are a manifestation of archaic 'Celtic behaviour' in remote and backward areas or the use by Tacitus of a series of familiar Celtic stereotypes. A further possibility, that primitive warfare exhibited many similarities irrespective of time, place, and ethnicity, has also to be borne in mind.

The Warrior and his Equipment

The classic Celtic image is provided in Strabo's oft-quoted description:

The whole race . . . is madly fond of war, high spirited and quick to battle, but otherwise straightforward and not of evil character. And so when they are stirred up they assemble in their bands for battle, quite openly and without forethought, so that they are easily handled by those who desire to outwit them.

When they are aroused, he says,

they are ready to face danger even if they have nothing on their side but their own strength and courage . . . their strength depends on their mighty bodies, and on their numbers . . . to the frankness and high-spiritedness of their temperament must be added the traits of childish boastfulness and love of decoration. They wear ornaments of gold torques on their necks, and bracelets on their arms and wrists, while people of high rank wear dyed garments besprinkled with gold. It is this vanity which makes them unbearable in victory and so completely downcast in defeat.   (*Geog.* 4. 4. 2)

Here then are displayed all the characteristics of the Greek or Roman vision of a Celtic warrior: he is ferocious, impetuous, boastful, flamboyant, and mercurial—not a foe to be lightly tangled with.

The weapons carried by the warrior were a sword, usually fastened on the right side, and a spear. Some used bows and arrows, slings, or throwing clubs. The normal means of protection was the shield, but sometimes helmets

63 Detail of a brooch, possibly of Iberian origin, showing a naked Celtic warrior complete with a typical set of armour, attacking a lion. Private collection.

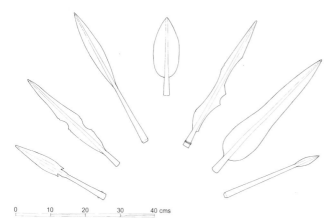

0   10   20   30   40 cms

64 Spearheads recovered from the site of La Tène in Switzerland. The variety of forms suggests a degree of specialization in the use of the spear in the hunt and in warfare.

65 The excavation of Maiden Castle, Dorset, England, exposed a pit containing about 20,000 carefully chosen pebbles to serve as sling stones for the defence of the fort in the first century AD. The ammunition dump lay just inside the strongly fortified east gate.

were worn and less often tunics of ring mail. All these pieces of equipment, mentioned in the texts, are reflected in the archaeological record and in the surviving iconography, though it is sometimes possible to detect regional variations. Among the Parisii of Yorkshire, for example, the sword was sometimes worn across the back and had therefore to be drawn over the shoulder from behind the head.

Iron swords in sheaths of iron, bronze, wood, or leather were the symbol of the warrior and as such were often personalized by elaborate decoration applied to the sheath or by stamps beaten into the blade (Fig. 87). Polybius is scathing of the quality of the swords used at Telamon in the third century. They were good for cutting but not thrusting and became easily bent during battle, requiring the warriors to pause and bend them back into shape with the foot, he reports. While there was, indeed, a variation in quality, and some made of softer iron may have been ineffective, the description may owe something to the fact that swords were often deliberately bent before being ritually deposited and it may have been the results of ritual activity rather than battle that Polybius was noting.

Throwing and thrusting spears were equally important, and a considerable variety of spearheads have been found, the different weights and shapes suiting them to different purposes. The large collection recovered from the ritual site of La Tène presents a variety of lethal designs with serrated, flame-shaped, and hollow ground blades designed for easy penetration. One version, with a notched blade, conforms to the type described by Diodorus Siculus with 'breaks throughout the entire length so that the blow not only cuts but also tears the flesh, and the recovery of the spear rips open the wound' (*Hist.* 5. 30).

Bows and arrows are not often mentioned and are rare in the archaeological record, but a scatter of bronze arrowheads of trilobate kind, a type common among the Scythians, may have been brought back to western Europe by mercenaries and migrants who had learnt to use them in the east. That it was not used in any of the recorded conflicts implies, however, that archery never achieved much favour in the Celtic world.

The sling is also only mentioned in passing and does not feature in any set-piece battle. In Britain, however, there is ample archaeo-

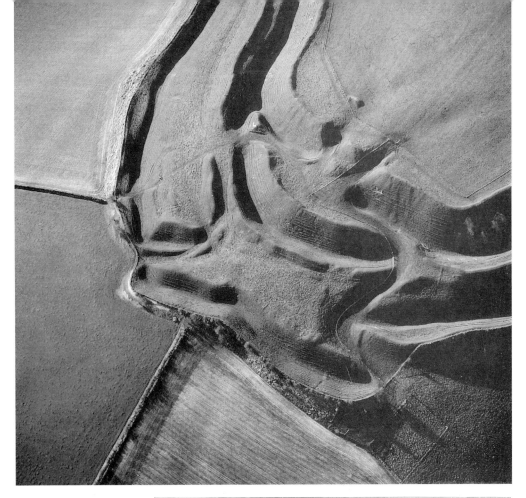

66 *Above*: Aerial view of the east gate of Maiden Castle, Dorset, England. The complex earthworks extending down the slope in front of the gate would have forced any attackers to weave backwards and forwards, exposing themselves to constant attack from strategically placed sling platforms. The fort was probably attacked and taken by the Second Legion in AD 43.

67 *Right*: The east entrance of Maiden Castle, showing the arrangement of the sling platforms.

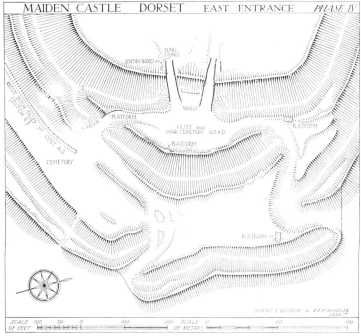

MAIDEN CASTLE DORSET EAST ENTRANCE *PHASE IV*

SLING STONES

SENTRY-BOXES

WALLS

PLATFORM

PLATFORM

HUTS AND WAR-CEMETERY 43 A.D

PLATFORM

PLATFORM

CEMETERY

PLATFORM

HUNTLY S GORDON & R.E.M.WHEELER 1934~5

SCALE 100   50   0   100   200   SCALE 0   50   100
OF FEET   OF METRES

logical evidence for its use as a defensive weapon at hill forts. Huge stockpiles of carefully selected sling pebbles found near the gates of Maiden Castle and Danebury were kept in readiness, and the design of the gates and earthworks seems to reflect the use of the sling to drive away attackers. That slings were also used in attacks upon hill forts is specifically mentioned by Caesar in describing Gaulish warfare, in which the missile volley was employed to drive defenders from the ramparts. In such contexts, slings would have been particularly effective, but much less so in open warfare.

The principal form of personal protection used by the warrior in battle was the shield, described by Diodorus as man-sized and decorated in individual fashion, some with projecting bronze animals of fine workmanship. A visual impression of the variety of decoration achieved is provided by the piles of armour depicted on the Roman arch at Orange. The most effective form of shield was made of leather or wood or a combination of the two. The ritual deposit found in a bog at Hjortspring on the Danish island of Als contained a number of wooden shields made out of planks with circular holes to take handholds with the knuckles protected by wooden umbos. Shields of this kind would have been effective but heavy. A far more efficient model is that typified

96

69 Simple wooden shield from a votive deposit buried in a ship at Hjortspring on the island of Als, Denmark. The shields are made from planks of wood with holes, covered by umbos, to provide a hand-hold. Nationalmuseet, Copenhagen.

70 *Far left*: Shield discovered in a bog at Clonoura, Co. Tipperary, Ireland. The shield is made of thin sheets of wood covered with leather and bound around the edge with leather strips. The central umbo protecting the hand-hold is also of leather. The construction means that the shield, while very resilient, is light to hold. The surface exhibits battle scars. National Museum of Ireland, Dublin.

71 *Left*: The Chertsey shield, recovered from the River Thames at Chertsey, Surrey, England. Elaborate metal-faced shields of this kind may have been made specifically for display or ritual deposition. Third or second century BC. British Museum.

72 Helmet found in a warrior's grave at Ciumeşti, Romania. It bears a fearsome bird with movable wings, which would flap when the wearer ran, and staring eyes of red glass. Early third century BC. Muzeul Naţional de Istorie, Bucharest. The horned helmet from the Thames near Waterloo Bridge, dating to the first century BC or early first century AD, would also have made its wearer look dominating. British Museum, London.

by the shield found in a bog at Clonoura, Co. Tipperary, in Ireland. It was composed of a thin sheet of wood covered back and front with leather providing a light and highly resilient form of protection, the umbo was also of leather. A shield of similar structure can be reconstructed from the archaeological evidence surviving in a burial at St Peter Port, Guernsey, but in this case the protective umbo was of iron, in the corrosion products of which traces of the wood and leather body of the shield were preserved. In all probability this type was in widespread use, though it is usually only the metal fittings that survive. Among the more elaborate examples are those covered in sheet bronze with bronze umbos, often highly decorated. Examples from the Thames, at Chertsey and Battersea (Pl. V) and from the River Witham were probably votive offerings and may indeed have been made as such. Such pieces were more appropriate to the parade than to warfare.

Bronze helmets were a feature of warrior equipment. Diodorus mentions that some possess 'long projecting figures, lending the appearance of enormous stature to the wearer. In some cases horns form one piece with the helmet, while in other cases it is relief figures or the foreparts of birds or quadrupeds' (*Hist.* 5. 30). This is amply borne out in the archaeological record, with finds of helmets with sockets for projecting elements and, in the case of one helmet from Ciumeşti in Romania, with an attached bird complete with flapping wings. The horned helmet from the Thames at Waterloo Bridge conforms to the general description, while small castings of bronze boars found in many parts of Europe are most likely to have been helmet attachments. Boar-crested helmets as well as others with birds and horns are shown worn by the warriors depicted on the Gunderstrup cauldron.

Diodorus also mentions that some warriors wear iron breast plates of chain mail. Seated figures of stone from the sanctuary of Roquepertuse (Fig. 163) and a stone statue of a Gaul from Vachères (Basse-Alpes) (Pl. VI), dating to the late first century BC, are shown wearing chain mail, and actual examples have been found in a few burials, including that of the warrior provided with the bird-crested helmet, who was buried at Ciumeşti.

One of the features of Celtic warfare which impressed itself upon the classical mind was the fact that some warriors fought naked except for the sword belt and a gold neck torc. In his description of the battle of Telamon in 225 BC Polybius distinguishes a particular detachment—the Gaesatae—who fought in this way. 'Very terrifying, too, were the appearance and gestures of the naked warriors in front, all in the prime of life and finely built men, and all in the leading companies richly adorned with gold torcs and armlets' (*Hist.* 29. 5–9). Polybius believed that they discarded their clothes because they thought that they would be a hindrance in battle, but this is likely to be a rationalization. In all probability nakedness had a ritual significance. The Gaesatae ('spear-men') were distinguishable as a distinct group and at Telamon appear to have been a lately arrived mercenary force. Their ritual nakedness may have been a demonstration of their oneness as a fighting body. Nakedness in battle is again referred to in Galatia in 189 BC, when the Tolistobogii and Trocmi took off their clothes before battle with the Romans exposing their podgy white bodies, which enhanced the vividness of their wounds as they were cut to pieces by the Roman force.

73 Detail from the cauldron found at Gunderstrup, Denmark, showing mounted warriors wearing helmets, one with a bird crest, the other with a boar. First century BC? Nationalmuseet, Copenhagen.

The vision of the naked Celt is a recurring theme in Graeco-Roman art, as is witnessed by the copies of the Pergamene statues, but it also appears much earlier on the Bologna funerary stela of the fifth century BC, which shows a naked Celtic foot soldier in conflict with a mounted Etruscan (Fig. 54). In sum, the evidence leaves little doubt that to fight naked was a comparatively common occurrence in the Celtic world.

Another recurring theme in the literature and in art is the wearing of the torc in battle. The torc had a deep religious significance. Deities are usually shown wearing torcs (Pl. XI) and the seated god on the Gunderstrup cauldron, in addition to wearing a torc, holds one in his hand. Torcs are also a component of ritual deposition, as is witnessed, in particular, at Snettisham in Norfolk (Pl. XXII*b*). The torc will have given the wearer the sense of being protected by the gods—it was a symbol of his life and being. When, in 361 BC, the Roman Manlius confronted a Celtic chieftain in single combat, the Celt fought naked but for his shield, two swords, and his torc and armlets. Manlius killed him and took his torc, acquiring, in doing so, the name 'Torquatus'. Nearly 200 years later, in 191, when the Roman army defeated the Celts at Bologna, the spoils included 1,500 gold torcs. Even as late as AD 60, when the British queen, Boudica, led her troops into battle, she wore a cloak and a gold torc, and carried a spear.

The Celtic war chariot impressed a number of observers. Diodorus describes how 'for journeys and in battle they use two-horse chariots, the chariot carrying both charioteer and chieftain. When they meet with cavalry in battle they cast their javelins at the enemy and then descending from the chariot join battle with their swords'. The absence of any reference to chariot warfare in Gaul during Caesar's campaigns suggests that as a means of fighting it was no longer of significance. When, however, he crossed the Channel to Britain, he found the chariot much in evidence. He was sufficiently impressed by the novelty of the tactics involved that he gave an extended description of British charioteering, stressing in particular the agility of the charioteer, who, by virtue of long practice, could run out along the chariot pole between the horses and could check and change direction in a moment. The speed with which chariots could move the combatant from one point of the field to another was particularly effective and led Caesar to make the shrewd observation of a military man that 'They combined the staying power of infantry with the mobility of cavalry.' In Britain his chief opponent Cassivellaunus was able to muster 4,000 chariots, which, if used together, must have been a formidable sight.

Sufficient is known of these machines from the archaeological remains of their metal fittings and from depiction on contemporary coinage to appreciate their lightness and efficiency. The chariot was essentially a platform, carried on a pair of iron-tired, spoked wheels c.0.9 metres in diameter, linked by a pole and yoke to two small ponies. The sides were low double hoops of bent wood or wickerwork, while the front and back were open for ease of access. The war chariot of this kind was a specialized version of the two-wheeled vehicle which became popular in the Celtic world in the fifth century BC and was used from then on in funerary ritual. Its ultimate inspiration may well have come from the Etruscan world.

There is no reason to assume that the funerary vehicles were war chariots. Structurally they were similar, but it is more likely that the vehicle used in burial was a parade vehicle symbolizing the high status of the deceased, though it might have been possible to convert one to the other.

Diodorus, as we have seen, says that, when the chariot teams meet with opposing cavalry, the combatants first throw their javelins and then descend from the chariot to join battle with their swords. Caesar adds that the chariots then moved off but returned when necessary to pick up the warrior and carry him to another part of the field. The chariot driver was evidently a skilled person and of vital importance to the well-being of the warrior he served. Diodorus records that the élite 'bring into battle as their attendants free men chosen from among the poorer classes whom they use as charioteers and shield bearers in battle' (*Hist.* 5. 29).

A remark of Pausanius' throws some further light on the battle order. He mentions the *trimarcisia* (literally 'three riders') as a Celtic fighting unit, implying that the warrior élite were accompanied by two supporters. In this case we are dealing with a cavalry unit. The supporters would stay behind the ranks as battle proceeded ready to dash to their master's assistance if he needed a fresh horse or was wounded and, if he were seriously injured, to take his place in the battle line.

74 *Above*: Chariot depicted, somewhat stylistically, on a coin of the northern Gaulish tribe, the Remi. First half of first century BC.

75 *Below*: A Celtic war chariot shown in action on the reverse of a Roman denarius minted in *c*.48 BC. The charioteer drives the horses, while the noble warrior, naked but armed, looks for action.

The chariot team and the *trimarcisia* imply a close and practised relationship between fighting men bound by obligation and honour, much as a knight and squire worked together in medieval warfare. In this context it is possible to understand the depth of the antagonism between the British queen, Cartimandua, and her husband Venutius when she left her husband in favour of Vellocatus, who was described as his 'armour bearer'. Not only was she publicly dishonouring Venutius, but she was weakening him by removing a trained and trusted member of his fighting entourage.

The Battle

The most informative description of the anthropology of the Celtic battle is provided by Diodorus Siculus (presumably using Poseidonius as a source):

When the armies are drawn up in battle-array, they [the chiefs] are wont to advance before the battleline and to challenge the bravest of their opponents to single combat, at the same time brandishing before them their arms so as to terrify their foe. When someone accepts their challenge to battle, they loudly recite the deeds of valour of their ancestors and proclaim their own valorous quality, at the same time abusing and making little of their opponent and generally attempting to rob him beforehand of his fighting spirit. (*Hist.* 5. 29)

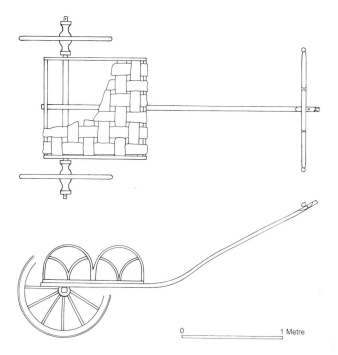

76 Reconstruction of a Celtic chariot (after Stuart Piggott). The essence of the vehicle is its light flexible construction designed for speed and easy manœuvrability.

A further detail is added by Athenaeus (also quoting Poseidonius) when he notes that 'The Celts have in their company even in war, companions whom they call parasites. These men pronounce their praises before the whole assembly and before each of the chieftains in turn as they listen.' It was no doubt this pattern of behaviour that led Diodorus to the generalization that 'They frequently exaggerate with the aim of extolling themselves and diminishing the status of others. They are boasters and threateners and given to bombastic self-dramatization' (*Hist.* 5. 31).

Taken together, and rid of the prejudice inherent in the style of the sources, these statements provide a vivid insight into the nature of Celtic warfare in its classic form, before frequent contact with Mediterranean armies brought about changes. Conflict was endemic: it was embedded in the social system, but was constrained, as it was and is in many societies, by conventions which attempted to limit hostilities to selected heroes. Through them all society could, vicariously, indulge in battle. The drawing-up of the two opposing forces, with women and children looking on from the rear, provided the occasion. The individual heroes would then issue their challenges, the tension heightened by eulogies of prowess. In these tirades the satirizing of an opponent in public could be a potent weapon. Once the challenge was accepted, the combatants would engage in full view of the assembled mass. It is quite conceivable that in such a situation, after a succession of contests, the result would be obvious and all could disperse. On other occasions growing tension could give rise to a more widespread engagement.

This pattern of structured aggression leading to a general mêlée is evident in the gladiatorial contest held in the amphitheatre of Pompeii during the reign of Nero between contestants provided by Pompeii and Nucria. Dissatisfaction with the result led the spectators supporting the two sides to engage in open, and bloody, conflict. It is much the same chemistry that today leads supporters to invade the football pitch.

The theme of single combat in the battle situation recurs in Livy's *History*. In 361 BC the Roman Manlius engaged in single combat with a Celt who goaded his opponent by poking out his tongue and laughing. Manlius used his short Spanish stabbing sword to good effect against the heavy Celtic slashing sword. In another tale, referring to 348, the tribune Valerius confronted a Celtic chieftain, having first gained permission from the consuls to take up his opponent's challenge. As battle commenced a crow perched on Valerius' helmet and attacked the Celt's eyes and face before returning to the helmet to watch the resulting combat. The Celt, weakened by the demonstration of divine disfavour, collapsed and was killed. For this Valerius gained the cognomen 'Corvinus'. The parallelism between the two stories may suggest the repetition of a single incident or even a fictitious embroidery, but the fact that Livy had access to the tradition suggests that single combat was a feature of fourth century Celtic behaviour in Italy. As Celtic forces faced the armies of Mediterranean states, so fighting tactics will have changed and single combat will have become increasingly irrelevant. The general onslaught now became the norm, and the fierceness and power of the Celtic charge became legendary.

One of the recurring themes in the classical sources is the noise of the Celts in battle. The Celt who faced Manlius preceded the combat with a war dance and battle chant which almost certainly had a magico-religious significance. Similarly the war trumpets—carnyxes—used in the opening stages of conflict were probably employed as much for ritual reasons as to strike fear into the enemy. Diodorus' description is brief. 'Their trumpets again are of a peculiar barbarian kind; they blow into them and produce a harsh sound which suits the tumult of war' (*Hist.* 5. 30), but the theme is taken up more dramatically by Polybius in his description of the battle of Telamon (225 BC). He tells how the Romans were terrified by the fine order of the Celtic army and 'the dreadful din, for there were innumerable hornblowers and trumpeters and, as the whole army were shouting their war-cries at the same time, there was such a tumult of sound that it seemed that not only the trumpeters and the soldiers but all the country round had got a voice and caught up the cry' (*Hist.* 29. 5–9). While it is too easy to read things into this picturesque description, it may have been intended to communicate the idea of the Celtic troops calling up the gods of the land in their cause. This same sense of panic was instilled into the Roman force who faced a Celtic mob supported by their Druids shouting dreadful imprecations as they prepared to attack the Druidic sanctuary on Anglesey in AD 59.

There is nothing specifically Celtic about the use of horns or battle cries. After all, Joshua used musical instruments to good (no doubt symbolic) effect when he paraded around the walls of Jericho. Why the classical sources tend to emphasize this raucous noise is that it was alien to the more ordered and considered Greek and Roman approach to battle—it served to characterize the barbarian.

The strength of the Celtic attack lay in the ferocity of the first onslaught. It was a power generated by many things, a belief in an afterlife, a desire to gain glory, and a battle hysteria created by the building crescendo of noise and chanting, often enhanced still further by alcohol—in fact the usual methods which fighting forces through the ages have used to give courage at the moment of battle. But the fury, by its very nature, lacked control: it was impetuous but without any forethought or planning. Thus, when the onslaught was held and turned, there was no strategy in reserve to cope, and desperation set in. The misery of the Celt in defeat was recorded on a number of occasions. At Telamon, after Roman successes, some of the Celts, 'reduced to utmost distress and complexity . . . in their impotent rage rushed wildly on the enemy and sacrificed their lives, while others, retreating step by step on the ranks of their comrades, threw them into disorder by their display of faint-heartedness'. This same theme recurs in the aftermath of the battle between Agricola and the native war leader Calgacus and is told vividly by Tacitus:

On the enemy's side each man now followed his bent. Some bands, though armed, fled before inferior numbers, some men, though unarmed, insisted on charging to their deaths. Armour, bodies, severed limbs lay all around and the earth reeked of blood; and the vanquished now and then found their fury and their courage again.   (*Agricola* 37).

The unpredictability and unreliability of the Celt who could at one moment be fierce and bombastic and at another flee in a deranged panic were part of the stereotype which classical writers chose to perpetuate, but that there were many occasions of steadfast heroism is not in doubt. Caesar's description of his battle against the Nervii in the second year of his Gallic War serves to redress the balance:

When their front rank had fallen, the next stood on the prostrate forms and fought from them; when these were cast down and the corpses were piled up in heaps, the survivors, standing as it were upon a mound, hurled darts at our troops, or caught and returned our javelins.   (*De Bello Gallico* 2. 27)

As a result of this engagement, the tribe was almost annihilated. Of the 60,000 who could bear arms, only 500 survived. Even allowing for Caesar's exaggeration, the battle of the Sambre was an heroic last stand.

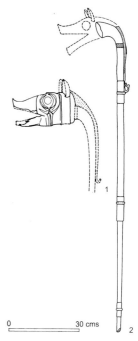

0   30 cms

77 Above: Parts of war trumpets (carnyxes) from Deskford, Banffshire, Scotland (left), and Tattershall Ferry, Lincolnshire, England (right). Trumpets of this kind are shown on the Gunderstrup cauldron and on various Celtic coins.

78 Below: Detail from the Gunderstrup cauldron showing three men blowing war trumpets (carnyxes). First century BC? National-museet, Copenhagen.

Heroism is a leitmotif in classical accounts of Celtic warfare. Wounds were a source of pride and might even be opened up further by the bearer if considered to be too insignificant. Failure, particularly of a war leader, was unacceptable. The stark sculpted image of the Celt committing suicide by the body of his wife, adorning the temple of Athene at Pergamum (Pl. II), would have reminded the Graeco-Roman world of the Celtic moral code. The recorded suicides of failed Celtic leaders are many: Brennus fleeing from Delphi, Florus and Sacrovir after the failed rebellion in Gaul, and Boudica in Britain are among the more famous. Against the social context of Celtic warfare, this is easily understood. The battle was a means of creating and enhancing warrior prowess. It was a public event in which achievement could be seen, judged, and remembered: failure subjected to the same scrutiny was socially unacceptable and demanded the honourable solution.

Celtic warfare evolved in different places at different rates. Boudica and Calgacus were using methods and equipment abandoned in the more central areas of the Celtic world several centuries earlier, and it is doubtful if the war chariot was ever seen in Ireland, in spite of its frequent appearance in the heroic vernacular literature. Similarly, the Nervii who so bravely opposed Caesar would have developed their fighting methods against neighbours and Germans, in contrast to the Volcae Tectosages of southern Gaul, whose ancestors were conversant with the hoplite army of the Greeks. Although Celtic warrior equipment remained remarkably similar across considerable areas and through time, subtle changes can be detected. By the third century BC the standard panoply became increasingly heavy, involving, it is estimated, up to five times more metal per man than two centuries earlier. The Celt at this stage was a heavily armed infantryman. The shield had developed a more elaborate and efficient umbo, and the chain by which the sword was slung from the belt had become a heavy complex structure brilliantly designed to keep the sword in place, however the body moved, to prevent the sheath from encumbering the warrior's feet. Thus equipped, and adopting the technique of the furious frontal onslaught, the Celts were able to deal efficiently with Mediterranean armies organized on the model of the Macedonian phalanx.

During the third century cavalry began to play a significant part in Graeco-Roman warfare, and the Celts' familiarity with the horse, which was long established, made them a sought-after addition as specialized mercenaries. Hannibal was to make good use of heavily armed Celtic cavalry during the Second Punic War. The growing importance of the cavalry is reflected in a marked increase in the length of the sword, many examples of which, by the end of the century, had reached 80–90 centimetres—too long for comfort in infantry fighting.

The battle of Telamon in 225 BC in many ways marks a turning-point. It is the last recorded battle on the continent of Europe in which the chariot appeared, and one in which Celtic cavalry, separately deployed, was to play a significant part. Thereafter, as cavalry became increasingly important, it is likely that the chariot began to decline, disappearing altogether by the beginning of the first century BC except among the Insular Celts. During Caesar's campaigns in Gaul, detachments of Gallic cavalry were widely used on both sides, and after romanization Gaul provided some of the most effective cavalry *auxilia* in the Roman army.

The Feast

Central to the establishment and maintenance of the social equilibrium was the feast. The feast was a social gathering at which status and prestige were demonstrated, flaunted, and challenged. The Poseidonian tradition provides an outline of procedure. On a formal occasion the men sat in a circle with the most influential member, judged on the basis of military prowess, nobility of birth, or wealth, occupying the central position. Beside him sat the host and next, on either side, the others in the order of their distinction. It appears that each man had two retainers present: his shield man, who took up a position behind his master, and his spear man. The spear men dined together but in the same room as their masters.

Poseidonius (in Athenaeus, *Deipnosophistae* 4. 40) records three behavioural practices. The first is the hero's portion, in which the beast is cut and served according to status. 'When the hindquarters were served up, the bravest hero took the thigh piece and if another man claimed it they stood up and fought in single combat to death.' This, he notes, was the practice in 'former times'. It is a motif which is to be found several times in the vernacular tradition of Ireland, in famous stories like Bricriu's feast and Mac Datho's pig. The second, which may have grown out of the first, was outright aggression. Sometimes single combat took place, as a result of which people could be wounded or killed. The third practice was more extreme. A man might pledge his life for gifts of gold, silver, or amphorae of wine. When the deal had been done, he would distribute the gifts among family and friends and would then lie stretched out face upwards on his shield, 'while another standing by cut [his] throat with his sword'.

These anecdotal scraps belie the social complexity of the feast but provide some indication of its importance in Celtic society. The feast was evidently a highly structured affair organized rigorously according to status. The arrangement of the participants and the serving of the meat provided the occasions for the definition of the social hierarchy and its public affirmation. If anyone felt demeaned by the ordering, he would contest it, and the ensuing conflict could lead to single combat and death. In any event, the contest would be resolved in the public arena, and thereafter the new order would be known and observed. Clearly, then, the feast provided the opportunity for the aspiring young man to make his claim and to demonstrate the power and the following to sustain it. The feast may well have been the moment when a warrior would propose to lead a raid and would gather support from those present. The size of his following would depend upon his status and the degree of inebriation of the assembly.

79 Bronze cauldron with its iron suspension chain and hooks found at the site of La Tène, Neuchâtel, Switzerland. Third or second century BC. Cauldrons of this kind would have formed the focus of the feast. Musée Cantonal d'Archéologie, Neuchâtel, Switzerland.

Just such a practice is recorded by Tacitus among the Germans. Failure to meet assurances made at the feast would bring disgrace.

In such a context the need for the individual to proclaim his virtues is evident. The Poseidonian tradition is possibly referring to this in recording that the Celts frequently exaggerate with the aim of extolling themselves and diminishing opponents. Others could be employed to do it for them, such as the 'parasites' who accompanied their masters in war and peace to pronounce their praises to the whole assembly and, no doubt, to denigrate their lord's rivals by satire. The bards are to be distinguished from these dependent followers. They were part of the skilled élite—the entertainers and 'poets who delivered eulogies in song'. The value of the praises of such men would be greater than that of the subservient parasites, and one can anticipate the tension that there must have been at a feast when the bard started to perform to see whom he would choose to praise and how he would use his skills to balance his eulogies between those he considered to be worthy of them. Part of his skill would have been to keep his audience on tenterhooks until the last moment. To cultivate such men was important to an aspiring leader. The Arvernian chief Louernius was well aware of this when the bard who arrived late at his feast composed a song to the chief's greatness, lamenting his own late arrival. Louernius was sufficiently judicious to throw the bard a bag of gold as he ran behind his chariot and was rewarded by another song based on the theme that even the 'tracks made by his chariot on the earth gave gold and largess to mankind'. It would have been in Louernius' interests that this song remained prominent in the bard's repertoire!

The feast which Louernius prepared and the gold which he liberally distributed is a fascinating demonstration of the 'potlatch'—the system by which an individual's status was enhanced by the public dispersal of wealth in the form of gifts, often, but not invariably, of food and drink at feasts. The more that was given away, the greater the giver's reputation, and the more he would, in turn, acquire through gift. At its most basic level, the potlatch provided a simple redistributive mechanism by which surpluses could be spread throughout the community. Often, however, it necessitated the destruction of wealth. The dedication of works of great craft skill, like the Battersea shield, or of great value, like the Snettisham gold, to the gods provides an example of wealth destruction within the religious context. Similarly, the burial of valuable goods with the dead was the public affirmation of the lineage's ability to destroy wealth. The feast itself, with the consumption of huge quantities of expensive imported wine, of which the Celts were so inordinately fond, was another form of public wealth destruction.

In a system in which individuals used the potlatch as a means of competing for status there would, inevitably, have been a tendency towards escalation. It is probably in this context that we should attempt to understand the Poseidonian account of the individuals who submitted themselves to death having acquired and distributed rich gifts. By sacrificing their lives solely in the interests of being able to redistribute the gifts they had received to their friends and kin, they were indulging in an extreme form of potlatch. The heady competitive atmosphere of the feast, the liberal consumption of alcohol, and a belief in the afterlife will all have contributed to the individual's willingness to submit to death in the interests of renown.

Hospitality to strangers is another leitmotif of Celtic society, and the Poseidonian tradition refers to the need to offer food and drink before finding out about a visitor's business. The rigorous rules which no doubt covered hospitality were manipulated by the Romans more than once in tricking and slaughtering Lusitanians and Celtiberians in Spain and by Mithridates in the massacre of the Tetrachs in Galatia. In all these cases the Celtic peoples were bound by custom and tradition to a system involving trust which their opponents simply abused for their own advantage.

The Social Hierarchy

That Celtic society was strongly hierarchic is evident from the archaeological record of burials. It is also reflected in Caesar's stark generalization that in Gaul only two classes were of any significance, the Druids and the knights, the rest being little better than slaves. The knights were constantly involved in warfare, their status being reflected by the number of dependants and clients they could command. Caesar's sketch is a gross oversimplification, but it reflects a simple basic structure which may well have lain behind the social systems of many of the Celtic communities. The social hierarchy graded from those who could command huge entourages, men like the Helvetian Orgetorix whose 'household' numbered 10,000 excluding his dependants and debtors, to the semi-free, who were roughly equivalent to a medieval bondman. Within this spectrum would have been carefully distinguished social classes about which little is known. No doubt the law gave a degree of rigidity to the system, but there would have been much visual symbolism to make the social distinction readily apparent in such things as settlement style and dress. These symbols of status, and indeed the social system itself, would have differed with place and time, but one may suppose that the possession of a panoply of arms was a ready and universal means of distinction, similarly the wearing of a torc and arm rings. Another hint is provided by Poseidonius when, describing tonsorial styles, he remarks that 'the nobles shave the cheeks but let the moustache grow freely so that it covers the mouth'. This may well have served to distinguish the élite from the others who shaved entirely or grew short beards. The prominence of the moustache on Celtic iconography and Graeco-Roman representations of Celts may suggest that the practice was widespread among the Celtic élite. Caesar's reference to the fact that the Britons painted their bodies with woad allows that body decoration may have been common and carried with it social messages. The use of tattooing among many societies, including the contemporary Scythians, is a reminder of the significance of this form of communication.

The importance of bonds of obligation among the Gauls, operating at a number of different levels, is frequently referred to by Caesar. At one level, clientage in its various forms could bind retainers to individual members of the élite, but at a different level it could relate tribes one to another. This was clearly the case in Gaul in the first century BC. By Caesar's time the Sequani had established themselves as paramount, with the help of the Germans, and thus had acquired as clients many of the smaller tribes, who previously had looked to the Aedui, taking the sons of their chieftains as hostages. When Caesar appeared and offered the Aedui the support of Rome, the hostages were returned and the clients flocked back to the Aedui, together with new clients impressed by the power the Aedui derived from their friendship with Rome. At the same time, the Remi, thought to be clients of Rome, received clients of their own who wished to ally themselves to the Roman cause but were not prepared to do so as clients of the Aedui. This broad pattern of changing allegiances seems to have been the norm in Gaul and was probably widespread in the Celtic world.

Clientage, at the tribal or personal level, implied obligations on both sides. As Caesar succinctly put it: 'The leaders do not allow their clients to be oppressed or defrauded, otherwise they lose their influence with their clients.' The clear implication here is that clientage was an agreement entered into willingly by both parties. Both were probably bound by strict rules as well as by the anticipation of mutual benefit.

The taking of hostages, referred to above, was equally widespread. It should not, however, take with it the connotations of the modern world. Among the Celts, hostages were usually young men of noble families from one tribe who lived and served with another as a guarantee of agreed behaviour: it was, in fact, a bonding mechanism. Caesar made ample use of the system during his conquests in Gaul, accepting or requesting hostages whenever agreements were reached. The case of the Treveri is instructive. In 54 BC, suspicious of the motives of one of the Treverian leaders, Indutiomarus, Caesar ordered the chief to attend his camp and to bring 200 hostages with him. 'The hostages were delivered, and included his son and all his relatives who had been specified by name. I reassured Indutiomarus about their safety and encouraged him to stay loyal.' At the same time 4,000 Gaulish cavalry arrived from all parts of Gaul, each group with its own leaders in charge. Those whose allegiance to Rome was in any way in doubt Caesar decided to take with him, as hostages, on his British campaign. Dumnorix, a chieftain of the Aedui, refused to join and fled with his cavalry, but was pursued, captured, and executed, even though he was brother of the Aeduan leader Diviciacus, a staunch Roman ally.

Although it can fairly be argued that Caesar's use of hostages may have been extreme because of the unusual nature of events, he was simply adapting a practice common among the Gaulish tribes to his own benefit.

Two other aspects of the bonding system—fosterage and marriage—deserve to be mentioned. The placing of children with foster parents is a theme constantly referred to in the Irish vernacular literature, where the close bonds between foster brothers are used to heighten literary effect. In all probability fosterage was adopted by Celtic communities quite widely, though there is very little positive evidence for it outside the Insular literature. There is, however, one somewhat obscure reference by Caesar. In writing of the Gauls he says that they differ from other peoples in 'that they do not allow their sons to approach them in public unless they have grown up to the age of military service, and they think it a disgrace for a boy under this age to sit in public within sight of his father' (*De Bello Gallico* 6. 18). Poseidonius, however (through Diodorus Siculus), mentions that at meals they are served by their youngest grown-up children, both boys and girls. The apparent contradiction can be resolved if the meal is considered to be a private occasion, when such intimacy is permissible. Whether or not this passage of Caesar's is an ill-understood observation of the taboos associated with active fosterage is unclear, but it could equally be that fosterage had, by this stage, died out in Gaul and all that remained were pale echoes reflected in symbolic behaviour patterns.

Women clearly occupied a more significant position in Celtic society than they did in the Graeco-Roman world and for this reason the classical sources give some prominence to observations about them, though in no systematic way. The Poseidonian tradition notes the beauty of Gallic women, describing them to be as tall and as strong as their husbands though the fourth-century Roman writer Ammianus Marcellinus, in a memorable piece of descriptive writing of the Celtic woman raised to anger, implies that as a fighter she is more than equal to the male. A tendency to promiscuity is noted. 'They generally yield up their virginity to others and this they regard not as a disgrace, but rather think themselves slighted when someone refuses to accept their freely offered favours' (Diodorus Siculus, *Hist.* 5. 32). To this, Caesar, writing of the Britons, adds that wives are shared between groups of ten or twelve men, especially between brothers, fathers, and sons. Once more the literary references are likely to be ill-observed and misleading, content simply to convey an impression of 'the barbarian'. Behind this probably lies a complex structure of male–female relationships beyond the comprehension of monogamous Mediterraneans. Something of the intricacies of these bonds are preserved in the Irish vernacular literature. In the Tàin Queen Medb is prepared to offer intercourse in the interests of friendship or gain without any sense of shame, while in the Old Irish Laws three grades of wife are recognized.

In Gaul, females had legal rights in marriage. A joint account was kept of the marriage wealth, composed of the bride's dowry, an equal sum contributed by the husband, and any interest accruing. Whoever survived the marriage inherited the total. The equity of the arrangement must, however, have been somewhat diminished by the fact that the husband had the power of life or death over his wife and children and if husbands died in suspicious circumstances wives could be interrogated under torture. We owe this insight to Caesar without being able to test the veracity of his account or the extent of the practice.

Marriage provided an important means of social and cross-tribal bonding.

The Helvetian Orgetorix, for example, in attempting to consolidate his power base, gave his own daughter in marriage to the Aeduan leader Dumnorix, while Dumnorix married his half-sister and other female relatives to prominent men in other tribes. A little earlier, the sister of the king of Noricum had been married to the German leader Ariovistus to cement a political alliance in the face of the Dacian advance. This use of the female relative, in the manner of a hostage bonded by marriage, was no doubt as widespread among the Celts as it was later to become among the royal households of Europe.

Women do not appear in positions of overt political power in Gaul at the time of Caesar's campaigns, unless he chooses not to record the fact, but in Britain Cartimandua of the Brigantes and Boudica of the Iceni were potent leaders, and the large bulk of Boudica, her harsh voice, and the mass of red hair falling to her knees, resplendent in gold torc and bright cloak, remains a lasting image of Celtic female power. Whether we are looking at the aberrant behaviour of a peripheral backwater in a time of unnatural stress or the survival of a phenomenon once more widespread throughout the Celtic world, it is difficult to say. The dominance of females in the Insular literature might, however, be thought to support the latter.

It must readily be admitted that any consideration of Celtic social systems is likely to be biased, not only by the prejudices and preconceptions of the Graeco-Roman sources but by the narrow time span and geographical area over which they range. None the less it is possible to construct an outline of the way in which society articulated itself. We must, however, constantly remind ourselves that no general scheme can ever hope to apply to all Celtic societies at all times.

6
The Arts of the Migration Period

Two things in particular stand out from viewing the entirety of the archaeological record from the La Tène period in Europe, the broad cultural similarity that can be seen over vast tracts of country and the dazzling inventiveness of what can broadly be called La Tène (or Celtic) art. We must be careful here to distinguish the technology of construction and manipulation of materials from the love of pure decoration. The two are strictly separate but they may come together to enhance each other and create a greater whole. Take, for example, the simple functional fire-dog—a piece of wrought-iron furniture for the hearth. It was essentially a framework for controlling roasting spits, but its projecting ends were frequently decorated with enormous skill to create the spirited essence of horned bulls' heads. In another medium, the large pottery jar from Saint-Pol-de-Léon in Finistère is an elegant and functional vessel, but it has been transformed into an object of beauty by a series of flowing scrolls and arabesques lightly incised on the body before firing.

The fire-dog and the pot are both visually highly satisfying to the modern eye—there is something about Celtic art with which we can easily empathize—but this should not persuade us into the facile belief that simply by describing and classifying we can understand. The quintessential bovine head on the fire-dog is a symbol, but of what? The sanctity of the hearth? The spirit of the beasts being roasted? The power of fire and of the smith's magic? We can never know. So it is with the decorated pot. To the archaeologist it is an item first to admire and enjoy and then to analyse stylistically, but the response of the original owner would have been totally different. One has only to consider decorated pots from Africa, whose meanings have been transmitted to us in language by their makers or users, to understand that form and decoration can have an immense subtlety of significance in their contemporary society, symbolizing func-

80 & 81 Iron furniture from a rich grave at Welwyn, Hertfordshire, England, second half of the first century BC. The lower picture shows the detail of a fire-dog, a pair of which would have stood on either side of the hearth. British Museum, London.

111

82 *Above, left:* Pottery vessel found in the barrow of Kernevez near Saint-Pol-de-Léon, Finistère, France. The style of decoration is closely similar to that adopted by metalworkers in the fourth century BC. Musée des Jacobins, Morlaix.

83 *Above, right:* Stone statue of a deity wearing a neck torc from Euffigneix, Haute-Marne, France. The boar figure carved in relief on the body is probably a symbol of the deity's strength. First century BC? Musée des Antiquités Nationales, Saint-Germain-en-Laye, Paris.

tion, status of owner, gender, sexual relationship, and so on. It is totally beyond the abilities of the art historian or archaeologist to say what the owner of the Saint-Pol-de-Léon pot was attempting to communicate. All that we can be tolerably sure about is that communication was intended.

If, then, we reject 'art for art's sake' as a starting-point (and with it the even less acceptable 'art for art historians' sake'), it is pertinent to ask how readily understood was the symbolism at the time? Was it known to all or only to a few, like the skilled men whose magic went into its creation?

The remarkable iron helmet of the early third century BC found in the chieftain's tomb at Ciumeşti (Fig. 72) provides an interesting example. On its crest stands a bird of prey, with articulating wings, staring fixidly with its violent red eyes at anyone who approached the wearer. It is a startling reminder of the story of the single combat between Valerius and the Celt (see p. 102). The symbolism of the bird on the helmet of the Ciumeşti chieftain would have been widely understood. So, too, would the symbol of the boar, found on helmet crests (Fig. 73), on the Witham shield (Pl. X), on a sword blade from Switzerland, on the statue of the god from Euffigneix, and in a variety of other contexts. The primeval strength and ferocity of the beast would have been considered to give strength and protection to the wearer, and it is likely that the boar, like the crow, would have been understood to be a war god in animal form. The shape-shifting of gods and the semi-divine to appear as animals is a recurring theme in the Irish and Welsh vernacular literature.

Herein might lie a clue to another aspect of Celtic art—the appearance of human and other faces either directly or obliquely and half hidden in Celtic designs on, for example, the Battersea and Witham shields (Pls. V and X), but also on a host of other items when carefully observed. The art historian Paul Jacobsthal once referred to this as the 'Cheshire Cat Style'—sometimes the cat appears in the tree, sometimes just the grin of the cat. He went on to describe it as the mechanism of dreams. Perhaps here, too, we are seeing the shifting shapes of Celtic mythology where visions appear and disappear and nothing is quite as it seems.

84 Human faces hidden in the decoration of two terret rings from northern France, now in the Musée Nationale des Antiquités, Saint-Germain-en-Laye, Paris. The half-visible face has been referred to as 'the Cheshire Cat Style'. After drawings by Paul Jacobsthal.

The skilled men, who were able to design and execute these timeless works of art, were clearly far more than just craftsmen. They carried with them a deep knowledge of mythology. The symbols which they used and the combinations in which they used them were a form of communication. They were the repository and the perpetrators of ancient skills and beliefs and as such they themselves would surely have been regarded as being above normal men.

Materials and Methods

The skills of the metalworker in bronze and gold were already long established by the beginning of the Iron Age. They involved casting, sheet working, and other forms of hammer working. Casting was normally by the *cire perdue* (lost-wax) method, best exemplified by the collection of metalworking debris found in an early first-century BC context at the settlement at Gussage All Saints in southern England, where sets of horse harness and vehicle fittings were being manufactured. The first stage involved the modelling of the desired item in beeswax using small bone spatulae. When complete, the wax form was invested with a refractory clay with at least two vents, one surrounded by a funnel or 'gate'. Next the whole would have been warmed, to melt the wax so that it could be poured out for reuse, before the clay mould was baked. Once the mould was hardened, molten bronze could be poured through the gate to fill the interior void. When it had cooled, the mould would be broken open and the cast item removed for fine trimming, filing, and polishing. What is perhaps most noteworthy is the comparative simplicity of the process, given the skill of the craftsman. Wax was reusable, and bronze could be melted down from scrap in crucibles. The only materials consumed were charcoal for the fire and clay for the moulds. In this way, using closed moulds, or, for more simple items, open moulds, a wide range of artefacts could be produced.

Sheet bronze working was in some ways a more skilled process. To begin with the sheet of appropriate size and thickness had to be beaten out by hand from a metal billet, constantly annealing the metal to prevent it from becoming brittle. In the process the sheet might be moulded into vessel shape or kept flat. The most common form of decoration was by inscribing, chasing, or repoussé working. In the last two cases the sheet being worked would have had to be attached to a suitably pliable backing material. A necessary preliminary to decoration of whatever kind would have been the laying-out of the design with lightly scribed lines, often using compasses, sometimes involving highly elaborate constructions, as the intricate pattern on the open-work discs from the Marne vividly demonstrates. Bone trial pieces found at Lough Crew, Co. Meath, in Ireland show how craftsmen tried out designs in rough first.

Other items such as brooches could be made by hammering out a billet, constantly annealing to retain malleability, drawing out, winding, flattening, and folding as required.

Finished items could be further enhanced by attaching or insetting other materials of which coral and red glass were favoured throughout most of the period. These substances were either attached with small pins or fixed, cloisonné-style, in pre-made cells. In the later stages the art of enamelling was developed, allowing elaborate multicoloured finishes to be achieved which were particularly favoured for horse harness mounts. The skills of the bronze workers were also those used by goldsmiths and silversmiths.

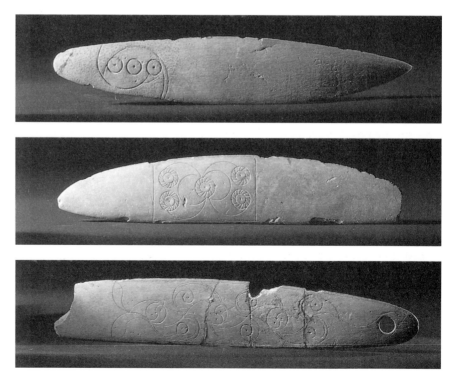

85 Bone trial pieces, possibly used by a craftsman to work out designs to be used on a metal object. Found in cairn H at Lough Crew, Co. Meath, Ireland. National Museum of Ireland, Dublin.

Iron became of increasing importance after its first widespread introduction into barbarian Europe in the eighth century. Though occurring naturally over far more extensive areas and in far greater quantity than copper and tin, its extraction required a more complex technology and a higher temperature for the chemical change to take place. Once this had been achieved, the spongy iron bloom had constantly to be reheated and beaten to remove slag. Finally, when the iron was pure enough, a number of blooms would be beaten together to form an ingot of sufficient size to allow tools and weapons to be forged.

86 A selection of iron-smith's tools from Nikolausberg, Austria, dating from the fourth or third century BC. Iron forging skills developed during the La Tène period have been little improved upon since. Museum Carolino Augusteum, Salzburg.

Large numbers of ingots are known, most of them dating to the later stages of the La Tène period (Map 23). A common form in central and western Europe is the double pyramidal type, thick in the centre with the ends drawn out. In Britain the most common form is the sword-shaped bar, with the flanges of one end beaten round to form a hollow tube. Both forms and others were developed to demonstrate the quality of the iron, because if the metal had been too impure it would have been impossible to beat out ends or form the tube without cracks appearing.

It is clear that ironsmiths had a detailed understanding of the qualities of their material and the appropriateness of different qualities to different functions. This is particularly apparent in the swords of the La Tène period. Metallurgical analysis has shown that for cutting blades different qualities of iron were used, layering it to provide a high-quality cutting edge of steel which was usually well tempered. The boars' stamps on the sword from Port in Switzerland and the name Korisios with its attached stamp on a sword from the same site are possible examples of craftsmen's personal marks being a guarantee of quality. There is no better example of the ironsmith's technical skills than the tunics of ring mail which occasionally come to light in graves, but for the smith as an artist the fire-dogs are pre-eminent.

87 Detail of a stamp on an iron sword blade found at Port, Bern, Switzerland. Below the stamp is the inscribed name KORISIOS. Whether the marks indicate the maker, owner, or have some other meaning is unclear. First century BC. Bernisches Historisches Museum, Berne.

In addition to the metalworker's products, one must not overlook those of the other men of skill: the glass workers, the wood carvers, the sculptors, the potters, and the woad painters (or tattooists). All created original works which in their different way transmitted the rich images of Celtic artistic expression and symbolism.

The Origins of Aristocratic Art

The earliest examples of Celtic art appear in the fifth century, accompanying the élite burials of the Moselle and Marne. Inevitably, in the first faltering

IX *Facing*: One of a pair of wine flagons from a burial(?) at Basse-Yutz, Moselle, France. They are examples of early native craftsmanship of the early fourth century BC, reflecting the initial stages in using Etruscan forms and decorative motifs, together with ideas from the east and from the traditional repertoire, to create something distinctively 'native'. The vessels are inlaid with red enamel and coral. British Museum, London.

stages, it was the imported Mediterranean wine-drinking equipment which provided the model and the stylistic stimulus. The bronze beaked flagons from the burials of Kleinaspergle, Dürrnberg, and Basse-Yutz (Pl. IX), all clearly based on Etruscan ideas, differ in form and in the treatment of the decorative detail to such a degree that they must all have been manufactured by local craftsmen working for aristocratic patrons. Yet all three are sufficiently different in their interpretations to show that a variety of regional influences were at work.

The grave from Kleinaspergle (found in a side chamber, the main grave having been robbed) provides an interesting range of items reflecting the development of Early Style art. The grave goods included an Italic cordoned bucket, an Etruscan stamnos, a locally made beaked flagon, two gold drinking horn terminals, a gold-repaired Attic cup, and a fitting probably for a belt. The drinking horn terminals were ornamented with rams' heads in a style that is reminiscent of 'eastern' animal art, while the flagon, even with its highly original interpretation of the human head at the base of the handle, is clearly of Etruscan inspiration. The gold patching on the Attic cup and the belt plaque incorporate plant motifs—palmettes, lotus-buds, and lotus-blossom, which, though original in their transformation, are a grammar learnt from the Greek world. In this one burial then, dating to the middle of the fifth century, we can see the first stages in the use of disparate inspirations from the classical Mediterranean world and the east being brought together and moulded into something new.

The Basse-Yutz flagons (Pl. IX) (a pair possibly from a single grave) were accompanied by two Etruscan stamnoi and probably date to the second half of the fifth century. The general concept of the flagons is evidently Etruscan, but the sharp high shoulder and concave sides are very unclassical. From its Hallstatt ancestry comes a band of coral interlace set around the base and a small duck riding on the spout. Less certainty attaches to the inspiration for the animals shown on the rim and handles of the flagon, but the dashed pellets and spiral joints may point to an eastern ancestry.

The Dürrnberg flagon shares the high-shouldered shape of the Basse-Yutz vessels but is otherwise altogether different. The handle attachment embodies a stylized head, with bulbous nose, lentoid eyes, and swept-back hair of a kind that was to recur many times in Celtic art, framed by vegetal renderings which have evolved from the classical palmette. On the handle a beast appears to hold a severed head in his mouth, while further around the rim a curious quadruped lurks. Once again we might see in the beasts some inspiration from the east.

Taken together, these fifth-century flagons provide a glimpse of an art style in the making—Etruscan vessel forms are mutating and already Greek palmettes and lotuses are disintegrating into more loosely structured plant forms. Echoes from the Hallstatt past are still dimly to be discerned; a new distinctive animal menage is beginning to intrude and the iconography of the 'Celtic head' is now becoming defined.

The Marne region at this time, while sharing in the general development,

develops characteristics of its own, most notably an emphasis on plant motifs and a preference for open-work ornaments. This is particularly clear on the open-work mounts for the chariot pole or yoke from the burial at La Bouvandeau. Geometric compass-work designs also develop, while a different tradition of highly accomplished engraving incorporating classical palmettes can be recognized on a few élite items such as the pointed helmet from Berru (Pl. XIV) in the Marne and the Etruscan beaked flagon, enhanced by a Celtic engraver, now in the museum at Besançon.

In the Moselle region the high point of artistic achievement in the fifth century was attained by the goldsmiths, whose masterpieces included the open-work gold covering of a hemispherical wooden bowl, found in barrow I at Schwarzenbach in Saarland (Pl. XIIIa), with its two registers and a basal disc decorated with transformed palmettes, lotus motifs, and triskels. A similar piece, possibly once ornamenting a drinking horn, from Eigenbilzen in the Belgian Limburg, is closely related in style and craftsmanship and could be taken for the work of a Moselle 'master'. Schwarzenbach has also produced four gold plaques displaying clean-shaven human faces framed by a 'comma-shaped' headdress similar to the depiction of the head on the handle of the Kleinaspergle flagon. Closely related items of gold-sheet decoration have been found further east at Dürrnberg and at the warrior grave of Chlum in Bohemia.

The pre-eminence of the Middle Rhenish goldsmiths is further demonstrated by a brilliant array of neck and arm rings which combine the plant motifs of the sheet-gold workers with superbly modelled fabulous and semi-fabulous beasts and human heads. One of the most spectacular of their products is the arm ring from Rodenbach found with an Etruscan flagon and basin and an Attic kantharos. The arm ring has a central moustached face, closely similar to that on the handle attachment of the Basse-Yutz flagon, flanked on either side by pairs of recumbent carpids looking over their backs to another human head behind them. The style of the beasts, with their legs folded up beneath them and their turned-back heads, vividly recalls Scythian gold-work of the sixth and fifth centuries, some items of which found their way as far west as Hungary.

The Rodenbach arm ring is not alone. Related pieces have been found in female graves at Besseringen and Reinheim and in a hoard of seven gold rings from Erstfeld in Switzerland, all seven evidently the product of a single work-

X *Facing:* Bronze shield found in the River Witham near Washingborough, Lincolnshire, England. The end roundel illustrated in detail shows the careful interplay of repoussé and inscribed decoration. The roundel is 'carried' on the head of a fabulous beast. Third or second century BC. British Museum.

88 Open-work bronze disc from the vehicle burial at Somme-Bionne, Marne, France. Late fifth century BC. The disc, which was part of a set of harness fittings, demonstrates the skills of the bronze-worker in setting out complex geometric designs. British Museum, London.

89 A diagrammatic representation of the decoration on a flagon from an unknown location but probably north-eastern France. The flagon is Etruscan in form but the decoration is Celtic. Early fourth century BC. Musée des Beaux-Arts, Besançon, France.

90 Gold arm ring from the princely grave of Rodenbach, Kr. Kaiserslautern, Germany. The decoration is characteristic of Early Style and incorporates squatting backward-looking cervids similar in form to Scythian animal art. The disembodied heads are common in Celtic art of this period. Historisches Museum der Pfalz, Speyer.

shop. The iconography of the Erstfeld rings is complex in the extreme, with a variety of humanoid, animal, or bird figures bound interminably in apparent conflict. That it had a meaning we cannot doubt, but how to interpret the contorted scenes is beyond recovery.

Together the items of élite art, created by master craftsmen in the Marne–Moselle region in the fifth century, represent the first innovative steps in the development of a Celtic art style. Though they display an evident variety, there is a sufficient degree of cohesion for art historians to use such portmanteau phrases as Early Style or Early Strict Style to contain the full repertoire. The influence of the Graeco-Etruscan world is still easily discernible. The much debated 'animal art' or 'eastern influence' is less certain. It could have been inspired by a few imported items, perhaps of carved wood, for which the Scythian artists were famous, but, as some commentators have emphasized, fabulous animals were very much a part of the Etruscan repertoire and there is little

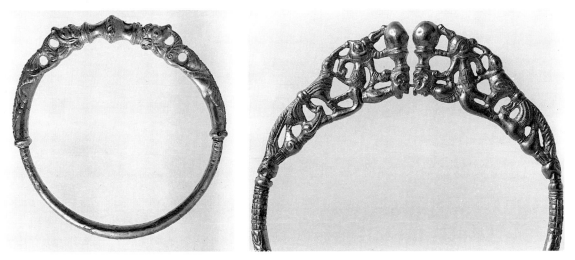

need at this early stage to suppose there to have been a strong eastern component.

Celtic Art in the Fourth Century: Influences from the Po Valley

The development of Celtic art styles in the fourth century BC have been variously characterized. Earlier attempts used the rich 'princess's' grave from Waldalgesheim, near Bonn, as a type assemblage against which to compare fourth-century products, and some observers even went so far as to propose a 'Waldalgesheim master'. Others have been content with a less constricting terminology, referring to the development as an Early Free Style. However, the more descriptive phrase, Vegetal Style, best captures the principal and distinctive characteristics of the products of the period, since the overriding motif is the running tendril or linked band of lyre-palmettes. Animals and human heads recede into the background. They do not entirely disappear but rather lurk in the vegetation, from which, disguised, they occasionally peer out.

The centre of innovation is no longer the Rhine–Moselle region but the Marne, Switzerland, Hungary, and the Po Valley, and it is the relationship of the last with the broad northern zone that raises interesting questions. It is now widely believed that the Celtic groups in the Cisalpine region, notably the Boii and the Senones, were responsible for integrating Graeco-Italic ideas with Celtic and transmitting the result back to the innovating centres north of the Alps. This interpretation would imply that close social links were maintained between the Celts who had emigrated to the south and those who remained in their northern homelands.

One artefact type which well exemplifies this is the jockey-cap helmet with a neck-brim, hinged side pieces, and central plume attachment. Helmets of this kind were usually made of iron, with an internal fabric lining and an exterior decoration of bronze or gold panels ornamented in repoussé. Three have come

91 Gold neck rings from a hoard found at Erstfeld, Canton Uri, Switzerland, dating to the late fifth or early fourth century BC. The complex interweaving of the figures and motifs is a theme running throughout Celtic art. Schweizerisches Landesmuseum, Zurich.

92 Designs from various
La Tène artefacts.

Nos. 1–7, Early Style, all
La Tène I.
1 Bronze disc, Ecury-sur-
Coole, Marne; 2 Bronze
bowl, Saulces-Champen-
oises, Ardennes; 3 Helmet,
Amfreville-sous-les-Monts,
Eure; 4 Pot, Prunay, Marne;
5 Bronze flagon in Besançon
Museum; 6 Bronze strainer
in Morel Collection;
7 Bronze brooch from
Prosues, Marne.

Nos. 8–11, Vegetal Style.
8 Flagon, Waldalgesheim,
Mainz-Bingen; 9 Torc,
Jonchery-sur-Suippes,
Marne; 10 Pot, Saulces-
Champenoises, Ardennes;
11 Bucket, Waldalgesheim,
Mainz-Bingen.

from northern Italy, from Monte Bibele, Gottolengo, and an imprecisely located example from Umbria, and another was found in an elaborate grave at Canosa di Puglia in Apulia (Pl. IV*a*). All four, which were evidently made in northern Italy, display the Vegetal Style of decoration, which is at its most luxuriant on the Canosa example. The lower register shows, alternately, reversed palmettes linked in a continuous band with fleshy S-shaped leaves, while in the upper register half palmettes alternate with lyre palmettes. The style is closely similar to that displayed on a disc from Auvers in the Marne, and on the flagon at Besançon (Fig. 89), as well as the painted pot from Prunay (Marne), implying a close relationship between the craftsmen of the Po Valley and Marne in the fourth century.

Two jockey-cap helmets of very similar kind have been found in France, one

120

from Agris (Pl. XIIIb) near Angoulême and another from the Seine at Amfreville-sous-les-Monts, the latter being made of bronze, while the former, of iron covered with gold, could, technically, be a north Italian product.

Another item which serves to link the Celtic communities north and south of the Alps is the buffer-headed gold torc. An example found in the cemetery of Filottrano in the Italian territory of the Senones, decorated with a central palmette combined with twinned foliage, is of a type found widely in temperate Europe, with examples coming from Bohemia, Austria, the Rhineland (Waldalgesheim), and probably the Marne region. Within this closely related series the Filottrano torc is seen to be an early example, showing the initial stages in combining Greek and Celtic motifs. The suggestion that the style developed and spread north from Italy is further supported by scabbard decoration found at Filottrano and Moscano di Fabri-

93 Bronze discs covered in sheet gold decorated in repoussé and inlaid with coral. From Auvers-sur-Oise, Val d'Oise, France. Early fourth century BC. The decoration is characteristic of the Vegetal Style of northern France. Cabinet des Médailles, Bibliothèque Nationale, Paris.

ano, which is considered to be the origin of a type displayed on several scabbards in northern France and on one from Bohemia. Taken together, the evidence is strongly suggestive that artistic developments among the Italian Celts were readily transmitted northwards to enhance the work of the craftsmen who served the Transalpine Celtic élite and in whose schools many regional variations began to develop. The vast spread of territory over which the Vegetal Style is found is a reflection of a social mobility occasioned by the warrior movements of the time.

Developments in the Third and Second Centuries

For much of the third and early second centuries BC the society of Celtic Europe was characterized by small communities whose menfolk equipped themselves as warriors and may well have spent time away from the home base engaged in raiding expeditions. There was, therefore, a high degree of mobility in both the geographical and the social sense: some archaeologists have even gone so far as to characterize this as a period of democratization. In such a context it was the swords of the warriors and the ornaments of their women that were to carry forward the development of the metalworker's art.

The large numbers of decorated sword scabbards that survive allow distinct schools or styles to be proposed, though inevitably in such cases art-historical classifications are at best broad oversimplifications.

One of the most distinctive series of swords is found concentrated around

Lake Balaton in Transdanubia and is accordingly referred to as the Hungarian Sword Style. Of the various motifs used, 'dragon-pairs' are the most distinctive. The two facing S-shaped dragons are really a variant of the simple lyre motif. Dragon-pair swords, though concentrating in Hungary, are very widely distributed, reaching as far afield as England, Spain, Romania, and Italy. By the second century the rigid bisymmetric motifs merge, giving way to more asymmetric designs, which flow across and down the scabbard.

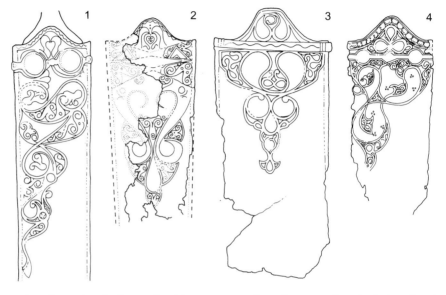

94 Examples of the Hungarian Sword Style of scabbard decoration. Swords (left to right) from: Batina, Croatia; Sremska(?), Serbia; and Bölcske-Madocsahegy, Hungary (both right-hand examples). Various scales. (After R. and V. Megaw.)

Another school of swordsmiths was at work at the same time in Switzerland (Fig. 26). One of the favoured motifs here is that of birds' heads which grow out of triskel or lyre motifs. The Swiss compositions are more symmetrical and restrained than the Hungarian.

The Hungarian and Swiss Sword Styles are little more than the archaeologically recognizable manifestations of a specific form of craft production which spread across Europe and, over two centuries or so, will have been practised and developed by a multitude of craftsmen, their individual creations being carried far and wide by their warrior patrons to be admired and sometimes emulated in distant lands.

The sword styles and related pieces are sometimes referred to as the Free Graphic Style, to distinguish it from its more three-dimensional manifestation, the Free Plastic Style. Plastic decoration is the method appropriate to the decoration of neck, arm, and ankle rings and for decorative fittings attached to vehicles or bronze vessels.

Knobbed anklets, hinged for ease of fitting, are especially distinctive, the knobs providing hemispherical surfaces which are ornamented in three dimensions often with triskels terminating in buttons or studs. The same plastic concepts were put to good use to create the human, animal, and grotesque heads which brighten up the yokes and linch pins of chariots or stare from the rims or handle attachments of vessels like the cauldron found in the Danish bog at Brä with its fearsome guardian bird.

Free Plastic art, particularly that which incorporates animal forms, is very different from that of the decorated sword scabbards. It uses the methods (of casting) and also the ethos of the earlier styles of the fifth and fourth centuries; even so it has moved a long way from its origins. These cast pieces and the graphic decoration on sword scabbards and spears are far more than just ornament to amuse. There can be little doubt that they were all deeply symbolic, denoting status, lineage, and power, warning off adversaries and providing protection. The sword, the chariot, the cauldron, and the human body were redolent with visual messages which the Celts themselves would have well understood.

The Impact of Scythians and Thracians?

During the sixth and fifth centuries Transdanubia developed a strong eastern, horse-focused culture which may have been, in part at least, the result of new peoples moving in from the region of the Pontic Steppe. To free it from preconceptions which might be implied by ethnic names such as Scythians or Sigynnae, it is usually referred to as the Vekerzug culture, after a type site producing distinctive horse burials. The maintenance of strong cultural links with the Pontic Steppe region produced, on the eastern borders of the Early La Tène cultural province, a rich source of concepts and iconography, and from the fourth century, when Celtic groups extended eastwards, there was much mingling of populations. In such a situation one might expect eastern Celtic culture to have absorbed some elements from the indigenous culture.

If one excludes the dragon-pairs on the swords, assuming them to have developed from the Etruscan lyre motif, then there is remarkably little metalwork that can be regarded as showing eastern characteristics, with the exception of a bronze drinking horn terminal from Jászberény-Cseröhalom which ends in an open-mouthed dragon wearing a torc. Hungarian pottery, on the other hand, embodies many reflections of its complex cultural ancestry. Most dramatic is a pottery vessel from Lábatlan, inscribed on the neck with a scene in which a cervid is being attacked and brought to the ground by two fierce quadrupeds, presumably wolves. The composition is redolent of the struggling animal theme so prevalent in steppe art.

Much of the Lower Danube Valley down to the Black Sea and the territories

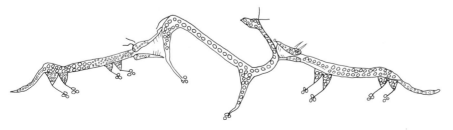

95 Scene of struggling animals in a Scythian Style inscribed on a pottery vessel from Lábatlan, Hungary. Magyar Nemzeti Múzeum, Budapest.

123

on either side was occupied by a complex group of tribes who may collectively be called Thracians. From the fifth century onwards the Thracian tribes developed a characteristic art style of their own based on an amalgam of Greek, Scythian, and eastern, ultimately Persian, ideas (Fig. 141). For the most part it was an aristocratic art designed to provide prestige vessels for the feast and armour for parade. The juxtaposition of Celtic and Thracian tribes in the Middle Danube created conditions of contact between the two cultures, varying from trade and the exchange of gifts to the acquisition of booty by raiding.

Several items, found in western La Tène contexts, may be thought to show Thracian influence. The ram-headed drinking horns from Schwarzenbach have already been mentioned. Drinking horns and ram-headed terminals were both prevalent in Thracian culture, and another drinking horn from Weiskirchen, on the Saar, decorated in gold stamped with sphinxes, may conceivably have been made in a Black Sea workshop. Their appearance in the Rhine–Moselle area could have been the result of a diplomatic gift between the nobility of the two regions. The Rodenbach arm ring, with its pairs of rams looking over their shoulders, though presumably of local manufacture, would have been familiar to a Thracian or Scythian.

From the early third century, when the Scordisci became firmly established in the Middle Danube as direct neighbours of the Thracian Triballoi, regular diplomatic relations must have become the norm. Surprisingly little has yet been found to give substance to the exchange, but two items must be considered. The first is a silver-plated iron torc of massive proportions found at

96 Torc of iron covered in silver from Trichtingen, Baden-Württemberg, Germany. The style of the piece with the confronting bovine heads and the use of silver suggests an origin in the Middle Danube region. Second century BC. Württembergisches Landes-museum, Stuttgart.

Trichtingen in south-western Germany. The high technical quality of the silver plating might suggest an eastern craftsman, while the iconography, incorporating two facing bulls' heads as terminals, is evidently Thracian. There can be little doubt that the torc was made somewhere along the Lower Danube. By what process it reached southern Germany it is impossible to say but its massive size and the fact that both beasts wear torcs, a sign of sovereignty, suggest that it could have been a diplomatic gift symbolizing a treaty of friendship between two equal élites.

The second item is the justly famous Gunderstrup cauldron recovered from a bog in Jutland (Pl. XI). While the cauldron form and certain pictorial details, in particular the depiction of warrior infantry and cavalry, are decidedly Celtic, much of the iconography and the use of silver and of gilding are Thracian. The most reasonable explanation for this remarkable piece is that it was made by Thracian craftsmen thoroughly conversant with the Celtic world. Whilst it could have been a gift, of great value, from the king of the Triballoi to his equal among the Scordisci, a more attractive hypothesis is that it was made and used as a symbol of lasting friendship, and perhaps even joint rule, between the two ethnically different polities.

The fact that the cauldron was eventually deposited in a Danish bog and the Trichtingen torc ended up in Germany is an interesting comment on the mobility of valuable items in the Celtic world. To this same list we may add an animal-ornamented silver gilt disc from Helden in Holland which is stylistically and technically of Thracian manufacture, and the remarkable collection of metalwork including phalarae and greaves recovered (but subsequently lost again) in the eighteenth century, on the tiny island of Sark near the Channel Island of Guernsey. Judging from contemporary illustrations, the collection is likely to have come ultimately from the Lower Danube region. The Helden and Sark finds were probably buried in the late first century BC or early first century AD, but this says little of their date of manufacture or the route through which they passed to their final place of deposition.

What survives in the archaeological record presently available is only a minute tithe of the works of high artistic merit which must have been moving about Europe displayed for all to admire. The visual stimulation for the inventive craftsman must have been immense.

The Art of the Sculptor

The art of the sculptor is art in the service of the gods. Here we will consider the range and style of the work rather than its religious context, which is the theme for a later chapter. Although a number of notable stone sculptures have been recovered, mainly from western Europe, in reviewing them we should bear in mind that they probably represent only a pale reflection of the sculptor's art, much of which is likely to have been in wood and therefore tends not to survive.

The earliest piece so far to come to light is a unique, roughly life-size carving in the round of a warrior, found lying at the edge of a barrow at Hirschlanden (Fig. 52) near Hohenasperg. If, as seems highly likely, the statue once topped the barrow and was contemporary with it, then it must date to the late sixth century. The figure is shown as naked except for a two-thonged belt holding a short dagger of Late Hallstatt type, a neck ring, and a conical hat very similar to that made in birch bark and worn by the Hochdorf chieftain in death. The figure is carved from local sandstone but in style is highly reminiscent of contemporary

97 Carved stone pillar from Pfalzfeld, St Goar, Germany. Each side bears a head with a leaf crown and triple-pointed beard. Fifth or fourth century BC. Rheinisches Landes-museum, Bonn.

carvings from the Abruzzi region and from Nesazio Pola in Istria, suggesting that the inspiration, and perhaps even the sculptor, came from the Etruscan south, whence, at this time, the élite of the Middle Rhine were receiving many cultural influences.

A group of sculptures from southern Germany dating to the fifth or fourth century is more obviously of native work, embodying as it does a religious iconography that is also reflected in broadly contemporary metalworkers' art. The most obviously 'La Tène' of the pieces is a four-sided pillar from Pfalzfeld. Each of the sides, framed by cabling, bears a stylized human head carved in high relief. The heads wear the so-called 'leaf crowns'—a common motif presumably of religious significance—and appear to be sprouting three-pointed beards. Between the heads and the frames the space is filled with running scrolls and lyre patterns composed of S-shaped motifs.

The leaf crowns are a feature shared with two other items from the region, a fragmentary stone head from Heidelberg and a stone pillar figure from Holzgerlingen. The Heidelberg head is a dramatic piece with piercing circular eyes and a furrowed brow which enhances the ferocity of his stare. The Holzgerlingen pillar statue, carved similarly on two opposite faces, is altogether simpler, with the facial features, and right arm folded across the stomach, heavily schematized. None the less, standing originally some 2.5 metres, it would have presented a terrifying vision. Another pillar sculpture, from Waldenbach, not far from Holzgerlingen, is rather different in style. Only the base now survives, but the complex curvilinear pattern with which it is decorated in low relief is characteristic of the fourth or third century. Little remains of the figure which comprised the upper part of the pillar except for a well-sculpted arm and hand. Together the southern German group of sculptures suggests a long-lived and varied tradition.

A second group of religious sculptures comes from Provence and helps to characterize the Celto-Ligurian culture of the region—a long-established folk culture overlain and modified by influences from the nearby Greek colonies

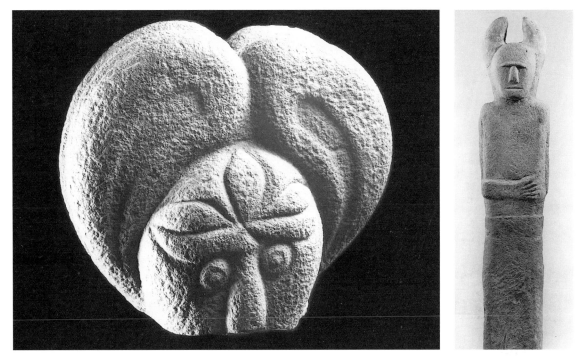

98 *Above*: Stone head of a deity from Heidelberg, Baden, Germany, wearing a leaf crown. Late fifth or early fourth century BC. Badisches Landesmuseum, Karlsruhe.

99 *Above, right*: Statue of a god from Holzgerlingen, Böblingen, Germany. The figure, Janus-like, faces two ways. The heads once shared a leaf crown which has since broken and been restored. Sixth or fifth century BC. Württembergisches Landesmuseum, Stuttgart.

100 *Below, right*: Carved pillar from Waldenbuch, Böblingen, Germany. The figure at the top is missing except for an arm. Fourth or third century BC. Württembergisches Landesmuseum, Stuttgart.

and also from the Celtic world. A recurring theme is the cult of the severed head. This is most dramatically represented by a pillar carved with a series of heads, presumably from a sanctuary, which was found reused as a door sill in the *oppidum* of Entremont, near Aix-en-Provence. A carving of four severed heads in a pile is a further image of the cult. Not far away, at Roquepertuse, an array of religious sculptures has been recovered, including columns with niches for severed human heads, and a lintel carved with a frieze of horse heads (Fig. 164) upon which probably once stood a dramatic stone carving of a bird of prey. Another notable find was a pair of stylized Janus-heads sharing a single leaf crown. Both Entremont and Roquepertuse also produced elegant renderings of life-sized human figures seated cross-legged. In the trabeated architecture of the Roquepertuse sanctuary and the seated figures (Fig. 163) we are

127

101 Black and red painted pottery of the Early La Tène period from graves in the Champagne.
1: 'Le Champ la Guerre', Prunay; 2: 'Quartier Saint-Basles', Prunay; 3: 'Culvidame', Bussy-le-Château; 4: 'Le Mont de la Forche', Lavannes.

clearly seeing the influence of the Greek world, but the severed heads and Janus-like deities provide a firm link with the Celtic symbolism.

An even more fearsome image was found at Noves in the Lower Rhône Valley. The 'Tarasque' of Noves, as it is called, is a squatting beast clasping severed, bearded heads in its forepaws whilst devouring a body of which only the arm protrudes from its jaws. A somewhat similar rendering, from Linsdorf in Alsace, is an indication that the imagery had a wide geographic spread.

In addition to these two highly distinctive regional groupings of sculpture, a number of individual items have been found widely scattered. A small stone figure from Euffigneix (Fig. 83) in the Marne evidently depicts a deity, wearing a torc, and is identified by a vigorous rendering of a boar against his body. Another god figure, again wearing a torc, but this time holding a lyre, was discovered at Paule in western Brittany. It is probably also in this same category of deities that we should place the famous head from the religious site of Mšecké Žehrovice (Pl. VIIIa) in Bohemia. He, too, wears a torc, but is considerably larger in scale than the two French figurines. These few surviving isolated examples are a reminder of both the diversity and the extent of Celtic sculpture. Similar icons and their wooden counterparts must have pervaded all parts of the Celtic sphere.

Ceramic Art

One of the most striking characteristics of La Tène culture is the frequent, and often highly elaborate, decoration of pottery using motifs common to those of the metalworker. An example of this is the popularity and widespread distribution of pottery with stamped decoration (Map 24) which was produced in several centres from the fifth to the third centuries, concentrating in a broad zone from the Moselle to Transdanubia but extending as scattered outliers even further. The high technical quality of this ware and standardized range of motifs and motif arrangements are strongly indicative of a shared set of cultural values and a degree of centralization in production. Outliers of the generalized style in western Brittany (Fig. 122) raise interesting questions about the nature of contact at this time.

By the fourth century the Breton potters had begun to develop a highly distinctive curvilinear style of decoration, at its most sophisticated on vessels from Saint-Pol-de-Léon (Fig. 82), Pendreff en Commana, Kélouer Plouhinec and Blauet (Fig. 123). The lyre patterns and running S-scrolls are highly accomplished reflections of the very best of the metalworker's repertoire developing in the Marne and Moselle regions. The striking similarity raises the question of the mechanism by which these visual concepts spread. The simplest explanation is that the Breton masters were using imported metal vessels as the source, and the discovery of inscribed bronze vessels of this quality from Cerrig-y-Drudion (Fig. 124) in Wales shows that such pieces had a mobility. Even so the transmission of metalworkers' designs to a subtly curving ceramic form required exceptional skill.

The same range of abilities was demonstrated by the potters working in the Marne region. Already in the fifth century pottery was being decorated, usually with geometric incisions, but more adventurous compositions were making an appearance, such as the facing S-shaped beasts, or dragon-pairs, on the beaker from La Cheppe. In the fourth century a far more elaborate style had developed in which the red-fired vessel was painted in black in such a way as to leave intricate curvilinear patterns appearing in the red body colour. The close similarity between the design on the pedestal vase from Prunay and that on the helmet from Canosa di Puglia leaves little doubt of their common artistic ancestry. A slightly later vessel from Bussy-le-Château, probably dating to the early third century, uses the same reversal technique, but the running scroll is more developed. Clearly, in the Marne region painted pottery served as a prestige item for several generations, during which the ceramic artists remained in the forefront of artistic development.

The inscribed curvilinear decoration of Brittany and the painted version of the Marne are two of the most impressive examples of potters' art in the Early and Middle La Tène period, but other regions could boast more modest output. In the south-west of Britain, for example, a number of different production centres created their own simplified versions of curvilinear decorated pottery, perhaps influenced by their neighbours across the Channel in Brittany, while in Northamptonshire a different curvilinear style of pottery decoration developed. In Hungary, on the other hand, potters favoured more plastic forms of decoration in the form of human or animal heads usually at the attachment of handles to the vessel. In this they will have had in mind the heads attached to metal vessels.

Many of the fine creations of ceramic art are likely to have been prestige goods produced by skilled craftsmen for an élite, perhaps specifically as grave goods, but their more lowly value, when compared with metalwork, and their general fragility will have mitigated against movement, by gift or exchange, far from their territory of origin. Below this level of production were far more humble pots, essentially the folk art of the ordinary people, produced to serve everyday needs, to symbolize the ethnic unity of the community, and to demarcate aspects of their social relationships.

102 *Right*: Pottery vessel from La Cheppe, Marne, France. Second half of fifth century BC. Each of the two zones of decoration shows pairs of confronting monsters. Similar dragon-pairs frequently ornament the hilt ends of sword sheaths. Musée des Antiquités Nationales, Saint-Germain-en-Laye, Paris.

103 *Above*: Painted pottery vessel from the cemetery of Fosse-Minore at Caurel, Marne, France. The bold curvilinear decoration is painted in red. Second half of fourth century BC. Musée des Antiquités Nationales, Saint-Germain-en-Laye, Paris.

An indication that decorative motifs of originality and vigour were a regular part of everyday existence is provided by the wooden vessels preserved at the lake village of Glastonbury in Somerset. At this level we might reasonably begin to wonder whether decoration might here be being used for no reason other than to give pleasure.

The Art of the Die Engraver

The debt of Celtic art to inspiration gained from the Mediterranean extends to the specialized sphere of die engraving as the essential creative preliminary to the striking of coins. Coin manufacture began in the Celtic zone at the beginning of the third century BC, the impetus coming, in part, from the flood of

130

Hellenistic coinage brought back from the Mediterranean by Celts who had served as mercenaries, and in part from the Greek colonies around the Golfe du Lion. The gold or silver coin was a convenient method of payment for service or reward for faithful clientage and as such it soon gained widespread popularity.

Silver was the favoured medium in the Middle and Lower Danube, the Balkans, northern Italy, and southern France, while gold was preferred in the north in a zone stretching from Bohemia to southern Britain. Different regions favoured different prototypes. The most popular in the Middle Danube was the tetradrachms of Philip II of Macedon (359–36), which had a head of Zeus on the obverse and rider on the reverse, but in the west the model was Philip's gold stater, with the head of Apollo on the obverse and a charioteer and team on the reverse. Between the two, in the Upper Danube and Bohemian region, the gold stater of Alexander the Great with helmeted Athene and a winged Victory provided the prototype. Why these different preferences developed is impossible to say—it need mean little more than the accident of what models were to hand when the decision was taken to begin a particular local series.

104 *Above*: Gold stater of DVMNOL TIGIR SENO of the British tribe, the Corieltauvi who occupied much of Lincolnshire. The original coin is 19 millimetres across. To make a die on this small scale indicates the great skill of the die-carver.

The coins minted in the Greek cities around the Golfe du Lion proved popular prototypes in the west. The didrachms of Rhoda were widely copied in south-western Gaul in the basin of the Garonne, while the communities of the Po Valley favoured the model provided by Massilliot drachms.

The processes involved in manufacturing coins were comparatively simple. To begin with the appropriate amount of metal had to be exactly weighed out and reduced to a blank by melting in a proformer. In the first-century rectangular sheets of baked clay with rows of deep indentations were used, so that fifty or more blanks could be produced at any one time. The blank (or flan) was then placed between two engraved dies, one firmly fixed to a base the other held in the hand, and the foot of the hand-held die was struck a heavy blow impressing both designs onto the flan.

105 *Below*: Silver minim of the Atrebates, a tribe which controlled much of central southern Britain (Hampshire, West Sussex, and Berkshire). The original coin is only 9 millimetres in diameter.

The huge array of Celtic coinage available for study leaves little doubt that from the third century BC there existed a distinct class of craftsmen highly skilled at the intricate art of die cutting. Not only were these craftsmen technically accomplished, with steady hand and fine eyesight, but they were creative artists in their own right. The vitality and sense of movement they were able to create, particularly when dealing with the horse and chariot, are remarkable. The freedom (and constraint) of the die provided the stimulus for a creativity which, in many instances, surpassed that achieved by craftsmen working on larger scales. The art of the coin engraver deserves far more attention than it has been afforded by numismatists intent on classification.

The Broader Context

Celtic art, because of its energy and novelty, has justly achieved fame, but to remove it, as has so often been done in the past, from its social context and to treat it in the manner of modern art-historical analysis, is entirely inappropriate. Celtic art was functional and served a variety of ever-changing needs. Its practitioners carried with them not only skill but a deep knowledge of society's beliefs and values expressed in symbols. That knowledge was potent and it must surely have been revered and feared. For this reason it is quite likely that the craftsman existed in a world outside the bounds of the closed community.

To attempt to understand the nature of a society through an observer-imposed interpretation of its art is a dangerous game. But is it too spurious to see in the tightly sprung tension of the art of the fourth and third centuries something that would have appealed to the reckless warrior hordes, or in the enigmatic faces which peer from the stylized foliage an image that had meaning for those who believed in the shape-shifting of the gods?

XI The Gunderstrup cauldron found dismantled in a bog near Roevemosen, Aars, Denmark. Although some of the figures appear to represent individuals wearing Celtic armour and the deities wear torcs in the manner of Celtic gods, much of the detail derives from Thracian art, and the use of silver, of which the cauldron plates are made, is common in the Thracian world and rare among the Celts. It is probable that the cauldron was made in the Middle Danube region in the second or first century BC and transported in some unknown manner to its Danish bog. Nationalmuseet, Copenhagen.

XII A pair of limestone heads wearing a 'leaf crown'
found at the sanctuary of Roquepertuse, Bouches-
du-Rhône, France, together with a range of religious
sculpture dating to the third or second century BC.
Musée d'Archéologie, Château Borély, Marseille.

7

Iberia and the Celtiberians

THE questions raised by the origins and nature of Celtic settlement in the Iberian Peninsula bring into sharp focus many of the general issues considered in Chapter 1, in particular the relationship between language, ethnicity, and archaeology. Classical writers describing Iberia frequently refer to the presence of Celtiberians, the Celtic language was spoken in some areas, and social systems existed which bore similarities to those of the historical Celts in temperate Europe; yet the material culture differed markedly from that of the La Tène type. In considering the problem in the Peninsula, therefore, it is necessary to dissociate La Tène material culture from the concept of 'Celtic' and in doing so the nature and significance of the Celtic language are inevitably raised.

The Landscape and Culture of Iberia

Before considering the matter of Celtic societies in the Peninsula, something must be said about the landscape and the broader cultural context within which the enquiry lies. The roughly square mass of the Iberian Peninsula can, at a highly simplified level, be regarded as a flat plain tilted down to the west. Because of this the east and south coasts present their somewhat austere mountainous backs to the Mediterranean while the western, Atlantic, coast is lower and more accessible. Iberia is also effectively isolated from the rest of Europe by the Pyrenees and their westward extension—the mountain ranges of Cantabria. This basic structure determines that most of the major rivers of Iberia—the Duero, Tagus, Guadiana, and Guadalquivir—flow westwards to the Atlantic; the Ebro and the Segura are the only significant east-flowing rivers.

The position of the Peninsula, between the Atlantic and the Mediterranean, as well as its varied relief, has a direct effect on climate, the north and west being significantly wetter and cooler than the south and east. This, in turn, conditions vegetation—the south-east has a Mediterranean climate, allowing the growth

133

and ripening of olives and vines, while the north and west are essentially temperate with much deciduous woodland. The Peninsula is also a rich source of metals, the most prolific zone being the 'pyrite arc' extending from the copper- and silver-rich Sierra Morena in the south to Galicia and the Cantabrian Mountains in the north-west where tin and gold are concentrated. These geomorphological factors, in their various ways, have all had an effect on the ethnic and political development of the region.

The communities of the east Mediterranean first began to establish links with Iberia, either directly or indirectly, in the Late Bronze Age, an interest reflected in a few sherds of Mycenaean pottery found in Andalucía. It may have been in the wake of these early exchanges that the first Phoenician contacts were established with the south-west, but it was not until the eighth century BC that the Phoenician port-of-trade at Gadir (Cádiz) developed as the base for regular and intensive exchanges between the east Mediterranean entrepreneurs and the metal-rich kingdom of Tartessos occupying the region of the Lower Guadalquivir and the valleys of the Rio Tinto and Odeil. In the seventh and sixth centuries a string of Phoenician settlements were set up along the southern coast as far east as Guardamar, and as a result the native culture of Andalucía underwent an 'orientalizing' phase.

Greek contact with the south is attested as early as c.630, when Kolaios, a native of Samos, explored the markets of Tartessos and came back a rich man. It was also during the latter part of the seventh century that the Greeks from Phocaea began to explore the north-western shores of the west Mediterranean from the Rhône to the Segura, an exploration which culminated in the foundation of Massalia c.600 and the creation of other colonies around the Golfe du Lion with Emporion (Ampurias) founded not long after. Greek trading interests extended well down the coast of Levantine Iberia, at least to the Segura mouth, where a fortified base was set up at La Picola in about 430 BC. Further to the south and west Greek trading interests penetrated the zone first developed by the Phoenicians, but the nature of the interaction is obscure.

From the eighth century until the middle of the third century the orientalizing and classicizing effects of intensive trade on the Mediterranean coastal zone of Iberia, from the Straits of Gibraltar to the Ebro Valley, contributed to the development of Iberian culture. Large nucleated settlements, many of them already occupied in the Late Bronze Age, developed the characteristics of Mediterranean cities; a distinctive art style represented in vase painting, sculpture, and metalworking emerged; and the social system developed a degree of complexity which, by the fourth century, can reasonably be called a state system. That a distinctive script emerged to express the Iberian language was no doubt a consequence of increasing socio-economic complexity. It was at this time that military forces, armed with round shields and falcatas (short swords with a single curved cutting edge), took on the appearance of hoplite armies and were in demand as mercenaries throughout the Mediterranean.

In short, the Iberians of southern and eastern Iberia can best be regarded as a

Mediterranean people sharing in the broader development of the region throughout the middle of the first millennium. After the mid-third century, when the Barcid dynasty from Carthage began to build a power base in southern Iberia, following Carthaginian failures in the First Punic War (264–241), the Iberians became caught up directly in Mediterranean power struggles—an involvement which led to the gradual annexing of the entire Peninsula by the Romans over a period of two centuries following their destruction of Carthaginian power and the capture of Cádiz in 206 BC.

The Atlantic zone presented an altogether different picture. Already during the second millennium the Atlantic communities had developed close contacts one with another along the length of the Iberian seaboard and had established wider links with the network which bound the communities of western France, Brittany, western Britain, and Ireland together in a series of overlapping spheres of interaction. It is unlikely that long-distance voyages were the norm along the Atlantic front: exchanges at this time were probably down-the-line between neighbours, but in this way commodities, especially metals, could be moved over considerable distances.

The Atlantic bronze industry received a new impetus when the Phoenicians established themselves on the Atlantic island of Cádiz. The consuming demand for tin, which was to be had in quantity in Galicia, Brittany, and Cornwall, and the ready accessibility of gold from these regions and from Wales and Ireland would certainly have led the entrepreneurs of Cádiz to encourage their native counterparts working the Atlantic sea-ways to bring supplies to the Phoenician port. As the Phoenician presence became established, Mediterranean sailors began to explore the Atlantic for themselves. In this way, it seems, enclaves were established around the coast at least as far north as the estuary of the Tagus and south along the African coast to Mogador. In all probability a few more enterprising ships' masters ventured further. The sixth-century sailing manual known as the *Massilliot Periplus* gives directions and advice for sailing into the Atlantic at least as far north as Britain and Ireland. On one such journey, in the late fourth century, Pytheas, a Greek from Massalia, reached Britain and probably beyond and managed to return safely to record his experiences.

In spite of the infiltration of the Atlantic sea-ways by Mediterranean influences, the indigenous culture, deeply rooted in the Bronze Age, remained strong. In the north-west of the Peninsula continuous development throughout the second half of the first millennium led to the emergence of a highly distinctive Castro culture characterized by defended hilltop settlements (*castros*), decorated pottery types, and stone sculptures. This community was among the last to submit to Rome in the first century BC.

The north-east of Iberia, and in particular the Ebro Valley and the coastal regions of Catalonia, developed a Late Bronze Age culture which exhibited close parallels with Urnfield developments in temperate Europe. The cultures on the two sides of the Pyrenees were sufficiently similar to suggest that close contacts were maintained, possibly involving limited movements of people. At

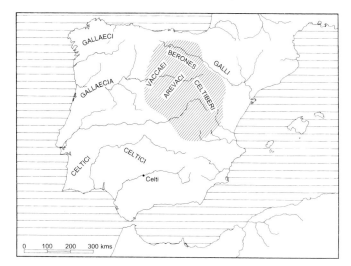

106 The Iberian Peninsula, showing the focus of Celtiberian culture with the names of the principal Celtic tribes.

the very least the Iberian communities readily absorbed the beliefs and material cultural assemblages of their northern neighbours interpreting them in a local manner. The extension of Greek influence along the coast of northern Catalonia, following the establishment of Emporion in the sixth century, helped to integrate this coastal zone into a Ligurian sphere which spread around the Golfe du Lion.

This brief overview of Iberia in the first millennium BC has left the centre of the Peninsula unaccounted for. Here lived indigenous groups who spoke Celtic and were to develop the distinctive characteristics of Celtiberian culture.

Celts and Celtiberians through Contemporary Eyes

Direct evidence for the existence of Celts in Iberia is provided by the classical historians. The earliest of these is Herodotus, who, writing in the mid-fifth century BC, makes oblique and somewhat confusing references to the Celtic presence. In one passage he mentions that they were the most westerly people in Europe next to the Cynetes, who appear to have been the inhabitants of the extreme south-west of the Peninsula. Elsewhere he says that the Celts lived beyond the 'Pillars of Hercules'—the area known to us as the Straits of Gibraltar. Both comments provide a reasonable geographical precision and leave no doubt that Herodotus' informants believed there were Celts in western Iberia. When Herodotus notes that Celts lived around the source of the Danube and that the Danube rose near Pyrene—a place name thought to be connected to the Pyrenees—he was presumably conflating two different scraps of information into a single incorrect perception.

The third-century writer Eratosthenes also comments on Celts in Iberia, contrasting their prominence in his own time to the situation two centuries earlier when they had been less numerous or at least less important. From the beginning of the second century *Celtiberes* or *Celtiberi* began to be referred to with increasing frequency in the various conflicts in which the Romans were engaged in the Peninsula. According to Diodorus, no doubt quoting Poseidonius, 'Celtiberes are a fusion of two peoples and the combination of Celts and Iberes only took place after long and bloody wars' (*Hist.* 5. 33). This may be nothing more than a helpful rationalization but it was widely believed. Indeed Martial, who was born in Bilbilis in Celtiberian territory in AD 40, several times refers in his writing to 'we who are descended from Celts and Iberians'. Diodorus characterizes the Celtiberes, saying that they were very warlike but were noted for their hospitality, since they regarded strangers as being under divine protection. He goes on to say that 'some have shields of lightly-constructed Celtic type; others a round shield of the kind more familiar in the Greek world. The iron of their two-edged swords, shorter than the Celtic great sword, is capable of cutting anything' (*Hist.* 5. 33).

Other authors contribute to the generalized Graeco-Roman view of the Celtiberian, emphasizing the dual attribute of military ferocity and hospitality. Support of the chief in battle was demanded of every warrior and to survive him was a criminal act: death in battle was glorious. One tantalizing account says that they believed that the souls of those who died in battle and were eaten by vultures went straight to heaven. Here, just possibly, is a reference to the rite of excarnation. Among at least one tribe, the Vaccaei, land and the harvest were the property of the community, and every year land was reapportioned to those who worked it. Many other anecdotes are recorded, such as Celtiberians drinking wine mixed with honey or cleaning their teeth with stale urine, but these add little to our understanding other than local colour. Taken together, then, the ancient sources are consistent in their belief in the Celtic ethnicity of the societies they encountered beyond the northern and western borders of the more civilized Mediterranean-facing Iberians of the south and east.

The Celtic Language

The origin and development of palaeohispanic languages present highly complex problems which have provided a fertile field for study and debate among scholars. It is only fair to stress that that debate continues and many issues are still unresolved. At the very simplest level, however, it is possible to divide much of the Peninsula into two broad linguistic zones based on the common occurrence of distinctive typonyms. In the south and east there exists a concentration of place names ending in *-il(t)i*, *-il(t)u*, which are thought to be non Indo-European and from their distribution clearly correspond to the region that was culturally and historically that of the Iberians. Over much of the rest of the country names ending in *-briga* are comparatively widespread; these reflect the area over which a Celtic language was spoken.

When examined in more detail, however, something of the complexity of the situation becomes apparent. The zone of non-Indo-European place names extending from southern Portugal to the Levantine–Catalan region can be divided into several different groups.

107 The distribution of Celtic place names in Iberia gives some idea of the area of the Peninsula over which the Celtic language was in use. Some of the Celtic name elements appear for the first time in Roman place names.

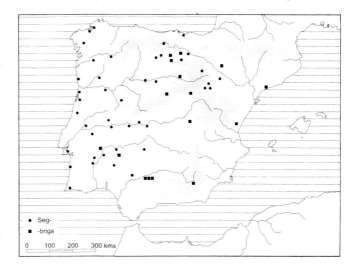

Seg-
-briga

0   100   200   300 kms

Similarly within the broad *-briga* zone several linguistic sub-zones can be defined, the most distinctive being the area of the Lusitani and Gallaecia on the Atlantic coast, which is thought by some linguists to represent an archaic form of Celtic, and the north of Galicia around Lugo and La Coruña. There are also significant differences in language east and west of a divide which runs approximately through Oviedo and Mérida. None the less, these groups all belong to the broadly defined Celtic family of Indo-European.

The questions which immediately arise are when and how was the Celtic language introduced into Iberia? Earlier linguistic studies have stressed that most of the Celtic which survives for study in Iberia is of the more ancient Q-Celtic form, suggesting an early penetration. There is, however, some evidence of P-Celtic in place names with the *-dunum* ending, suggesting to some linguists the possibility of a second penetration. Since the *-dunum* names were found over only a limited territory, concentrating mainly in Catalonia, it has been suggested that a later Celtic 'influx' through the Pyrenees was superimposed upon an already established and far more extensive Celtic-speaking region.

Interpretations of this kind must be regarded as oversimplifications. At best the linguistic evidence shows that Celtic, in various forms, was spoken over large areas of Iberia. It does not take with it a convincing chronology nor can it be used as a model for population movements.

It has been argued that the Celtic language had already evolved by the time that food-producing communities first moved into northern and central Iberia in the Neolithic period, but the view is not widely supported. An alternative is to see the language spreading as the result of a series of successive migrations in later prehistoric times, different 'waves' of Celtic speakers settling different areas. Yet another suggestion is that a limited influx of population took place in the north-east of Iberia, whence, as an élite language, Celtic spread to other regions. The simple reality is that we do not know, nor is it within the nature of the evidence ever to provide firm answers to these problems. All that can safely be said is that by the fourth century BC a Celtiberian spoke a language which had much in common with that spoken by many communities of western and central Europe, and by good fortune the Celtiberians sometimes had recourse to record transactions in their native language on metal plaques like that found at Botorrita, which contribute to a growing corpus of invaluable texts.

108 One of the longest inscriptions in the Celtiberian language was discovered at Botorrita near Saragossa in Spain. It was inscribed on both faces of a bronze plaque and is interpreted as a contract relating in some way to land ownership. Museo Arqueológico Nacional, Madrid.

The 'Arrival' of the Celts: Some Theories

The question of the 'arrival' of Celtic-speaking peoples in the Iberian Peninsula has understandably been the subject of much debate. In the nineteenth century it was usual to link 'Celts' with the construction of megalithic tombs, more because the megaliths were at that time the best-known elements of the archaeological record than for any more positive reason. In the 1920s and 1930s, as an awareness of the complexity of the archaeological record grew, it was suggested that the Celtic advent was reflected in the material culture of the Urnfields of north-eastern Iberia. This, it was argued, was directly related to the culture of western and central Europe, which was the homeland of the Celts. Further study refined the view, leading to the 'two-Celtic-waves' theory. This saw an initial wave arriving from north of the Pyrenees about 1000 BC, with a second, more complex invasion bringing in new peoples in the sixth century. Another version of the same general theory held that there was only one phase of incomings, some time in the eighth century. However, the demonstration that the Celtiberian zone and the distribution of the Iberian Urnfields were exclusive and that the language spoken in the Urnfield area was not Indo-European did much to undermine the traditional view. More recently some commentators have attempted, somewhat unconvincingly, to demonstrate that the Celtic incursion was the result of movements of the La Tène Celts.

Current Spanish work accepts that these monocausal explanations are over-simple. Invasionist theories are rejected in favour of a model based on the assimilation of selected cultural elements by the indigenous élites. The model proposes the existence of a cultural 'substratum' embedded in the Atlantic Bronze Age which had already absorbed some linguistic and ideological traits common to the historical Celts. Among the distinguishable characteristics are a language form in which place and personal names retain an initial P and are closely related to the later Lusitanian language, circular houses, burial rites involving the excarnation of the dead, and religious locations associated with natural phenomena such as mountains, springs, rivers, and woods. This 'proto-Celtic' culture gradually developed, in the highlands of the Iberian Mountains and the Eastern Meseta, into the culture of the historical Celtiberians, as a result of absorbing influences emanating from the Mediterranean fringe. From the homeland of its genesis, Celtiberian culture spread to northern and western Iberia, being readily assimilated by the 'proto-Celtic' substrate, but in the extreme north and west—the area of the Castro culture—the 'proto-Celtic' culture remained largely untainted.

This interpretation raises a number of interesting questions and possibilities. In its reliance on an Atlantic Bronze Age 'proto-Celtic' culture, it opens the possibility for developing a model which embraces the whole of Atlantic Europe—a matter to which we will return in the next chapter. The view that classic Celtiberian culture was an amalgam of the indigenous 'proto Celtic' with an overlay of Mediterranean influences is precisely what has been suggested, in

Chapter 3, as the process behind the emergence of the La Tène Celtic culture of temperate Europe.

The Archaeology of the Celtiberians

The homeland of the Celtiberians lay in the north-eastern part of Iberia stretching from the southern flank of the Ebro Valley to the Eastern Meseta. To the north lay the territory of the Urnfield culture, to the west the loosely linked communities of the Atlantic Bronze Age, while to the east and south, along the Mediterranean fringe, the distinctive Iberian culture was soon to emerge as contacts with the east Mediterranean states intensified. The Celtiberian zone therefore lay on three peripheries and inevitably benefited by absorbing cultural elements from all three.

The harshness of parts of the territory, particularly the plains of the Meseta, desiccated during the summer months, necessitated a degree of transhumance in the pastoral economy. The flocks and herds were taken to upland mountain pastures before the heat came and were brought down again in autumn. Such conditions allowed a gradual increase in population and led to the emergence of an élite reflected in a series of rich graves furnished with short swords, spears, and round shields, redolent of the warrior-based nature of society.

The principal burial rite was urned cremation, adopted from the Urnfield cultural zone to the north-east, but other elements came from the south and east, including geometric painted pottery, fibulae with two-part springs, and belt hooks, all characteristic of Tartessian culture. The short antennae-hilted

109 *Above*: Antennae-hilted sword from Alcacer do Sal, Portugal, is typical of swords of the sixth to fourth centuries BC in use in the Celtiberian region. Museu Nacional de Arqueologia e Etnologia, Lisbon.

110 *Right*: The *oppidum* of Los Cogotas, Avila, Spain, is one of the better-known defended settlements of the Celtiberian region of Spain. It has been extensively excavated as the result of which the arrangement of the interior buildings has been identified in outline allowing this artist's reconstruction to be offered.

iron sword was, however, a development specific to the north, extending, with regional variations, over the Celtiberian area and the Ebro
Valley, and across the Pyrenees into Languedoc
and Aquitania.

From the sixth century BC the influence of
stimuli from the cultures of the Mediterranean
littoral and the developing Iberian hinterland
intensified. By the fourth century the Celtiberians were using rotary querns and the potter's wheel. Celtiberian script, derived from
Iberian, was in use by the third century, and
large *oppida*-like settlements—again probably
an Iberian inspiration—began to develop at
about the same time or a little later.

To what extent Celtiberian culture received
significant influences from the La Tène cultural
zone it is difficult to say. A scatter of La Tène
artefacts have been found in Iberia, most notably the collection of third-century weapons
from the burial at Quintana de Gormaz, which
included a scabbard decorated with dragon-
pairs. This array of material shows that contacts
existed with communities north of the Pyrenees,
but it need not imply anything more than
processes of gift exchange. Nor does the adoption of the torc as an item of prestige display
mean more than a sharing of belief or value sys-

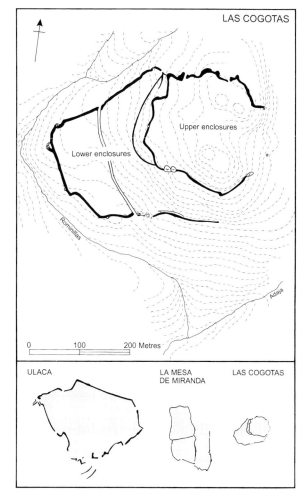

111 *Above*: The defences of
Los Cogotas enclose in total
some 14.5 hectares but only
the upper enclosure was
intensively occupied.
Though large, it is by no
means the largest of the
oppida in the Ambles Valley
as the lower plans will
demonstrate.

112 *Left*: Gold torc of the
fourth–second centuries BC
from Vilas Boas, Portugal.
Museu Nacional de
Arqueologia e Etnologia,
Lisbon.

141

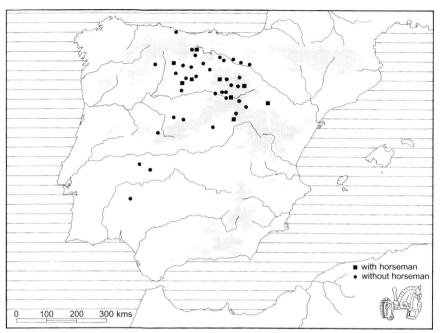

113 Distribution of horseman fibulae, typical of the Celtiberian area of Spain. The style is local but the basic structure of the brooch is found throughout much of western Europe.

tems. The silver torcs of the Meseta and the gold torcs of the north-west are distinctively Celtiberian in style, as are the widely distributed horse-and-rider fibulae.

The possibility that groups of La Tène Celts may have moved south into Celtiberian lands, as raiders, settlers, or mercenaries, cannot, however, be ruled out. Celtic war bands may have attached themselves to the incursion of the Cimbri in 104 BC and Caesar specifically mentions the arrival in Lérida, in 49 BC, of 6,000 Gauls, including Gallic cavalry, Ruthenian archers, and their families. The contribution of these and other possible intruders to Celtiberian culture seems to have been minimal.

The Expansion of Celtiberian Culture

From its homeland in the north-east of the Peninsula, Celtiberian culture spread to many other areas of the country. This is best exemplified by the extent to which the Celtic language was spoken, as is demonstrated by the distribution of place names with the suffix -*briga* or the prefix *Seg*- (Fig. 107).

Archaeological evidence from grave finds suggests an extension of Celtiberian culture westwards to the territory of the Vettones in the fifth century BC, and to Estremadura and the far west, where the surname *Celtius* was used to indicate ethnic origin. According to Pliny, some Celtiberians from this region moved south to settle in Baetica, whence they became known as the *Celtici*: one of the towns, Peñaflor, was called *Celti* in the Iberian and Roman period. Pliny as well as other writers record further movements to the north: the *Celti praestmarici* settled in northern Portugal, the *Gallaeci* moved to the extreme north-

114 *Left*: Stone relief of a warrior from Osuna, Andalucía, Spain. The warrior holds a typical Iberian falcata (single edge sword) in his right hand, but his elongated shield is of La Tène type and quite unlike native Iberian round shields. Third or second century BC. Museo Arqueológico Nacional, Madrid.

115 *Above*: Detail of the decoration of a painted pottery vessel from Liria, Valencia, Spain, showing a warrior holding an elongated shield of La Tène type. Third or second century BC. Museo Prehistórico de Valencia.

west (modern Galicia), while the *Galli* settled in the Ebro Valley. That all these groups were known by ethnic rather than tribal designations is an indication that the Celtiberian expansion is more likely to have been the result of military élites taking over the power structure of the peripheral tribes than of large movements of population. Beyond this zone raids may have penetrated still further into the territories of the more advanced Iberian communities, and it was in these regions that Celtic mercenaries, like those depicted on the stone relief from Osuna or the pot from Liria, will have found employment. In rare sculptures, like the stone head from Córdoba, we may be glimpsing an icon of a Celtic deity.

Celtiberians and the Classical World

The value of the Celtiberians as mercenary troops was well appreciated by the Carthaginians, who employed substantial detachments in their various campaigns. Celtiberians were also used in the Roman armies, which entered Spain in 218 BC at the beginning of the Second Punic War, though they proved to be somewhat unreliable. By the end of the second century, with Carthage defeated and Rome now developing its hold over the Iberian lands, Romans and Celtiberians had become all too familiar with each other's strengths and weaknesses.

116 Stone head carved in a style very similar to Celtic stone heads found in southern Gaul. From the region of Córdoba. The very simplicity of the depiction makes it difficult to argue that the object was actually carved by a craftsman with knowledge of 'Celtic' iconography, but the head stands out in marked contrast to Iberian and Roman work in this region of Andalucía. Museo Municipal de Córdoba.

For the next seventy years, in a long-drawn-out war of attrition, enlivened by peace treaties and revolts, Rome was drawn deeper and deeper into the territories of the Celtiberians and Lusitanians. Some indication of the devastating scale of the conflict is provided by Tiberius Gracchus, who could claim to have destroyed 300 Celtiberian hill towns in his single expedition of 179–8 BC. A brief respite followed, but after the revolt of the Celtiberians and Lusitani in 154 a further series of bitter engagements ensued, the native opposition being rallied and brilliantly led for a time by the Lusitanian war leader Viriathus. The final stage began in 143 BC, by which time the Lusitanian campaign had been separated from that against the Celtiberians, and culminated in 133 with the destruction of the Celtiberian stronghold of Numantia after a long and bitter siege. Although it was to take more than a century for the whole of Iberia to be brought under Roman control, the destruction of Numantia and the selling of its survivors into slavery effectively marked the end of organized Celtiberian resistance.

During the second century Rome had come to understand and respect the Celtic peoples of Iberia. They were characterized as fearless, ferocious warriors who fought with a total disregard for their own safety: their cavalry was awe-inspiring and they were capable of producing charismatic war leaders like Viriathus. They were also bound by their overriding belief in the sacred nature of hospitality.

In stressing the valour and hospitality of the Celtiberians, the Roman writers were providing a familiar caricature of the Noble Savage, but there can be little doubt that these aspects were deeply embedded in the social system of the Celtiberians. It was this, as well as their language, which allowed the classical authors to believe them and the Celts of temperate Europe to be one people.

117 A wolf's head made from baked clay found at the native hill town of Numantia, Spain. The head is the mouth of a trumpet similar to the carnyx. Second to first century BC. Museo Arqueológico Nacional, Madrid.

8
The Communities of the Atlantic Façade

THE Celtic language was spoken throughout much or most of western Europe to the very fringes of the Atlantic and survives now in a vital spoken and written form as Gaelic, Manx, Welsh, Breton, and, until recently, Cornish. Over much of this same region distinctive elements of the La Tène material culture are to be found, and there is ample evidence that local craftsmen, working in metal or clay, were thoroughly conversant with the grammar and spirit of Celtic art. For these reasons, then, one may assume that western Europe was an integral part of the wider Celtic world.

But behind this broad linguistic and cultural similarity lay a more complex pattern. In the opening paragraph of the first book of his *Commentaries on the Gallic War*, Caesar offers a sketch of the ethnic structure of Gaul:

Gaul as a whole consists of three separate parts; one is inhabited by the Belgae, another by the Aquitani, and the third by the people we call Gauls, though in their own language they are called Celts. In language, customs, and laws these three peoples are quite distinct. The Celts are separated from the Aquitani by the river Garonne and from the Belgae by the Marne and the Seine.   (*De Bello Gallico* 1. 1)

The reference is admirably clear and explicit, and, while it may well contain a degree of oversimplification either through ignorance or to aid the audience, there is no reason not to accept it as a fair summing-up of the situation in the mid-first century BC. The archaeological evidence provides some support for this threefold division, but the broad swath of territory designated 'Celtic' by Caesar can be further divided into Armorican Gaul, occupying the entire Atlantic zone from the Seine to the Garonne, Narbonnaise Gaul, comprising Provence and Languedoc from the Alps to the Pyrenees, and a central zone which subdivides roughly along the Loire Valley into an Arvernian and central eastern region.

Further west, Britain and Ireland pose an altogether different problem. No ancient author ever described the inhabitants of the islands as Celts, though Caesar says of the occupants of Kent that their way of life was very like that of the Gauls. The earliest surviving reference is to be found in the *Massilliot Periplus*, a source probably of the sixth century BC, preserved in the *Ora Maritima* of Avienus. Here Britain is described as *insula Albionum* and there is mention of *gens Hiernorum*—the race of the Irish. The underlying Celtic forms are *Albiones* (roughly 'people of the living surface world') and *Ierne* ('people of the fertile earth'). The account of the voyage of Pytheas, which took place about 320 BC, makes no use of these ethnonyms, employing instead a transliteration of the Gallo-Brettonic *Pritani* to describe the British—a name which has persisted ever since. Taken together, this evidence is usually thought to imply that the earlier form of Celtic (Goidelic) was replaced by the later (Brythonic), in Britain but not in Ireland, between the sixth and the beginning of the third centuries. The reasoning has further been extended by suggesting that the appearance of Brythonic Celtic is the result of social contacts between Britain and Gaul reflected in the development of Insular Celtic art. As a simplified model this may be broadly acceptable, but, as we will see, the situation is likely to have been far more complex. A point of particular relevance, however, is that in Ireland and Britain the Celtic language was already established by the sixth century.

The situation in Brittany is less clear. Modern Breton is based on Brythonic Celtic, very similar to that spoken in Wales and, until recently, Cornwall. Since the Armorican peninsula is known to have received settlers from south-western Britain in the fifth century AD, it has generally been assumed that the Breton language developed from that spoken by the incoming population. This is, however, likely to be an oversimplification. Archaeologically Armorica, south-west Britain, and south Wales formed a broadly linked cultural zone in the first millennium BC and must have shared a similar Brythonic Celtic. Although the Roman interlude in Armorica seems to have imposed itself rather more heavily than that in the south-west of Britain or in Wales, there is no reason to suppose that the indigenous Celtic language was totally replaced by Latin. In other words, the British migrants in the fifth century AD are likely to have encountered a native population able to communicate with them in the language shared by their ancestors five centuries before, even though it must have undergone a degree of transformation. In the rest of Gaul, where romanization was far more intense, Latin had, by the fourth century, begun to oust Celtic. Even so, that St Jerome could note the similarity between the native language of the Treveri and that of the Galatians suggests that Celtic survived in spoken form in parts of Gaul other than Armorica until the Migration Period.

The principal question to emerge from this brief introduction is when and by what processes did the communities of western Europe become Celtic? The traditional view, held until the 1960s, was that the answer lay in one or more major migrations. More recently it has been suggested that the Celtic languages of the west simply evolved *in situ* from an indigenous Indo-European base. On both archaeological and linguistic grounds, neither generalization is acceptable. By reviewing a selection of the evidence, it may be possible to come closer to an understanding of the issues involved.

The Nature of the Atlantic Fringe in the Bronze Age

To take the broadest view it may be said that the communities of the Atlantic fringe of Europe formed a single cultural zone, linked by the sea. It differed significantly from the central zone of temperate Europe and from the Mediterranean zone, yet all three were bound by networks of contact channelled along corridors determined, to a large extent, by the opportunities created by geography. Most of these corridors were threaded by navigable rivers—the Rhine, Seine, Loire, and Gironde—but other nodes, such as the trading port of Gadir (Cádiz), provided essential points of articulation.

That cultural links along the Atlantic sea-ways extend back far in time is evident from the archaeological record. As early as the fourth millennium BC, megalithic tombs, of the type known as passage graves, developed on a broad front from Portugal to Ireland, and within this zone common symbols recurred, carved on the orthostats of the tombs. While no one any longer conjures up visions of migrant 'Megalithic Saints' proselytizing along the Atlantic façade, the similarities are such that the different communities must have been developing their belief systems in the general knowledge of what was happening elsewhere. A flow of ideas implies movements, however limited, of people, and it may well be that the exchange of rare commodities, such as fine stone axes, between neighbouring polities provided the mechanism.

Continued contact was maintained throughout the second millennium and began to intensify as copper and later bronze became generally available. Along the maritime networks a distinctive burial practice spread, characterized by single inhumations accompanied by grave sets including decorated beakers. It was during this time that centres displaying élite dominance emerged in Brittany and Wessex. Cultural contact was maintained through gift exchanges which saw fine stone axes, gold, amber, and faience beads pass between them across the intervening channel.

Contacts intensified still further in the Late Bronze Age, after about 1300 BC. From then, until c.600 BC, bronze in various forms—as its

118 Atlantic Europe, indicating the main cultural zones in the second half of the first millennium BC.

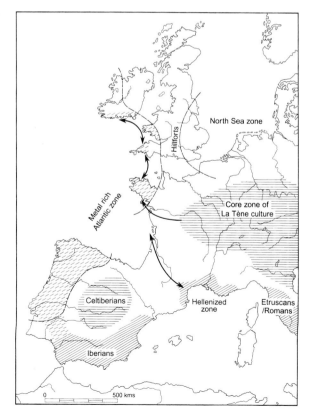

raw metal components, as scrap, or as finished weapons and implements—moved in increasing quantity, and over greater distances, than before. The evidence derives almost entirely from the distribution of artefacts, but includes rare examples of shipwrecks, such as the vessels carrying French-made implements to Britain which foundered off the cliffs of Dover and in Saltcomb Bay in Devon in about the tenth century BC. Artefact distributions are at best a surrogate for understanding the movement of people and can offer only a crude indication of direction and intensity of contact. Thus the Sicilian-made shaft-hole axe found in the sea near the southern British port of Hengistbury is not necessarily evidence of a Mediterranean adventurer visiting Britain in the eighth century BC. At best it indicates the geographical extent of contact and hints at the complexity of the social processes involved.

The copious evidence for the movement of bronze in the Late Bronze Age also raises the question of the movement of skilled people able to judge the quality of metal and, in some remote areas, to introduce the technology of extraction or manufacture. The individuals who cast a range of bronze items at Dun Aengus on the Aran Island of Inishmore off the Galway coast and at Jarlshof on Shetland 170 kilometres north of Scotland must have travelled in small boats with their metal, beeswax, refractory clay, and skills.

It would be possible to call upon an array of varied evidence to demonstrate local interactions, but sufficient will have been said to show that, for at least three millennia, the communities of the Atlantic had maintained a degree of contact such that many aspects of culture, especially belief systems and technological skills, were held in common. The contact would mostly have been between adjacent communities, with few venturing further afield, but in this way, from one neighbour to another, ideas would quickly have spread.

The principal change which can be discerned within this *longue durée* is an intensification in the volume of bronze moving through the system after the beginning of the Late Bronze Age. It is difficult to discern an internal cause for this, and the simplest explanation would be to suppose that the metal-rich Atlantic zone was being increasingly drawn into the bronze-consuming world of the Urnfield and Nordic cultures. Here, in central and northern Europe, bronze was used up in great quantities as furnishings for the burials of the dead and as gifts to the chthonic deities whose worship demanded the deposition of valuable items buried in pits in the ground or thrown into bogs, springs, and rivers. As the Atlantic communities began to respond to the demand, developing new networks of communication along which the metals could pass, aspects of Urnfield material culture, learned from the contact, began to be absorbed into the Atlantic system—so too did the belief systems which required the deposition of wealth on a considerable scale. The Late Bronze Age was, therefore, the time when the technology and ideologies of the central European Urnfield world were introduced to the communities of the Atlantic fringe.

The Mediterranean states will have been made aware of the potential of the

XIII*a* *Above*: A cup from the princely burial at Schwarzenbach, Rhineland, Germany. The vessel is enlivened by an external application of open-work embossed gold leaf characteristic of the Early Style of Celtic art which closely copies Etruscan designs. Second half of fifth century BC. Staatliche Museen Antikensammlung Preussischer Kulturbesitz, Berlin.

XIII*b* *Left*: Helmet made of iron and bronze covered with gold and inset with coral from Agris, Charante, France. Fourth century BC. The decoration is characteristic of the Vegetal Style of Celtic art. Musée de la Société Archéologique et Historique de la Charante, Angoulême.

Atlantic zone by the Phoenician enclave at Gadir (Cádiz), and it was probably as the result of Phoenician activity that Atlantic bronzes were carried into the western Mediterranean. Their appearance, scattered though they are, reflects an increasing awareness of the potential of the Atlantic zone among the communities of the Mediterranean.

Within this sweep of territory, extending over 30,000 kilometres from the Straits of Gibraltar to the Shetlands there developed a number of distinctive cultural zones (Fig. 118) which, because of their geographical proximity, maintained close links and shared socio-cultural attributes.

Occupying a central place in this Atlantic continuum were the sea-girt peninsulas of southern Ireland, south Wales, south-west Britain, and Armorica. It was a region composed, for the most part, of old hard rocks heavily mineralized, its Atlantic face washed by the Gulf Stream, which ensured a mild but damp climate. What encouraged continued contact between these four promontories was the attraction of their metal resources, principally copper, tin, and gold.

A second system included the coastal region of Gaul, between the Seine and the Rhine, and the adjacent shores of Britain from Hampshire to East Anglia. Here the most evident medium of exchange was bronze, either in the form of finished items or as scrap, but behind this archaeologically visible material no doubt lay exchanges in many other commodities. Further to the north cultural similarities suggest that the communities of north and west Scotland, the Northern and Western Isles, and the north-eastern part of Ireland formed another closely related zone.

South of Armorica it is possible to distinguish two distinctive cultural zones: the north-west corner of Iberia, including Galicia, Asturia, and Cantabria, with its highly localized settlement types and copious supplies of gold and tin; and a south-western zone, stretching from the Tagus to the Lower Guadalquivir, characterized in the Late Bronze Age by engraved stelae and burnished pottery. This region was rich in copper and silver.

XIV *Facing*: Bronze helmet from a vehicle grave at Berru, Marne, France. Early fourth century BC. Musée des Antiquités Nationales, Saint-Germain-en-Laye, Paris.

119 Carved stela, possibly of Late Bronze Age date, from Ategua, Andalucía, Spain. The central part of the scene illustrates a two-wheeled vehicle pulled by paired quadrupeds with another standing by. At the bottom are human figures, one group of whom seems to be dancing. The scene is probably part of a funerary ritual. Museo Municipal de Córdoba.

The Development of the Atlantic Communities: 800–200 BC

The attraction of Atlantic metal resources is apparent from the *Massilliot Periplus*. In it is a reference to islands in the Atlantic called the Oestrymnides, 'rich in the mining of tin and lead. A vigorous tribe lives here, proud-spirited, energetic and skilful. On all the ridges trade is carried on.' The account describes the native boats made of leather hides sewn together, and goes on to locate the Oestrymnides at two days' sailing distance from Ireland, which would place them in either Cornwall or Brittany. Avienus says that the Tartessians

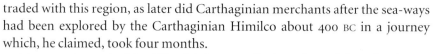

traded with this region, as later did Carthaginian merchants after the sea-ways had been explored by the Carthaginian Himilco about 400 BC in a journey which, he claimed, took four months.

A later explorer, the Massilliot ship's master Pytheas, braved the Atlantic sea-ways in about 320 BC, venturing even further. His reference to Belerion—the Land's End peninsula—suggests that he may have been following the established tin route, but he gives no further details. However, the Sicilian historian Timaeus, who was roughly contemporary with Pytheas and may indeed have used Pytheas as a source, recorded some additional facts which survive now only in a confused and muddled account in Pliny's *Natural History*. An island called Mictis is mentioned where tin is produced and the Britons sail to it in vessels of wickerwork covered with hide. Much the same story is taken up by Poseidonius (quoted by Diodorus Siculus), though the island is called Ictis and is joined to the mainland at low tide. 'Here the merchants buy the tin from the natives and carry it over to Gaul and after travelling overland for about thirty days they finally bring their loads on horses to the mouth of the Rhône' (*Hist.* 5. 22). It is not immediately clear which route was being used, but the general assumption is that the tin was shipped either to the mouth of the Loire, where the port of Corbilo was said to be located, or to the Garonne. Both estuaries, Strabo tells us, were ports of embarkation for Britain.

The tin trade described by the ancient sources is best seen as a specific development of the long-established Atlantic exchange network, manipulated now, either directly or indirectly, by Mediterranean entrepreneurs. It need have changed little except for the introduction into the native systems of concepts and possibly artefacts from the Mediterranean region. On this matter the archaeological record is not particularly informative but two small bronze figurines, one from Sligo in Ireland, the other from Aust in the Severn Estuary, may be imports from southern Spain. There is also a close similarity between fibulae from Mount Batten in Devon and Harlyn Bay in Cornwall and types manufactured in Aquitania and the Garonne estuary region. In addition to this some at least of the comparatively large number of Greek and Carthaginian coins discovered in Armorica and southern Britain are likely to have been contemporary imports.

The Mediterranean penetration of the Atlantic systems seems to have focused particularly on the tin-rich areas of Armorica and Cornwall with a probable extension to southern Ireland where gold was to be had. But that there was also direct interest in the tin and gold production of Galicia is indirectly indicated by the extension of Phoenician activity along the Portuguese coast and the discovery of Mediterranean trade goods, including Greek pottery, at a number of coastal locations in the north-west.

Whilst the Mediterranean world was learning how to exploit the Atlantic trading system, the complex network of exchange which linked the western European communities to the innovating core of the Urnfield élite in western central Europe continued to develop in the subsequent Hallstatt C period (*c*.750–600). The distribution of the typical Hallstatt C slashing sword, known after the type site of Gundlingen, together with the winged chapes which adorned the ends of the scabbards, give a vivid impression of the direction and intensity of these contacts (Maps 3 and 4). The more common bronze version is found in the Low Countries and northern France between the Rhine and the Seine, in the Loire Valley, and in the basin of the Garonne. It also occurs quite widely in Britain, where the form is copied and modified by local craftsmen, and is scattered across the face of Ireland. In Britain and Ireland the majority of the swords from known findspots occur in rivers, lakes, or bogs in just those locations where weapons were customarily deposited throughout the latter part of the Bronze Age.

A range of other élite equipment in bronze echoes this pattern: bronze cauldrons and buckets (both with distinctive British/Irish varieties), bronze horse gear, razors, pins, and other trinkets. In other words the full panoply of élite display, except for the ceremonial vehicle, finds its way, selectively, into the hands of the western communities. What is particularly interesting is that the élite items were incorporated in different ways into the cultural systems of the west. In the Low Countries, for example, swords and horse gear were deposited with cremation burials under barrows according to the indigenous rite. In the Garonne–Tarn region, urned cremations accompanied by personal jewellery or weapons were also normally buried beneath low barrows continuing indigenous practices. In Britain and Ireland, on the other hand, deposition was usually in watery contexts and less often in hoards. Evidence of this kind demonstrates not only how the alien goods were adopted and adapted by the western communities who received them, but also how extensive were the mechanisms which bound the polities of the Atlantic zone to those of the Hallstatt C chiefdoms of west central Europe. The network, which had developed throughout the Late Bronze Age, was now being even more intensively exploited. The view, frequently expressed up to the 1960s, that the distribution of Hallstatt C material represented invasions or migrations of warriors from the centre is not supported by any of the evidence and is best disregarded.

In the subsequent Hallstatt D period (*c*.600–450 BC) there was a significant change in the pattern and intensity of interaction. One possible explanation is that developing contact between the Late Hallstatt élite and the Mediterranean states diminished the desire to maintain traditional links with the west, or, more precisely, such links as there were were refocused.

The range and quantity of centrally produced (or inspired) Hallstatt D goods in northern France, the Low Countries, Britain, and Ireland dropped dramatically. In Britain, apart from a single antennae hilted sword and a bronze cauldron, the only distinctive items are a small number of bronze daggers which were avidly copied by local craftsmen and were mainly deposited in the Thames. Similar daggers from the Low Countries and northern France suggest that these display pieces were items of exchange in the sixth and fifth centuries. The same pattern can be seen in Aquitania, where native craftsmen copied the

120 *Facing, above*: Small bronze figure identified as coming 'from Sligo' in Ireland, considered to be an import from Iberia in the fourth to first centuries BC. National Museum of Ireland, Dublin.

121 *Facing, below*: Small bronze figure found at Aust, Gloucestershire, England. The style of the figure is Iberian, the closest parallels coming from Andalucía, dating to the fourth or third century BC. The Aust figure may have arrived in Britain via the Atlantic trading systems. British Museum, London.

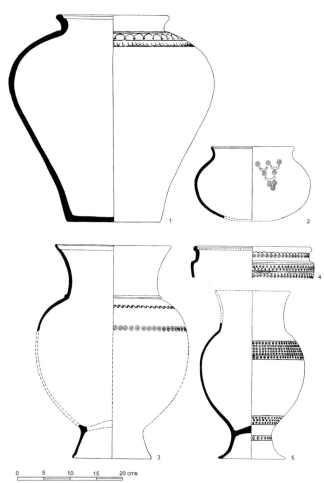

0   5   10   15   20 cms

122 Stamped pottery from
Brittany dating to the fifth
century BC.
No. 1 from Pludual, Côtes
d'Armor; no. 2 from
Kerhillio, Morbihan;
no. 3 from Roz-an-Tré-
Men, Finistère; no. 4 from
Mané Rouillard, Morbihan;
no. 5 from Saint-Martin-
des-Champs, Finistère.

Hallstatt D dagger form, the local version in this region accompanying the dead to the grave. Once again the alien concept was adopted and adapted technically and culturally to suit indigenous demands.

In Armorica the picture was altogether different. Items of Hallstatt C type are noticeably absent and there is little evidence of significant contact with west central Europe, but in the late sixth and early fifth centuries the situation changed. Imported metalwork is rare (not least because soil conditions are not conducive to preservation), but two notable items, a fragment of a bronze oinochoe from a cemetery or shrine at Tronoën and a decorated dagger scabbard from Kernavest–Quiberon, represent alien élite goods. Even more dramatic is the development of a highly distinctive style of stamp-decorated pottery which belongs, in general, to a broad category of stamped pottery found throughout central Europe in the fifth and fourth centuries (Map 24). The inspiration for the Breton vessels probably came from Late Hallstatt metalwork, like the Kernavest scabbard, but the origin and chronology of the style is still unclear.

If it is accepted that the Breton stamped wares reflect intensified links with west central Europe (and the argument is by no means decisive), then this could be seen as a reflection of the growing importance of the Armorican peninsula in providing access to the metal-producing Atlantic system. It would be easy from here to transport metals along the Loire to the western extension of the Late Hallstatt chiefdom zone in Burgundy. The development of the Loire corridor would also explain the rise of Bourges as an élite centre (see p. 65).

Having once established a direct route to Brittany, which occupied the centre of the Atlantic system, the peninsula appears to have remained a zone of innovation into the Early La Tène period. The intensity, and indeed the nature, of the contacts are difficult to characterize, but the remarkable ceramic art of Armorica in the fourth century (Figs. 82 and 122) is witness of the willingness and ability of local potters to accept the most up-to-date ideas developed by metalworking craftsmen in the Marne and Moselle regions. The inspiration which the potters received would almost certainly have been through the medium of imported metalwork. Of this virtually nothing has survived in the archaeological record except a fragment of helmet found at the sanctuary of Tronoën, but it is possible that the metal vessels, which were eventually deposited in a cist burial in Wales at Cerrig-y-Drudion, could have passed through Brittany. Tronoën has also produced the only Early La Tène swords, albeit fragments, so far found in Brittany.

Northern France, the Low Countries, and Britain received a flow of goods throughout the Early La Tène period. The rite of élite burial distinguished by two-wheeled vehicles, which had developed in the Marne and Moselle regions in the late fifth century, was adopted in four peripheral areas: in the Lower Seine Valley, the Ardennes, the Haine, and Yorkshire. What initiated these trends is difficult to say. A population movement is one possibility but is by no means required of the evidence, which could equally well be explained by supposing that local élites with access to the knowledge of vehicle burial (and possibly the vehicles themselves as diplomatic gifts) simply adopted the fashion as a means of self-aggrandizement. Once established it would have generated its own momentum. Other gifts that passed through the exchange network included daggers, swords, shields, and spears, as well as trinkets such as fibulae. All were copied by native craftsmen and accepted into the local repertoire.

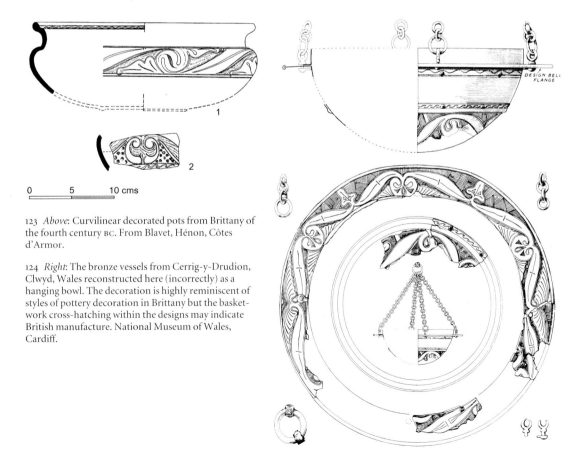

123 *Above*: Curvilinear decorated pots from Brittany of the fourth century BC. From Blavet, Hénon, Côtes d'Armor.

124 *Right*: The bronze vessels from Cerrig-y-Drudion, Clwyd, Wales reconstructed here (incorrectly) as a hanging bowl. The decoration is highly reminiscent of styles of pottery decoration in Brittany but the basket-work cross-hatching within the designs may indicate British manufacture. National Museum of Wales, Cardiff.

It is simplest to see the distribution of these Early La Tène items as reflecting a continuation of the systems which had been established in the succeeding Hallstatt D period. In other words, the pattern of contact in northern France, the Low Countries, and Britain continued little changed over a period spanning the sixth to fourth centuries. Thus the British craftsmen, who in the sixth century began to modify imported Hallstatt D daggers, and were the heirs of the makers of British Hallstatt C swords, were themselves succeeded by craftsmen who responded to new styles of La Tène daggers when they arrived on the island.

For Ireland during this time, the archaeological evidence suggests an altogether different picture. In the Hallstatt C period it is apparent that the island played a significant part in the exchange networks which bound the Atlantic communities together and received an inflow of élite items from west central Europe. The fact that Ireland is specifically named in the *Ora Maritima* is an indication of its prominence. But from the beginning of the sixth century until the end of the second century BC there is little trace of any contact with continental developments, and indeed the dendrochronological evidence shows that over large areas forests were regenerating—an observation suggestive of a dramatic decline in population. In other words, after the sixth century Ireland seems to have become a backwater for almost half a millennium.

The folk movements which were underway by the beginning of the fourth century in west central Europe disrupted the long-established networks of exchange which had developed throughout Europe. In Brittany, north-western France, the Low Countries, and Britain there is a marked diminution in the volume of centrally produced goods and ideas absorbed into local repertoires. Each of the regions developed its own distinctive culture in relative isolation and it is not until the second century that extensive networks of exchange begin to develop once more.

Archaeology and Language

The archaeological evidence from Atlantic Europe for the period from 1300 to 200 BC allows three phases to be recognized. In the first, from c.1300 to c.600, the Atlantic system of exchange was at its most dynamic. During this time the entire system north of Galicia was actively bound in a complex network of reciprocal exchange to the Urnfield and Early Hallstatt systems of west central Europe. Meanwhile in the south of Iberia the Phoenicians and possibly the Greeks were creating ties with the Mediterranean system.

In the second period, from c.600 to c.400, the intensity of the east–west contacts slackened noticeably, with Ireland now left outside the system. This diminution may have been caused by a reorientation with new networks developing through Brittany, linking the West Hallstatt chiefdoms more directly with the metal-rich core of the Atlantic zone. It was at this time that Mediterranean interest in Atlantic products increased.

In the third and final period, *c.*400–*c.*200, with much of Europe in the throes of disruptive migratory movements, the Atlantic system was left to develop without significant external contacts, except for a continued, and possibly increasing, interest by Mediterranean entrepreneurs.

There can be little doubt that the intensity and duration of these reciprocal exchanges between western central Europe and the communities of the Atlantic fringe led to a convergence in many aspects of culture. Similar élite goods were accepted over large areas, technologies and craft skills were shared, and decorative symbols may well have been understood by communities separated by considerable distances. There was also a common attitude to the gods, who required valuable equipment to be deposited in their honour in rivers, bogs, and lakes or raw materials to be buried in the earth. Taken at this level, the degree of cultural similarity over huge territories is remarkable. It is a similarity born of long and intimate contact. All parts of the Atlantic zone as far south as south-western Iberia shared this common culture until the sixth century BC.

So much for archaeology: we must now turn to language. That the Atlantic communities spoke Celtic is well established. The generally accepted view is that the Celtic spoken in Ireland was an early form of Celtic—Goidelic or Q-Celtic—whereas in the British Isles and France the later Brythonic or P-Celtic was dominant. If the difference between Q-Celtic and P-Celtic is significant and if that difference has chronological implications, then one reasonable interpretation would be that Ireland received its Celtic language roughly at the same time as the rest of the Atlantic zone but did not share in the development or spread of the later form of P-Celtic which replaced the earlier linguistic form in France and the British Isles.

The possible correlation of archaeological and linguistic data is self-evident. The question which arises is whether the network of cultural interrelationships, so clearly demonstrated for the entire region in the period *c.*1300–600, provides a suitable context for the Celtic language in its more archaic form to spread from its west central European homeland to the Atlantic zone without having to invoke the *deus ex machina* of 'invasion' or 'folk movement'? The acceptance of élite systems and their symbolism and the sharing of complex technologies, as well as religious concepts and practice, imply ease of communication. It is not at all unreasonable to suppose that it was within this context that the Celtic languages became widely adopted in the west.

This view, of the progressive celticization of the Atlantic province, could also help to account for the development of an early form of Celtic in the Iberian Peninsula. If Celtic was the lingua franca of the Atlantic sea-ways, it may have been from the western coasts of Iberia that the inland Celtiberians developed their language and the Lusitanians theirs. Herodotus may not have been so misinformed when, in the fifth century, he wrote that the Celts were the most westerly people in Europe next to the Cynetes (who occupied southern Portugal).

After the re-formation of the sixth century, the cultural isolation of Ireland will have ensured that the more developed form of Celtic did not penetrate to a degree sufficient to alter the established forms, whereas in Britain and Armorica and the rest of western France, two more centuries of continuing contact with the innovating areas of west central Europe brought in new forms enhancing and modifying the Celticness of an already thoroughly celticized zone.

Regional Variations among the Communities of the Atlantic Zone

In spite of the broad similarities which bound them, the communities of the Atlantic fringe exhibited a considerable cultural variety. Some aspects of this are worth considering to provide an indication of the diverse social systems which could exist in peripheral areas away from the main centres of innovation and movement.

The metal-rich core provides a good starting-point. The Armorican peninsula, south-western Britain, south Wales, and southern Ireland—all essentially peninsulas surrounded by the Atlantic—share many physical characteristics in common, and aspects of their culture suggest that links between them were maintained throughout much of the formative period (1300–600 BC), though little is known of southern Ireland after this.

Culturally the communities of the Armorican peninsula provided the focus, especially after the sixth century BC, when close contacts developed with west central Europe and, as we have argued above, the symbols and grammar of Celtic art were readily adopted by local craftsmen. It was during this time that a distinctive Armorican Iron Age culture developed among a population concentrated more in the coastal zone than in the centre of the peninsula. The principal settlement form was the enclosed farmstead of family or extended family type, comprising one or more small subrectangular houses. Some larger and more complex sites may represent a hierarchic structure. A frequently occurring feature is the souterrain—an elongated chamber or series of chambers tunnelled out of the soft bedrock and entered from the surface through one or more shafts. The function of souterrains is much debated, but the explanation most likely lies in a storage use, possibly involving a belief in the power of the chthonic deities to preserve and protect stored commodities. The distribution of souterrains, which have been found in considerable number in Brittany (largely because tractors

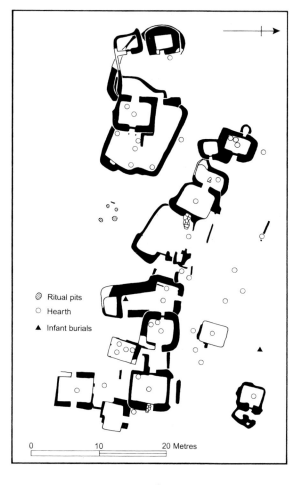

125 The village at Goulvars on the Quiberon peninsula, Morbihan, Brittany. The rectangular style of house-building is typical of the La Tène period in Armorica.

⊘ Ritual pits
○ Hearth
▲ Infant burials

0   10   20 Metres

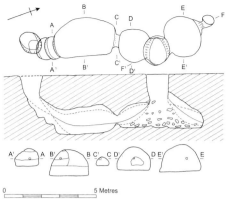

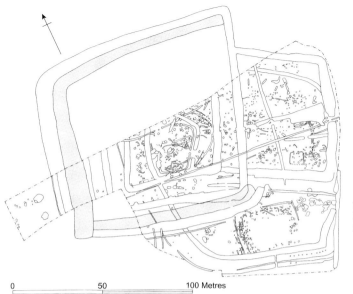

127 *Above*: Souterrain at Lauban en Kerfourn, Morbihan, Brittany. These underground chambers may have been used for storage, perhaps of seed grain.

126 *Left*: The defended settlement of Saint-Symphorien, Côtes d'Armor, in Brittany, was discovered during road-building and has been the scene of a major excavation. It is a complex multiperiod site of the La Tène period. Among the finds was a stone carving of a god playing a lyre.

128 *Below*: The distribution of souterrains in Brittany reflects the distribution of known settlements of the Middle La Tène period, since, where excavation has been on a sufficient scale, they are usually found to be a component of rural settlements.

introduced particularly in the post-war period caused the hollowed chambers to collapse) provides a striking impression of the extent of the classic Armorican Iron Age culture and its sharp boundary with the rest of France.

The second settlement type is the defended coastal promontory, generally called cliff-castles (Pl. XVII). These occur in some numbers, particularly around the northern and western coasts. Little is known of their internal features or chronology, but it is clear from Caesar's accounts of his Armorican campaign in the mid-first century BC that cliff-castles were widely used at that time. While it is possible that their substantial defences endowed them with a higher social status than the more normal farmsteads, there is no direct evidence that this was so and a ritual function is not unlikely.

Another highly distinctive aspect of the Armorican Iron Age is the prominence of standing stones (stelae) scattered widely in the landscape. Of the many hundreds which are known, two types can be distinguished: tall pillar-like stelae and shorter hemispherical stones. All were worked with some care to create smooth surfaces, the tall types being columnar, faceted, or ridged. A few, most notably the low stela from Kermaria, near Pont-L'Abbé, and the tall example from Sainte-Anne-en-Trégastel, were carved with curvilinear and rectilinear designs, a reminder that many of the others could also have

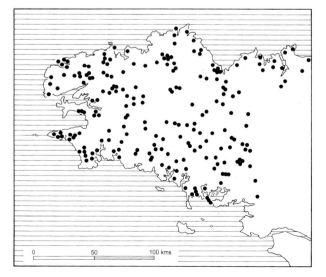

been decorated with paint. The function of the stelae is unknown, but their prominence in the landscape may suggest that they served as religious foci or boundary markers, perhaps both. The distribution of these stones is closely comparable to that of the souterrains, the two features serving to define western Armorica as a culturally distinct zone.

The culture of the south-western peninsula of Britain reflects that of Armorica but has its own defining characteristics. There is a preference here for pottery decorated with curvilinear motifs, though the British south-western decorated wares are less exuberant and refined than contemporary Breton wares.

The settlement pattern has close similarities to that of Armorica, with defended enclosures for the family or extended family (in Cornwall called 'rounds') and cliff-castles around the coasts. In Devon the rather more elaborate multivallate enclosures, usually sited on hill slopes not far from a permanent water supply, might suggest a different kind of social organization, perhaps based on the importance of cattle. Underground stone-built storage chambers, called fogous, are the Cornish equivalent to the Breton souterrains.

129 An Iron Age stela from Kermaria en Pont-L'Abbé, Finistère, France, is one of a small group of decorated stelae from Brittany. The style suggests that it may be of fourth century BC date. A very large number of other stelae exist in Brittany, but, though carefully finished, they are usually plain.

Much the same array of settlement types occurs across the Severn Estuary in south Wales, extending across to the south-west of the country. Here the enclosed homestead type is characterized by Walesland Rath (rath being the generic name for this type of enclosure in Wales and Ireland), where total excavation demonstrated a simple arrangement of circular houses in the centre with storage buildings around the periphery, the individual structures being replaced on a number of occasions. The material culture of the south Welsh Iron

Age communities is not prolific but includes the sporadic use of decorated pottery imported from across the Severn.

The one noticeable difference between Armorica and the British south-western communities is the absence of stelae, though the possibility must be allowed that in Britain a similar socio-religious function may have been served by wooden pillars no longer extant.

Ireland remains something of a mystery in this period, but certain characteristics link it culturally to the communities of the south-west. Cliff-castles, all undated, occur around all the coasts, particularly the south and west, and a small number of carved stone stelae have been recovered, the best known and most elaborate being the Turoe stone from Co. Galway. One structural feature, which has been much debated, is the *chevaux de frise*—a zone of close-spaced angular stones laid out in advance of the walls or ramparts of fortified enclosures. One of the most dramatic example of this from Ireland is at Dun Aengus on the Aran Island of Inishmore (Pl. XVII*a* and *b*). Other examples are known in the west of Ireland, north-west Britain, and south Wales, and are closely comparable to sites in north-west and central northern Iberia. It is tempting to suggest an Atlantic origin and dissemination of this style of defensive definition, but the angular stones may be nothing more than local manifestations of a more widespread system employing sharpened wooden stakes, an impressive example of which has been excavated at Castell Henllys in south-west Wales.

The great stone-built fort of Dun Aengus is one of a group of stone forts focused on the Aran Islands and the nearby limestone uplands of the Burran. Although similarities in style were conditioned by the use of limestone for building, these western stone forts must reflect a strong local cultural tradition as well

130 Aerial view of Clovelly Dykes, north Devon, England. The many lines of roughly concentric earthworks are typical of the 'multiple-enclosure' forts of south-western Britain. Some of the enclosures may have served as paddocks for cattle.

131 The landscape of south-west Wales is scattered with small defended enclosures called raths. Walesland Rath in Dyfed is one of the few excavated examples. The central area was occupied by a succession of circular houses, while around the perimeter were arranged four-post storage structures. Occupation spanned the third and second centuries BC.

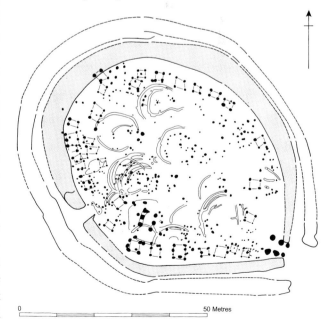

0   50 Metres

as the ability of society to mobilize labour on a massive scale. Little dating evidence has yet been obtained except at Dun Aengus where it can be shown that the site began its life as an extensive settlement in the Late Bronze Age before the massive stone walls were erected.

The northern extension of the Atlantic zone leads to the west and north coasts of Scotland and the Islands—the Inner and Outer Hebrides, the Ork-

132 Granite monolith from Turoe, Co. Galway, Ireland carved in a curvilinear style which suggests a possible date in the first century BC.

neys, and the Shetlands. This zone shares a cohesive culture which can be called that of Atlantic Scotland. Its most notable characteristic is the proliferation of massive stone-built settlements—brochs or duns—in which the desire to monumentalize by grandiose building has gone far beyond the need for physical comfort or even protection. These structures are clearly a statement symbolic of the social status claimed by the lineages who occupied them. At what stage this monumentalization began is not easy to define, but there is sufficient evidence now available to show that the structural tradition can be traced back to the Late Bronze Age. The material culture of Atlantic Scotland is limited and indigenous in the extreme, suggesting a high degree of cultural isolation throughout most of the Iron Age, though there is evidence of developing contact along the Atlantic sea-ways in and after the first century BC.

This brief review of the north-western part of the communities of the Atlantic zone has shown something of the variety of cultural responses reflected in the archaeological evidence. The clear impression given is of a cultural focus in Armorica linked to mainstream European development with increasing regionalism and increasing isolation the further one ventured north. The one essential characteristic binding these communities together was a similar social structure based on the family unit or lineage group. There may, in some regions, have been variations in status or communal works such as hilltop enclosures, perhaps defining the meeting places of the larger community at annual festivals when flocks and herds needed to be gathered in, but evidence for large agglomerations of population is noticeably absent.

The eastern part of Britain, from the Yorkshire Moors to the Thames Valley, presents a very varied landscape, divided by a number of large rivers flowing eastwards into the North Sea. Within this zone a broad cultural similarity can be recognized, although regional variations persist. In the ninth and eighth centuries a glimpse of an élite society is provided by large, circular, defended enclosures containing substantial circular houses. A little later, from the fifth to the third centuries, the distribution of locally made daggers and anthropoid hilted swords, centred within this zone, is a further indication of a privileged class served by able and inventive craftsmen.

Broch of Mousa, Shetland

Broch of Dun Troddan, Inverr

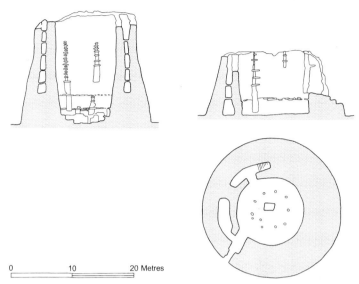

0   10   20 Metres

133 The brochs of Scotland and the Scottish islands reflect a local tradition of house-building in which the simple idea of the circular house has been transformed into a massive walled structure sometimes of tower-like proportions far outgrowing defensive needs. Brochs may have originated as early as the fifth century BC and may have continued to develop at least to the first century BC.

In the late fifth, or early fourth century, the élite occupying the area of the Yorkshire wolds, just north of the Humber, adopted the burial practice of their peers in northern France and the Low Countries—the burial of a two-wheeled vehicle and an array of personal gear with the dead man or woman and the definition of individual burials by placing them within square ditched enclosures. The practice, once introduced, persisted at least into the second century BC.

Continued contact with the Continent brought to Britain items of metalwork decorated in the Vegetal Style. These were copied and developed by local craftsmen producing prestige goods for the élite of eastern Britain throughout the third and second centuries. For the most part it was the equipment of the warrior that was selected for embellishment, in particular sword scabbards like those from Wisbech, Cambridgeshire, Standlake, Oxfordshire, the River Witham near Lincoln, and the élite burial at Wetwang Slack in the Yorkshire wolds. A few decorated shields are also known, including the bosses from the Thames at Wandsworth and from the River Witham. It is also possible that the decorated pony cap from Torrs in Scotland, together with the engraved drinking-horn terminals, which had at some stage been incongruously attached to it, were products of eastern British craftsmen. Most of these valuable products were dedicated to the gods of rivers, but a few accompanied prominent people to their graves. Among these we may include, in addition to the Wetwang Slack sword, a decorated canister, also from a grave at Wetwang Slack, and an armlet, from what was probably a female burial, found at Newnham Croft in Cambridgeshire. The corpus of the surviving material is impressive and leaves little doubt that the socially varied communities of eastern Britain were dominated by élites served by skilled craftsmen in much the same way as their continental neighbours.

161

The settlement pattern, as it is at present known, throws little light on social status after the eighth century. Enclosed homesteads are known but a number of much larger and more straggling settlements have been discovered, suggesting sizeable communities, of village-like proportions and complexity. Settlements in the Yorkshire wolds have been found to extend for considerable distances along the principal trackways.

The social systems in eastern Britain, with their élite gear and nucleated settlements, contrast noticeably with those of the west, but are far more closely paralleled by those of northern France and Belgium, where the distribution of prestige warrior metalwork, the vehicle burials of the Lower Seine, the Haine, and the Ardennes, and large open settlements like Haps in the Netherlands reflect, though with regional differences, much the same overall structure.

A third area of Britain—the central southern zone—presents an altogether different picture to that of both the west and the east. Its most obvious characteristic is the dominance of hill forts—hilltops of some 5-10 hectares enclosed by substantial defences sometimes multivallate and with elaborate entrance earthworks. The hill-fort-dominated central southern zone extends from the south coast, between Devon and East Sussex, in a band of decreasing width to north Wales, with outliers spreading into Northamptonshire. It is a region of different landscapes and encompasses a number of communities demonstrating their separateness through different styles of pottery decoration: the common link between them is the hill fort.

134 *Top, left:* Bronze sword scabbard found at Wisbech, Cambridgeshire, England. The decoration is a rather faltering British version of the Vegetal Style and probably dates to the third century BC. Wisbech and Fenland Museum Cambridgeshire.

135 *Left, and below left:* Bronze sword scabbard sheath from the River Thames at Standlake, Oxfordshire, England showing the Vegetal Style of decoration. The basketry cross-hatching on the upper mount is typically British. Late fourth or early third century BC. Ashmolean Museum, Oxford.

136 *Right:* Bronze shield boss from the River Thames at Wandsworth, Middlesex, England. The decoration resolves itself into two birds with wings stretched. It is brilliantly executed in a combination of repoussé and incision. Second century BC?

Although a number of excavations have shown something of the variety within the general 'hill-fort' category, some generalizations can be offered. The earliest of the forts at present known, dating to the end of the Bronze Age, concentrate in the Welsh borderland, but by the sixth century the phenomenon has spread to the Wessex region, extending into the south-east (Surrey and Kent) by the third century. In some areas, such as central Wessex, it is possible to show that over time the number of forts in active use decreased, but the strength of those surviving, and the intensity of their use, was enhanced.

Functionally, the forts seem to have served their region in a variety of ways, providing central places where the different needs of the community could be articulated. Some, like Danebury and Maiden Castle, were intensively used for settlement, production, and storage on a large scale. The extent to which the forts were designed to provide defence is debatable. The enclosing earthworks and the structure of the developed gates would certainly have offered efficient protection, but there may well have been an element of display involved. However, that some were actually defended and attacked is clear from the excavated evidence. At Danebury, for example, large numbers of sling stones were hoarded on at least two separate occasions, in the third century and again in the early first century, and after both phases there is evidence of burning at the gates, the last burning marking the abandonment of the fort. Other forts offer similar evidence, and at Bredon Hill in Gloucestershire the mutilated remains of bodies were found at the entrance.

137 Pony cap with drinking horn terminals attached from Torrs, Dumfries and Galloway, Scotland, as originally found. The decorated terminals of the two drinking horns had been attached at some date to a repoussé-decorated pony cap. Though the context of the curious marriage of these disparate items is uncertain, the style of both elements is typical of that of a skilled school of craftsmen working in eastern Britain in the third or second century BC. National Museum of Scotland, Edinburgh.

The hill forts are only one aspect of the settlement pattern. Elsewhere the contemporary countryside was densely scattered with farmsteads, many of which showed continuous occupation over centuries. Most of the farmsteads seem to have been of family size and were therefore probably centres of single estates practising a mixed farming with a heavy emphasis on cereal production; a few larger agglomerations indicate a scatter of more substantial communities.

Apart from the massive nature of the hill forts, there is very little evidence in this central southern zone for a hierarchy or an élite, but the heavy emphasis on the intensive working of the land and the production of grain might indicate that status was measured by land or livestock. In the second century the two-wheeled chariot, represented by decorated bronze fittings for the vehicle and the bronze harness attachments for the horses, becomes far more evident. Whether the vehicle was simply an indication of status or a means of warfare is impossible to say, but most likely it served as both. The virtual absence of elab-

138 The Iron Age hillfort of Uffington Castle, Berkshire, England, with the carved hill figure—the White Horse of Uffington—nearby. The hill fort was constructed in the sixth or fifth century BC and subsequently modified when one of its gates was blocked. The hill figure has been suggested, on the basis of some scientific dating evidence, to be a little earlier in origin.

orate weaponry is at first sight puzzling, but it could be that this was simply a reflection of the fact that prestige weapons were not consigned to rivers or burials within this region and therefore stood less chance of survival.

The developments in central southern Britain are in marked contrast to those in the west and east. One possible explanation is that the central southern zone was a border region between the metal-producing west and the warrior élites of the east. The instability of such a region, perhaps under threat of continuous raids from the eastern zone, may well have led to the need to develop and maintain fortifications.

Similar hill-fort-dominated zones dating to the fourth to second centuries can be seen elsewhere in west central Europe, especially in the region between Trier and the Rhineland, where again it could be their border position, between the fully developed La Tène warrior élites in the south and zones with totally different socio-economic systems to the north, that created a 'marcher' society.

The western coastal area of France from the Charante southwards to the Pyrenees has produced a varied range of archaeological evidence for the period 1300–200 BC. It is, however, clear from the distribution of Late Bronze Age tools and weapons that the region played a significant part in the networks of exchange during this period, and the Garonne–Gironde axis provided an easy route linking the Atlantic to the Mediterranean. It was certainly an important corridor for the trans-shipment of tin after the sixth century.

In the sixth and fifth centuries a distinctive Aquitanian culture can be recognized, largely from the evidence of cremation cemeteries. Grave goods included local versions of anthropoid hilted swords and fibulae with elongated springs and ornamented feet. Although both types are local products, they were evidently inspired by widely distributed west central European forms. What is more significant perhaps are the general similarities which the Aquitanian forms share with those south of the Pyrenees in north-west and north central Iberia. The two regions must have shared systems of exchange linking them through the western Pyrenean passes.

The discovery of a remarkable series of gold torcs in Haute-Garonne, Tarn, and Gironde, dating to the third and second centuries, decorated in an exuberant form of plastic art, has been linked to the possible migration of Tectosages in the aftermath of the Celtic expedition into Greece. Whatever the origin of the inspiration for these pieces (and Middle Danube parallels can be quoted), they are likely to have been of local manufacture, utilizing gold extracted from the gold-rich sands of the Tarn Valley. The social context of these items is obscure, but their discovery in hoards suggests a religious motivation for their deposition, although this does not exclude their production under élite patronage.

To what extent these western French communities had become celticized it is debatable, but the fact that Caesar regarded them as ethnically separate from the Celts of Gaul may suggest that they retained a strong indigenous identity throughout.

Although the Iberian Peninsula has already been considered separately in Chapter 7, it is necessary here to offer a brief comment on the cultural development of the north-west—the area of present-day Galicia. The area is rich in metals, in particular tin and gold, for both of which it became famous in the ancient world. Its cultural links were, traditionally, Atlantic, although during the first millennium a series of closer contacts developed with the Celtiberian peoples of the interior. The socio-economic system seems to have become warrior-based, the most evident settlements being the fortified hilltop enclosures, known locally as castros which gave the culture its archaeological name—the 'Castro culture'. Stone-built round houses, which

139 In central southern Britain, in a zone spreading from the south coast of England to the north of Wales, strongly defended hill forts dominated the Iron Age landscape in the period from the sixth to first centuries BC. Not all hill forts were in use for the whole time. After the early third century a few sites rose to dominance while the rest were abandoned. The hill-fort-dominated zone may have been a 'marcher' area between the Atlantic communities of the west and the more socially complex communities of the eastern zone.

* 3-15 acres
○ over 15 acres

0   200 kms

140 The *oppidum* of Citânia de Sanfins, Paços de Ferreira, Portugal, is one of the best known of the castros of northern Portugal and north-west Spain. The defences enclose an area of 15 hectares. The careful internal planning is based on a main north–south street with side streets dividing the interior into eighteen rectangular 'insulae' which are subdivided into smaller units for the individual households. Regular planning of this type was learned from the Romans who, by the end of the second century BC, had established themselves over much of Iberia. The individual houses of circular plan and their method of construction were, however, entirely native.

dominate the settlement pattern, and the use of *chevaux de frise* around some of the castros, have been used to stress the cultural links between Galicia and the northern areas of the Atlantic province, but how significant these structural similarities are it is difficult to judge. Recent work on the Castro culture has shown it to have been an indigenous development rooted in the second millennium. Many settlements originated in the period 1000–700 BC at a time when maritime links generated by the exchange of metals were strong. From about 700 BC Phoenician influences show that the indigenous culture was being progressively integrated into Mediterranean systems. After the middle of the millennium regional differentiation becomes apparent among the settlements, and at some the extension of their boundaries suggests an increase in population. Parallel with this it is possible to detect an increase in items of both male and female prestige and the appearance of rather closer cultural links with the communities of the Meseta which might be related to the folk movements of the Turduli and Celti towards the north-west referred to by Strabo. Increasing contact with the Roman world, particularly after the campaign of Decimus Brutus in the region in 138–6 BC, provided the stimulus for further change. It was at this time that those settlements in favoured positions began to take on

166

distinctly urban characteristics, with well-defined street grids and public open spaces.

Taken together, the array of disparate evidence for the communities of the Atlantic zone, presented in summary here, emphasizes the highly individual nature of each of the major regions within this broad Celtic-speaking zone. Maritime links bound them in systems of reciprocal exchange which waxed and waned as internal and external stimuli had their different effects. Superimposed upon this was a network of east–west contacts, linking the Atlantic to the developments of the La Tène cultural heartland of west central Europe. Each of the Atlantic cultures responded in an individual way.

9

The Communities of the Eastern Fringes

THE classical sources and the archaeological evidence taken together leave little doubt that by the end of the fourth century BC Celtic communities were well established in the lands of the Middle Danube and some groups seem to have moved eastwards from the Tiza into Transylvania. As a generalization we can regard the Carpathian mountain range, which swings in a broad arc south then west to join the mountains of the Balkans, as the effective limit of expansion by the mid-fourth century. The Iron Gates—the gorge through which the Danube flows from its middle reaches to the lower part of its valley, where it now defines much of the border between Serbia and Romania—were still, at this stage, closed to Celtic expansion.

Eastern Europe before the Celts

The cultural development of eastern and south-eastern Europe beyond this mountain barrier was complex. The most potent force was, of course, that of the Greek city states, which, standing together in the period 513–479 BC, had managed to halt the western advance of the Persian armies under first Darius and later Xerxes. This episode, which saw a massive Persian presence in the Lower Danube Valley for much of the forty years of threat, had a significant effect on the development of Thracian society. The Persian Grand Army moved with its treasure and its finery and an entourage of craftsmen who could serve the needs of the élite. Inevitably the Thracians were to learn much from the example: eastern values and the accompanying symbolism were adopted and adapted by the local craftsmen to serve their own masters, and there emerged a highly distinctive regional style of aristocratic metalwork in silver and silver-gilt, blending ideas derived from the east, from the nomadic cultures of the steppe, and from the Greek cities which fringed the western shores of the Black Sea. Thracian art, in its fourth–second century manifestation, was the eastern counterpart of Celtic art and is its equal as one of the great indigenous artistic developments of late prehistoric Europe.

The Greek cities of the western Black Sea coast provided an interface with the Greek world through which a wide range of raw materials and products could be exchanged. After the Persian incident, trade intensified: corn, slaves, furs, and metals flowed out of the Thracian hinterland and wine and prestige goods of Greek manufacture flowed in. As Thucydides noted: 'you can accomplish nothing with the Thracians without giving gifts.' It was a situation with many parallels in the west Mediterranean and in Iberia, and it was during this period that the Thracian élite began to become archaeologically recognizable through their elaborate burials richly furnished with the accoutrements of status and wealth. No doubt the competition engendered would frequently have expressed itself in raiding and more extended bouts of warfare. The impression given by the designs on the prestige metalwork of the period is of an élite intimately involved with feasting and hunting. These pursuits—statements of nobility and prowess—were as much a part of the Thracian social fabric as the raid was of the Celtic.

By the beginning of the fourth century BC it is possible to identify distinct 'kingdoms' and their kings. One of the most powerful were the Odrysae of central Thrace, whose close links with Athens, both political and economic, contributed to their strength and ascendancy. In the early fourth century one of their kings, Kotys, seems to have been acknowledged by other lesser polities as having extensive powers beyond the territorial limits of his own kingdom.

141 Bridal decoration in silver-gilt from Letnitsa, Bulgaria, showing a Thracian rider wearing scale armour. The rider's hair is tied in a topknot—a style noted as Thracian by Homer in *The Iliad*. The horseman warrior, sometimes a rider god, is a frequent motif in Thracian art. Narodnija Archeologičeski Museg, Sofia.

The broadly defined Thracian culture, within which at this stage we can include other specific groups named by the classical authors such as the Getae and Dacians, extended northwards along the coast of the Black Sea into Moldova. Beyond this, stretching around the northern shores of the Black Sea in the vast expanse of the Pontic Steppe, a somewhat different cultural configuration was developing which can, for convenience, be called Scythian or Scythio-Sarmatian. We saw earlier (pp. 46–7) that this region had been occupied by nomadic and semi-nomadic groups known to the classical writers as Cimmerians but that during the eighth century BC they were coming under increasing pressure from groups living on the Volga who, historically, were called Scythians. The picture given by Herodotus of the replacement of the Cimmerians by the Scythians is a considerable oversimplification and may have been little more than the movement of a Scythian élite westwards into the northern Pontic zone. What is clear, however, is that the eighth and early seventh centuries were a period of upheaval and folk movement which resulted in hoards of dislocated horse-riding warriors, distinguished as Cimmerians and Scythians by contemporary sources, pouring through the Caucasus southwards into Asia Minor, where they became involved as mercenaries and freebooters in the struggle between the Assyrians and the kingdom of Uratu.

By the sixth century the 'Royal Scyths' were firmly established in the Crimea and in the steppe zone to the north and, through the Greek colony of Olbia at the mouth of the Bug, had developed close contacts with the Greek world, with which a lively trade developed. The highly skilled craftsmen working throughout the length of this Greek interface produced a range of exquisite items, most notably in gold, for the Scythian élite who were buried in the great royal tombs such as Čhertomlyk and Solocha. When Herodotus visited Olbia in about 450 he was able to observe Scythian culture at first hand and to provide a vivid description of the complex processes involved in the burial of the Royal Scyths.

Scythian culture developed a distinctive and original character in the sixth and fifth centuries, and many aspects of this northern Pontic culture spread south, to be absorbed into the eclectic culture of the Thracian tribes, and west into the Middle Danube region, especially into the Great Hungarian Plain and Transylvania. These influences may have been the result of the migratory movements of populations or élites or simply of intensifying systems of exchange. By the fifth century, however, many of the communities of the Great Hungarian Plain, extending westwards along the Danube into Slovakia, had adopted a style of horse-riding and a material culture which bore many similarities to that of the people living around the Black Sea fringe.

The pattern of folk movement from the east, reflected in the early movement of Scythians from the Volga to the northern Pontic zone, was repeated again at the end of the fifth century BC, when the Sauromatae (Sarmatians), who emerged as an ethnically identifiable group in the region east of the Don, moved westwards into Scythian territory. One classical text, Pseudo-Hippocrates, suggests that this expansion took place about 400 BC. Certainly, by 338 another text, Pseudo-Scylax, could refer to the *Syrmatai* as the tribe now occupying the old Scythian lands west of the Don. That the transference of power was not peaceful is suggested by the archaeological evidence, which shows that a number of Scythian settlements on the Lower Dnieper were destroyed in the late fifth or early fourth century. Whilst there may well not have been a significant replacement of population, it is clear that the Scythian élite—the Royal Scyths—were ousted from much of the territory; some retained power in the Crimea while others established themselves in the Dobruja at the Danube mouth, whence it seems that forays were made deeper into Thracian lands. What emerged in the Pontic Steppe was a complex culture deeply rooted in indigenous systems, which can best be called Scytho-Sarmatian.

The political and social upheaval around 400 BC dislocated the economic systems which sustained the port city of Olbia. Cut off from its traditional customers on the mid-Dnieper and from the exchange networks which brought raw materials from the Urals and beyond, the city suffered a decline, though it maintained control of the coastal strip between the estuaries of the Dnieper and the Dniester.

The growth of Macedon as a significant political and military force in the area began in the mid-fourth century BC, when, under Philip II (359–336), Macedonia began to expand northwards into Thrace. Expansion continued with Alexander, who, in 335, crossed the Danube to lead his armies against the Getae, and it was on this occasion that his famous meeting with the embassy of Celtic chieftains took place. After Alexander's departure to the east in 334 the Macedonian interest in the north continued, and in 331 (or 326) detachments of Scytho-Sarmatians came to the aid of Olbia, when Zopyrion, one of Alexander's generals, then governor of Thrace, mounted an attack on the now weakened city.

In the political and social chaos which followed Alexander's death in 323 the Macedonian hold on Thrace collapsed. The power vacuum was to some extent filled by the rise of the Odrysae, who, under their king Seuthes III, made good use of their central position in the Balkans to command the trade which was intensifying with Greece, particularly along the Maritsa valley route. Even so the sudden demise of the power of Macedon, which had to a large extent held south-eastern Europe in a state of stable equilibrium, created an entirely changed situation which, as we saw in Chapter 4, provided new opportunities for Celtic expansion.

Asia Minor before the Celts

In Asia Minor the ethnic and political situation was no less complex. In the period of turmoil which followed the collapse of the Mycenaean system, migrating communities moved from Europe into Asia Minor, trekking across the Hellespont or sailing the Aegean. It was in this way that the early Greeks established their colonies along the Aegean coast. One of the migrating groups was the Phrygians, whose homeland is thought to have been Thrace. It is possible that they were involved in the destruction of Troy VIIa and the Hittite capital of Hattusa some time about 1180 BC at the time of their settlement in north central Asia Minor. They became archaeologically recognizable by the middle of the eighth century, and in the period c.725–675 the Phrygian empire had developed into a regional power, under King Midas, with its capital at Gordion. The stability of the area was undermined by the conflicts between Assyria and Uratu and by the incursions of horse-riding hordes from the Pontic Steppe (the Cimmerians and Scythians) at the beginning of the seventh century. At this time Gordion was destroyed by Cimmerians and the power of the Phrygians collapsed. Many factors—the rise of the Greek cities on the west and north coasts, the land-locked nature of their territory, the comparatively poor quality of the land, and the eventual dominance of Persia—contributed to the Phrygian decline. By the third century they were regarded as effete, good only at embroidery and best used as slaves.

The degree of stability which had been maintained in Asia Minor by the Persian domination after the mid-sixth century was finally shattered by Alexander's 'liberation' and by the chaos of rivalries left in the wake of Alexander's death. After c.330 BC Asia Minor, like the Balkans and the Pontic zone, was destabilized to such an extent that migrant Celts would find little resistance and even, in some regions, a misguided welcome. This opportunity, together with continued population pressures in their homelands, were two of the more significant factors that encouraged the eastern advance of the Celtic tribes.

In Chapter 4 we outlined the main historical framework for the Celtic presence in the east. Populations and bands of fighting men moved comparatively freely over large territories. They came from the mid-Danube region, and, while identified as Celts, or more usually Gauls or Galatians, by the historical sources, they are likely to have been of mixed ethnicity. Intermarriage and allegiances will undoubtedly have made the Celts who moved into the Balkans and Asia Minor significantly different from those who a century earlier had penetrated the Po Valley. None the less, since they were recognized as 'Celtic' by their contemporaries and, some at least, appear to have spoken a Celtic language, we may legitimately consider them here.

Celtic Settlement in Thrace

The Celtic expansion from the Middle Danube was underway in the early third century. In 281 BC, in a major thrust to the south and east, the capital of the Odrysae at Seuthopolis was sacked and the way was clear for the historic attack on Delphi. It was in the aftermath of the expedition into Greece that a Celtic settlement, the kingdom of Tylis, was established in Thrace. According to Polybius, the kingdom was not far from Byzantium, but a later source, Stephen of Byzantium, says that Tylis was further away near Mount Balkan. It is difficult to

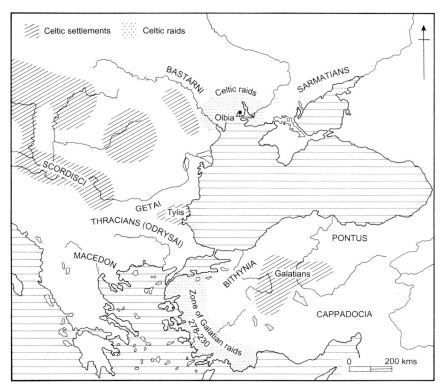

142 Map to illustrate the principal areas of Celtic settlement in eastern Europe and Asia Minor and the neighbouring political or tribal entities.

offer greater precision and the thin scatter of items of La Tène metalwork are no sure guide. Indeed it is possible that throughout the third century the Celts maintained a high degree of mobility within a much larger territory. Certainly in 227 BC one group had reached Chersonesos (Gallipoli) but was defeated by Antigonos II. At any event, Celtic power in Thrace was finally destroyed in 213–12 BC.

Since the Celtic presence in Thrace lasted for only two generations, it is unlikely to have left any substantial trace, nor is there any reason to suppose that its material culture was closely comparable to that of the west central European La Tène culture. The few La Tène objects recovered from Thrace need be little more than gifts arriving by exchange from the west, and their distribution does not necessarily reflect that of the Celtic group.

One outstanding discovery does, however, deserve mention. At Mezek, in the valley of the Maritsa River, which runs south through the Rhodope mountains, a settlement and cemetery were discovered. The principal tomb was a tholos type, with a circular corbelled chamber (the tholos proper) reached by a long passage or *dromos*, the entire structure being embedded within a substantial tumulus. The style

143 The Thracian tholos tomb of Mal-tepe, Mezek, Bulgaria. It was possibly reused for a Celtic burial in the third century BC.

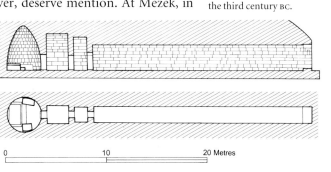

of the burial is Thracian, its architectural refinement being the result of techniques coming ultimately from the Greek world. The original burial, dating to the end of the fourth century BC, is likely to have been of a Thracian chieftain but the tomb was later used for a second burial in the third century. The new interment was accompanied by a group of decorated bronze fittings appropriate to a chariot, which may well have been placed in the grave. Stylistically the fittings are Celtic and may be paralleled by contemporary material found in Bohemia and Moravia.

The Mezek 'chariot burial' nicely points up the problem. Was it the burial of a Celtic chieftain, his lineage laying claim to territorial legitimacy by choosing

144 Linch pin and other fittings from the third century BC burial in the Thracian tomb of Mezek, Bulgaria. Narodnija Archeologičeski Muzeg, Sofia.

an indigenous royal tomb for the interment, was the chariot a diplomatic gift from a Celt to a Thracian, or was it a Celtic chariot captured by a Thracian? There is, of course, no certain answer, but the questions highlight the complex of relationships which could have occurred between Celt and Thracian in the region during the third century. The absence of any systematic body of archaeological evidence and the lack of anything more than a few passing references in contemporary sources make it impossible to assess the nature or extent of Celtic settlement in Thrace or of its impact on Thracian culture.

Celts in the Pontic Region

That groups of Celts moved east of the Carpathians into the Ukraine and Moldova now seems tolerably certain, since their presence is specifically mentioned on a marble inscription from Olbia put up in honour of Protogenes. It is dated to the late third or early second century BC but may well be referring to events earlier in the third century—a time of great instability in the region. It records that 'The Galatians and Scirians had formed a union and had assembled large forces and intended to arrive in the winter' and that 'The Thisamatiae, Scythians and Saudaratae, who were likewise afraid of the Galatians' savagery, sought shelter within the city walls.' Protogenes, one of the wealthy inhabitants of the city, received his honour for paying for the building of a defensive wall along the river and port side of the city, which had previously been unprotected.

145 Bronze coin of the Bosporan king, Leucon II. Although the symbols are the subject of debate, the shield resembles the Celtic-style long shield. The use of these weapons as symbols could reflect an unrecorded event when Celtic peoples came into contact with the Bosporan kingdom. National Museum, Moscow.

Additional evidence of a Celtic presence is provided by a number of Celto-Illyrian hydronyms and place names such as Gallitsyja and Galich found in western Ukraine which are suggestive of settlement on a more permanent basis than that of merely a roving war band.

The archaeological record is also informative, producing an array of La Tène metalwork, mainly brooches and bracelets, of which a significant number came from Scythian graves. Among the more diagnostic of the metalwork are items belonging to the Duchcov–Münsingen phase dating from the mid-fourth century to roughly the middle of the third century, spanning the period of the historical migrations of the Celts into Greece and Asia Minor.

If we accept the presence of a Celtic population in the Moldova–Ukraine region, the question arises from which direction did they come? One possibility is that it was a northwards move from Thrace, but it is equally possible that the penetration came from the west from the area of Celtic settlement in Transylvania. At any event it was probably the state of disruption caused by the Sarmatian destruction of Great Scythia that provided the opportunity. Another group which took advantage of these troubled times was the Bastarnae, probably of Germanic origin, who are first mentioned in the region in the later third century. It may have been they who constrained the opportunities for a further and more intensive Celtic penetration.

The nature of the Celtic presence in the northern Black Sea littoral is unclear.

175

146 A plaque of bronze inset with enamel from Kerch, Ukraine. First century AD showing the influence of motifs adapted from Celtic art. Ashmolean Museum Oxford.

The place names and the Protogenes inscription show that they remained a cohesive entity, but the archaeological evidence could imply at least a degree of assimilation in the confused Sarmato-Scythian culture of the region. The Celtic swords in Scythian graves, like that at Verkhnjaja Tarasovka in the Lower Dnieper Valley and the Celtic fibulae and bracelets from other Scythian cemeteries, may well represent the exchange of weapons and women between élites. The familiarity of the Greek town dwellers with Celts is also suggested by a number of terracotta figures depicting Celtic weaponry.

Further to the east, east of the Sea of Azov including the basins of the rivers Don and Kuban, a scatter of 'Celtic' items has been found, most notably Etrusco-Celtic helmets of Montefortino type. Although these were probably made in the fourth and third centuries, most have been found in Sarmatian graves of the second and first centuries. Various explanations may be offered for the processes by which the helmets were transported, and they and the other items need not imply a Celtic presence. It may be relevant, however, that Greek geographers considered Meotide (the Sea of Azov) to be the frontier of the Celtic world. In such a situation it would not be unreasonable to argue that the helmets and other prestige items such as bronze vessels were the result of gift exchange between Celtic communities and their Sarmatian neighbours on the other side of the sea.

Sufficient will have been said to show that there are grounds for accepting a Celtic presence in the north Pontic region, but the nature of the community, its size, and its longevity as a distinct ethnic entity remain uncertain. Only one settlement, at Bovshev on the Dniester, and one grave, at Zalesye in the Pripyat estuary near Chernobyl, may reasonably be regarded as 'Celtic'. The remaining thirty or forty items are all stray finds. In a minimalist view, the Celtic presence need have been no more significant or long lasting than the Thracian kingdom of Tylis.

The Galatians

The Galatians of Asia Minor provide an interesting example of a Celtic community which retained an ethnic integrity after its initial settlement in the early third century BC and yet appears to have adopted the material culture of its new homeland with little or no reference to that of its roots.

The history of the Galatians has been outlined above (Chapter 4), and need not be repeated here. Suffice it to say that the historical view records the movement of some 20,000 people, only half of whom were fighting men, into Asia Minor in 278–7 BC under the leadership of Leonorios and Lutorius. They came, we are told, at the invitation of King Nicomedes of Bithynia to serve the king in his conflicts with his neighbours. After fifty years or so as mercenaries in the service of different factions and as raiders in their own right, they were eventually settled in Phrygia in the vicinity of Ankara.

Livy, no doubt following Polybius, gives an account of the migrants at the time of their arrival. They were divided into three tribal groups, all speaking the same language, the Tolistobogii, the Trocmi, and the Tectosages, each of which laid claim to a territory over which to rampage and raid. It was in this mobile phase of their occupation that they provided mercenary services for any Hellenistic potentate prepared to employ them. After a major defeat in about 232 BC, the Celtic peoples were compelled to concentrate in Phrygia. The Tectosages were already in the Ancyra region and the other two tribes were settled nearby. An agreement with the Pergamene king, Attalus, recognized the Celts' right to the land they now occupied in return for an agreement to cease raiding the Pergamene kingdom and other spheres of Pergamene interests. In reality this left only the lands to the east as legitimate for punitive exploitation and it was probably at this time that some territorial expansion took place east of the River Halys. The agreement with Attalus marks the point at which Galatia—the land of the Galatae—became a recognized territory, and we can henceforth speak of the inhabitants as Galatians.

The Galatians by this time must have become ethnically mixed. The élite lineages may well have been descended from the original migrant families of two generations past, but the indigenous population of Phrygia will now have been absorbed, if only in a subservient position, into the Galatian state.

The social structure of the Galatians seems to have remained little changed from its earlier form. According to Strabo, each of the three tribes was divided into four parts, which were called tetrarchies, and each had its own overall leader (tetrarch) to whom a judge, a war leader, and two subordinate commanders were answerable. A council, representing the twelve tetrarchies and composed of 300 men, met at Drunemetom. Among its duties was to pass judgment on murder cases. The system has interesting similarities to the organization of the Celtic Gauls described by Caesar. There is the same separation of leadership between a civil and a military leader and the recognition of a distinct judicial class. A supreme council was also a feature of Gaulish society. Originally it seems to have met once a year under some form of Druidic authority in the territory of the Carnutes, but Augustus refounded it as the *Consilium Gallarium* and required it to meet at Lugudunum on 1 August at the Altar of Rome and Augustus. The name of the meeting-place of the Galatians' council—Drynemetum—also implies a religious focus, since *nemeton* is a Celtic word for a sacred place and is suggestive of a controlling religious authority.

How long this essentially Celtic system of social organization lasted among the Galatians is difficult to say. Strabo, writing about the turn of the millennium, specifically mentions that in his time power had passed first to three rulers, then to two, and finally to one, in contrast to 'the organization of Galatia long ago'. This may have been as a result of Roman encouragement or duress, but there are clear signs of change earlier. In 189 BC we learn that Ortagion, a chief of the Tolistobogii, wanted to unite the Galatians under his leadership, but his attempts met with little success and a few years later a number of social units are mentioned each with its own chiefs.

A century later the old system of tetrarchs still appears to have been in force. The glimpse is provided by a treacherous incident orchestrated by Mithridates IV. In 88 BC, in a bid to take control of Asia Minor, he effectively destroyed Galatian opposition by inviting the Galatian chiefs to meet him at Pergamum. Of the sixty who turned up all but one were massacred. Those who did not attend were picked off in individual attacks, only three tetrarchs managing to escape.

The massacre of the tetrarchs may well have been the deciding factor in bringing about far-reaching changes in the old social order. Not only did it greatly weaken the ruling élite, but it showed that divided leadership was inefficient in dealing with the problems of the rapidly changing world. Perhaps even more important was that the incident drove the Galatians to the Roman side, and it was in the interests of the Roman state to encourage a more unified leadership.

Very little is known of Galatian ritual or religion. The existence of Drunemetom is a hint that sacred locations existed, presided over, perhaps, by a Druidic priesthood, but there is no direct evidence of this. What is clear is that the indigenous cults were assimilated by the Celts. Such was the case of the worship of the Mother Goddess at Pessinus. In the late second century BC the high priest, known by the ritual name of Attis, was a Celt whose brother, Aiorix, bore a characteristically Celtic name. It is evident from a later, Roman, inscription that half the college of priests at the temple were of Celtic birth. The sanctuary at Pessinus was, however, a thoroughly hellenized place. Strabo refers to it as having been built up by the Pergamene kings 'in a manner befitting a holy place with a sanctuary and also with porticoes of white marble'. Yet, in spite of their acceptance of native cults and practices, the Galatians could revert to a more typically barbarous practice, as they did in 165 BC when, following the conclusion of a war with Eumenes, the most important of the prisoners were sacrificed to the gods, while the less favoured were dispatched by spearing. In this incident we may be witnessing a resurgence of the Celtic belief in the need to sacrifice the best of the spoils of war to the deities.

The fighting practices of the Galatians were, as we have seen, vividly depicted by Pergamene artists in an array of victory monuments. Their fierceness and ferocity in battle were legendary. In 189 BC a Roman army, under the command of Cn. Manlius Vulso, moved against the Tolistobogii and Trocmi and won a decisive victory at Olympus near Pessinus. Livy gives a detailed account of the engagement using the occasion to provide his reader with a series of familiar stereotypes about the Celt as a fighting man (*Hist.* 38. 19–30). Thus from the mouth of the commander, in his set-piece pre-battle oration, comes direct reference to incidents from the Celtic invasion of Italy in the fourth century. That Livy should emphasize the comparison in this way shows, at the very least, that he was acutely aware of the similarities of the two peoples, even though he may have overstressed or oversimplified them. Yet even allowing for these potential distortions, several interesting points emerge. The Galatians, it appears, were still using the rather archaic type of Celtic shield, 'long, but not wide enough for the size of their bodies and . . . flat in surface', and they still adopted the practice of fighting naked, a point vividly described by Livy: 'Their wounds were plain to see because they fight naked and their bodies are plump and white since they are never exposed except in battle.' There is no reason to suppose that these observations were not specific to the event. Together they show that patterns of behaviour in battle had changed little, in spite of nearly a century of experience in Asia Minor. Even so, Livy could report the Roman commander as saying: 'The Gauls here are by now degenerate, a mixed race, truly described by their name Gallogrecians.'

In his brief review of Galatian territory, Strabo (*Geog.* 12. 5) makes no mention of towns. The Trocmi, he says, have 'three walled garrisons', Tavium, Mithridatium, and Danala; the Tectosages command the fortress of Ancyra; while the fortresses of the Tolistobogii are Blucium and Peïum, the former being the royal residence of King Deïotarus, and the latter where he kept his treasure. Strabo's use of 'fortress' is clearly intended to imply that these sites were not towns in the classical sense. He does, however, say that Tavium was 'the emporium of the people in that part of the country' and he uses the same word in describing Pessinus in the border region to the west of Galatia. By 'emporium' he was presumably seeking to stress the market functions of the two places. If we can accept Strabo's distinctions, the implication is of an essentially non-urban society focused on a series of fortified enclosures and with an economy articulated at a few trading centres, at least one of them sited at a major shrine. The towns of the Phrygian indigenes were left to decay. By the time of the Roman annexation in 25 BC, Ancyra, Pessinus, and Tavium were sufficiently important to become the capitals of the three tribes.

Several Galatian fortresses have been located. Blucium has been tentatively identified with the fortifications partially excavated at Karalar 35 kilometres north-west of Ankara. A nearby tomb with a funerary inscription showing it to have belonged to King Deïotarus (son of the king of the same name who was an ally of Rome) provided some assurance of the identification. Peïum, the second of the Tolistobogii strongholds mentioned by Strabo, is thought to lie in the meander of the river Girmir Bay at Tabanlıoğlu Kale. The deeply incised river provides the site with more than adequate protection on three sides, while the neck of the promontory is defended by a wall protected by multiangular bas-

147 The treasury of the Galatian king Deïotarus is situated at Peïum in Anatolia on a ridge protected on two sides by a loop in the valley of the River Siberis. The masonry of the fortifications is typical high-quality late Hellenistic work.

tions built in fine Hellenistic masonry. The strength of the defences would be entirely appropriate to a fortress guarding the king's treasure. The quality of the architecture of Peïum (if correctly identified) is a reminder that the Galatian élite were well able to use Hellenistic building techniques, even if their fortified sites were typical Celtic 'hill forts' in size and location.

The material culture of the Galatians has not been extensively studied, but sufficient is known to suggest that indigenous styles and technologies were adopted from the beginning. Distinctive items of La Tène metalwork are at present limited to four bracelets and twenty brooches from the whole of Asia Minor. While a few items appear, as would be expected, in Galatia and on the Aegean coast, the densest concentration lies in the south-east of the country in Cappadocia, a pattern which might suggest that Celtic raiding parties ranged over a wider territory than might be supposed from the classical sources.

The Galatians provide a fascinating example of a Celtic people who maintained a high degree of ethnic identity over several centuries, even though they must have represented a minority in their territory. Their persistence as a recognizably 'Celtic' people must be the result of élite dominance. As a powerful warlike group, thrown together by migration and periods of mercenary service, they were easily able to dominate the effete Phrygian inhabitants of the land in which they eventually settled without feeling the need for recourse to material symbols of their ethnicity.

The Celts in Egypt

The Celts who burst onto the Hellenistic world in the 280s and 270s BC were, as we have seen, largely absorbed into the armies of the contending dynasts of Asia Minor, but the renown of the Celt as a fighting man was already well known in the eastern Mediterranean. It is hardly surprising, therefore, to learn of Celts in Egypt as early as 274 BC serving in the army of Ptolemy II Philadelphos. In all

XV Aerial view of the hill fort of Las Cogotas on the edge of the
northern Meseta in the province of Avila, Spain. The site was first
occupied in the Late Bronze Age but received its first fortifications
(the upper rampart enclosing the two summits) in the fifth century
BC. The lower enclosure was added later. Close-spaced rectangular
houses were found in the upper enclosure while the lower enclosure
contained evidence of pottery manufacture.

XVI The Celtiberian hill fort of Numantia, in the Ebro valley in north-eastern Spain, had taken on the appearance of a Mediterranean town by the beginning of the second century BC, with a regularly laid out street grid defining insulae of closely packed houses. The settlement stood out against Roman advances and was eventually taken by Scipio in 133 BC after a long siege during which time, it is said, the inhabitants were forced to resort to cannibalism.

probability they were recruited from the horde that broke into Asia Minor in 278, but that they may have arrived in Egypt some time before is not impossible. They soon proved to be unreliable allies. Believing that Ptolemy was caught in an impossible position between his half-brother Magas in the west and Antiochos I in the east, they rebelled, buoyed on by the prospects of the wealth to be gained by looting the cities and sanctuaries of Egypt. They had, however, misjudged the situation: Ptolemy reacted swiftly, driving some 4,000 of the mercenaries onto an island in the Sebennytic branch of the Nile, where, Pausanius tells us, 'They perished by hunger and each other's swords'.

This was by no means the end of the Celtic presence in Egypt. It was normal in third-century Egypt for troops, no longer needed for active service, to be settled and given land to cultivate, usually in the Fayum. These cleruchs ('sleepers') were, in theory, expected to retain their military skills and to be immediately available when called upon. Among the cleruchs living in the Fayum was a detachment of Celts whose presence is demonstrated by a wooden shield, preserved in the dry desert conditions. In 217 BC, when Egypt was threatened by

148 *Far left*: Wooden shield of Celtic type, well preserved in the desert atmosphere of the Fayum oasis, Egypt, where a group of Celtic mercenaries were given land in the third century BC. Services des Antiquités, Cairo.

149 *Left*: Small terracotta figure of a Celtic warrior from Egypt. Third century BC. British Museum, London.

the Seleucid king Antiochos III, Ptolemy IV called the 'sleepers' to his defence. Among the 50,000 or so troops who were eventually amassed were 6,000 'Gauls and Thracians', of whom 2,000, of unspecified nationality, were newly re-cruited. Some of the cleruchs who took part were, according to Polybius, the sons of original settlers. In the event the Ptolemaic force won a resounding vic-tory at Raphia in Gaza. It is tempting to think that the small terracotta of a resplendent Gaul found in Egypt proclaims Gaulish successes at this time.

Gauls still retained their identity throughout the second century BC and their presence is recorded from time to time: they helped besiege the rebel town of Abydos in 186–5 and were among the garrison resident at Hermopolis Magna towards the end of the century. Whether these detachments had families in the Fayum and returned there when not on military duty is difficult to say, but that other communities existed is implied by funerary stelae naming Gauls and sometimes depicting Celtic shields, found in the necropoli of Alexandria. One wonders whether the old fighters living in the desiccating atmosphere of the Fayum oasis in the mid-third century told their incredulous children stories of the fertile Danube plain or the pine-clad slopes of Mount Parnassos remem-bered from the time when they had camped in its shadow waiting to pillage Delphi.

10
Religious Systems

In describing the Irish and Welsh vernacular sources for Celtic religious beliefs, the Irish scholar Proinsias MacCana, in a memorable phrase, referred to the 'fertile chaos of the insular tradition'. 'Fertile chaos' perfectly characterizes the enormously rich array of partial and confusing evidence available to us from a wide variety of sources reflecting on the religious beliefs of Celtic peoples. It may fairly be said that there is more, varied, evidence for Celtic religion than for any other aspect of Celtic life. The only problem is to be able to assemble it in a systematic form which does not too greatly oversimplify the intricate texture of its detail.

The Greek and Roman texts provide a number of pertinent observations, but these are at best anecdotal, offered largely as colourful background by writers whose prime intention was to communicate other messages. The most comprehensive account is that given by Caesar in his description of Gaulish society. Though useful, its summary nature could lead to confusion if it was not balanced against other evidence. Similarly the immensely rich vernacular literature of the Insular Celts must be approached in the awareness that Celtic religion was not necessarily consistent across Europe, nor was it unchanging. The very 'Insular' nature of the sources and the fact that what comes down to us has passed through the emasculating filter of a Christian monastic perspective demand particular care when such material is used as a basis for generalization.

The archaeological record produces an equally varied mix of data. Iconography in the form of stone and wood sculptures is not particularly plentiful, but, if Celtic art in its broader sense is taken into account, as it must be, the variety of symbols and images is greatly multiplied. In addition to this we have evidence for belief systems embedded in burial practice, in a great number of votive deposits, and in religious structures such as shrines and shafts. From this huge mass of disparate evidence, sometimes distorted and usually partial, some semblance of the religious systems of the Celts can be reconstructed.

It is necessary to stress at the outset the complexity of the problem. Three factors, in particular, contribute to it: the substratum of religious beliefs coming through from the earlier prehistoric period; the relative isolation of certain regions for periods of time; and the impact of rapid social and economic change on those communities in closest proximity to the Mediterranean world. Together these factors will have created a disparity of belief systems taking, from the general gene-pool of concepts, different combinations of characteristics and emphasizing them in different measure. Yet behind this variety, broad structural similarities can be detected.

There can be little doubt that religious concepts, prevalent in the second millennium BC, appear, albeit dimly, in some of the beliefs and practices of the Celtic communities in the later first millennium, yet there does seem to have been a significant transformation across much of Europe some time in the second half of the second millennium. Simply characterized, the earlier systems, with their strong solar symbolism, were evidently focused on the solar and lunar cycles, the significance of which underlies the orientation of some at least of the megalithic tombs, circles, and alignments of the third and early second millennia. By the end of the millennium these early monuments, many of them long-lived, had been largely abandoned, and instead an emphasis had developed on the deposition of items of value placed in pits in the ground or thrown into rivers, springs, and bogs. This focus on deposition intensified throughout the first millennium. Deposits of this kind imply a more earth-related belief system which may be best understood as a corollary to the increased emphasis which was now being placed on the organization of the land and its productive capacity. A greater reliance on crops and herds would have meant a greater interest in marking the seasons. Thus the seasonal calendar may have begun to replace, at least in emphasis, the solar and lunar calendar.

Some memory of these earlier beliefs may have been caught up in the myth of the Hyperboreans who were believed to have lived in the distant north. Hecataeus, who wrote in the sixth century BC (and is quoted by Diodorus), said that they occupied a large island in the ocean facing the country of the Celts and there, in a magnificent circular temple, worshipped the sun god. One may reasonably wonder if this is a reference to Britain and more specifically to Stonehenge, about which the ancient world must have had some knowledge even though there is no evidence that it was in active use much after the middle of the second millennium.

The Nature of the Celtic Gods

At first sight the Celtic world was pervaded by a multiplicity of gods and goddesses, of whom the names of more than 200 have been recorded. But if we accept that individual deities could have been known by several titles or epithets, then, in theory at least, the plethora of divine personages might be reducible to a more manageable system.

Julius Caesar attempted to do so in a famous passage in Book 6 of his *Commentaries on the Gallic War*. Having introduced the topic by telling us that the Gauls as a whole were extremely superstitious, he goes on to correlate the Celtic gods, whom he does not name, with their Roman counterparts. The most popular was Mercury 'and they have very many images of him'. He is regarded to be the inventor of all arts, and also presides over travel and commerce. The other deities include Apollo, who averts diseases, Minerva, who instructs in industry and craft, Mars, who controls warfare, and Jupiter, who 'has supremacy among the gods'. Caesar's rationalization is clearly an oversimplification designed to explain the essentials of the Celtic gods to his Roman audience, but as such it offers a useful guide.

A rather different approach was taken by Lucan, who, in *Pharsalia*, names three Celtic deities—Teutates, Taranis, and Esus—who were propitiated by human sacrifice. The victims of Teutates were to be drowned, those of Taranis burnt, and those sacrificed to Esus hanged. The Celtic names are informative. Teutates means 'the god of the tribe' from the Celtic *teutā* 'tribe'; Taranis is probably a sky god whose name comes from the Celtic *taran* 'thunder'; while Esus means 'good' in the sense of all-competent. It is reasonable, therefore, to equate Taranis with Jupiter as a deity of the sky and Esus (the all-competent) with Mercury ('inventor of all arts'). In another guise Esus may have been synonymous with Lugh, a widely revered deity in the Celtic world whose name is preserved in a number of place names such as Lugudunum (Lyons) and Luguvallum (Carlisle). In Ireland Lugh (whose associated description means 'skilled in many arts together') conquered the evil creatures of the other world and was celebrated at the harvest feast of Lugnasad held on 1 August.

Less certainty attaches to the other correlations. It is, however, likely that the tribal deity, Teutates, who was the protector of the tribe in times of war, is to be seen as roughly equivalent to Mars in Caesar's list. His Apollo and Minerva find no parallels in Lucan's classification but may be recognized among the Celtic gods. Minerva is most likely to be a generalization for a formidable troop of female deities who appear under various names as the consorts of male gods of the tribal kind, as protectors of springs and rivers, or simply as *Matres* or *Matronae*—the divine mothers. Caesar's Apollo is probably the Celtic Maponos—the divine son—whose cult is known in Gaul and Britain and may be associated with healing springs.

If the Celtic deities are approached through the vernacular literature of Ireland, a rather different perspective is achieved. Here the essential structure was a dualism between the male tribal god and the female deity of the land. The male deity was the Dagda, which means the good (that is all-competent) god who served as the protector of the tribe. He was all-embracing and included among his functional attributes control of warfare and the provision of wisdom. The Dagda's counterpart and consort was the Morrígan, a native goddess frequently referred to as 'the Queen of Demons' in the Irish texts but also known under other names such as Macha and Maeve, and often associated with the symbolism of the horse. She is both fertile and destructive. The coming together of the Dagda and the Morrígan on the night of the festival of Samain ensured the continuing prosperity of the tribe and the fertility of the crops and animals in the coming year.

This simple binary opposition, which is probably of ancient origin, was complicated by further deities who may have been introduced at a later stage. Thus Brigit was the daughter of the Dagda. She was a potent fertility force and seems also to have had powers of healing and wisdom. Another latecomer, portrayed as such in the mythological tracts, was Lugh, who, like the Dagda, was good at all things. It is tempting to see in this pattern a simple early system, which may date to pre-Celtic times, becoming overlaid by levels of complexity and apparent conflicts as the celticization of Ireland proceeded. This would explain how it was that the all-competent characteristics of the Dagda were to some extent replicated by those of the newcomer, Lugh, and how the fertility/healing powers of Brigit could be understood to differ from those of the Morrígan. If one allows that the early Irish binary system represented the continuation of an ancient pan-European tradition, which in continental Europe developed more rapidly to become the Graeco-Roman pantheon and the Celtic ensemble, then the Mercury/Lugh/all-skilled god may be only a continental version of the early Insular Dagda, while the Minerva/Brigit/fertility-curative deity could be the continental manifestation of the Irish Morrígan. Reintroduced into Ireland at a later date in their evolved form, they were accepted as different gods. Clearly such suggestions must remain in the realms of speculation, but they have the advantage of opening the mind to something of the complexity of the situation.

Various approaches have been made to attempt to systematize the Celtic pantheon by scholars who, like Caesar and Lucan before them, have felt the need to understand the structure which lay behind the apparent chaos. On the one hand, it has been argued that Caesar was wrong to attempt to separate divine functions. Leaving aside the female deities, the male tribal gods were more or less polyvalent in that they were competent at all things and they were also polymorphic, appearing in many guises and answering to a variety of names. In this view the male tribal god was one. Other scholars have regarded this as an oversimplification, a view which was neatly summed up by Proinsias MacCana when he wrote:

one cannot but reflect that if the Celts were monotheists at heart, then they were remarkably successful in disguising this, for not merely have they fractured their single godhead into a multiplicity of aliases, but they have also invested some of these with a convincing air of individuality.

For him, while Caesar's account was wrong to imply that a pantheon of Celtic gods with specific names occurred all over the Celtic world, it was none the less a useful typological index to the principal classes of deity that a traveller in Gaul in the first century BC might encounter. Thus, in addition to the male tribal god, one might expect to find Lugh (Mercury), Taranis (Jupiter), Maponos

(Apollo), Brigit (Minerva), Ogmioc (Hercules), Cernuunos ('the horned one'), Epona (the horse goddess), and others cropping up almost anywhere.

Caesar adds one tantalizing detail to his account of Celtic religion. 'The Gauls claim that they are all descended from Dis Pater; they say this is the tradition handed down to them from the Druids.' Dis Pater, the Roman god of the dead, provides an understandable eponymous ancestor. As the first man alive, he was first to die and thus to acquire control of the underworld, and it is to him that the spirits of the dead return after their earthly life. In Celtic mythology and in the Irish Insular tradition, as Donn 'the brown or dark one', he stands aside from the other gods.

One further aspect deserving of consideration is the prevalence of triplism in Celtic religion. This is best understood to be an expression of extreme potency rather than of any coming-together of three disparate elements. The 'power of three' was frequently expressed in iconography, as, for example, in the three-faced stone head from Corleck, Cavan, in Ireland or the tricephalic deity depicted on the pot from Bavay in northern France, but it is also found as a recurring motif—the triskele—in Celtic art. The concept is made even more specific in Romano-British and Gallo-Roman religion in the form of the *Deae Matres* or the *Matronae*—the three mother goddesses—who together form a unity representing strength, power, and fertility. Another but less widespread female trinity are the *Saluviae*, who preside over springs. Male deities are less prone to triplism, but inscriptions to the *Lugoves* in Switzerland and Spain may well refer to a triple form of Lugh. In the Insular literature of Ireland triplism is a recurring theme. The great goddess, the Morrígan in her plural form, the Morrígna, resolves into three: Morrígan, Badb, and Nemain. Brigit and Macha also occur as triads. It is tempting to wonder if the threefold division proposed by Lucan, of Esus, Teutates, and Taranis, is a further expression of Celtic triplism.

Sufficient will have been said in this brief summary to have justified describing the Celtic gods as a subject of 'fertile chaos'. Certainly by the first century BC, when the first coherent evidence from classical sources, inscriptions, and iconography begins to appear, a bewildering variety of deities present themselves, some strictly local others with a wider geographical distribution. No doubt there would have been an accompanying mythology explaining

150 Small plaque of schist from Cleveland Walk, Bath, England, crudely carved with three female figures probably representing the 'three mothers', a triad of deities. The piece is undated but is probably Roman. Triads of mother goddesses were comparatively common in the west of Britain in the Roman period, probably reflecting an earlier Iron Age tradition. Roman Baths Museum, Bath.

the supernatural community and this will have varied in emphasis and content from region to region. The many-layered complexity of it all is well exemplified by the mythologies which survive embedded in the Irish and Welsh vernacular literature.

It would be unwise to try to structure Celtic religion more rigidly than we have here, given the long period of development, the great geographical range, and the variety of indigenous and external influences to which it was subjected. Yet, among the multiplicity and mobility of titles and powers exhibited by the Celtic gods, it is possible to detect an underlying structure of simple binary oppositions: male/tribe/sky/war against female/place/earth/fertility. The coupling of the two produces balance, harmony, and productivity and has to be enacted on a regular annual cycle determined by the seasons.

Seasons and Festivals

151 The fragmentary bronze calendar found at Coligny, Ain, France. It is divided into sixteen columns each of four 29- or 30-day months, containing a total of sixty two months. Propitious or unpropitious times are indicated and the dates of two festivals are recorded. First century AD? Musée de la Civilisation Gallo-Romaine, Lyons.

The Insular literature and the remarkable calendar found at Coligny near Bourg, dating to the late first century BC, enable an approach to be made to Celtic concepts of time. The Coligny calendar, inscribed on sheets of copper alloy, is divided into sixteen columns each subdivided into four months except for the fifth and ninth columns each of which contain two lunar months and one intercalary month needed to adjust the system to the realities of actual time. The months are divided alternately into 29 and 30 days, making a year of 354 days. Each month is also divided into a light half and a dark half, the divide

signified by the word *Atenoux* ('returning night'), and the months are divided between those that are auspicious and those that are not, with the abbreviations MAT ('good') and ANM ('not good'). The days are numbered and some are also marked by abbreviations which must have been significant for those who were informed: there are indicative signs for the festivals of Beltane (1 May) and Lugnasad (1 August). Considerable similarities to the Greek calendar suggest a possible source of inspiration.

That time was rigorously ordered need occasion no surprise in a society whose economic basis was agrarian and pastoral. To be able to chart the passage of time and to know when to initiate essential processes, such as sowing the crop and moving animals to upland pastures, lay at the very basis of existence.

The Irish literature provides the most detailed insight into the divisions of the year into seasons. The end of the old year and the beginning of the new was marked by the greatest of the ceremonies, *Samain*, which took place on 1 November. It was a liminal time between the two years and as such was dangerous: the spirits of the dead could roam free. It was on this occasion that the male god Dagda and the female goddess, usually Morrígan, came together, and through their intercourse the well-being of the tribe and fertility of all their enterprises were assured. In some versions of the myth the goddess, now an old hag, was revitalized by the union and became young and beautiful once more. Samain was the time when all the important communal acts, meetings, and sacrifices took place. The strength of tradition which lay behind the festival has ensured its survival as Hallowe'en and its Christianized version, the festival of All Souls.

The next festival, *Imbolc*, which took place on 1 February, is less well known. In all probability it was associated with the goddess Brigit, a goddess of fertility, learning, and healing (cognate with Minerva). In Christian mythology the Celtic Brigit became a saint: her festival falls on 1 February and is still celebrated widely in Ireland. In terms of the agrarian year it probably signified the beginning of the period of lactation of ewes, when the sheep could be moved to upland pastures.

Next came *Beltane*, held on 1 May, a ceremony associated with the Celtic god of fire, Belenus. The fires lit on this occasion may have been used to fumigate cattle before they were turned out to graze on the summer pastures.

Finally on 1 August the festival of *Lugnasad* was held, presided over by the god Lugh. The timing might suggest that it was when the propitiatory offerings had to be made to the chthonic deities in anticipation of a fruitful harvest. In Gaul in the first century BC this was the occasion when the Council of the Gauls met, a fact neatly manipulated by the Emperor Augustus when, in 12 BC, he relocated the Gaulish *consilium* requiring it to meet annually at the Altar of Rome and Augustus at Lyons. In doing so he was demonstrating the unity of Gaul and Rome, by equating himself with Lugh.

The Irish sources enable us to recognize the overall structure of seasonal festivals in its most complete form in relation to the main events of the agricultural and pastoral year. The Coligny calendar, in indicating only the festivals of Beltane and Lugnasad, might be thought to imply that here, in the most civilized part of the Celtic world, some of the old beliefs and practices had already fallen away. The suggestion would not be inconsistent with the other socio-political changes which were already underway in Gaul. The issue is a reminder of variations possible across the Celtic world.

Time was crucial to the proper enactment of ritual. This is made clear by Pliny's famous description of the rituals attendant on the cutting of mistletoe from the sacred oak. It had to be done by a white-robed Druid using a golden sickle and afterwards a suitable sacrifice had to be made, but more important to the present discussion is that the act had to be carefully timed: 'it is gathered with a great deal of ceremony, if possible on the sixth day of the moon. . . . They choose this day because, although the moon has not yet reached half-size, it already has considerable influence' (*Nat. Hist.* 16. 249). In this context one can understand why the monthly cycle with its dark and light halves and its propitious and unpropitious days had to be recorded and accessible to those whose task it was to attend to supernatural matters.

152 Coin showing the Altar of Rome and Augustus at Lyons, consecrated in 12 BC as the focus of imperial power in Gaul. Here the annual meeting of the Gallic Council was held.

Man and the Gods

In most societies interactions between the natural and supernatural world are ordered by ritual and mediated by specialists and so it was in the Celtic world. The principal mediators were called Druids (*druides, druidae* in Latin; *druad* in Old Irish; *dryw* (singular) in Welsh), which is thought to mean 'knowledge of the oak' or, less likely, 'deep knowledge'. Another group of religious practitioners were called by Strabo *vates* (*fáthi* in Old Irish), which probably originally meant 'seer' or someone who was inspired by the gods to understand that which was invisible.

Caesar gives the most comprehensive, and in many ways the most convincing, account of the function of the Druidic class (*De Bello Gallico* 6. 13–14). Druids belonged to the social élite and had control over all sacrifices, both public and private. It was they who gave rulings on all religious questions. They were also called upon to act as judges in criminal cases and in disputes about boundaries and inheritances. To enforce their judgements they were able to ban any defaulter from taking part in sacrifices—an easy thing to accomplish, since they were the sole intermediaries—and in doing so they cut off the individual from the gods, thus making him unclean and excluded from normal social intercourse: 'no one will go near or speak to them for fear of being contaminated.'

Among the Druidic class in Gaul one man was elected as supreme and held the position for life. There was an annual meeting held in the territory of the Carnutes, which was considered to be the centre of Gaul, where all the major issues were settled.

190

The Druids enjoyed various benefits: they were exempt from tax and were not required to offer military service, though Diviciacus, brother of the ruler of the Aedui, who Cicero assures us was a Druid, was also a fighting man. The privileges of the class attracted many pupils, who would be required to spend twenty years studying the doctrine, committing everything to memory. Caesar believed that emphasis on memorizing the teachings was designed to train the mind. This may well be, but there must also have been the desire to keep the lore exclusive to the initiated. In this way the Druids maintained their hold over the population.

Caesar offers one final and intriguing observation: 'It is thought that the doctrine of the Druids was invented in Britain and was brought from there into Gaul: even today those who want to study the doctrine in greater detail usually go to Britain to learn there.' If one can accept the factual accuracy of the second part of this statement, it might suggest that the power of the Druids in Gaul had decreased by Caesar's time largely as a result of the social changes which were taking place, and that in Britain, where a more undeveloped form of Celtic society remained, Druidism was still strong. That this was so is suggested by Tacitus' account of the destruction of the Druids on the island of Anglesey by the Roman army in AD 59. None of this, however, need be seen to support Caesar's report that Druidism originated in Britain, though there is no inherent reason why this should not have been the case.

One of the functions of the Druids was to officiate during sacrifices to the gods, and there is ample evidence to suggest that among the commodities sacrificed were human beings. For this reason, in the writings of the classical authors, Druidism was associated with human sacrifice, which the Roman world claimed, somewhat disingenuously, to find abhorrent. In describing Druidic altars on Anglesey as 'soaked with human blood', Tacitus could hope to offer justification for the destruction of the priestly class. What is more likely to have been at issue is not so much the upset to Roman susceptibilities caused by human sacrifice as the fear of the Druids as the unifying force able to galvanize Celtic opposition. It may have been no coincidence that the trouble which broke out in the otherwise peaceful region of Gaul in 53 BC started among the Carnutes, where the Druids held their annual pan-Gaulish assembly. It may also have been no coincidence that the rebellion of Boudica in eastern Britain began in the immediate aftermath of the Roman attack on the Druidic centre on Anglesey. In both cases the Druids may have provided the spur to rebellion.

Human sacrifice among the Gauls is mentioned by several classical writers. Lucan's commentaries distinguish the particular mode of death which the different gods preferred: the victims of Taranis were burnt, those of Teutates were drowned, while those of Esus were hanged. The same methods of dispatch were enumerated by Poseidonius (and reported by others), though without specifying the preferences of the different gods. Strabo, quoting Poseidonius, says: 'They used to shoot men down with arrows, impale them in the temples, or, making a large statue of straw and wood, throw into it cattle and all sorts of wild animals and human beings and thus make a burnt offering' (*Geog.* 4. 4. 6). Burning victims alive is mentioned by Caesar, probably quoting the same source. It is interesting that Strabo uses the past tense, which might suggest that the practice had died out in Gaul by the first century BC. Britain, however, still upheld traditional values. Not only were victims sacrificed on the altars of Anglesey, but Boudica chose to impale captives taken during the rebellion of AD 60, though whether out of sheer ferocity or as offerings to the gods of war is not clear.

A distinction should be made between human sacrifice made to propitiate the gods and that performed in the interests of divination. Diodorus Siculus, probably quoting Poseidonius, is informative. When enquiring into important matters, he tells us:

They devote to death a human being and stab him with a dagger in the region of the diaphragm and when he has fallen they foretell the future from his fall and from the convulsions of his limbs and, moreover, from the spurting of the blood, placing their trust in some ancient and long continued observation of these practices.   (*Hist.* 5. 31)

A little earlier in the same passage Diodorus describes auguries, based on sacrificed animals, which are made by 'seers', taking care to distinguish these practitioners from the Druids. By implication, therefore, it is the 'seers' who were likely to have been most closely involved in the human sacrifices, even though the Druids must have been present.

Convincing evidence of human sacrifice is surprisingly rare in the archaeological record. In the case of the body placed in a bog at Lindow in Cheshire in the first or second century AD, there is tolerable certainty of ritual death. He had been strangled, hit on the head, and his throat cut all in rapid succession. This is surely an example of the threefold death referred to in the Irish vernacular literature. Less certainty attaches to the complete bodies thrown into disused corn storage pits at various sites in southern Britain, most notably at the hill fort of Danebury. Whilst the victims could have been dispatched on the spot before deposition, some at least could have been stoned to death *in situ*. Bog burials and pit burials may well represent offerings made to chthonic deities, the different places of deposition reflecting perhaps different deities.

The concept of dedicating material to gods was well established in the Celtic world. The belief system is neatly encapsulated by Caesar:

When they have decided to fight a battle, it is to Mars that they usually dedicate the spoils they hope to win; if they are successful, they sacrifice the captured animals and collect all the rest of the spoils in one place. Among many of the tribes it is possible to see piles of these objects on consecrated ground. It is most unusual for anyone to dare to go against the religious law and hide his booty at home, or remove any of the objects that have been placed on such piles. The punishment laid down for that crime is death by the most terrible torture.   (*De Bello Gallico* 6. 18)

It may be that in this section Caesar was relying on Poseidonius. Strabo used the

153 The body of a man buried in a peat bog at Lindow, Cheshire, England. The man had suffered a violent bang on the head and strangulation, and his throat had been cut. The three ways of death suggest that he may have been a propitiatory offering to the gods. Probably first century AD. British Museum, London.

154 Human body buried in a disused storage pit in the hill fort of Danebury, Hampshire, England. There was no indication of how and where the individual died, but it is possible that the large rocks which originally covered most of the body were the cause of death. Here again we are probably witnessing a propitiatory burial. Third or second century BC.

same source for his discussion of the great treasure at Toulouse believed to have come from the sack of Delphi, which was eventually appropriated by the Romans. Part of it was stacked up in temple enclosures and part had been thrown into sacred lakes. The temple at Toulouse was highly revered by the local inhabitants and for this reason the treasure stored there was considerable. Religious taboos kept it entirely safe until the Roman Conquest, and even then the despoiler, Caepio, suffered a succession of misfortunes at the hands of the gods.

The beliefs lying behind these two accounts were widespread and are well reflected in the rich archaeological record. The most famous of the sites which can reasonably be regarded as a religious location is La Tène on the edge of Lake Neuchâtel in Switzerland (Figs. 23–7). Although there has been much debate about the nature of the site, there can be little doubt of its ritual connotations. The principal structure was a timber pier running out into the lake, which served as a platform from which votive offerings were thrown into the water (Fig. 25). The range and quantity are impressive. In addition to 269 spearheads, 166 swords, and 29 shields, there were hundreds of brooches and an array of other items including wooden yokes, bronze cauldrons, iron ingots, knives, razors, belts, and so on. La Tène is by no means unique. A similar pier built out into the River Witham was found at Fiskerton in Lincolnshire, and from the sediments around were recovered a number of metal artefacts, including a La Tène I sword in an iron scabbard, though the radiocarbon dates suggest that the structure may have begun earlier. Much the same arrangement was found at Flag Fen in Norfolk, where a timber platform, reached by means of a bridge, served as a place from which weapons, with a few tools and other items, were thrown into the surrounding water over a long period from c.1600 to 200 BC.

This same general concept is inherent in the famous ritual site of Llyn Cerrig Bach in Anglesey, where a rock outcrop served as the place from which a wide range of items, principally war gear, was thrown into a lake in the late first century BC or early first century AD.

In none of these cases is there any need to suppose that there was only one act of deposition. Indeed, there is positive evidence to show that the dedications took place over a period of time, perhaps on a seasonal basis or when a particular event, past or pending, demanded a propitiatory response. The examples cited so far were all well-defined locations focused on a structure or natural feature. The possibility of less focused deposition also exists. Very large quantities of artefacts, mainly weapons, have been found in European rivers with no evident concentration at any specific location. This pattern could be the result of deposition from the river bank or from boats—the river itself, rather than a specific location along it, being the sacred place. The Thames provides a particularly impressive example, with concentrations of weapons spanning the period from the Late Bronze Age to the end of the Iron Age. Many of the items—like the Battersea and Wandsworth shields, the spearhead from Datchet, and the Waterloo Bridge helmet—were prestige goods of considerable value, and it remains a strong possibility that they were made specifically for

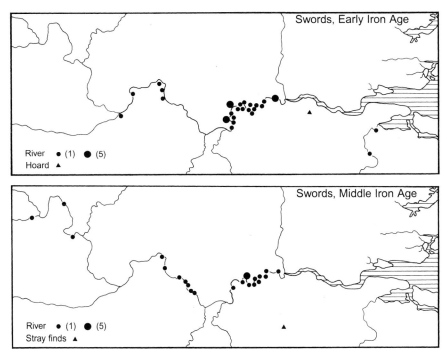

155 The Thames may well have been a sacred river in the Late Bronze and Iron Age. From it have come a remarkable number of items of prestige metalwork. The maps show the distribution of Iron Age swords pointing to a slight change in the focus of deposition between the Hallstatt and La Tène periods.

parade purposes or for ritual deposition. Given the apparently scattered nature of these river deposits and the exceptional quality of some of the pieces, the belief system underlying their deposition must have differed from that governing the more normal array of warrior equipment dumped at one location. What binds the two types of behaviour is the underlying belief that the gods needed to be propitiated by dedicating war gear to them in watery locations. It was a long-lived tradition which began in Europe in the sixteenth century BC and continued unabated until the Roman Conquest in those areas reached by the Roman armies. Rich finds as far north as Denmark, most notably the collection of weapons deposited in a boat in a bog at Hjortspring on the island of Als in the third or second century BC, are a reminder that placating the gods in this way was not the sole preserve of the Celtic regions.

Other types of propitiatory deposit are also known. The description of the sacred treasure at Toulouse is an indication that items of considerable value could be dedicated. Such deposits have occasionally been recovered. At Niederzier in the northern Rhineland, for example, a hoard of gold consisting of two torcs, an armlet, and forty-five coins were found together in a bowl buried next to a post which was considered by the excavators to be of cult significance. The total weight of the gold amounted to 321.84 grams, which was almost one Roman pound (327.45 grams). This type of mixed deposit composed of various combinations of torcs, arm rings, and coins occurs widely. At Tayac (Gironde) almost 4 kilograms of gold were recovered made up of a massive torc, ingots, coin blanks, and coins. At Fenouillet (Haute-Garonne) six torcs (Fig. 60) were found, while at Lasgraisse (Tarn) two examples came to light.

This same pattern of deposition extends to eastern England. A hoard from Ipswich (Suffolk) contained six torcs, but the most informative site is Snettisham in Norfolk (Pl. XXII*b*) where chance finds and, later, systematic excavation exposed twelve individual deposits over an area of some 1.2 hectares. The deposits varied in size. One of the original finds, producing the famous Snettisham torc, in addition yielded another torc, a bracelet, and a gold quarter stater. Among the more recent, scientifically excavated, deposits were five separately buried groups together producing sixty-three torcs of gold, silver/gold, silver, and bronze. The sheer concentration of material in a small area and certain details of deposition—for example, that some of the pits contained two deposits separated from each other—leave little doubt that the motive for deposition was ritual. Snettisham with its apparent lack of boundary features and absence of structures, other than the votive deposits, provides a fascinating insight into the kind of 'natural' sacred place implied by certain of the classical texts. It is tempting to see Snettisham as little more than a clearing in a forest protected only by its sanctity and the religious taboos restraining the people.

The great deposits of weapons and of treasure are likely to represent a 'tribal' response to the deities, either one related to a particular momentous event, or a continuous process of reverence, but it is evident from the archaeological record that everyday life was pervaded by the need to propitiate the deities, and there will have been very many acts of deposition carried out by the community and the individual throughout the year. Evidence for this level of response has come from the large-scale excavations of the hill fort of Danebury, in central southern Britain. Here, in common with much of southern Britain and northern Gaul, grain, presumably seed grain, was stored in pits. When the storage phase was over and the pits ceased to have a functional use, propitiatory offerings were placed in them. The range of material offered is impressive. In addition to the complete human bodies mentioned above, which may have been sacrificial victims, parts of human bodies have been recovered, including severed heads. The most common deposit comprised domestic animals in whole or in part. While the sheep, cattle, and pigs could have been animals offered by virtue of their value to the community as food, other animals including dogs, horses, and ravens are more likely to have had specific ritual significance. This is most noticeable with horses, which were usually represented either by a single articulated leg or by a skull, sometimes in combination with dogs. Other deposits include small collections of tools or horse gear, whole pots, grain, and quernstones. Clearly, in these deposits we are glimpsing only

156 A hoard of sheet-gold neck rings, an arm ring, and gold coins from Niederzier, Düren, Germany. First century BC. This recurring combination of objects, found in hoards in Belgium and Britain, suggests adherence to a particular propitiatory ritual. Rheinisches Landesmuseum, Bonn.

XVII*a Facing*: The stone fortifications of Dun Aengus cling to the edge of the island of Aran, Ireland, while the Atlantic waves pound far below. The fortifications, still undated, have been shown to be multiperiod and post-date an extensive Late Bronze Age settlement.

XVII*b Inset*: A barrier of closely spaced angular rocks placed to hinder the approach of men or horses to the fort of Dun Aengus, Aran, Ireland. This kind of defensive cordon is known as *chevaux de frise* and is widespread in the west from Iberia to Scotland.

the archaeologically recognizable elements of a highly complex pattern of behaviour. It is possible to imagine a whole range of offerings, including hides, wool, cheese, and so on, which would have left no archaeological trace.

The positions in which these deposits are found in the pits is informative. The majority are from the bottommost layer, before any erosion had taken place, but some pits had secondary deposits placed after a phase of erosion. The implication is that there was a fixed pattern in the timing of the depositions. It is tempting to see this as related in some way to seasonality and possibly to one or more of the seasonal festivals.

The most convincing explanation for this complex pattern of behaviour would be to regard the storage of the seed corn in pits as representing a belief in the power of the chthonic deities in preserving the corn during the liminal period, when it is dormant, and ensuring its fertility when sown. Once, therefore, the seed had been taken from the pits for sowing, it would have been necessary to make an offering to the deity in anticipation of a productive harvest. The second deposition might represent an offering of thanks. For spring-sown seed, the appropriate seasonal festivals would have been Lugnasad and Samain.

For societies for whom the productive capacity of the land was of vital importance, it is easy to understand how propitiatory offerings specific to the community's central concern became dominant. In times of stress, such as a succession of bad harvests, the intensity of sacrifice will have increased. It is probable that societies more reliant on flocks and herds will have developed different systems. In the case of upland areas, deposition in bogs seems to have been a significant pattern of behaviour. In this context, the discovery of 'bog butter' in the bogs of Ireland and Scotland is interesting. It is not unreasonable to see in these kegs or cloths of butter the offering to the deities, by a pastoral community, of part of its valued product in expectation of a satisfactory milk yield. Other items found in bogs, including wooden containers and bronze vessels, may again reflect the importance of the uplands for milk production.

Groves, Springs, and Shrines

Sufficient will have been said to show that offerings to the gods were made throughout the landscape—both the natural and the domestic landscape. There were also specifically designated sacred locations, known by the Gallo-

XVIII *Facing:* The River Thames has produced a spectacular array of extremely fine Iron Age metalwork much of which was probably thrown into the water as offerings to the gods. The shield boss from Wandsworth is a considerable work of art. It is decorated in repoussé style with two large birds whose flowing wings develop into tendril motifs. Second or first century BC. British Museum.

157 The carcass of a dog and the leg of a horse buried together in a disused storage pit in the hill fort of Danebury, Hampshire, England. This combination of dog and horse recurs on a number of occasions and is suggestive of a distinctive ritual belief. A range of other animal burials was also recorded. The practice of animal burial was widespread in southern Britain and northern France and may represent thank offerings to the chthonic deities for protecting the seed corn stored in the pits.

Brittonic word *nemeton*, which, like the cognate Latin *nemus*, means a sacred clearing in a wood or a sacred grove. The word recurs throughout the Celtic world, from the Galatian *Drunemeton* to *Nemetobriga* in Spain and *Aquae Arnemetiae*, the sacred spring at Buxton in Derbyshire. In Old Irish *fidnemed* refers to a shrine in a forest.

Tacitus, in his description of the rout of the Druids on Anglesey in AD 59, writes of 'groves sacred to savage rites' which were cut down, 'for their religion encouraged them to drench their altars with the blood of prisoners and to find out the will of the gods by consulting the entrails of human beings'. But the most evocative description of a grove, in this case in southern Gaul, is provided by Lucan in his poem *Pharsalia* and deserves to be quoted in full.

A grove there was untouched by men's hands from ancient times, whose interlacing boughs enclosed a space of darkness and cold shade, and banished the sunlight from above . . . gods were worshipped there with savage rites, the altars were heaped with hideous offerings and every tree was sprinkled with human gore. On those boughs . . . birds feared to perch; in those coverts wild beasts would not lie down; no wind ever bore down upon that wood, nor thunderbolt hurled from black clouds; the trees, even when they spread their leaves to no breeze, rustled of themselves. Water, also, fell there in abundance from dark springs. The images of the gods grim and rude were uncouth blocks formed of felled tree-trunks. Their mere antiquity and the ghastly hue of the rotten timber struck terror. . . . Legend also told that often the subterranean hollows quaked and bellowed, that yew trees fell down and rose again, that the glare of conflagrations came from trees that were not on fire, and that serpents twined and glided round their stems. The people never resorted thither to worship at close quarters but left the place to the gods. For, when the sun is in mid-heaven or dark night fills the sky, the priest himself dreads their approach and fears to surprise the lord of the grove. (*Pharsalia* 3. 400–25)

For all its poetic licence, Lucan's description, which so brilliantly conjures up the sense of stark panic, may be regarded as a reasonable evocation of a sacred place and the hold which it will have had over the local population. Lucan goes on to mention that Caesar had it cleared 'for it grew near his works', though it was more likely that he wished to destroy the power of the place. An interesting parallel is provided by the sacred spring of Sulis at Bath, where hot mineral water still gushes out of the ground at the rate of a quarter of a million gallons a day. Very soon after the Roman invasion of AD 43, a road, presumably of military origin, was driven through the sanctuary within 30 metres of the spring itself. Twenty years or so later, by which time the province had been firmly grasped, the road was removed and the land returned to the deity, now conflated with the Roman goddess Minerva: there is some suggestion in the archaeological record that a grove was replanted nearby at this time.

The archaeological demonstration of sacred groves is likely, by the very nature of the places, to be difficult, but, as we have suggested, there is a possibility that deposits like that found at Snettisham may indeed represent just such a place. The thermal springs of Bath and Buxton are other contenders.

Reverence for springs was widespread. Among the best known are two Gaulish examples, the shrine of Sequana at the source of the Seine in Burgundy and Chamalières near Clermont-Ferrand. Both have produced a remarkable array of votive offerings in the form of small wooden carvings or, less common, embossed plaques of metal. The symbolism of many of these items, emphasizing as they do limbs, internal organs, and eyes, leaves little doubt of the underlying belief in the curative power of the waters. Such a belief is also implied by the way in which the thermal springs at Bath and Buxton developed. That the figurines from the sanctuary of Sequana date to the first century AD might suggest that the sophistication evident in the depiction of that part of the body which required the deity's attention was something which developed late, perhaps as a result of Mediterranean influence, but the sanctity of the springs must go back to an earlier period. It is significant that the majority of them for which the dedication is known were presided over by female deities, but this is entirely appropriate to the generalized Celtic belief which related earth and place to goddesses. The continuation of this belief pattern is shown by the large number of wells and springs in the west of Europe which continue to be associated with female Christian saints, and in this context it is not irrelevant to point out that the majority of the French river names are feminine.

The sacred nature of lakes and bogs should also be remembered. The collections of war gear at Llyn Cerrig Bach (Anglesey), Hjortspring in Denmark, and La Tène in Switzerland have already been mentioned, and it is clear from deposits comprising a range of metal items of the eighth to the sixth centuries BC from the lake of Llyn Fawr in south Wales and from numerous bogs in Ireland that the tradition was long established and need not be exclusively associated with weapons. Geneva provides another example of a lakeside sanctuary. Here an inlet from the lake was found to contain a collection of human remains especially skulls, and a massive statue carved from an oak tree and dated to *c*.80 BC may well have been one of the cult figures which dominated the sanctuary. Its somewhat gaunt appearance is a reminder of Lucan's haunting description.

Reverence for the chthonic deities, inherent

158 The sanctuary of Sequana at the source of the Seine, Côte d'Or, was used during the Late Iron Age and Roman period as a healing sanctuary. A large number of votive offerings were found, among which were simply carved wooden figurines presumably intended to represent some aspect of the suppliant. Some indicated by emphasis the parts of the body requiring divine cure. Musée Archéologique de Dijon.

159 Timber idol erected at the port of Geneva, Switzerland, c.80 BC. The port was constructed between 123 and 120 BC, based on dendrochronological dates, at the time when the Romans were establishing a firm presence in Provence. The development of the port may have been encouraged by rapidly increasing trade with the Roman colonists. Musée d'Art et d'Histoire, Geneva.

in the worship of watery places, also finds an expression in the digging of shafts or wells, which are found throughout Celtic Europe. The tradition is evidently an ancient one and it is likely that the shaft found at Wilsford near Stonehenge, dating to the Middle Bronze Age, represents the same belief system. A slightly later example, of the Late Bronze Age, from Swanwick in Hampshire, is said to have contained an organic deposit identified as blood.

The majority of the shafts from continental Europe date to the later stages of the Iron Age and many of them lie within rectangular ditched enclosures (*viereckschanzen*) (Map 27). That at Holzhausen in Bavaria was some 90 metres across. In one corner was a timber structure, possibly a shrine, together with three shafts 2.5 metres in diameter and 40 metres deep. One of the shafts contained an upright wooden stake associated with material thought to have derived from decayed flesh or blood. The *viereckschanze* of Fellbach-Schmiden in Baden-Württemberg has proved to be particularly informative. Within the enclosure, in addition to burials, there was a well, the lower part of which was waterlogged, creating conditions for the preservation of the timber lining and of organic remains within the filling. According to the dendrochronological date, the timbers were cut in 123 BC. Parts of a timber structure which surrounded the top of the shaft had fallen in and were preserved. These included a group of remarkable wooden carvings of animals (Pl. XXI), one a rampant stag, another comprising two goats standing on their hind legs and clasped about the waist by a central human(?) figure, now missing. On the bottom of the shaft were two almost complete pottery vessels. The shaft probably served as a well, presumably for ritual purposes, before it was abandoned and filled. Whether the well was associated only with the activities attendant upon the burial or whether it continued to have a function after burial was complete remains unclear.

Viereckschanzen, with or without burials, have tended to produce little archaeological material other than that which might have been thrown into shafts, if they occurred. This implies that, whatever activity went on within them, the deposition of votive offerings was not normally part of the ritual. The contrast with the numerous kinds of sanctuaries which have been excavated is striking. Broadly speaking there are two basic sanctuary types: the Celto-Ligurian sanctuaries of southern Gaul and the northern Celtic type which cluster densely in a broad zone extending from Germany to Britain.

The southern Gaulish type is best known from the sites of Roquepertuse (Bouches-du-Rhône) and Entremont near Aix-en-Provence. At Roquepertuse two separate elements survive: large seated figures carved in stone, which are now thought to be prominent members of the aristocracy, and the stone elements of a stone and timber architectural complex incorporating the famous Janus-heads (Pl. XII), a stone bird of prey, a frieze carved with simply delineated horse heads, and stone pillars carved with niches to take severed human heads. Most of the ensemble dates to the third century BC and the sanctuary was abandoned after it was destroyed by fire at the beginning of the second century.

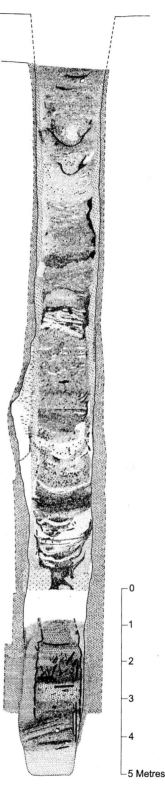

160 *Above*: Aerial view of the rectangular ritual enclosure (*viereckschanze*) at Neufahrn, Baden-Württemberg, Germany. Enclosures of this sort dating to the Late Iron Age are widespread in Germany and parts of northern France.

161 *Right*: Ritual shafts are a recurring feature in Late Iron Age Europe. In the case of those dug to beneath the water level it is difficult to be certain whether they were dug as wells or for ritual purposes, but use as a well does not preclude ritual connotations. The shaft from Fellbach-Schmiden, Baden-Württemberg, Germany, was associated with a *viereckschanze* (a rectangular ritual enclosure) and produced well-preserved wooden sculptures. Württembergisches Landesmuseum, Stuttgart.

162 *Below*: The bottom part of the ritual shaft or well at Fellbach-Schmiden during excavation, showing the wooden stag *in situ*.

0
1
2
3
4
5 Metres

164 Frieze simply carved with a row of horses' heads from the sanctuary of Roquepertuse, Bouches-du-Rhône, France. Traces of paint remain. Third or second century BC. Musée d'Archéologie Meditér-ranéenne, Marseilles.

Many of these same elements recur at Entre-mont, where the architectural features include a vertical pillar carved with severed heads and another fragment with a carved severed head flanked by niches for real severed heads, of which some fifteen examples were found, some still bearing nail holes for attachment. Other sites in the region have produced fragments of similar sculpture as well as human heads.

To what extent the religious sites of the Celto-Ligurian area differ significantly from those of the rest of Gaul is difficult to say. The availability of easily carved limestone and prox-imity to the Greek cities of the Mediterranean coastal zone will have had some influence, but the principal elements of iconography—the squatting figures and the Janus-heads—are known in other parts of the Celtic world and the collection of human heads among the Celts was an often-repeated anecdote among Greek and Roman writers. It is simpler, therefore, to re-gard the Celto-Ligurian sanctuaries as a region-al manifestation of a more widespread pattern of beliefs.

In the northern Gaulish zone the normal type of sanctuary by the Late Iron Age was a rectan-gular or circular building of timber usually set within a rectangular *temenos* defined by a ditched or fenced boundary. Excavations at Gournay-sur-Aronde (Oise) have provided a detailed insight into the form and development of a sanctuary of this kind and the rituals prac-tised there. The sanctuary occupied a spur overlooking a stream which flowed from a small lake. The earliest building dates to the fourth century BC, and thereafter the site was continuously used and modified until the end of the first century BC, when the timber structures were burnt and the site levelled. The sacred nature of the loca-tion remained in folk memory until the fourth century AD, when a Gallo-Roman temple was built precisely over the original shrine.

Throughout, the pre-Conquest shrine was surrounded by a ditch of rectan-gular plan later enhanced by an external palisade. From the fourth until the first century BC the focus was a large oval-shaped pit, in which the remains of sacrificed cattle had been placed. It first lay in the open within a setting of

163 *Far left*: Stone sculpture of a seated figure from the sanctuary of Roquepertuse, Bouches-du-Rhône, France. Third or second century BC. Musée d'Archéologie Meditérranéenne, Marseilles.

165 Bronze statue of a seated deity from Bouray-sur-Juine, Essonne, France. The figure has hoofed feet like a deer and wears a neck torc; the eyes were of glass paste. First century BC–first century AD. Musée des Antiquités Nationales, Saint-Germain-en-Laye, Paris.

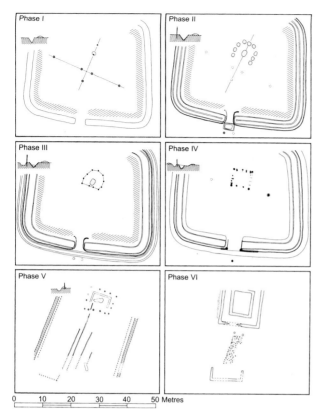

Phase I

Phase II

Phase III

Phase IV

Phase V

Phase VI

0   10   20   30   40   50 Metres

166 The temple site excavated at Gournay, Picardy, France, remained in use over a considerable period, for much of the time focused around a ritual pit. The ditch, created in period II, formed the receptacle for extensive ritual depositions comprising weapons and animals. The sanctity of the site was still recognized in the Roman period, when a typical Romano-Celtic temple was built in masonry.

upright posts placed some distance away. Later it was enclosed on three sides by three sets of three pits containing a range of offerings. In the next stage the pits were replaced by a setting of timbers, which may have served as uprights to take a roof over the central pit. In the early first century BC the building was reconstructed in timber in a more regular rectangular form and was rebuilt again *c.*30 BC, this time of daub on stone footings surrounded by an ambulatory of light posts.

Throughout the life of the sanctuary the *temenos* ditch was used as a repository for sacrificed offerings, including some 2,000 broken weapons and large quantities of animal bones, which were found to have been placed in successive layers, each representing a distinct act of sacrifice.

The continuity of the sanctuary over a long period of time, from the pre-Roman Iron Age well into the Roman period, is a phenomenon widely recognized across the northern part of the Celtic zone. Among the sites where structural evidence of the early sanctuaries has been found beneath later Roman shrines may be listed Uley (Gloucestershire), Worth (Kent), Hayling Island (Hampshire), Vendeuil-Caply (Oise), Saint-Germain-le-Rocheux (Chatillon-sur-Seine), and Schleidweiler (Trier); many others have produced evidence suggestive of a long continuity.

The evidence from Gournay-sur-Aronde and Vendeuil-Caply, only 30 kilometres apart, show that in this region of Belgic Gaul, from the fourth century until the beginning of the first, the religious structures—pits and upright posts—were essentially open air; the concept of a regular roofed structure was a first-century BC development. A similar open-air sanctuary dating to the third century BC was discovered at Libenice in Bohemia. Here the *temenos* was created by a continuous ditch defining an elongated rectangular area at one end of which a standing stone and two large post-holes provided the ritual focus. The possibility that the posts were carved into god-like figures is suggested by the discovery nearby of two bronze torcs which might have been worn by the wooden images. A series of pits, dug one at a time and refilled, seem to have been associated with successive libations, while deposits of animal bones and the burial of a female indicate the variety of sacrifices offered.

The evidence from Britain differs only in that rectangular buildings appear before the first century. The best known is the rectangular *cella* with its post-built ambulatory found at Heathrow (Middlesex) within a rectangular enclosure. Other examples of rectangular- or square-built structures have been found in the hill forts of Danebury (Hampshire) and South Cadbury (Somerset) and at Lancing Down (Sussex). All are thought to have served as shrines during the British Middle Iron Age (*c.*300–100 BC).

Another feature of the British evidence is the prevalence of circular temples. This is most clearly demonstrated by the first-century BC structure found on Hayling Island, a large building 15 metres in diameter set within a rectangular ditched enclosure. The entire structure was rebuilt in stone, after the Roman invasion, in the late first century AD. A circular shrine, this time built with drystone wall footings, was found in the centre of the hill fort of Maiden Castle (Dorset). This, too, was replaced in masonry in the Roman period. Although circular shrines of the Iron Age are not yet known in continental Europe, circular Gallo-Roman temples suggest that earlier prototypes may once have existed.

In Ireland, circularity was the prime characteristic of religious sites. Four

167 *Below, left*: A rectangular ditched enclosure excavated at Heathrow Airport, Middlesex, England, in 1944, was found to contain a rectangular timber building with a slighter 'ambulatory' around it. The plan is highly reminiscent of later Romano-Celtic temples. The date would appear to be Middle or Late Iron Age.

Heathrow, Middlesex

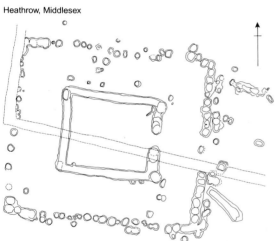

Late Iron Age

Early Roman

0   10   20 Metres

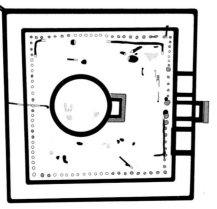

168 *Left*: The temple at Hayling Island, Hampshire, England, in use from the first century BC, was rebuilt in masonry by the Romans in the late first century AD, the Roman structure reproducing the form of its predecessor.

169 *Above*: Aerial view of the sacred site of Tara, Co. Meath, Ireland. The large enclosure, the *Rath na Riogh*, contains a number of monuments, the most prominent being two smaller enclosures and a Bronze Age burial mound—the Mound of the Hostages. Beyond the enclosure, close to the church, is the Rath of the Synods, which was in use during the first century AD; the parallel banks beyond are known as the Banqueting Hall. Tara was important in early Irish history as the place where kingship was legitimized.

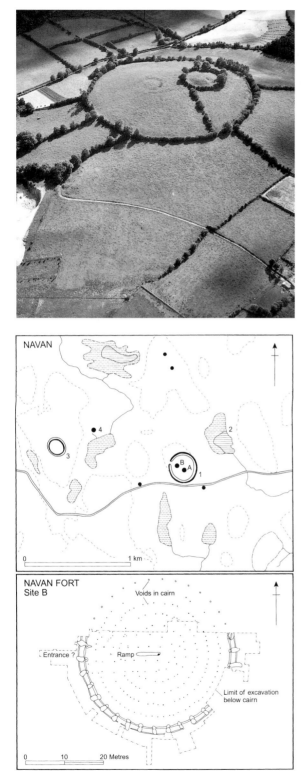

great ritual centres are known from the vernacular literature and all have been identified on the ground as surviving complexes of earthworks: Tara (Meath), Cruachain (Connacht), Dún Ailinne (Co. Kildare), and Emain Macha, or Navan Fort (Co. Armagh). All were associated with rites of kingship in the early historic period, but Tara was pre-eminent.

The complex of Emain Macha is best known archaeologically. The focal point is an oval enclosure of 5 hectares set within a ritual landscape which included a natural lake, from which four bronze horns and a number of human skulls were recovered, and an artificial pool known as 'the King's Stables' which appears to have been dug for ritual purposes c.800 BC. The enclosure itself contained two prominent circular monuments. One was a ploughed-out ring barrow, the other survived as a mound 50 metres in diameter and 6 metres high, but as excavation showed it was altogether more complex. The earliest occupation comprised a series of circular buildings associated with a range of prestige goods dating from c.700–100 BC: the assemblage included the skull and jaw of a Barbary ape which it is tempting to interpret as an exotic Mediterranean import, though whether as a living beast or simply a severed head is unclear.

In 94 BC (a precise date based on the dendrochronological evidence) an oak tree was felled and set up as the centre post of a massive circular structure nearly 40 metres in diameter composed

170 *Top left*: Aerial view of Navan Fort in Co. Armagh, Northern Ireland. Navan is the Emain Macha of the Irish epics. The crest of the hill was occupied by a remarkable timber structure 40 metres in diameter built around a single oak felled in 94 BC. The structure was embedded in a cairn of stones and the exposed parts set on fire.

171 *Left*: The map shows the ritual landscape dominated by the enclosure known as Navan Fort (1), overlooking the lake of Loughnashade (2), where four large bronze horns and a number of human skulls were found. Other sites are Haughey's Fort (3), and an artificial pond known as the King's Stables (4), which produced finds of Late Bronze Age date. Other archaeological sites are shown as black spots. The detailed plan shows the massive timber structure dating to 94 BC found under mound B within the fort.

of six concentric settings of posts, some 275 timbers in all, arranged in radial sets in a manner highly suggestive of a structure designed to be roofed. No evidence of internal activity was found and the floor was kept absolutely clean. The standing structure was then embedded in a stone cairn piled up inside to a maximum height of 2.5 metres, and that part of the building which projected above the cairn was set on fire. After the conflagration the cairn was covered by a mound of cut turves, raising the height by a further 2.5 metres. The motivation for this remarkable programme, involving the mobilization of huge social effort, defies explanation, except as a ritual act of momentous proportions.

The excavation of Dún Ailinne provided a further insight into Irish ritual sites. Here the hilltop was defined by an enclosure of 16 hectares. A succession of three substantial timber structures occupied a central position. The first was a circular palisaded enclosure 22 metres in diameter. This was replaced by a more elaborate circular structure with concentric settings of timbers which the excavator suggests supported platforms of different heights looking inwards. A smaller enclosure formed an annex, while radiating palisades and posts created a monumental funnel approach. In the final stage concentric palisades defined a circular area 37 metres in internal diameter. Within the centre of this was a circular building 5 metres in diameter surrounded by a setting of massive free-standing timbers probably 3–4 metres in height. After a period, during which there was intensive burning near some of the posts, the entire structure was dismantled. Subsequent use suggests that the site was given over to periodic, perhaps seasonal, meetings involving feasting. The dating evidence shows that the entire sequence belonged to the period from the third century BC to the second or third century AD.

The size and form of the structures at Dún Ailinne leave little doubt that they served a centralizing ritual function. It is possible that the creation of the mound at Emain Macha and the demolition of the final structure at Dún Ailinne were broadly contemporary and mark a significant change in the ritual use of these sites.

The monumentality of the Irish religious sites sets them apart from their British and continental European counterparts. The

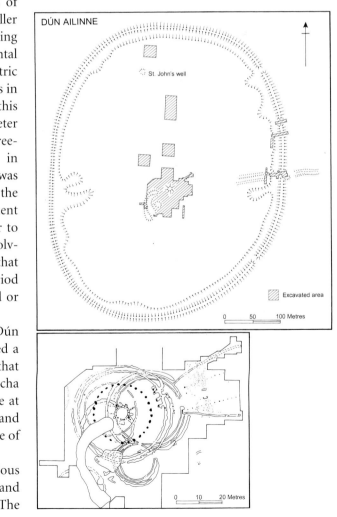

172 Dún Ailinne, Co. Kildare, Ireland, was one of the ritual centres mentioned in the Irish vernacular literature. The centre was occupied by a complex of timber buildings.

huge timber structures, and the enclosing earthworks which invariably have the banks outside the ditches, are features which hark back to Neolithic and Early Bronze Age times and provide a firm reminder of the strength of indigenous traditions in more remote areas of the Atlantic fringes.

In this context it is worth recalling the carved stelae—standing stones—of Armorica, which occur in their columnar and hemispherical forms throughout the Breton countryside (Fig. 129). That they were regarded as religiously powerful is demonstrated by the Christianization which many of them suffered by having Christian symbols, usually the cross, carved on them or by being moved bodily into the precincts of a church. These Iron Age stelae clearly belong to a belief system which can be traced back to the standing stones of the megalithic period.

Some echo of the outlandish rites of the distant fringes is provided by Poseidonius' anecdotal tale (quoted by Strabo) of an island lying off the mouth of the Loire occupied only by women 'possessed by Dionysus'. Once a year they removed the roof of their temple and replaced it with a new roof within the day. During this ceremony one of the women was chosen for sacrifice. She was 'torn to pieces by the others, and they carry the pieces around the temple crying out "euoi" and they do not cease until their madness has passed away' (Strabo, *Hist.* 4. 4. 6). Presumably this behaviour was judged to be sufficiently unusual for Poseidonius to have mentioned it.

Sufficient will have been said to indicate that built temples existed throughout the Celtic world. The archaeological evidence adds firm support to the references about religious structures given by the classical writers. When Diodorus Siculus writes of 'temples and sanctuaries' and Plutarch tells us that Caesar's sword was hung up in a temple of the Arverni, they were presumably referring to the quite sophisticated timber structures of the type represented at Gournay, the sanctity of which was to be remembered for many centuries to come.

Attitudes to Death

The archaeological evidence derived from the excavation of cemeteries is sufficient to suggest that a belief in the afterlife may have persisted throughout much of the Celtic world. Caesar makes the matter explicit by reporting that the Druids attach particular importance to the belief that after death the soul passes from one body to another. In this he, like other commentators, is probably following Poseidonius, and rationalizes his observation by supposing that the doctrine was favoured because it made the warrior fearless in battle.

The burial tradition most widely practised in continental Europe from the seventh to the first centuries BC was inhumation, the dead person being provided with the equipment appropriate to his or her status as perceived by the lineage responsible for burial. This qualification is necessary to remind us that the burial rite, at least of the élite, was an occasion for the lineage publicly to display its prestige to the assembled company. Rich burials, like those of the West Hallstatt chiefdoms and their successors in the fifth century, and those of the northern Celtic zone in the first century BC and early first century AD, reflect societies in which command of prestige goods was considered to be an attribute of status. For most of the period from the beginning of the fourth century to the end of the second status was expressed in terms of warrior equipment reflecting a rather different set of values.

The change to cremation, which becomes evident in much of Celtic Europe late in the second or early in the first century BC, implies a significant shift in belief, though it is not apparent what caused it. It may be little more than the resurgence of a long-established view of the spirit being released into the sky. An alternative possibility is that the custom was an emulation of Roman practice. The move to cremation, together with the formalization of temple buildings and the development of *oppida*, may be seen as part of the package of changes which spread through much of the Celtic world in the last decades of the second century BC.

The probability that much of the British Isles adhered to a somewhat different belief system is suggested by the virtual absence of any form of burial over much of the country before the beginning of the first century BC, with the exception of the cemeteries of the Arras culture in Yorkshire and the cist burials of the South-West peninsula. The simplest explanation for this is that the normal method for dealing with the dead body was by excarnation—that is, the exposing of the body in some area set aside for the purpose. The bones would either be left there in the open or selectively brought back to the settlement for curation or use in other rituals. Some such explanation accounts both for the absence of evidence for regular interments and cremations and for the presence of human bones in settlement contexts. It is quite possible that excarnation was widely practised in other parts of Europe alongside other rites: its archaeological invisibility makes the issue difficult to judge.

The curation of human remains is dramatically reflected in the Celtic attitude to the head. Diodorus Siculus, presumably quoting Poseidonius, offers the standard disapproving view seen through the classical eyes:

They cut off the heads of enemies slain in battle and attach them to the necks of their horses. These blood-stained spoils they hand over to their attendants and carry off as booty, while striking up a paean and singing a song of victory, and they nail up these first fruits upon their houses just as do those who lay low wild animals in certain kinds of hunting. They embalm in cedar-oil the heads of the most distinguished enemies and preserve them carefully in a chest and display them with pride to strangers, saying that for this head, one of their ancestors, or his father or the man himself, refused the offer of a large sum of money.   (*Hist.* 5. 29)

In comparing the human head taken in battle with that of wild animals caught in the chase, Diodorus demeans the Celtic practice whether by ignorance or design. But behind the second part of the quotation one can discern something of the importance of the head in Celtic society: to own and to display a distinguished head was to retain and control the power of the dead person, which was the inheritance of the lineage. Refusal to part with such a trophy is understandable in that it would diminish the holder's power. Behind this might also lurk the belief that the head, once freed from its captor or his successor, would be able to work against them.

Reverence for the power of the head lies behind the story told by Livy of the battle between the Boii and the Romans during which the Roman consul, Postumus, was killed. His body was carried to the most prestigious temple of the tribe and there decapitated, the skull being cleaned and mounted with gold to serve as a cup in the deity's honour. Evidently the skull of such a distinguished enemy was a gift appropriate to a god. It is in this context that the skulls found in the Celto-Ligurian sanctuaries are probably best interpreted. Their power added to that of the god and was prevented from working against those who brought about the death. Behind what the Greek and Roman writers saw as a caricature of Celtic barbarism lay a complex pattern of values and beliefs.

That the Celts were, in Caesar's words, extremely superstitious seems fair comment. The gods, in their various guises, were everywhere and controlled everything. They could communicate with man through augury and could be cajoled or persuaded by sacrifice, but no contact was possible without the oversight of a trained practitioner—a Druid. Stated in these simple terms, Celtic religion was much like any other in its basic form. It is only in its vibrant mythology, still vivid in the Irish vernacular literature, that the rich complexity of the inherited lore can be glimpsed.

11

The Developed Celtic World

THE migratory movements which began towards the end of the fifth century BC were largely, but not entirely, over by the beginning of the second century, by which time the immense energy spent on conquest and raiding was being turned to more productive activities. The result was that throughout the Celtic world intensification in production and exchange becomes evident on an unprecedented scale. The reasons for these changes are complex, and their pace and trajectory differed from place to place and over time, and yet the generalization holds good for a vast territory from the Middle Danube to south-eastern England and from northern Iberia to Bohemia. In attempting to draw out the causal threads running through these developments we must begin by considering the impact of the extension of Roman influence, both direct and indirect, on the communities around the Mediterranean core.

Rome survived the threat of the Second Punic War (218–202 BC) and in the aftermath embarked on the first significant stage of its territorial expansion. On all fronts—in Iberia, southern Gaul, the Po Valley, Illyria, and Asia Minor—Rome confronted Celtic peoples. While the pace and nature of the interactions varied, the barbarian periphery cannot have failed to have undergone some change as a consequence of contact with the energetically expanding economy of the Mediterranean. These factors, together with the internally generated social dynamics of the different Celtic communities, led to the emergence of societies very different from those existing at the height of the migration period.

The Extension of Roman Power: 200–60 BC

The Second Punic War was a turning-point in Rome's relations with the wider world. Before the war began, Rome's interests were focused on peninsular Italy and the seas around, the command of which required the control of the islands to the west and the coasts of Illyria to the east. The conflict with Carthage totally changed the perspective. As a result of Hannibal's energetic campaigns, Rome was led to appreciate the strategic importance of controlling the Po Valley; her armies were actively involved in the south-east of the Iberian Peninsula, and were regularly using the land route through Provence and Languedoc; while in the east, in the Balkans and Asia Minor, the potential dangers of political instability there were fast becoming apparent. To maintain and develop the Italian core it was becoming necessary to control a much more extended periphery.

This was not just for reasons of military security. Active campaigning in distant territories provided a context for young men to gain experience and to advance in the Roman social system. Indeed there are interesting comparisons to be made between the importance of the raid in maintaining social hierarchies in the Celtic world and overseas campaigns in providing the aspiring Roman with a context in which to progress his career through a display of military excellence. Nor should the economic importance of overseas territories to Rome's development be underestimated. New territorial gains could yield raw materials and slaves in desirable quantity. For example, huge amounts of gold, silver, and copper were extracted from Iberia in the six years following the destruction of Carthaginian power, and Caesar's campaigns in Gaul are estimated to have provided a million slaves, most of them destined for the Roman markets. The other great advantage of overseas territories was that they could provide markets for surpluses produced on the estates of the Roman aristocracy. The quantity of north Italian wine offloaded in Gaulish markets in the early first century BC is thought to have been in the order of 100,000 hectolitres a year. Interactions on this scale must have had an effect on native communities in the areas peripheral to Roman activity.

Roman expansion into the Po Valley was rapid after the defeat of Hannibal. Traditional fear of the Celts, intensified by an awareness of the weakness of Rome's northern borders and the value to a potential enemy of the large pool of willing mercenaries provided by Cisalpine Celtic settlements, focused Rome's attention on the need for rapid conquest of the entire Po Valley. A series of determined campaigns ensued. In 197 BC the Cenomani were defeated at the Minico and forced into a treaty of friendship, and the next year the Insubres were overcome at Como. In a later rebellion, aided by the Boii, the Insubres were again unsuccessful, and in 194 the Boii were finally subdued, as the result of which many of them retreated northwards back into Transalpine Europe. Further campaigns in the west against the Ligurians and the east against the Carni during the next few years extended Rome's power to the southern fringes of the Alps. By the end of the 180s BC the process of latinization was well underway and surplus native manpower was finding itself in Roman employ both as auxiliary troops and as farm workers called *accolae galli*.

The romanization of Cisalpine Gaul meant that the routes through the Alps were now firmly under Roman control, and, with the instability of the Po Valley at an end, trade could begin to develop in a more regular and organized manner. For the Alpine and Transalpine Celts the new political geography of the south meant the beginning of a period of dramatic socio-economic development.

In Iberia the capture of Cádiz in 206 BC marked the end of Carthaginian colonial involvement and the beginning of Roman influence, while the foundation of the two provinces of Hither and Further Spain in 197 BC formalized the process. For the next sixty-four years, until the capitulation of Numantia in 133, Rome was in a state of almost constant war with the native tribes on the provincial borders, most notably the Lusitani and the Celtiberians. These hostilities, and the Social War which followed in the early first century BC, part of which was fought on Spanish soil, mitigated against the development of significant trading systems between the native and Roman zones, and it was not until Caesar arrived in 61 BC that the west of Iberia began to be brought under Roman control. By this stage, however, even the remote north-west—the region of the Castro culture—had begun to absorb the concepts of Roman urbanism, following the expeditions into the region of Decimus Brutus in 138–136, which initiated the opening-up of the Atlantic fringes.

The long and painful wars against the native Iberians in the second century BC and the Social and Civil Wars of the first century created the need for a constant movement of men and supplies to and from the Peninsula, a movement enhanced by the outflow of raw materials from the highly productive Spanish provinces. Although direct contact by sea was an option, the overland route through southern Gaul was preferred, especially for the movement of troops and military equipment. Thus, throughout the second and first centuries Roman convoys passed through Provence and Languedoc across the now thoroughly hellenized coastal zone. The needs of the military quartermaster and the entrepreneurial activities of civilians travelling with the armies opened up the

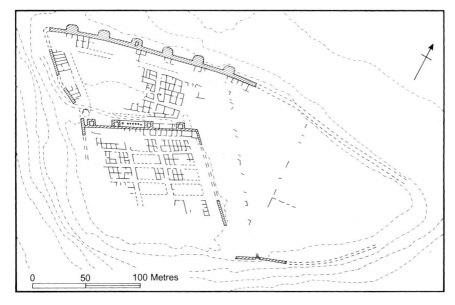

173 The hilltop town of Entremont, Bouches-du-Rhône, France, was the capital of the Saluvii, who occupied the territory in the region of Aix-en-Provence. The town was defended by a stone wall with bastions which derives its inspiration from the Greek city walls of the southern French coast. Entremont was destroyed by the Romans in 123 BC.

0   50   100 Metres

174 *Above*: The *oppidum* of Entremont was defended with stone walls and bastions based on Greek models. The urban layout within was carefully planned. Fourth to late second centuries BC.

175 *Below*: The native *oppidum* of Nages, Gard, France, was defended by stone walls with bastions reminiscent of Greek defensive architecture. The regular layout of the parallel streets is a characteristic of Greek urban planning, which can only have been learned from the Greek cities of the coastal zone. Third to first centuries BC.

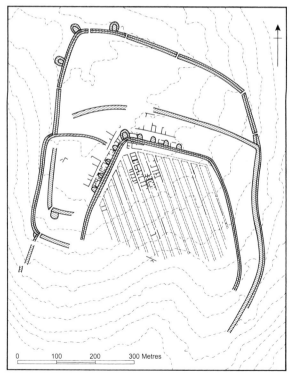

zone to Roman commerce. In this way the Celto-Ligurian inhabitants absorbed many aspects of Roman culture. This is demonstrated by the Mediterranean styles of architecture adopted by the inhabitants of the hill forts of Ensérune, Entremont, and Nages.

In crossing southern Gaul the Roman entrepreneurs will have become increasingly conscious of the two great axes of trade—the Rhône route to the north and the Aude–Carcassonne Gap–Garonne route to the west. The large native settlements at Tolosa (Toulouse) on the Garonne and Vienna (Vienne) on the Rhône were no doubt thoroughly explored by the more adventurous at an early stage in the contact period.

The mutual interdependence of the native and Roman systems worked well, until increasingly serious raids mounted by the tribes of the Maritime Alps and Lower Rhône Valley against Roman convoys and Greek cities alike led, inevitably, to annexation in 123 BC. After this the Province of Transalpina was formally established.

Thus, while in Iberia Celtic-speaking peoples were locked in a seemingly interminable conflict with the Roman armies, in the west the early second century BC saw the establishment of an interface between the Roman and the Celtic worlds stretching from the Adriatic to the Pyrenees. Along the 1,100 kilometres of this cultural frontier social and economic interactions developed, increasing in intensity as the Italian economy became more and more dependent on the periphery.

In the eastern Mediterranean and the east the situation was different. The mountains of the Balkans formed an effective barrier between the Adriatic and the Middle Danube regions, sheltering the Celtic communities from Roman interference, apart from brief campaigns against brigands in the Upper Sava Valley between 156 and 129 BC. In the Lower Danube Valley the Thracians acted as a buffer against the developing Roman interest in Greece and Macedonia until the middle of the first century AD, when Thrace finally became a Roman province.

The situation in Galatia was different yet again. Here, as we have seen, the Galatian state remained independent and, to a large extent, isolated, even after its decisive defeat by the Romans in 189 BC. Following the massacre of the Tetrarchs by Mithridates IV in 88 BC, the Galatians became increasingly pro-Roman until their territory was annexed by Pompey in 67 BC. During the century or more of contact between the two peoples there is little evidence of significant acculturation, but the allegiance which developed between the later Galatian leaders and the Roman authorities implies a close political relationship at least by the first century BC.

The Roman Economy and the Celtic World

During the second century BC the Roman economy was undergoing major transformations. The reasons were various and complex. One of the principal factors was the need to maintain substantial citizen armies to forward Roman interests abroad. This meant that men who would otherwise be engaged in rural activities were required to spend long periods away from home and were therefore unable to work the land. For many of those who survived and returned home, farm work retained little attraction. This encouraged a gradual drift to the cities and in particular Rome, leaving farms abandoned and land uncultivated. As the urban proletariat grew, so the smallholdings were bought up and gradually amalgamated into estates of increasing size. By the end of the second century large tracts of land were held by comparatively few owners. One of the reasons for the growth of big estates, in addition to the availability of cheap land, was that for the senatorial class land provided a convenient and socially acceptable form of investment. To be involved directly in the trading of commodities was not considered to be a proper pursuit for a man of status, though in all probability many ignored or circumvented the convention. To own land, on the other hand, was desirable. The physical extent of the estate or estates was a ready indicator of a man's prestige. More to the point, the yield provided a cash return on the money invested in the original land purchase.

The estates required large bodies of agricultural workers. With extensive rural depopulation, labour for hire was not readily available. A more certain way to fuel productivity was with slave labour. Slaves were cost effective, not least because they could breed in captivity and slaves could be sold. By the beginning of the first century BC the reliance of the Roman economy on slave labour was considerable. One estimate is that in the early first century BC there were 300,000 Gaulish slaves in Italy alone, a total which required to be topped up at the rate of 15,000 a year.

There is one further factor to be weighed. For the most part those estates, too far from Rome to deliver fresh fruit and vegetables to the city, had to rely on producing corn, oil, and wine. Of these, manufacture of wine soon became the most popular, no doubt because of ease of production and profit margin, but overproduction led to pressure to develop new overseas markets.

From this brief, and greatly oversimplified, sketch, two things stand out: the need to maintain a steady flow of slaves; and the need to create new markets in which to dispose of surpluses not required in Italy.

While the Roman economy became increasingly dependent on slaves to fuel its productive capacity, its need for raw materials, and in particular gold and silver to serve as currency in the increasingly complex economic system, also increased. Copper, tin, and high-quality iron were always in demand. Other imports listed by contemporary writers such as Strabo include hides, furs, amber, hunting dogs, and other exotic animals. These raw materials would have been sought in the newly won territories and in the barbarian hinterlands beyond. Thus from the beginning of the second century BC Rome became more and more dependent upon sources of supply beyond its immediate control.

Romans and the Society of the Celtic Periphery

There can be little doubt that the imperative of Roman needs impinged significantly upon the barbarian world, such was the energy of the Roman state. But the Celtic north was also undergoing social change, in part *sui generis*. Opportunity for raiding was now far more restricted, not only by the growing power of Rome in the south but by the rise of the Dacian state in the east and what may be interpreted as the population increase now underway among the Germanic peoples of the north. New systems were evolving for the display of power among the élite. The entourage remained important: the size of a leader's 'following' was seen as an indicator of his status. In earlier times, as we have argued above (pp. 88–90), the raid provided the opportunity to lead and the feast was the occasion for the display of status before the assembled company. But times had changed, and Poseidonius (through Strabo), in describing the feast among Celts with whom he was familiar, could assign it to 'former times'.

What seems to have replaced this early system, at least in parts of Gaul, was a form of potlatch—a process of conspicuous giving and consumption, enacted publicly so that the company could gauge the wealth of the host and benefit from his generosity. The account which Poseidonius gives of an event staged by the Arvernian chief Louernius is informative. In a bid for status he built a large square enclosure and there stockpiled food and set up wine presses to feast all comers over a period of many days. He also drove about the countryside in his chariot scattering 'little pieces of gold and silver' to the horde who followed eagerly in his wake. To be able to mount such a display of largess Louernius was evidently in command of considerable resources. Thus the control of goods and raw materials, and the facility to manipulate them to produce luxury exotics such as wine to dispense to clients, now became essential for the aspiring leader. The development of *oppida* controlling route nodes, and thus the movement of goods, might be seen as one of the more visible elements in the complex package of social change now coming about in the Celtic world.

Whether or not the 'little pieces of gold and silver' which Louernius threw to his followers were coins or bullion is unclear, but the development of coinage played a significant part in the new system. Gold and silver coins were used for gift exchange rather than commerce in the capitalist sense. Since they were stamped with the symbols of the issuing authority, often in the first century BC actually mentioning the king by name, the coin, however acquired, would be seen to emanate ultimately from this authority. It was part of the largess which he distributed to his people, and the current holder was therefore beholden to him for his initial generosity. The sporadic mintings of coins were, quite possibly, occasioned by the desire of the issuer to legitimize his claim to leadership.

The proximity of the Roman world introduced another new factor into the political and social dynamics of the periphery. A tribal leader could ally himself and his following to the Roman state—that is, he could become a client of Rome. In doing so he would acquire prestige and power by virtue of the protection which the Roman patron would offer. In the same context an aspiring young warrior might place himself and his fighting entourage in the hands of Rome to serve as auxiliaries in the Roman army, much as his ancestors might have been engaged in a less formal way as mercenaries by Mediterranean powers. Knowledge of Roman fighting methods and acceptance of Roman ways would have provided another opportunity to demonstrate social superiority.

The kingdom of Noricum provides an informative example of the relationship which could develop between Celtic and Roman society. The kingdom lay in the eastern Alps in an area roughly coterminous with present-day Austria. It began as a group of loosely allied Celtic tribes but achieved a degree of unity

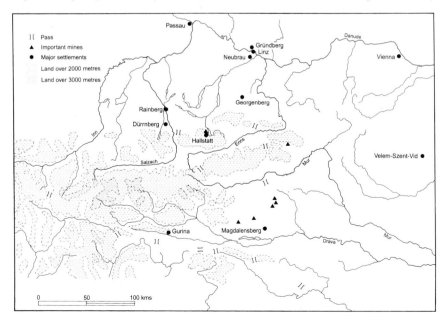

176 The kingdom of Noricum in the second and first centuries BC.

217

some time during the second century BC under the hegemony of the Nori of central eastern Carinthia. Noricum lay astride the east Alpine trading routes, but it also commanded rich supplies of iron, which were worked locally into a fine steel, well known in the Roman world as *ferrum Noricum*. Relations with Rome began in 186 BC and developed amicably, until the region was eventually annexed in 15 BC. Throughout this period trade intensified. In about 70 BC a local coinage was developed in southern Noricum to serve as a medium of exchange.

The capital of Noricum, Virunum, was located on the Magdalensberg, near Klagenfurt, close to the major route leading northwards from Aquileia. The native *oppidum* was sited on the highest point of the mountain. It was here that the royal residence was located, and, inevitably, the *oppidum* served as the principal administrative centre of the kingdom. Just below the native town there developed a ghetto occupied by resident Roman traders. Excavation suggests that it was established as early as the beginning of the first century BC and continued to grow. By 30 BC the lower settlement could boast a large forum and masonry-built houses constructed and decorated in purely Roman style. These were the residences of traders linked to enterprises based in Aquileia. When, in 15 BC, Drusus and Tiberius began to annex the Alpine territories, Noricum, now thoroughly romanized, was absorbed with ease.

Roman relations with the Celtic tribes of Gaul were no less intense. The constant Roman presence in the south of the country after *c.*200 BC will have provided ample opportunity for Roman entrepreneurs to develop lucrative trading links with native communities living around the fringes of the Roman sphere of influence. At the hill fort of Nages, in the Vaunage not far from Nîmes, it is possible to trace the impact of the Mediterranean world through the increasing quantities of imported pottery, both fine wares and transport vessels, found in successive stratified layers throughout the duration of the settlement's habitation beginning about 300 BC and ending about AD 10.

One of the most desirable of the Roman imports was wine. The Celts' love of wine was legendary in the Roman world. Diodorus Siculus (quoting Poseidonius) sums up the stereotype in a famous account:

They are extremely partial to wine and glut themselves with the unmixed wine brought in by merchants. Their desire makes them guzzle it and when they get drunk they either fall into a stupor or become manic. For this reason many Italian merchants, with their usual love of money, regard the Celtic passion for wine as a source of treasure. They transport the wine by boat on the navigable rivers and by cart through the open country and they get an incredibly good price for it: for one amphora of wine they get a slave—a servant in return for a drink!   (*Hist.* 5. 26)

Whilst it is always necessary to treat texts of this kind with caution, archaeological evidence amply bears out the huge volume of Roman wine which was transported to Gaul in distinctive amphorae of Dressel 1 type. Two trading ports have been identified, one near Toulouse in the Garonne Valley, the other on the Saône at Cabillonum (Chalon). At Chalon, it is estimated that 24,000 amphorae were discarded in the river, while the farm land at Vieille Toulouse is still so thick with amphora sherds that even today ploughing is difficult. Both locations must have functioned as trading ports where the wine, transported by the merchants in amphorae, was decanted into other containers, either barrels or skins, for movement inland. At other sites deeper into Celtic territory the discovery of large numbers of amphorae show that sometimes it was moved further without decanting. Several of these sites, such as Bibracte, Jœuvres, Essalois, and Montmerlhe, were native fortifications. To such places the Italian wine may well have been carried by Roman merchants and there exchanged for slaves and other commodities with the local élite, who could then dispense the wine to their followers.

The exchange rate noted by Diodorus—an amphora of wine for a slave—need not be taken too literally: it may have been little more than a neat literary flourish. But if it is an accurate record of relative values, then comparative data suggest that the Celts were getting a poor deal: in Rome the trader might expect to get the equivalent of half a dozen amphorae of wine for a healthy Gaul.

The development of the wine trade can be charted from the relative frequency of amphorae in dated archaeological contexts. In southern Gaul Italic amphorae make their appearance in small number about 200 BC and increase steadily throughout the second century BC, but it may well have been the annexation of southern Gaul by Rome c.120 BC that gave the impetus for the adventurous to seek more lucrative markets deeper inland (Map 28). The first of the distinctive Italic amphorae to be found widely in Gaul are the Dressel type 1A, the earliest known examples of which were recovered from the destruction levels at Carthage and can therefore be dated to 146 BC. It is quite possible, therefore, that wine was already reaching the Gauls of the interior as early as the middle of the second century BC. Thereafter the quantities increased dramatically, reaching a peak by the middle of the first century, when Caesar's conquest created new and extended marketing opportunities.

The distribution of Dressel 1A and the later Dressel 1B amphorae provides a vivid illustration of the Roman penetration of Celtic society in the west. The navigable rivers of Gaul, as Diodorus says, provided arteries along which the wine could flow. The long-established trading route along the Aude, Garonne, and Gironde to the Atlantic sea-ways—the route by which tin had been brought to the Mediterranean—was evidently busy in the late second and first centuries BC. Dressel 1A amphorae have been found on wreck sites off the Breton coast and at a number of settlements in Brittany. The further extension of the route can be traced, by amphora sherds, via the Channel Island of Guernsey to a major port-of-trade at Hengistbury Head on the coast of Dorset. Contemporary archaeological levels at Hengistbury have shown that other goods, including figs, raw glass, metal vessels, and unknown commodities transported in Armorican-made pottery, were reaching Britain at this time. Evidence for the production and refinement of metals—iron, gold, silver, and

177 Amphorae used to transport wine provide a clear indication of trade routes. Two amphora types, Dressel 1A and Dressel 1B, both made in Italy, are particularly useful in identifying the changing patterns of commerce in the second and first centuries BC. The 1A type was in common use from the mid-second to mid-first centuries BC. The 1B type became common in the second half of the first century BC. Musée de Saint Raymond, Toulouse.

bronze—and for the manufacture of shale bracelets, provides some tangible indication of British exports. Others, mentioned by Strabo a little later as the desirable products of Britain—hides, corn, hunting dogs, and slaves—can hardly be expected to leave much archaeological trace.

The evidence from Hengistbury is interesting in showing the impact which the Roman economy could have on distant communities. There is, however, no need to suppose that Roman entrepreneurs were actually sailing the Atlantic sea-ways. In all probability commodities moved back and forth within an indigenous network of exchange, but Roman demands may have influenced the intensity and focus of the exchanges. That the major port-of-trade on the south coast of Britain developed at Hengistbury rather than a port in the south-west peninsula might suggest that the emphasis was more on corn and slaves than on metals. The hill fort-dominated society of central southern Britain might have been a convenient source of slaves. It was probably for some such reason that Hengistbury became the port-of-call in the late second and early first centuries. It was short-lived, for after the Caesarian conquest of Gaul new systems of trade emerged (see pp. 247–50).

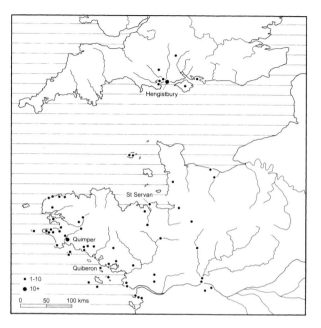

178 Distribution of Dressel 1A amphorae in north-western Gaul and southern Britain, indicating the trade axis operating in the early first century BC.

The head of the Adriatic provided another convenient route between the Roman world and the north. A Roman colony, established at Aquileia as early as 169 BC, led to the further development of an already important trading post on the route northwards along the eastern Alpine fringes to the Danube, in the vicinity of Sopron in north-west Hungary, thence to the Morava Valley and the far north. This was broadly the route along which Baltic amber was carried to the Mediterranean throughout the later prehistoric period, in Roman times, and into the early Middle Ages. The importance of Sopron as a route node is amply demonstrated by the large settlement and cemetery which developed there and flourished between the fifth and first centuries BC, its function eventually being continued by the Roman town of *Scarbantia*.

Between the head of the Adriatic and Transdanubia lay the hilly, even mountainous, country of the Julian Alps from which flowed the upper streams of the Drava and Sava rivers. In terms of modern political geography the region is roughly equivalent to Slovenia and north-western Croatia. It was through this territory, controlled by many Celtic tribes, among them the Taurisci, Carni, Istri, and Iapodi, that items of trade had to pass.

The Carni caused some disruption in 186 BC, when, intent on establishing new settlements, they moved west, forcing the evacuation of Aquileia, but they were eventually driven back in 183. Thereafter Roman relations with the area were not always harmonious. In 171, returning from an abortive attempt to reach Macedonia, a Roman army commanded by Cassius Longinus rampaged through the region taking large numbers of captives to sell as slaves. A formal complaint was presented to the Roman Senate by ambassadors from the Carni, Istri, and Iapodi, and the brother of the king of Noreia went to Rome as a representative of other Alpine tribes. The incident is interesting in that it demonstrates the nature of diplomatic relations between Celts and Romans at this time. A few decades later, in the 140s and 130s, Polybius records the discovery of gold in the territory of the Taurisci. Italian entrepreneurs joined the gold rush but were expelled as soon as the price of gold began to fall. Partly as a result of this a Roman force was sent into the area in 129 BC, gaining victories over the Taurisci, Iapodi, and Istri, and probably also the Liburni and Carni. Further expeditions followed in 115 BC.

Thus, although the relations between Rome and the eastern Alpine region were uneasy during the second century, a degree of equilibrium was eventually established allowing an active trade to develop. At the end of the first century BC Strabo could list the materials flowing through Aquileia as 'slaves, cattle, and hides'.

The situation further east is confused by the many different ethnic groups inhabiting the area and the mobility of many of them. As we have seen, the Celtic enclave in Thrace had been destroyed by the end of the third century and the Celtic communities which had penetrated Transylvania and the southern parts of Moldova and Ukraine had in all probability been absorbed or ousted, the former group into the emerging Dacian state, the latter by the Sarmatians and the Bastarnae. After the end of the second century it is unlikely that any recognizable Celtic community existed east of the Middle Danube Valley, except for the Galatians in their remote homeland in central Asia Minor.

The Dacians and the Germans

To the east of the Celts of the Middle Danube lay the Thracians and the Dacians, while to the north were many tribes regarded by classical writers as being ethnically German. While the Thracians mostly maintained friendly relations with their Celtic neighbours during the second and first centuries BC, the Dacians and certain of the so-called Germanic peoples made territorial inroads on the Celtic homelands.

The earliest recorded movement came from the north and involved two different tribes, the Cimbri and the Teutones, who migrated, sometimes singly sometimes together, through western Europe in the late second century BC, causing widespread disruption among the Celtic tribes and sending a chill of fear down every Roman spine (Map 29).

The origins of these tribes is obscure, though there is sufficient evidence to suggest that they came from north-west Europe bordering or close to the North

Sea. The long debate about their ethnicity—whether Celtic or Germanic—is, and is likely to remain, inconclusive. In 120 BC the Cimbri had moved against the kingdom of Noricum, where they were unsuccessfully opposed by a Roman force. In 114 they were ousted by the Boii in northern Hungary and moved south, where they became involved in various clashes with the Taurisci and Scordisci. Thereafter they thrust westwards into Gaul, inflicting further defeats on Roman armies at Bordeaux in 107 and Orange in 105. A brief expedition through the Pyrenees brought them into conflict with the Celtiberians. By the time they returned once more to southern Gaul, Gaius Marius, with a reformed Roman army, was ready to meet them. In two decisive battles, in 102 at Aix-en-Provence and 101 at Vercellae in northern Italy, the marauding barbarian forces were destroyed.

The significance of the invasion is difficult to judge. While it may not have caused extensive disruption among the tribes of western Europe, it served as a destabilizing element in that it demonstrated to local tribes that Rome was not always invincible.

A more serious threat to the eastern Celtic tribes was posed by the growing power of the Dacians. The origins of the Dacians are obscure. The earliest literary accounts of them refer to the first half of the second century BC, at which time they were successfully preventing the Bastarnae from moving into the Carpathians. Under King Rubobostes, in the 170s BC, their territorial control was said to be increasing, and it is generally assumed that this implies an expansion from their original homeland, in the plain of Wallachia north of the Lower Danube, into Transylvania, where they will have come into contact with long-established Celtic communities, absorbing them into the expanding Dacian state.

By the 80s of the first century BC the focus of Dacian power lay in Transylvania, with its centre in the Orăştie mountains to the south of the fertile valley of the Mureş. Here, under the leadership of King Burebista working in partnership with a religious leader named Deceneus, a number of disparate tribes, among them the Daci, the Getae, and the Buri, were welded together to form a single powerful state covering roughly the present area of Romania. After some twenty years of consolidation, Burebista was in a strong position, able to command, according to Strabo, 200,000 warriors.

In 60 or 59 BC he began a policy of expansion westwards, moving first against the Scordisci and then against the Boii and Taurisci (Map 30). His intention, Strabo tells us, was to win back ancient Dacian territory. The defeat of the Celtic tribes was so devastating that Strabo was able to write of the 'desert of the Boii'—a phrase open to several interpretations. The archaeological evidence, mainly in the form of distinctive Dacian pottery, suggests that the conquered territories extended across the northern Tisza region into Slovakia and possibly as far as Moravia. By expanding westwards Burebista was evidently seeking to take control of an important route node where the east–west Danube corridor was crossed by the north–south amber route. He then turned his attention eastwards to the Dobrudja, attracted both by the Greek cities of the Pontic coastal region and by the prospect of halting Roman advance north of the Danube.

Having established a massive power block from central Europe to the Black Sea, Burebista felt strong enough to intervene in international politics and in 48 BC he sent a message to Pompey, then at Heraclea Lyncestis in Macedonia, offering him the support of Dacia against Caesar. In the event Pompey was defeated at Pharsalus, and, before Caesar could take up the Dacian challenge, he was assassinated in 44 BC, at about the same time that Burebista met a like fate. The king's death signalled the end of Dacian expansion: the annexed territories were quickly lost and the Dacian homeland was split into a number of smaller polities ruled by *reguli*, leaving only a resistant core in the Orăştie mountains to provide continuous trouble for Rome until its final conquest early in the second century AD.

The Dacian expansion into the eastern Celtic territories in 60 BC caused considerable reverberations among the Celtic tribes of the Alpine region. The Boii who had been displaced from northern Hungary/Slovakia moved to the southwest into Noricum and besieged Noreia. They were repelled but entered Helvetian territory and subsequently were to join the Helvetii in their abortive migration westwards through Gaul. The alliance of the Boii and Helvetii posed a potential threat to the kingdom of Noricum and it may have been for this reason that Noricum forged a diplomatic bond with a Germanic tribe, the Suebi, by marrying the sister of Voccio, the king of Noricum, to the German leader Ariovistus. In such a circumstance it is possible to understand why, at this stage, Ariovistus was classed as 'king and friend' to Rome and why the Helvetii felt under threat from all sides. Ariovistus was also involved in Gaulish politics as an ally of the Arverni and Sequani against the Aedui and had, by 61 BC, settled a large group of his people in the territory of the Sequani (modern Alsace), further fuelling the tension and instability of the region. The complex situation in the Alps and its western fringes provided Caesar with ample excuse to begin his wars of conquest in Gaul.

It is difficult to judge how unusual the situation in the 60s of the first century BC was. The classical sources are sufficiently detailed to provide a picture of social disruption and migration. It is quite possible that this was a new development caused by the Dacian expansion and exacerbated by population pressures among the Germanic peoples of the north. But it may have been little more than the inherent instability of the Celtic tribal system brought into sharp focus by the sudden interest of the Roman world in the affairs of its northern periphery.

Intensification, Production, and the Emergence of *Oppida*

The century and a half after 200 BC saw a series of far-reaching changes in the Celtic world which are represented in the archaeological record as a dramatic increase in production and the rise of large nucleated settlements usually referred to as *oppida* (Map 26). The definition and significance of *oppida* have occasioned a considerable literature and there is little doubt that the debate will provide a fruitful area for continued investigation for years to come. The reason why there is so much uncertainty about these sites is that archaeologists have attempted to reconcile a categorization used, but not defined, by Caesar— the word *oppidum*—with a broad group of large settlements, usually defended, about which there is surprisingly little tangible archaeological evidence. Few '*oppida*' have received more than a cursory archaeological examination and very few have been examined on a scale appropriate to the questions being asked of them. It is hardly surprising, therefore, that there is confusion and disagreement not only about the social and economic processes which led to the development of these sites but even about the functions they performed.

Caesar's use of the word *oppidum* relates specifically to the Celtic sites he encountered during his Gaulish campaigns in the middle of the first century BC. It is, therefore, specific to time and place. He uses it to distinguish the larger settlement locations from villages (*vici*) and farmsteads (*aedificia*). Among these larger settlements he further distinguishes the towns within the Provincia, which he calls *civitates*, and a few other important locations, such as Gergovia, Alesia, and Avaricum, for which he uses the word *urbs*, from the general mass of *oppida*. Even in the light of our present imperfect archaeological knowledge it is clear that the word *oppida* is used to cover a number of sites of different size and different functions spread among tribes of very different social organization. There is no suggestion that *oppida* were necessarily tribal capitals: among the Helvetii there were twelve and the Bituriges had twenty. Even the small cliff-castles of the Armorican tribes 'on the far ends of spits and headlands' were described as *oppida*. Caesar, therefore, uses *oppida* as a convenient portmanteau word and as such it may be used by archaeologists.

Within this very broad category it is possible, archaeologically, to distinguish a class of large developed *oppida*. These may be defined as areas of land (usually in excess of 10 hectares) defined by a continuous boundary, man-made or natural, within which a variety of social, religious, and economic functions were performed of the kind needed to enable the systems, binding large communities, to articulate. A definition of this kind takes with it the implication that the *oppidum* was a focal centre in a larger territory (not necessarily that of the whole tribe): it had a political legitimacy and may have been a centre of regional authority.

The *oppidum* of Bibracte, in the territory of the Aedui, exemplifies this definition. It was prominently sited on a hilltop commanding an important route nexus. The defended area covered some 135 hectares and required over 5 kilometres of ramparts to be built and maintained. It was, Caesar said, 'by far the largest and richest *oppidum* of the Aedui'. Here envoys from other tribes were received by the chief magistrate and most of the tribal councils met during Caesar's Gallic campaigns, and here, in 52 BC, Vercingetorix was confirmed as supreme war leader by Gauls who had gathered from all over the country. Its

significance was such that the next year Caesar decided to spend the winter there. Excavation has shown that occupation began in the second century BC and continued until about 20 BC, by which time the focus of activity had moved to the newly founded Roman town of *Augustodunum* (Autun) 20 kilometres away.

179 The *oppidum* of Bibracte (Mont Beuvray), Saône-et-Lare, France, was the capital of the Aedui at the time of Caesar's conquest.

The *oppidum* of Manching, in the Lower Danube Valley in Bavaria, exemplifies other aspects of this type of settlement. It too was large, occupying some 380 hectares enclosed by a massive timber-laced rampart some 7 kilometres in length. Something of the communal effort involved can be appreciated when it is said that to make the nails which clenched the timbers is estimated to have required 60 tons of iron. This, together with the massive mobilization of resources needed to fell and carry the timber, hew the stone, and assemble the rampart and gates, gives some idea of the vitality of the community and the coercive power of the authorities. Within the enclosed area the central part was densely occupied with houses and other buildings laid out in an ordered manner bounded by paths and streets. Between this area and the ramparts was an open space which could have been used for pasturing livestock.

When it is remembered that only about 4.5 hectares of the site have been excavated (less than 3 per cent), the size and quality of the assemblage of artefacts recovered are remarkable. The tools reflect all the major craft and agricultural processes and there is clear evidence of manufacture on a large scale: iron extraction and forging; bronze-working to make a range of personal jewellery; the large-scale production of high-quality pottery; the manufacture of poly-

225

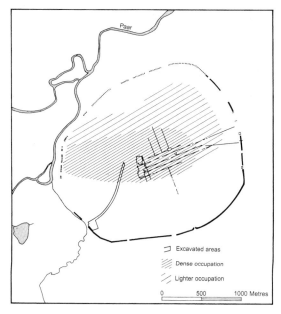

Excavated areas

Dense occupation

Lighter occupation

0   500   1000 Metres

180 *Above*: The *oppidum* of Manching, Ingoldstadt, Germany, is one of the best known of the *oppida* of temperate Europe, as a result of an extended campaign of excavation which examined a large sample of the densely settled area of the interior.

181 *Above, right*: An excavation conducted within the *oppidum* of Manching 1965 in advance of construction work. The pits, post-holes, and ditches, showing as dark marks cut into the bedrock, clearly demonstrate the regular rectilinear layout of the boundaries of the first century BC settlement.

182 *Right*: The nucleated settlement which developed on the banks of the Rhine (beneath the site of Basle, Switzerland) in the first century BC was first an open settlement. Later, after about 50 BC, the occupation moved to a new defended location on Cathedral Hill.

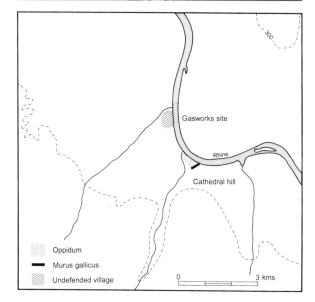

Gasworks site

Rhine

Cathedral hill

Oppidum

Murus gallicus

Undefended village

0   3 kms

226

chrome bracelets and beads from imported raw glass; and the casting of pellets of gold and silver from which coins were struck. There can be little doubt from the items produced, and from the distribution of the more distinctive types, that the craftsmen working in Manching reached an impressively large market area. In this sense Manching functioned as a service centre for its hinterland.

The excavations at Manching have been on a sufficiently large scale to provide some evidence for the development of the site. Occupation began in the third century with an agglomeration of small farms with their fields and pastures. Throughout the second century the population increased, and at the same time craft specialization and coin production speak of greater complexity. Some time in the 130s–120s BC, a time of insecurity exacerbated by the wanderings of the Cimbri and Teutones, there is evidence of destruction and a total rebuilding, this time within the protection of the massive defensive perimeter. Thereafter, for seventy or eighty years, the *oppidum* continued to develop, the defences being rebuilt or repaired on two occasions. After the middle of the first century BC decline set in, occasioned presumably by the rapidly changing political scene and the economic reordering consequent upon it.

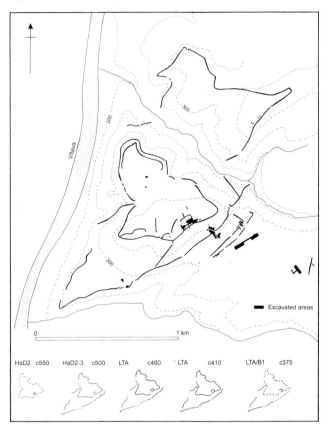

The development of Manching provides a convenient yardstick for comparing the archaeology of *oppida* and for showing the way in which such sites might develop from simple rural village beginnings, but it should not be taken as the only model for the evolution and functioning of *oppida*: different economic pressures and different political histories will have produced a variety of patterns.

Zavist, in the valley of the Vltava, south of Prague, offers a slightly different scenario. Here a hill fort flourishing in the fifth and fourth centuries BC provided a focus for the development of a much larger *oppidum*, in the second century covering an area of 150 hectares with a perimeter of 9 kilometres. The history of the site appears to have been troubled, and several phases of destruction have been noted, requiring one of the main gates to be rebuilt on five occasions. The population seems to have grown rapidly during the first century BC, when new enclosures were successively added to the original nucleus. Internal organization, like that at Manching, was controlled and regular streets were

183 The *oppidum* of Zavist, Bohemia, Czech Republic, has been the focus of a long campaign of excavations which has allowed the complex development of the defences to be disentangled.

XIX *Facing*: The city of Pergamum, in Aegean Turkey, was the capital from which the Attalid dynasty led the struggle against Celtic war bands in the third century BC. To monumentalize their victories they created many great buildings ornamented with sculptural compositions often depicting their enemies, particularly the Celts. One of the most impressive of these was the great Altar of Zeus excavated in the nineteenth century. All that now remains is the sad ruin of its stepped foundation: the superstructure is on display in Berlin.

184 *Below*: The *oppidum* of Kelheim, Bavaria, Germany, occupies a large area, but this is achieved by making good use of the River Danube and its tributaries in lieu of ramparts.

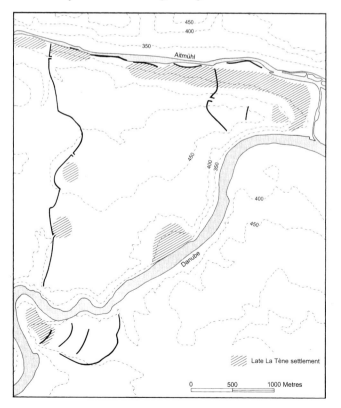

Late La Tène settlement

0   500   1000 Metres

maintained. Structures identified as farms occurred alongside other houses and there was ample evidence of craft production particularly of ironwork and the minting of gold and silver coins. Occupation ended in a disastrous fire in 25 or 20 BC, which may be associated with the Germanic penetration of Bohemia.

The sequence observed at Levroux (Indre) provides another example, like Manching, of an *oppidum* which begins as an open undefended village and was succeeded, some time about 80–70 BC, by a strongly defended settlement of some 20 hectares in extent. The difference is that at Levroux the two settlements are about 1.5 kilometres apart. The situation at Basle is much the same. Here an undefended settlement on the plain, on the banks of the Rhine, began in the third century BC. It seems to have been abandoned some time about 60 BC in favour of a fortified *oppidum* of about 5 hectares in area, 1.5 kilometres away, on the site now occupied by the cathedral. One possible historical context for this shift may have been the social turmoil which would have accompanied the migration of the local tribe, the Rauraci, in the company of the Helvetii, in 58 BC, and their subsequent defeat by the Romans. This same movement from open settlement to fortified hill site is reflected in the settlement pattern at Aulnat near Clermont Ferrand.

Whilst the evidence for the origins and development of *oppida* is still far from adequate, the picture which emerges suggests a gradual growth over time, beginning, in the third or second century BC, with open village settlements, which gradually acquired a range of specialized manufacturing skills until such time, in the first century BC, that the community decided, for reasons of status or sheer need, to defend itself. Thereafter, where local conditions permitted or demanded, the defences were refurbished or extended. The size and development of these *oppida* depended on a variety of factors, among which their position commanding raw materials or major route ways must have been particularly important. It is no coincidence that successful *oppida* like Manching and Kelheim were located close to rich supplies of iron, while Trisov in Bohemia had a prolific source of graphite in the immediate vicinity: graphite was extensively used in pottery manufacture. Other *oppida* commanded major routes: Staré Hradisko in Moravia was astride the amber route, as the quantities of amber found in the excavation bear witness, while Zavist, Bratislava, and

228

Berne could have controlled traffic along the Vltava, Danube, and Rhine, which they respectively overlooked.

Differences in size may to some extent have reflected the different status and prosperity of the community. Manching, at 380 hectares, is large by any standards, and the 9 kilometres of ramparts at Zavist, even though not all of the same date, reflect the colossal surplus effort available to the community. But enclosed area alone is not a direct measure of status. The remarkable 630 hectares of Kelheim and 1,500 hectares of Heidengraben were achieved by judicious use of comparatively short lengths of man-made defences cutting off promontories between the meandering courses of the Rhine and the Danube, while the coastal port of Hengistbury, before recent erosion, would have extended to some 120 hectares behind a single rampart only 600 metres in length, which cut off the promontory.

Although a variety of defensive techniques were used, most of the large *oppida* which have been excavated fall into one of two categories: a western European type called the *murus gallicus* style and a central European type known as the *pfostenschlizmauer* style. *Murus gallicus* is the phrase used by Julius Caesar to describe the type of fortification he commonly encountered during his Gallic campaigns.

Wooden beams are laid on the ground at regular intervals of two feet along the whole length of the wall and at right angles to it. They are fastened together on the inside and covered with a thick layer of rubble; at the front large stones are used to form a facing which fills the spaces between the timbers. When this first course has been laid and made firm, another is added. This is set on top in such a way that, although there is a two-foot space between its timbers as well, they do not touch those of the first course but are separated from them by a vertical interval of two feet.   (*De Bello Gallico* 7. 23)

He goes on to commend the regular appearance of the wall seen from the outside with its alternating timbers and stones running in straight rows at standard intervals from each other, noting that such a structure made a good defence, the stone protecting the wall against fire while the timbers provided resilience

XX*a Facing, above*: The Roman triumphal arch at Carpentras, Vaucluse, in southern France was probably set up in the early first century AD to commemorate a local victory against rebellious Gauls who are depicted in chains beneath a victory monument.

XX*b Facing, below*: The cliff-castle of Lostmac'h, Finistère, France. The multiple banks and ditches defend a promontory jutting into the Atlantic.

185 Section through the *murus gallicus* defence of Le Camp d'Artus at Huelgoat, Finistère, France, drawn by Sir Mortimer Wheeler. The position of the lacing timbers and the nails joining them was clearly observed.

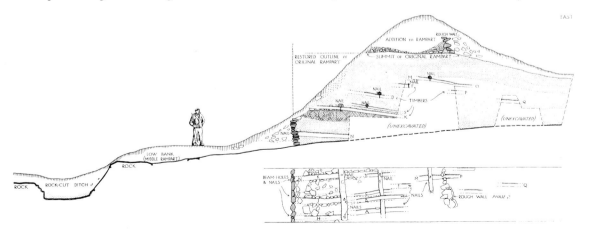

against the battering ram. About thirty structures of this type have been found and excavated. They are concentrated mainly in Gaul, but the style extends as far as the Upper Rhine and the Upper Danube. Most of those excavated exhibited the additional refinement of having the timbers fastened at the crossing point by large iron nails.

The second type of defensive structure—the *pfostenschlizmauer* or Kelheim type—involved creating a vertical front wall with large upright timbers set in post-holes 1–2 metres apart with the intervening spaces filled with drystonework. The verticals were tied back into the ramp of soil and rubble behind with horizontal timbers. This type of defence is characteristic of the eastern Celtic area stretching from just west of the Moselle to Moravia. The distributions of the two styles overlap in the Upper Rhine–Upper Danube area, and at Manching the Kelheim type of wall was adopted when the earlier *murus gallicus* was rebuilt.

A third distinctive type of defence has been identified in northern Gaul, distributed mainly, but not exclusively, north of the Seine and named after the fortification at Fécamp. Here the rampart was composed of tips of earth and rubble without timber structuring, its front face being steeply sloped. Added strength was provided by a wide flat-bottomed ditch. This type of rampart construction (but seldom the ditch type) was adopted in contemporary fortifications in Britain.

The gates of the *oppida* were usually elaborate structures set back at the end of a corridor or courtyard created by inturning the ends of the ramparts.

It is worth focusing on the salient characteristics of *oppida*. They are large nucleated settlements exhibiting a high degree of social organization reflecting the power of the hierarchy to mobilize surplus labour in the interests of the community. Many of them evolved from earlier undefended villages and in all a high percentage of the population was involved in productive activities generating manufactured goods for extensive hinterlands. The documentary evidence provided by Caesar makes clear that in some, like Cenabum (Orléans), Roman traders had taken up residence. The major *oppida* were also places where tribal assemblies could meet and where embassies from other tribes could be received. This list of generalizations suggests that by the middle of the first century BC many of the *oppida* had acquired the functions appropriate to urban centres and we might reasonably refer to them as towns.

186 Diagrammatic sections through ramparts of Fécamp type in Normandy and Picardy. Those tested by excavation were dump-constructed without timber or stone-wall strengthening. The wide flat-bottomed ditch is a distinctive characteristic.

Fecamp

Duclair

Cité de Limes

Tirancourt

Liercourt-Érondelle

0   10   20   30 Metres

The emphasis on command of trade routes and raw materials and on the production of consumer durables implies that the economic imperative was a significant factor in the emergence of *oppida*. It is reasonable, therefore, to suggest that one of the prime causes, perhaps even the initial catalyst, for the growth of these sites was increasing contact with Rome and the intensifying demands of the Roman economic system for manpower and raw materials after *c*.200 BC. In other words the *oppida* and the economic systems which they represented were a feature of the barbarian periphery adjacent to the Roman world. Trade preceded the flag: within another century Rome had absorbed most of the *oppida* zone.

Social Organization: Power and Prestige

For the Roman system to have been instrumental in causing change in the Celtic world implies that what it had to offer was acceptable in Celtic society. We have suggested above that this was indeed the case. With the raid becoming obsolete as a mode of élite expression, new forms of aggrandizement and display were developing which involved the manipulation of commodities, generated by systems of intensified production, either for direct use or for exchanges yielding Mediterranean luxuries.

Some reflection of this change in the style of power and prestige is reflected in Caesar's *Commentaries on the Gallic War*, which depict Gaulish society in a state of evolution. The situation among the Helvetii is informative. Orgetorix, we are told, was the richest and most distinguished man in the tribe, but he 'aspired to kingship' and, according to Caesar, attempted to persuade Casticus, a noble of the Sequani, and Dumnorix of the Aedui to do the same. 'The three exchanged an oath of loyalty, hoping that when each had seized royal power they would be able to control the whole of Gaul.' However, the conspiracy was discovered and Orgetorix was arrested to stand trial. If he were found guilty, the punishment would be death by burning. To evade the procedure Orgetorix called together his kin and clients (some 10,000 according to Caesar), but the magistrates amassed a force to oppose him, and in the chaos which followed he died, possibly by suicide. The incident is informative in that it shows that among certain tribes government by elected magistrates had replaced kingship, but such was the social instability that to aspire to kingship was regarded as a very serious offence. The point is again made when Caesar mentions in passing that Celtillus, an Arvernian and the father of Vercingetorix, had once been the most powerful man in the whole of Gaul and had been killed by his fellow tribesmen because he wished to become king.

The leadership of these more socially evolved tribes was in the hands of an annually elected magistrate, called the Vergobret by the Aedui, who had the power of life and death over his people. During his term of office the magistrate was forbidden to leave his country, and a further rule laid down that two members of the same family could not be appointed magistrates while both were alive or indeed might not be members of the council together. These strict controls were evidently designed to prevent an elected representative from leading a raiding force into another territory and to make sure that power did not concentrate in the hands of any one family. Regulations of this kind hint that the change from the old system to the new had only just got underway and that the elected magistracy was still a delicate growth.

These social changes seem to have been underway among the Gaulish tribes closest to the Roman Provincia and are likely therefore to have been conditioned to some extent by the Roman example. Elsewhere in Gaul kings were still much in evidence, though the system allowed for war leaders to be appointed to command the troops of more than one tribe when the need arose. Vercingetorix, who led the opposition to Caesar in 52 BC, is the prime example.

Caesar's sweeping generalization—that in Gaul only the knights and Druids were of any social significance—is useful in that it makes clear that the power lay with a social élite among which the mounted warrior was still a symbol of prestige. It designated the class from which the tribal leader and the war leader would be drawn. The size of the entourage which a man could call upon, because of lineage or clientage, was the demonstration of social prowess, if not any more of military power. His ability to maintain or enhance that following was now largely dependent on his ability to manipulate production and the wealth generated through trade.

The archaeological identification of the élite is not easy, nor is it clear whether or not they lived within the *oppida*. Rich burials which can reasonably be regarded as kingly have been found within the bounds of the *oppidum* of Camulodunum (Colchester), suggesting that in south-eastern Britain, in the early first century AD, the top echelons of the élite were closely associated with the growing urban nucleus. But not all of the aristocracy were *oppida*-centred, if the burial evidence can be taken as indicative. In south-east Britain there appears to be no close correlation between *oppida* and rich burials. Much the same can be said of burials found across northern Gaul. In the territory of the Treveri, for example, the élite burials of Goeblingen-Nospelt (Luxembourg) (Pl. XXII*a*) were 17 kilometres from the *oppidum* of Titelberg.

Rich burials of the types just referred to were not evenly spread throughout the *oppida* zone but are restricted to a peripheral zone in west and north-west Europe (Map 25). Within this region, from the late second century BC, warriors' tombs, some of them provided with a rich array of grave goods, begin to appear. Most contain fittings appropriate to the feast, such as amphorae of wine, jugs, basins, and paterae, frequently imported from the Roman world, as well as firedogs and other hearth furniture. A few were provided with parts of chariots or chariot fittings.

In Britain it is possible to recognize a hierarchy of burials. The simplest are cremations in pots, sometimes accompanied by other pottery vessels. Next come those provided with bronze-bound wooden buckets and occasionally other luxury items such as imported Roman bronze vessels. These are named after the type site at Aylesford in Kent. Rich female burials, of the same social level, were provided with decorated mirrors and sometimes bronze bowls. More elaborate are the Welwyn-type burials arranged in pits with amphorae and imported tableware. Finally there are the kingly burials such as Lexden, Colchester, and Folly Lane, St Albans, where the exceptionally rich grave goods were ritually destroyed, presumably at the point when the lying in state of the dead king was over and the body was ready for cremation.

In Gaul, especially in the central and western part of the territory, the richer burials were often accompanied by short swords with anthropoid hilts. Such swords are widely distributed from Hungary to Britain and may have been an emblem of a particular social class.

The appearance of this broad zone of élite burials from south-eastern Britain and western France across to Luxembourg suggests that the social system which they represent may have differed from that which had developed in the core of Europe, where the large *oppida* flourished. If so, then the totality of the evidence available to us might be taken to indicate three broad social zones: a core zone of tribes or early states which were adopting governments of elected magistrates; an intermediate zone of polities ruled by kings where large *oppida*, like those of the first zone, had developed; and a periphery where élite status was still being expressed in the ancient manner with sumptuous burial rites. Beyond, up to the Rhine, in central, western, and northern Britain and in Ireland, old social systems continued much as they had done for centuries. The army of Queen Boudica in AD 60 and that led by Calgacus in northern Scotland in AD 84 appear

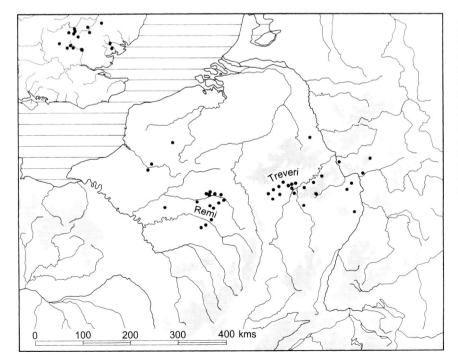

187 Élite burials of the Late La Tène period cluster in a broad zone from Kent to Germany. They are characterized by their use of imported wine-drinking equipment and wine amphorae coming from northern Italy and reflect a type of prestige goods economy developing in the second half of the first century BC. In Britain burials of this kind continue into the middle of the first century AD.

233

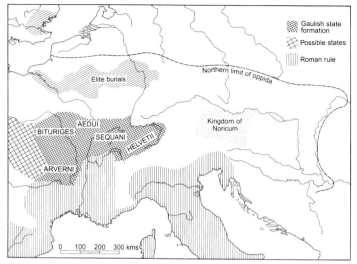

Gaulish state formation

Possible states

Roman rule

Northern limit of oppida

Elite burials

AEDUI
BITURIGES
SEQUANI
HELVETII
ARVERNI

Kingdom of Noricum

0 100 200 300 kms

188 Map indicating the different social zones in the early first century BC.

to have been organized in much the same way as the Celtic forces which met the Romans in Italy three centuries earlier.

Clearly, any such model is a generalization. The situation in the second and first centuries BC was by no means static. Society was changing. The tribes living in areas more distant from the influence of the Roman world inevitably evolved at a different rate from those in direct daily contact.

After 60 BC the pace of change, which hitherto had been regular with its own momentum and trajectory, was dramatically dislocated as Rome began its accelerated expansion northwards.

12

The Celts in Retreat

DURING the third century the Celtic world reached its greatest extent. In northern central Spain the Celtiberians had developed as a strong military force whose influence extended westwards to the Atlantic. To the north the Celtic language had long been spoken as far west as the Atlantic shores of Ireland, and elements of La Tène culture were well established among many of the Insular communities. South and east the Celts who had settled in the Po Valley and in central Asia Minor were harrying the Graeco-Roman world and earning their reputation as ferocious fighters. Smaller communities had spread around the northern shores of the Black Sea and others had penetrated northwards through the Carpathians into southern Poland. Isolated war bands had reached Delphi, mercenaries were operating in Egypt, and ambassadors had followed Alexander to Babylon.

The Second Punic War completely altered the balance of power in the Mediterranean. Rome moved into an expansive mode. From the end of the war in 202 BC until the capitulation of Numantia in 133 the Celtiberians and Lusitani were gradually brought under control. The first two decades of the second century saw the Roman armies win a series of major campaigns north of the Apennines paving the way for romanization, largely completed within a century. In Asia Minor the Celts of Galatia were brought to heel by the Roman army in 189 BC, after which, though still nominally free, their powers were progressively circumscribed.

In 133, the fall of Numantia in the west and the 'gift' of the Pergamene kingdom to Rome in the east, following the death of Attalus III, established Rome as a world power. Within a decade southern Gaul had been annexed, marking the first step in the systematic encirclement of the Mediterranean. At about the same time campaigns in the eastern Alps had extended Roman influence deep into central Europe. Along this immensely long interface, from the Pyrenees to the mountains of Illyria, the Roman world confronted Celtic tribes.

The Unstable Equilibrium: 130–60 BC

For seventy years or so the Roman frontier with the Celtic world retained a degree of stability, while complex systems of interaction developed. Trade, as we have seen, expanded quickly, while a host of treaty relations negotiated with individual tribes established a delicate network of obligations and expectations which could be manipulated to the advantage of any party with the wit to do so. It was a time of bonding and learning.

Inevitably there were tensions, and these erupted into bouts of outright aggression. In Transalpine Gaul, the initial campaigns against the Ligurians, the Salluvii, and the Vocontii in 124 and 123 BC, which led to the annexation of the coastal region, had quickened, to be followed up in 122 and 121, when Cn. Domitius Ahenobarbus routed the Allobroges and Arverni bringing under Roman control the Rhône Valley as far north as Geneva. The creation of a port on the lakeside with timbers felled between 123 and 120 BC is almost certainly to be seen as a native response to the new commercial opportunities which the Roman presence offered. Some years later a firm control was taken of the western trade corridor—the Carcassonne Gap and Garonne—when in 106 Caepio was sent with an army to put down a revolt among the Volcae and Tectosages. As a result Tolosa (Toulouse) was sacked, and thereafter the town and its territory were absorbed into the Province.

Old Greek cities of the coastal zone, new Roman creations like the colony of Narbo Martius (Narbonne) founded near a native town in about 118 BC, and the commercial annexation of important native centres like Tolosa, Vienna (Vienne), and Geneva provided the infrastructure necessary for the aggressive trading ventures of the Roman entrepreneurs who flooded into the Gaulish province. An interesting insight into these times is provided by the court case in which Cicero defended Fonteius, *praetor* of Transalpina, in 75–3 BC, against charges of extortion made by members of the local community. The details are slightly obscure, but in essence Fonteius stood accused of levying an unofficial tax, in his own interests, on the movement of Italian wine destined for the Celtic market. In his defence of Fonteius, Cicero is at pains to denigrate the accusers, playing on all the prejudices of a Roman Celtophobe—they are noisy and arrogant, their manners and language are uncouth, and they wear trousers! More to the point, their ancestors attacked Rome and Delphi. Thus they are barbarians and cannot be considered on the same level as a Roman citizen. If a civilized man like Cicero could present the Gauls in this way, even allowing for a lawyer's distortion, what must have been the attitude of petty officials and merchants?

A little later, in 63 BC, the Allobroges sent commissioners to Rome to complain of maladministration. The discontent among Celtic tribes was well known in Rome and an attempt was made to involve them in the conspiracy of Catiline, but in the event the Allobrogian emissaries decided against rebellion. The incident is interesting in that it shows how Roman factions might choose to manipulate Celtic discontent in their own interests, but it also demonstrates the reluctance of tribes who had experienced only two generations of romanization to disrupt the equilibrium which had emerged, even though they had serious grievances.

The situation in the fringes of the eastern Alps is less clear. The close relationship which had been established with the kingdom of Noricum created a degree of stability in the western flank of the region, but the main axis of communication which led northwards from Aquileia to the Sava Valley and beyond remained in the hands of native tribes, principally the Taurisci and Iapodes. When, from time to time, the flow of trade was threatened, Roman troops were sent in to restore order. In 129 BC a force reached Siscia (Sisak), but without attempting to take control of the land. Policing of this kind continued until the middle of the first century BC. In 88 the Roman commander Scipio Asiagenus moved further east against the Scordisci, who were decisively defeated but with no territorial advantage to the Romans.

For the last two decades of the second century many tribes in central and western Europe suffered disruption from the migratory movements of the Cimbri and Teutones, the names which classical authors give to a mobile horde which originated somewhere in the territory north of the Lower Rhine. While the composition and exact ethnic origins of these peoples remain unclear, that they emerged from the land broadly known to the Romans as *Germania* gave rise to the belief that they were Germans and thus were distinct from the Celts. The divide was a convenient one for commentators like Caesar and Tacitus to use, and for them the Rhine marked the boundary between the two peoples. The actual situation was far more complex and it is doubtful if any significant ethnic divide existed at least before the middle of the first century BC. Celtic tribes had long occupied the Middle Rhine, Bohemia, and Moravia, and Celtic enclaves had established themselves in southern Poland. Caesar also acknowledged that Germanic tribes occupied lands west of the Rhine and that there was some admixture with the northern groups of Belgae who lived between the Seine and the Rhine. While in terms of material culture, socio-economic structure, and language the inhabitants of the North European Plain differed from the Celtic communities further south, there was a wide zone between where one graded into the other.

One way to view Europe in the second century BC, as we have argued in Chapter 11, is to see it as a series of peripheries of decreasing social and economic complexity as one moved away from the Mediterranean. Close to the Roman frontier the groups were oligarchies practising an advanced market economy. Further out they were kingdoms focused on *oppida*. These graded outwards into a zone where status was still expressed by prestige goods burials and where many defended settlements suggest a more fragmented organization. Beyond this in the northern parts of Belgica and the North European Plain organization seems to have been simpler and the people more warlike. This last zone, broadly speaking, is that which the classical writers designated as 'German'. What can be deduced of Germanic society from Julius Caesar, and from

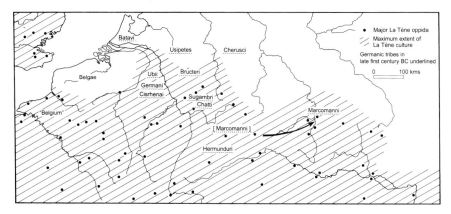

189 Map to illustrate the changing boundary between 'Celts' and 'Germans'.

the more specific accounts of Tacitus written 140 years later, gives the impression of communities differing little from the Celts of the fourth and third centuries. In other words, degree of social complexity cannot be taken as a distinguishing factor between Celt and German. If a single characteristic is required, it can only be language. But apart from recourse to chronologically ill-focused maps of Celtic and Germanic place names, there is no sure way of distinguishing which tribes were German-speaking. All we can do is to accept the ethnic identifications made by the Roman commentators.

The movement southwards of the Cimbri and Teutones is the first recorded movement of Germanic peoples into the territory of the Celts. It reflects an early stage in a series of southward expansions which culminated in the massive migrations between the third and the fifth centuries AD. Caesar's often-quoted rationalization, that Gaul would have to be taken over by the Romans if it were not to become Germanic, may have been an unbiased interpretation of the evidence he had before him.

In Gaul the situation reached a critical point when a German tribe, the Suebi, led by Ariovistus, crossed the Upper Rhine to support the Sequani in their struggle against the Aedui. The event helped to precipitate Caesar's intervention in Gaul. It was at precisely this time that Burebista led a huge force of Dacians westwards across the Great Hungarian Plain into Transdanubia, devastating the Boii and Taurisci, and establishing control of the crucial route westwards of the Danube Bend.

These two events, coming together in 60–59 BC, caused turmoil among the Celtic tribes of the Alps and Gaul.

The Conquest of Gaul: 60–50 BC

In 59 BC Julius Caesar was given command of the province of Cisalpine Gaul and Illyricum for an exceptional period of five years (which he later had extended for a further five years in 55 BC). To this province the Senate added Transalpine Gaul at the urging of Pompey. Thus in one stroke Caesar was provided with a brief that gave him control not only of the full sweep of the land approaches to Italy but also of virtually the entire frontier between Roman territory and the surrounding Celtic tribes. He was, therefore, able to choose whether to focus first on the Germanic threat in the western Alps or the Dacian threat in the east. His choice of Gaul may have been conditioned to a large extent by his perception of the immediacy of the problem, but it is difficult to believe that he was not influenced by his knowledge of geography, which would have told him of the circumscribed nature of Gaul and the ease, therefore, with which the entire territory could be annexed for Rome.

Another factor was surely economic. Gaul, as we have seen, provided Rome with an immensely valuable market where slaves and other commodities could be had in plenty in exchange for Italian agrarian surpluses especially wine. Some indication of the volume of this trade is given by the tens of thousands of Italian wine amphorae which found their way into free Gaul before the con-

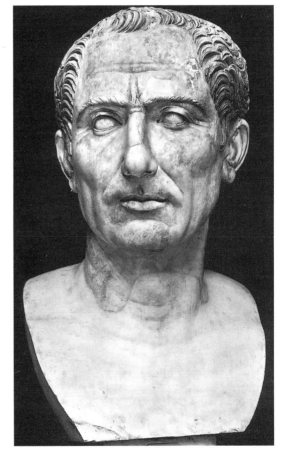

quest. When Cicero wrote, 'all Gaul is filled with traders, is full of Roman citizens', it was probably a fair reflection of the state of things. The threatened instability caused by Ariovistus' interference, to-gether with the imminent migration of the Helvetii and their followers, which would also have left a dangerous vacuum on the doorstep of Cisalpine Gaul, provided ample reason for Caesar to inter-vene. By driving the remnants of the Helvetii back to their Alpine homeland and winning a decisive battle over the massed Germanic tribes commanded by Ariovistus, he was protecting Roman commercial interests as well as establishing a *raison d'être* for campaigning in Gaul.

The subsequent course of the Gallic War was con-ditioned by many factors. The prime motivation was Caesar's need to establish military prestige and thus to build his power base, while at the same time amassing booty in order to pay his debts. The way he chose to pursue the war suggests a carefully devised strategy designed to leave the principal markets of central Gaul intact for the Roman entrepreneurs while taking control of the entire northern coastal region from the Loire to the Rhine. By doing this he would open up new markets with the British Isles, which were rumoured to be a prolific source of desirable raw materials. Thus, in his second cam-paigning year, 57 BC, he moved directly into Belgic territory, where, using the friendly Remi as a stable base, he moved first against a massed force com-manded by the Bellovaci, and then against the Nervii and the Aduatuci, suc-cessfully destroying all opposition and acquiring among the booty some 53,000

190 Julius Caesar, 100–44 BC, conqueror of Gaul. Museo Farnese, Rome

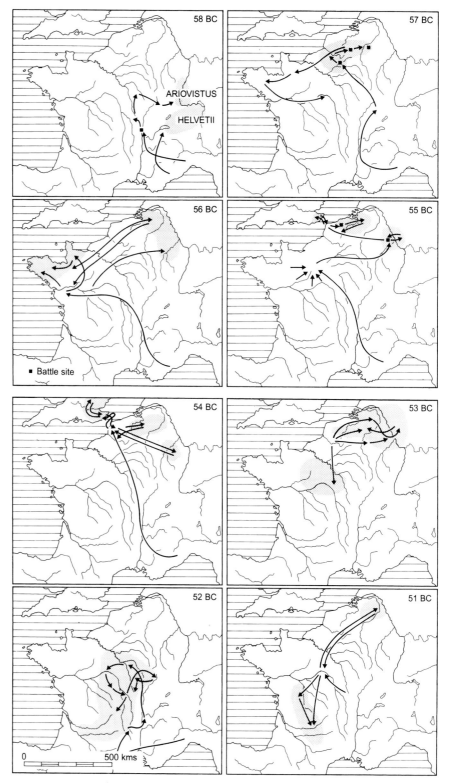

58 BC

ARIOVISTUS

HELVETII

57 BC

56 BC

■ Battle site

55 BC

54 BC

53 BC

52 BC

0   500 kms

51 BC

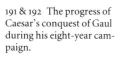

191 & 192 The progress of Caesar's conquest of Gaul during his eight-year campaign.

prisoners, who were sold as slaves. Whilst the Belgic campaign was being fought, Publius Crassus had been sent with a legion to the Atlantic seaboard, where he received the submission of all the major tribes of Armorica and Lower Normandy. The stage had been set for what may have been assumed to be the season of careful consolidation and planning needed for the invasion of Britain in 55 BC.

In the event rebellion among the Armorican tribes upset the plan. Their submission to Crassus had been nominal, and it may well have been news of the intended Roman invasion of Britain that sparked off the revolt. For centuries the Armorican tribes had had a close trading relationship with Britain: its imminent disruption by Roman intervention could have been sufficient cause to try to thwart Roman efforts through active opposition. In this context we may also understand why the Aquitani chose to rebel. They too were an integral part of the Atlantic trading system, since they commanded the crucial route node between the ocean, via the Gironde, to Tolosa and the Mediterranean. Any threat to siphon off the lucrative Atlantic trade was a threat to their livelihood. Although Caesar does not suggest a causative link of this kind, some such fear may well have spread the flame of revolt.

In the event Caesar had it well contained: Crassus was sent in spring to subdue the Aquitani, while Caesar moved against the tribes of Brittany with a specially constructed fleet, focusing his energies on the Veneti, who appear to have been the main instigators of the uprising. Sabinus, meanwhile, was given the task of bringing the tribes of Lower Normandy to heel. Caesar's treatment of the Veneti was particularly savage. All the elders were put to death and the rest of the fighting force who surrendered were sold as slaves. 'I decided that they must be punished with particular severity,' wrote Caesar, 'so that in future the Gauls would have greater respect for the rights of envoys.' No doubt the confiscated property and the proceeds of the sale of slaves were an added incentive to his wise decision to teach a salutary lesson.

There was just time at the end of the summer for a force to be sent to the maritime Belgic tribes, the Morini and Menapii, who had not previously come to terms. The control of this territory was crucial to the successful invasion of Britain, but it was too late in the season to complete the operation before the winter rains set in. Had the Veneti not rebelled, the whole of the coastal zone would probably have been firmly under Roman command and the preparation for the invasion of Britain well advanced. As it was, 'after ravaging all the enemy's fields and burning their villages and farm buildings', Caesar put his army in winter quarters spread out among the tribes of Lower Normandy.

At this stage in his command it was crucial for Caesar to be able to present some spectacular successes to the Roman people and to remind them of the potential dangers of the northern barbarians to the safety of Italy. In this way he would be able to gain agreement to the renewal of his command for another five years. Against this background it is possible to understand why, in 55 BC, he needed to take his force across the sea to Britain—an act which would have been regarded as verging on the superhuman—and across the Rhine into Germany to demonstrate not only his military skills but the ferocity of these northern peoples whose ancestors had, only fifty years before, reached the Po Valley.

In the fourth book of his *Commentaries* Caesar begins with a sketch of the warlike Germans, reminding his readers of the instability of the region. His description of the expansive power of the Suebi, driving other tribes like the Usipetes and the Tencteri from their lands to seek a new home south of the Rhine, is probably an accurate account of the volatile situation and provides sufficient justification for his concern on behalf of the stability of Rome. After building up a fearful picture of the might of the Germans in battle, and throwing in the incredible figure of 430,000 for the size of the enemy force, Caesar presents the justification for crossing the Rhine—the Ubii, on the German side of the river, had asked for Roman protection, saying that a show of strength and support would strike fear into the rest of the German peoples and, by implication, discourage them from further southward movements. In the event, Caesar spent only eighteen days across the Rhine, considering that he had done all that 'honour or interest required'.

The German expedition had deflected him from his planned invasion of Britain, but even though it was late in the season he decided on, what he presented in retrospect to be, a military mission of reconnaissance. 'I thought it would be very useful merely to have visited the island to have seen what sort of people lived there and to get some idea of the terrain and harbours and landing places.' He goes on to offer the interesting observation that very few people apart from traders crossed to the islands and they knew only the maritime regions. To prepare the way, while the fleet was being assembled, he sent a warship to reconnoitre and began to establish diplomatic relations with certain of the British tribes, using Commius, a chief of the Belgic Atrebates, as a mediator.

The campaign was not a particular success, in spite of Caesar's attempt to present it in a favourable light. He had clearly underestimated the strength of the British resistance and in particular the mobility of the British cavalry and chariots in battle. He had also seriously misjudged the effect of weather and tides in the Channel. To add to his difficulties, the Morini, in whose territory lay his European base port, attacked the returning troops, reflecting Caesar's lack of preparation. To make sure that the failures of 55 BC were not to be repeated, he set the army to work throughout the winter, preparing a fleet for the next year's campaign.

The planned invasion of Britain in 54 BC was again deflected by trouble close to the German frontier: this time the powerful Treveri had refused to acknowledge Caesar's authority, largely because of an internal power struggle which was going on for leadership of the tribe. The situation was serious enough to require Caesar's personal intervention. Further troubles with the Gaulish nobility in his train caused additional delays, but eventually, during the summer, a huge invasion force set off in a flotilla of 800 vessels. The size of the expedition and the enormous input of labour that the preparations had required are sufficient to demonstrate the importance which Caesar attached to the venture. Indeed it could well be argued that his main aim from the outset of the Gallic War had been to subdue Britain.

The picture which he provides of that part of the island through which he campaigned was of tribes involved in continuous bouts of warfare but sufficiently cohesive to be able to elect one of their number, Cassivellaunus, as supreme war leader against the Roman threat. Opposition was fierce and at one point, whilst campaigning north of the Thames, the Roman force was in danger of being cut off from base by the concerted attack of four Kentish tribes. Assessing the dangerous situation in the light of the damage which his fleet had sustained in a storm and the fact that the campaigning season was drawing to a close, Caesar decided to withdraw, having negotiated terms with Cassivellaunus. The nature of the arrangements are not reported in detail, except that hostages were given and Cassivellaunus agreed not to harass the Trinovantes. The archaeological evidence for what was to follow suggests that the Trinovantes of Essex were probably given some kind of special treatment by the Roman authorities, which may even have amounted to a trading monopoly, since it is in their territory that the greatest quantity of Roman luxury goods, hereafter, concentrates.

On his return in the early autumn of 54 BC Caesar found northern Gaul in a dangerous state. General unrest, exacerbated by a poor harvest, had flared into a rebellion led by Ambiorix, one of the élite of the northern Belgic tribe, the Eburones. It was a confused period of marching and countermarching, during which time a substantial Roman force under Sabinus and Cotta was cut off and destroyed and only by rapid action was Caesar able to retrieve what had promised to be a rout. So serious was the situation that Caesar decided to spend the winter with his troops near Samarobriva (Amiens).

It was a winter of discontent in Gaul. The annihilation of a Roman force had shown that Rome was not invincible: it provided hope for dissident elements throughout Gaul. 'There was scarcely a time', wrote Caesar, 'when I was not anxious, and not receiving some report or other about plans for a rising among the Gauls.' What is significant is that the discontent had spread far beyond the Belgic tribes. A force from Armorica threatened one legion based, presumably, in Lower Normandy, while the Senones and Carnutes, strong and influential tribes who occupied the territory between the Seine and Loire, ignored Roman instructions and were regarded as being in open revolt. Apart from the Aedui and Remi there was no one Caesar could trust. All the while the Treveri were actively stirring up trouble among their neighbours and the Germans across the Rhine, but their leader Indutiomarus was killed in a skirmish, whilst attacking the winter camp of Labienus. After this, wrote Caesar, 'my province of Gaul was somewhat more peaceful'.

With the winter not yet over Caesar moved decisively against the main centres of resistance. The northern Belgic tribes were the first to receive his attention with a rapid thrust against the Nervii. Following this success he sum-

XXI *Facing*: Wooden carvings found in the ritual shaft and well at Fellbach-Schmiden, Baden-Württemberg, Germany. The figures presumably decorated a structure built around the top of the shaft. The paired beasts, clasped about the waists by a central figure now missing, are a motif reflected in Celtic metalwork. Late second or early first century BC. Württembergisches Landes-museum, Stuttgart.

moned the Gallic Council. The Senones, the Carnutes, and the Treveri failed to attend—a failure which Caesar interpreted as an act of hostility. His first response was to bring the Senones and Carnutes to heel by a show of military strength, thus preventing the immediate threat of being encircled. Then he turned his energies against the Treveri and Ambiorix. First he moved into the territory of the Menapii at the Rhine mouth to establish control and thence to the Treveri, from where he crossed the Rhine again to harry the Suebi and to consolidate the subservience of the Ubii. After a brief stay he was back in the land of the Eburones engaging in systematic destruction and plunder, in which the Roman forces were joined by pillaging Gauls and by Germans who, seeing an opportunity, came from across the Rhine. It was an effective way to destroy the resistance of a people who would not come to battle.

The terror over, Caesar returned to the safety of the Remi, where he held an enquiry into the conspiracy of the Senones and Carnutes, bringing the proceedings to an end with the public execution of the instigator of the plot. The act was ill-judged, or at least ineffective. The unrest which had been simmering now boiled up, the Carnutes taking upon themselves the leadership of a revolt more serious than any that Rome had previously experienced. Caesar gives no reason why the tribe should have been such a focus of unrest, but we learn in another context that the annual assembly of the Druids was held there at what was considered to be the centre of Gaul. The place clearly had power in legitimizing pan-Gaulish decisions. Some such meeting, possibly under Druidic instigation, may have provided the context for concerted action. The rebellion began with the murder of the Roman traders who had settled in the principal *oppidum* of Cenabum.

News rapidly spread to the Arverni, where a member of the élite, Vercingetorix, set himself up as war leader. The event throws interesting light on the changing nature of Celtic society at the time. The Arverni were ruled by a democratically elected magistracy and, like many such tribes, were evidently aware of the ease with which the old social system, in which power was wielded by those who could command large entourages, could re-establish itself. The father of Vercingetorix, Celtillus, had actually been killed by his fellow tribesmen for wanting to become king. When Vercingetorix 'called his dependants together and had no difficulty in rousing their passions', he was taking the first step in elevating himself as his father had tried to do. It is understandable, therefore, that his uncle and other leading men in the tribe should try to restrain him. He was, in fact, expelled from the *oppidum* of Gergovia. But he persisted and gradually won over other Arvernians, soon gaining sufficient power to oust his opponents and set himself up as king. What we are witnessing, therefore, is the resurgence of the old social order made possible by the call for Gallic freedom. Once established, his support among other tribes grew rapidly, and he was acknowledged as supreme war leader.

Virtually the whole of central Gaul was up in arms against the Romans, placing Caesar in a very difficult position. His first action on reaching the Province,

at the beginning of the campaigning season of 52 BC, was to establish the security of the western part of Transalpina, which was most at risk. Next, by leading his troops through the Cevennes against the Arverni, he added a further safeguard to the Province while causing a considerable distraction to the rebels.

Then followed a long period of marching and countermarching through those parts of central Gaul which hitherto had been totally free of Roman military interference. One by one the major tribal *oppida* were besieged and fell. Vellaunodunum, capital of the Senones, capitulated, Cenabum of the Carnutes was taken and destroyed, and the Biturigan *oppidum* of Noviodunum surrendered. Next it was the turn of Avaricum, the largest of the *oppida* of the Bituriges, to suffer Roman encirclement. The resistance of the townspeople was paid for with savagery when the Roman troops entered. Of the population of 40,000 only 800 escaped. In dealing with the more urbanized tribes of central Gaul, Caesar's tactic was simply to pick off the population centres one by one. Such an approach would have been impossible among the tribes of Armorica and Belgica, where this degree of centralization had not developed.

In the weeks to follow, news of the close-run battle at Gergovia and the defection of the Aedui to the rebellion caused the uprising to escalate. Robbed of Gallic support and unable to bring in new troops from Italy, Caesar resorted to inviting German cavalry groups to join his force. They were soon to play a significant part in routing Vercingetorix's cavalry and forcing him to withdraw to the *oppidum* of Alesia in the territory of the Mandubii.

At Alesia the Gaulish rebel force was besieged (Figs. 12 and 13). In making his decision to defend himself on the hill, Vercingetorix was no doubt banking on the rapid arrival of a large relieving force which was now being amassed. According to Caesar, a Council of Gauls had been summoned but had rejected Vercingetorix's proposal for a universal call-up, instead deciding to proscribe the size of the force which each tribe was required to provide. Some forty-four different tribes are named, and the company, when finally assembled, amounted to 8,000 cavalry and 240,000 infantry. The supreme command of the force was divided between four war leaders, one from the Atrebates, two from the Aedui, and one from the Arverni. The coercive power of the Gallic Council in causing such a force to be created is impressive. Although it was, no doubt, due to the uniqueness of the occasion, the facts that individual tribes respected the will of the assembled chiefs and that so many men could so readily be called to arms are indications that the character of Celtic society, evident in the migration period of the fourth and third centuries, had not been significantly weakened by the socio-political changes which were already well underway in some parts of the country.

The rest of the story may be briefly told. The arrival of the relieving force and its defeat by the Roman troops were quickly followed by the surrender of the Gaulish force in Alesia. All the captives, other than Arvernian and Aeduian, were distributed as booty to the Roman troops and thus passed into the Roman slave markets. The 20,000 Arvernian and Aeduian prisoners were restored to

193 Vercingetorix, a noble of the Arverni, became war leader in 52 BC, spearheading the revolt of the Gaulish tribes against Caesar. He and his followers were eventually besieged at Alesia and forced to surrender to the Romans. After years in a jail in Rome he was strangled as part of Caesar's triumph.

The coin is a gold stater of the Arverni struck in central Gaul *c*.51 BC.

XXIIa *Facing, above*: The contents of a princely grave (tomb B) at Goeblingen-Nospelt, Luxembourg. Wine was provided in large amphorae and mixed and drunk from imported bronze vessels. The bronze-bound wooden buckets, similar to those found in southern Britain, are of local manufacture. Late first century BC. Musée Nationale d'Histoire et d'Art, Luxembourg.

XXIIb *Facing, below*: One of the deposits of gold and silver torcs buried in a pit at Snettisham, Norfolk, England. The surprisingly large number of deposits of this kind concentrated in a small area suggests that this may have been a location sacred to the gods. First century BC. British Museum, London.

194 The plateau of Alesia was chosen by Vercingetorix as a secure place from which to resist Rome. As a result of the interest of Napoleon III, a massive campaign of fieldwork and excavation was mounted between 1860 and 1865, bringing to light details of Caesar's siege works. After the capitulation of Vercingetorix to the Romans in 52 BC, the hill developed as a small town.

their tribes as a gesture of goodwill. Caesar himself decided to spend the winter in the Aeduian capital of Bibracte, to rebuild relations with the tribe and set Gaul in order. Vercingetorix was shipped to Rome, where, after spending six years in prison, he was strangled to add drama to Caesar's delayed triumph.

The war in Gaul was not yet over. During the winter Caesar had to deal with residual unrest among the Bituriges and the Carnutes. More serious trouble with the Bellovaci required firmer military action, after which Caesar turned his attention once more on the Eburones, where the rebel leader Ambiorix was still at large. His tactics were the same as those used on his previous campaign in the area. 'Detachments of legionary and auxiliary troops were sent out all over Ambiorix's territory, killing, burning, and pillaging; everything was destroyed and great numbers of the people were either killed or taken prisoner.'

The final acts were focused in the west, where certain of the tribes of Aquitania had mobilized forces. The campaign culminated in the siege of the native *oppidum* of Uxellodunum. When eventually the defenders surrendered, all those who had carried weapons had their right hands cut off but their lives spared, 'so that everyone might see how evildoers were punished'.

Thereafter mopping-up operations in various parts of the country extinguished any spark of resistance which had survived. Hirtius, who wrote the eighth book of the *Commentaries*, concludes by telling us that Caesar completed his activities in Gaul by handing out valuable presents to the surviving Gaulish leaders. 'He did not wish to impose any fresh burdens on them. Gaul was exhausted by so many defeats. Caesar was able to keep it peaceful by making the terms of subjection more tolerable.' The reality must have been far more stark. Of an estimated population of 6–7 million, about one million had been killed and another million sold into slavery. Among the remainder hardly a family would have been left unscarred. The resentment must have been deep and bitter.

With Gaul now brought to heel, it is likely that Caesar's attention would have turned to the problems posed by the expansion of Burebista, whose military ambitions had led him to annex great swaths of territory across what is now northern Hungary and to establish control of the narrow reaches of the Upper Danube. The Celtic *oppidum* of Bratislava seems to have been destroyed at about this time and a Dacian stronghold established nearby at Devin. The main westward thrust of this expansion came in 60–59 BC, at just the time that Ariovistus was causing trouble to the west of the Alps. The fact that Illyricum was added to Caesar's command is, in part at least, an acknowledgement that the eastern Alpine region was likely to require firm military action. After his Belgic campaigns in 57 BC Caesar had hurried back to Illyricum, quite possibly to give some initial consideration to the problems developing on the northern border of this part of his sphere of responsibility. The fact that he had seriously underestimated the resistance of the Gauls meant that he could not pursue any plan that might have been forming and at the end of the Gaulish War he was drawn immediately into the Civil War so that the Dacian problem had to be left in abeyance.

That Burebista remained a serious threat is, however, shown by his overtures of support to Pompey in 48 BC. Thus, once Pompey had been overcome and some semblance of stability restored to Rome with Caesar firmly in control, plans for a Dacian campaign, and for the wildly ambitious conquest of Parthia, could be pursued. Caesar's assassination in March 44 BC brought these grandiose schemes to an end.

Consolidation and Expansion: 50 BC – AD 10

For more than two decades Gaul was left to nurse its wounds with relatively little interference from Rome, while the continuing Civil War claimed everyone's attention. During this time native systems continued. At Bibracte, capital of the Aedui, buildings were replaced by more elaborate structures modelled on the Roman house, the artisan quarters continued to develop, and the *oppidum* began to take on the appearance of a Roman town. In the less advanced regions of the north the Mediterranean overlay was less evident. In the Aisne Valley, for example, the old *oppidum* of the Suessones at Pommiers seems to have been abandoned for a new settlement built in the bend of the river at Villeneuve-Saint-Germain, defended in native style by a rampart thrown across the landward approach.

While systems of government and the native economies were left more or less unhindered, except for the draining of the gold from the system by taxation, the economic demands of the Mediterranean were having a noticeable

195 *Oppida* in the Aisne Valley showing the three successive foci of population. Pommiers was occupied in the period up to Caesar's conquest; Villeneuve-Saint-Germain was a post-Caesarian development but was abandoned when the Roman town was established at Soissons by Augustus.

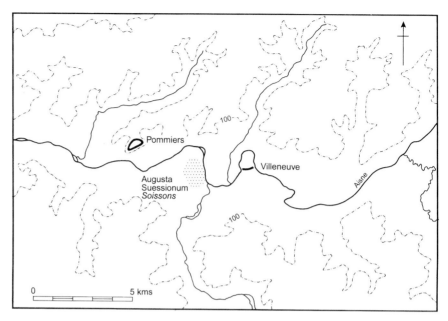

196 *Below:* The defended settlement of Villeneuve-Saint-Germain, Picardy, France, was protected on three sides by the River Aisne and on the fourth by a rampart and ditch. Internally the buildings were carefully laid out. Occupation in the second half of the first century BC was short-lived.

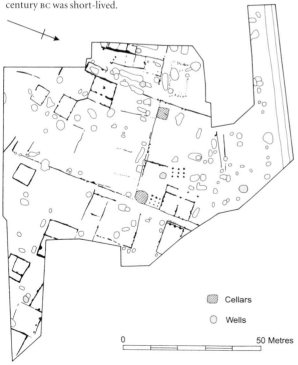

Cellars

Wells

0   50 Metres

effect. Lyons was the hub of Gaul. It was already tied firmly to the Mediterranean by roads and the River Rhône: from here new roads were set out to augment the old river routes. One road to the west linked the centre direct to the Atlantic ports. Two other road systems thrust northwards, one to the Channel coast at Boulogne, the other through the territory of the Treveri to the Rhine. Both routes were of considerable importance in opening up direct access to new markets and also providing a means of rapid contact with troop concentrations in frontier regions. No doubt those tribes, like the Treveri and Suessones, who were able to command the routes, could gain benefit from the volume of traffic and trade passing through. The distribution of the later Dressel 1B amphorae, which concentrate in these territories, provides a convenient demonstration of the benefits which this northern zone were now reaping. Many of the amphorae, together with the Italian bronze vessels necessary for wine-drinking, were finding their way into the graves of the native aristocracy. Once again the burials of the élite were being used to demonstrate the conspicuous consumption of a prestige goods economy. This system was to last in the region until the end of the first century BC.

Apart from a brief revolt in Aquitania in

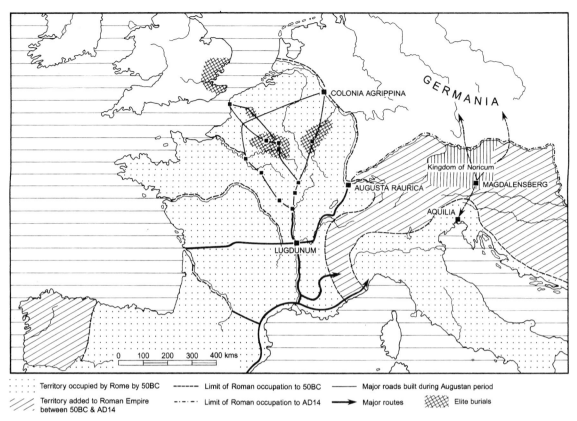

197 Map to illustrate aspects of the political geography of western Europe at the end of the first century BC.

39–38 BC, Gaul appears to have remained quiet. But widespread discontent arose in 27, when Augustus, who had successfully destroyed all opposition to his leadership of the Roman state, began to organize a census of Gaul as a preliminary to imposing a new system of taxation. The presence of the emperor himself prevented serious trouble from erupting and thereafter romanization moved on apace.

The regions of the Pyrenees and the Alps, still unconquered, were brought rapidly under Roman control. The Augustan campaigns in north-western Iberia and in particular the Cantabrian mountains from 25 to 19 BC tidied up one corner, and in doing so freed larger numbers of troops from frontier duties.

Augustus, as Octavian before becoming emperor in 27 BC, had already attended to problems in the eastern Alps. In 35 BC he had moved against the Iapodes and had pushed on into Pannonia, in the next year taking the key location of Siscia (Sisak in Croatia), which henceforth became the springboard for Roman campaigning in the region. In this way he was beginning to put into play plans which must have been in Caesar's mind. The campaign against the Dacians was finally launched in 29–28 BC by Marcus Lucius Crassus. With the Dobrudja under Roman control, much of the Balkans began to be taken in hand.

In 15 BC Tiberius and Drusus led a major offensive into the eastern Alps. Noricum was formally annexed and the Rhaetians and Vindelici brought into

249

the Roman sphere. The tribes of southern Pannonia, between the rivers Dráva and Sava, were the focus of Tiberius' campaigns between 13 and 9 BC, during which time the province of Illyricum was formally instituted. In this way the Celtic peoples of Transdanubia began to be absorbed into the expanding Roman world. In 7 BC Augustus inaugurated a victory monument at La Turbie on the coastal road around the Alpes Maritimes. On it he recorded his victory over forty-four Alpine tribes. The erection of the monument symbolized the end of free Celts south of the Rhine. The incorporation of a few surviving enclaves, such as the remaining Boii in northern Transdanubia, in the early first century AD, brought Celtic freedom to an end in continental Europe.

The expansion of the Romans towards the Rhine–Danube frontier in the second half of the first century BC took place in parallel with the more gradual expansion of Germanic peoples in the north and Sarmatians in the east. The continued southern pressure of the populations of the North European Plain, which Caesar was to stay temporarily in the 50s BC, continued with the Germanic settlement of the Celtic regions of Bohemia and Moravia between 16 and 8 BC. The germanization of these territories effectively brought to an end the large *oppida* and with it Celtic culture. Thus, while the strong Roman presence south of the Rhine–Danube axis prevented a further southward move at this stage, the territories on the north side of the rivers were open to settlement and filled rapidly with new tribes of Germanic origin. The absence of a firm ethnic frontier at the beginning of the first century BC had allowed a fluidity of movement. Once the Romans had established a firm control along the two rivers, the ethnic divide was rapidly intensified by the tide of incoming Germans building up against the barrier of the frontier. This pressure was to continue until, three centuries later, the power of the Romans to resist it began to give way.

In the east the constant outflow of horse-riding peoples from the steppes, north-east of the Black Sea, continued with the western migration of Sarmatians along the Lower Danube Valley into the region of the Great Hungarian Plain. The region was settled by a Sarmatian tribe, the Iazyges, in the early years of the first century AD. This movement was simply echoing the western migration of the Cimmerians and Scythians before them. The new settlers will have found themselves in an area where Celtic groups had long combined with indigenous populations. After the new wave of immigrants from the Pontic Steppe had established themselves little of Celtic culture remained. Henceforth the Middle Danube, flowing between Transdanubia and the Great Hungarian Plain, formed the boundary between the Roman world and the eastern barbarians. Under the Romans some vestiges of the Celtic tribal and social systems survived; beyond they disappeared totally.

Romanization and Rebellion: AD 10–40

The romanization of Celtic societies in Gaul, the Alpine regions, and Pannonia developed apace in the early first century AD. There had always been a tendency to ape selected behaviour emanating from the Mediterranean, and now Roman style and manners provided the Celtic élite with a mode of expression in their very midst. The adoption of Roman building styles by the Aeduian aristocracy at Bibracte is a clear example, and it was not long before the population had migrated from their hilltop fortification to the new Roman foundation of Augustodunum (Autun) in the valley 20 kilometres away, where all the principal comforts of Roman city life were to be had and where their sons could be educated in the Roman manner. Even in the rather more primitive north, the *oppidum* built by the Suessones after the conquest at Villeneuve was abandoned for the Augustan town nearby at Augusta Suessionum (Soissons), founded in the early years of the Principate (Fig. 195).

In the far west at Mediolanum Santonum (Saints) a triumphal arch was dedicated to the Emperor Tiberius and his heirs in AD 18 or 19 by Caius Julius Rufus, who records his ancestry back to his great grandfather—a Celt with the name of Epotsoviridos. His grandfather Otuaneunos had been given citizenship by Caesar and had taken the names Caius Julius. Family histories of this kind were by no means rare among the urban aristocracy of Roman Gaul. Whereas 100 years previously a Celtic chief, like Louernius, would have demonstrated his status by feasts and gift-giving, now the same end could be achieved by paying for public monuments and proclaiming the fact through the Latin inscriptions which adorned them.

There was little to prevent natives of Gaul from rising to positions of power within the Roman state. The Narbonnese province had long provided distinguished men. From the town of Forum Julii came L. Julius Grecinus, who gained the rank of senator under Tiberius. He may well have come from Celtic stock. His son Julius Agricola, born about AD 40, spent much of his life in the Celtic west, serving first in the army in Britain, then as governor of Aquitania. Later, as governor of Britain, he led the army into Wales and Scotland, with distinction in the period AD 78–84. Beyond the region of the old Province, in the Gaul conquered by Caesar, the social advancement of the native élite was significantly slower. It was not until a century after the conquest, in AD 48, that Claudius made his famous speech recommending that leading men of the Aedui should be admitted to the Roman Senate. Even then he met with ridicule from his peers.

For all the desire to emulate Roman ways and become part of the Roman system, there remained a deep-seated resentment which, given the scale and ferocity of Caesar's conquest, is hardly surprising. Natural sentiments of this kind were exacerbated by bureaucratic abuse—an ever-present feature of Roman civil administration. The provinces were an important source of wealth to provincial administrators whose terms of office were short and whose rapacity was, in consequence, intensified.

Unrest was recorded from time to time, but the most serious outbreak of violence came in AD 20, when two members of the Gallic aristocracy, Julius Florus of the Treveri and Julius Sacrovir of the Aedui, orchestrated an outright rebellion to Roman rule under the banner of Gallic liberty. The actual reasons were more prosaic: Roman officials were behaving in an arrogant and oppressive manner and many individuals had become bound by debt to Roman money-lenders. The rebellion was serious but came to little. In the event Florus was defeated during flight and committed suicide, while Sacrovir and his followers, who had seized Augustodunum, finally killed themselves having set fire to the town when defeat looked inevitable.

It is difficult to judge from the rather summary account of Tacitus how wide-spread the revolt was, but his observation that 'The seeds of rebellion were sown in almost every Gallic community' suggests that the situation may have been serious. These Gauls were, after all, the grandchildren of tribesmen decimated by Caesar, and there must have been much latent anger in the stories told of family exploits seventy years before. In the call for Gallic freedom and the sui-cides of the leaders in the face of defeat we are witnessing the last significant expression of the Celtic heroic ideal. The later revolt of Vindex and Civilis in AD 69–70 was an altogether more sophisticated act of political intrigue.

Into Britain: AD 40–100

Julius Caesar's brief campaign in Britain in 55 and 54 BC may not have achieved a great deal from a military point of view, but the treaty relations he established with the tribes of the east coast, north of the Thames, had a lasting effect on the social and economic development of the south-east. The tribes on either side of the Thames Estuary already had close relationships with their Belgic neigh-bours: indeed Caesar records that before the war Diviciacus of the Suessones had exercised authority in Britain, a fact which may suggest that Diviciacus was recognized as some kind of high king to whom tribute was due. During the war Britons fought with the Gauls, and the considerable number of distinctive Gallo-Belgic E coins minted as a war currency which found their way to Britain suggests that payment for services may have been made on an impressive scale.

With the war over these long-established links continued to be maintained, and parts of south-eastern Britain, in particular the territories of the Trinovan-tes and Catuvellauni, developed close economic ties with their Belgic neigh-bours, sharing the same range of imported wine and wine-drinking equipment and the same customs of display in elaborate burial rituals. Largely as a result of this contact, which involved the export of those goods for which Strabo tells us Britain was famous—metals, corn, hides, slaves, and hunting dogs—that part of the country south and east of a line roughly between the Humber Estuary on the east coast and Lyme Bay on the south developed systems of coinage mod-elled on continental types, while the heart of that region, south-east of a Solent–Wash axis, became politically and economically sophisticated with large nucleated settlements having many of the characteristics of the continen-tal *oppida*. Although this advanced core was composed of a number of tribes, by about AD 40 two main power blocks had emerged: north of the Thames the

Catuvellauni ruled by Cunobelin were dominant, while to the south the Atrebates held sway. Conflict between these two polities had been going on for some while, and disputed territories seem to have changed allegiance more than once, but the Catuvellauni were in the ascendancy and Tacitus could describe Cunobelin as 'great king of Britain'.

The treaties set up by Caesar, and no doubt later developments about which we know little, established bonds of clientage between the native tribes and Rome, and these were used to political effect. A number of British kings are recorded as being among the admirers of Augustus, and during the first decades of the first century AD several British rulers fled to Rome to ask for the help of the emperor in establishing their claims to power. The last recorded refugee was Verica, king of the Atrebates, whose flight, about AD 42, was caused by internal rivalries, possibly exacerbated by the increasing dominance of the Catuvellauni. The arrival of Verica provided the Emperor Claudius with the excuse he

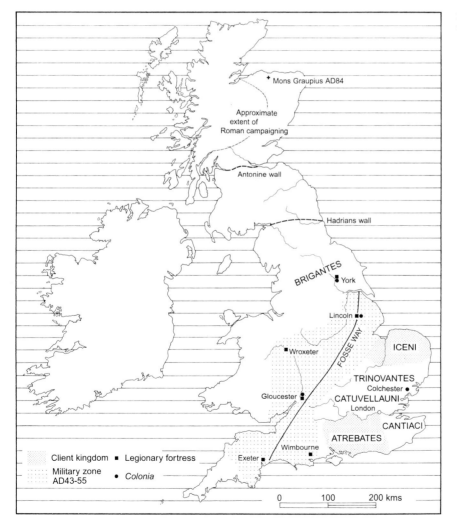

198 Britain in the first century AD.

needed to mount a British expedition—a flamboyant gesture which had been in the minds of the emperors since Caesar's time. The motives behind the plan, like those of Caesar before, were mixed. Roman economic interests would have been to the fore, but the challenge of the island and the desire to impress were not far behind. Whether there was any real need to interfere in British politics to support pro-Roman factions is doubtful.

The first aim of the invasion force was to capture the Catuvellaunian capital at Camulodunum and then to fan out across the core of the south-east to take control of the territories which had come either directly or indirectly under the authority of the Catuvellauni and Atrebates. This semi-urbanized zone with its large *oppida* would be easy to integrate into the Roman system. The less centrally organized tribes beyond, the Durotriges, Dobunni, and Corieltolavi, were also rapidly overcome, though not without considerable resistance from the Durotriges, and a military frontier zone was laid through all three territories, skewering them together with a military road—the Fosse Way—which ran from one military base at Exeter on the Channel coast to another at Lincoln on the east side of the island.

The organization of the province was put rapidly in hand. Most of the area seems to have been taken under direct state control, but two client kingdoms were created within: the Iceni of Norfolk were left under the authority of Prasutagus, a member of the royal family, while part of the Atrebates was put under the control of Cogidubnus, who, by virtue of his acquired names, Tiberius Claudius, presumably received his grant of citizenship from Claudius. Nothing is known of his ancestry but he may have been chosen from the Atrebatic aristocracy at the time of the invasion.

The opposition to the landing was orchestrated by Togodubnus and Caratacus, the two sons of Cunobelin (who had died a year or two before). Togodubnus was killed and Caratacus fled beyond the frontier area, into the Welsh mountains, where he stirred up an active resistance to Rome for a further eight years, thus providing an example of the way in which charismatic war leaders could assume the leadership of tribes other than their own.

To contain the military problems which the occupation of the south-east of the island posed, the provincial authorities negotiated a settlement with a conglomeration of tribes, known collectively by the name of the Brigantes, who occupied the whole of northern England from coast to coast and recognized the authority of a single ruler Queen Cartimandua. The coalition seems to have been unstable, and in AD 51 Cartimandua took a decidedly pro-Roman stance by handing over the war leader Caratacus to the Romans. The anti-Roman faction, led by her estranged husband Venutius, were no doubt incensed by the act. In the ensuing disarray a legion had to intervene to prop up the queen's authority. The unstable equilibrium was maintained for a further decade until AD 69, when Venutius gained control by fermenting a revolt among the queen's tribe and enlisting the help of other tribes in the anti-Roman cause.

While these events were going on, the English Midlands, Wales, and the south-western peninsula were taken under military control, the only significant opposition coming from the two major mountain tribes of Wales, the Silures in the south and the Ordovices in the north. Fighting was tough but the result inevitable. Far more serious was a revolt deep within the province led by Queen Boudica of the Iceni, wife of the client king Prasutagus. There had been a minor uprising in AD 48 when the tribe was disarmed but it does not appear to have been too serious. The events of AD 60–1 were on an altogether different scale. The immediate cause was the heavy-handed bureaucratic incompetence which followed the death of Prasutagus, when the authorities seem to have decided to terminate the client kingship, but the speed with which the revolt spread to most of the rest of the province implies a far more deep-rooted resentment caused by administrative abuses and the appropriation of tribal lands for the colonial settlement implanted in the *oppidum* of Camulodunum. A further factor, the impact of which is difficult to estimate, is that the revolt broke out at the precise moment that the Roman armies were in north-west Wales attacking the Druid sanctuary on Anglesey.

The revolt spread rapidly and was pursued with ferocity by the Britons, many of whom would have experienced the trauma of the conquest only seventeen years previously and the humiliation and abuse which had followed. The colony of Camulodunum, the town of Verulamium, and the port of London were destroyed and their inhabitants slaughtered. Boudica's plea to the goddess Andrasta for assistance, and the subsequent impaling of female victims, suggest that the old Celtic gods still had a firm hold on the people. The final battle, in which the British force was soundly beaten, with its chariots, noise, clamour, and boasting and its baggage trains from which the women and children could get a good view, would not have been out of place as a description of Celtic warfare four centuries earlier. The scale of the engagement can be judged from Tacitus' estimate that 80,000 British died. The reprisals to follow put back the development of the province for decades.

Meanwhile the situation in the north of Britain had deteriorated and Cartimandua had finally to be rescued. Thereafter Roman campaigns beginning in AD 71 brought much of northern Britain, up to the line later chosen for Hadrian's Wall, under Roman military control, and the scene was set for Julius Agricola, as governor of Britain (AD 78–84), to complete the subjugation of Scotland, fighting the last pitched battle against the army of Calgacus at Mons Graupius in the far north on the south side of the Moray Firth. It was the last occasion when a Celtic army used chariots against a Roman force. The circumnavigation of Scotland and the acceptance of the submission of the Orkney Islands brought Agricola's triumphant campaign to an end. Although the Roman hold on the north and west of Scotland was tenuous in the extreme and a withdrawal to the Tyne–Solway line was soon considered advisable, Mons Graupius marks the culmination of Roman military achievement against Celtic peoples.

The old socio-economic division of Britain at the time of the conquest

remained a significant fact of political geography throughout the Roman interlude. In the south-east the urban pattern continued and developed, even
though the Boudican revolt caused a major disruption. Tacitus could write of
this region:

Agricola gave private encouragement and official assistance to the building of temples,
public squares and private mansions. . . . he trained the sons of the chiefs in the liberal
arts and expressed a preference for British natural ability over the trained skill of the
Gauls. The result was that in place of distaste for the Latin language came a passion to
command it . . . and so the Britons were gradually led on to the amenities that make vice
agreeable—arcades, baths, and sumptuous banquets. They spoke of such novelties as
'civilization', when really they were only a feature of enslavement.   (*Agricola* 21)

Yet beyond, in the south-west, Wales, and the north, in spite of a network of
forts and roads, the life of much of the population changed little. City life failed
to gain a hold, traditional patterns of agrarian production and settlement continued, and the Celtic language with its rich oral tradition remained strong.
Whether it was Roman lack of enthusiasm for instigating what they perceived
to be unnecessary economic changes in the far-flung fringes or native resistance
to change and a dogged adherence to traditional ways, it is impossible to say.
The fact remains that in the western and northern fringes of the islands much
of Celtic life continued.

The Free Celts: Ireland in the First Century AD

Tacitus records the story of Agricola standing on the coast of western Scotland
and looking across to Ireland and saying that he thought it could be conquered
and held with a single legion. 'In soil, in climate and in character and civilization of its inhabitants [Ireland] is much like Britain.' He goes on to say that its
'approaches and harbours are tolerably well known from merchants who trade
there'. This much is evident from the quite detailed and accurate knowledge
which the geographer Ptolemy was able to gather for his *Geography* in the
middle of the second century, at least of the south, east, and north coasts. That
trade with Roman Britain did take place is evident from the array of Roman
objects, mainly trinkets of various kinds, found on Irish sites, and there is
evidence to suggest that a major port-of-trade was established on the sea-girt
promontory of Drumanagh, north of Dublin. There is, however, nothing to
imply a Roman military presence on the island and little to suggest any significant exchange of population.

Something of the vitality of Celtic society in Ireland in the last centuries BC
and first centuries AD can be gauged from the importance of the great ritual
centres of Tara, Emain Macha, and Dún Ailinne, and, by implication, Cruachain. These were the social foci for huge territories and the places where kingship was legitimized, but outside these centres remarkably little is known of
Iron Age society and economy. Indeed recent pollen analytical work has sug-

gested widespread forest regeneration in the second half of the first millennium BC, which may indicate a significant decline in population during this time.

There remains, however, the wonderfully rich vernacular literature committed to writing for the first time in a final, if somewhat emasculated, form in the medieval period. While accepting all the problems of interpretation which this literature carries with it—whether the sagas are specifically Irish or pan-Celtic and how to distinguish the various overlays of later material—there can be little doubt that in the *Táin*, the earliest written version of which dates to the eleventh century AD, we have a reflection, albeit perhaps a dim and distorted reflection, of a Celtic epic which may, in innumerable different versions, have been told from one end of Europe to the other. The survival of so much of this oral tradition is one of the miracles of Celtic studies.

13
Celtic Survival

BY the end of the first century AD most of the lands occupied by the Celtic peoples south of the Rhine–Danube line were under Roman occupation. To the north of the Danube the Celtic territories of Bohemia and Moravia had become Germanic, while further east in the Great Hungarian Plain and Transylvania the Celtic enclaves had been absorbed either within the Dacian state or by the incoming Sarmatian tribes. It was only along the extreme north-western periphery, in north and west Scotland and in Ireland, that Celtic-speaking communities continued to exist without the benefit of romanization.

Celts under the Romans: First Century BC to Fourth Century AD

The treatment of native Celtic societies by Roman administrators varied from region to region, but for the most part the newly imposed structures made good use of indigenous systems. Thus in Gaul the Augustan reorganization which divided the country beyond the Province (now Gallia Narbonensis) into Aquitania, Gallia Lugdunensis, and Gallia Belgica was reflecting directly the ethnic divides noted by Caesar when he distinguished between the Aquitanians, the Celts, and the Belgae. Below this tier of administration lay the individual *civitates*, which, almost invariably, were directly, or closely, related to existing tribal divisions, allowing much of the economic, social, and legislative structure of the indigenous systems to remain in place. Those native towns which were well sited to become nodes on the newly imposed road system simply continued, while others in less favourable locations withered away to be replaced by new towns: Bibracte gave way to Autun and Villeneuve to Soissons in the Augustan period.

In the south-east of Britain the situation was much the same, though in the early stages of the occupation two large tribal units were left under the direct control of client kings. In East Anglia the Iceni were ruled by Prasutagus until

258

his death in AD 60, and in the centre south a substantial part of Atrebatic territory was put under the control of Cogidubnus, who was styled 'rex' though he
had been made a Roman citizen by Claudius. Cogidubnus survived as ruler
faithful to Rome until the time of his death, probably early in the 70s. How the
client kings were chosen is unknown, but they were probably members of the
ruling native élite. In the fragmented tribal system north of northern Britain it
was left to Queen Cartimandua to attempt to maintain control under the protective eye of the Roman governor. These somewhat tenuous arrangements
were probably intended as temporary measures, and, with the deaths or (in the
case of Cartimandua) overthrow of the clients, the territories were formally
absorbed into the administrative structure.

The Roman system provided many opportunities for the native élites. The
willingness with which the Gauls took to Roman education is noted by a number of contemporary observers. In Britain, Tacitus describes the deliberate
process of romanization in a somewhat scathing passage already quoted (p.
256). The reality of all this can be seen in Britain in an impressive building programme in the late 60s and 70s AD, which saw the erection of the forum and
basilica at Verulamium, public baths at Chichester, and the palatial residence at
Fishbourne, while the native temple at Hayling was rebuilt to a similar plan in
masonry and the sacred spring at Bath aggrandized on a monumental scale.

Much of the building work undertaken in Gaul in the Augustan and Tiberian
period and in southern Britain in Neronian and Flavian times would have been
under the direction of the Roman provincial authorities and may well have
used military engineers and craftsmen, but building programmes provided the
native élites with a way to demonstrate their patronage: their natural inclination for competitive display could now be channelled into public works.

The integration of native communities into the Roman system seems to have
been thoroughly achieved throughout Gaul by the first century AD. Even in the
remote west, in the Armorican peninsula, each of the main tribal territories was
provided with an urban centre laid out on a regular grid system: Condate
(Rennes) for the Riedonies; Fanum Martis (Corseul) for the Coriosolitae; Vor-
gium (Carhaix) for the Osismi; Darioritum (Vannes) for the Veneti; and Con-
devicnum (Nantes) for the Namnetes. That none of these sites is known to have
been a native centre before the Roman period, taken together with their formal
planned layouts, suggests that the urban system may have been deliberately
imposed. Some native centres, like Camp d'Artus, were abandoned altogether,
while others, like Le Yaudet and Alet, remained in occupation though at an
undeveloped level. The romanization of Armorica is evident not only in the
imposition of towns but in the development of a network of quite opulent
villas.

In Britain the situation was different. In the economically advanced south-
east—that is, roughly south and east of the Fosse Way—the indigenous system
was easily adapted to Roman administrative needs, with flourishing *civitas* capitals developing from native centres accompanied by a rash of villa building in

XXIII *Facing*: The small settlement, remarkably preserved at Chysauster in Cornwall, comprises a group of cellular courtyard houses representing a local style of architecture which developed in the first and second centuries AD from native traditions and owed nothing to Roman ideas or techniques.

rural areas around about. In many cases these villas evolved from settlements dating back to the first century BC. The continuity is impressive. Yet beyond this favoured south-eastern core, in the periphery, life was very different. Much of Wales and the north remained in military occupation. Some easing of tension allowed legionary bases such as Gloucester, Lincoln, Chester, and York to be developed as *coloniae* to provide civilian urban foci, while others such as Exeter and Wroxeter developed as urban and administrative centres without the benefit of colonial status. But over much of northern Britain and Wales the romanized style of civilian development characteristic of the south-east failed to take hold. The only exception was the southern coastal strip of Wales fronting the Severn Estuary, where small towns were established at Caerwent and Carmarthen and a few villas developed from native settlements. In the south-west peninsula of Devon and Cornwall the lack of romanization, after a brief military occupation in the first century, is particularly striking. West of Exeter the native socio-economic system simply continued unhindered.

In Britain and Ireland, therefore, we can recognize three distinct zones: the romanized core, with its focus on the commercial and administrative centre of London, where an urban system was firmly in place; a peripheral zone, including the south-west peninsula, Wales, and northern Britain up to the Clyde–Forth line, which was under Roman authority but was substantially unromanized; and a free zone beyond, including the extreme north of Britain and all of Ireland, where native systems continued unhindered. The survival of Celtic culture was directly related to the intensity of romanization reflected in these three zones.

In Gaul and south-east Britain it is evident that Celtic society became heavily romanized, both by the adoption of Roman culture and by a mobility of population caused by trade and military and civil service. None the less,

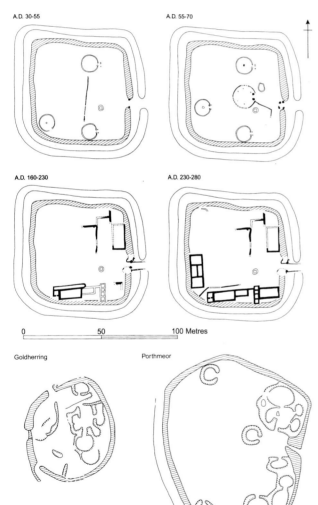

A.D. 30-55

A.D. 55-70

A.D. 160-230

A.D. 230-280

0   50   100 Metres

Goldherring

Porthmeor

0   50 Metres

199 *Above*: The Iron Age and Roman farmstead at Whitton, South Glamorgan, Wales, showing its development from the early first century AD.

200 *Below*: Native settlements of the Roman period in Cornwall. Two examples of stone-built courtyard houses constructed within enclosures ('rounds') which were probably of pre-Roman date.

elements of the Celtic belief systems remained—a reality vividly shown by the maintenance of many Celtic religious sites of great antiquity, temples such as Gournay and Hayling Island and sacred springs like those of Sulis and Coventina in Britain and Sequana in Gaul. A chance remark by Ausonius, writing in the fourth century AD, that Attius Patera, a professor in Burdigala (Bordeaux), came from a Druidic family, might reflect the continuation of a tradition of learning going back into pre-Conquest times. Certainly a sense of ethnic unity would have been maintained by the *Consilium Gallarium* and was put to good political use during the brief life of the virtually independent Gallic Empire which emerged in the turmoil of the late third century. In Armorica it is tempting to wonder if the refortification of the old Iron Age *oppida* of Alet and Le Yaudet might not have been, in part at least, a symbolic gesture recalling a Celtic past.

A question of some interest is the extent to which Celtic was spoken in Gaul and south-eastern Britain during the Roman period. The discovery of a number of inscribed lead 'curses' at the spring of Sulis Minerva at Bath shows that Celtic personal names remained much in evidence into the third and fourth centuries AD, and one example of an entire curse written in Celtic was recovered. A few other examples are known from Gaul, including curses thrown into the hot springs at Amélie-les-Bains and the spring of Chamalières. These few Celtic texts are interesting but they give no sure indication of the strength, or otherwise, of spoken Celtic in relation to the vulgar Latin which must surely have been widespread.

Away from the areas of intense romanization, in the south-west peninsula, Wales, Scotland, and Ireland, Celtic remained the dominant language throughout.

Ethnic Readjustments in the Fourth to Sixth Centuries

The Germanic raids into lands south of the Rhine and deep into Gaul in the late third century AD should be seen essentially as the continuation of south-thrusting pressures created by a growing and mobile north European population which first emerged into history with the Cimbri and Teutones of the late second century BC. Caesar's campaigns against Ariovistus and the subsequent creation of the Rhine frontier brought these incursions to a temporary halt but did nothing to stop the root cause. Pressures continued to build until the spectacular break-out in the mid-third century.

After a temporary respite the germanization of the Roman west continued, first with the deliberate settlement of Germanic peoples in frontier regions to provide buffer zones and later, in the early fifth century, with large-scale population movements into Gaul and south-eastern Britain. While the actual number of immigrants involved is difficult to estimate and the size of the indigenous populations who survived may have been greater than was previously supposed, the political, and to some extent the linguistic, map was totally changed.

XXIV *Facing*: Many of the Iron Age stelae of Brittany continued to be revered as sacred places well into Christian times. Some were moved into the precincts of churches, while others were carved with Christian symbols. This stela from Croas-Men at Lampaul-Ploudalmézeau, Finistère, had had its top removed and replaced by a Christian cross.

201 The village of Chysauster, Cornwall, England, consists of a number of simple cellular houses built of stone, laid out either side of a street. Each house was built in a similar way with a series of small chambers opening onto a central courtyard. Though a distinctive Cornish development dating to the Roman period, the basic plan owes far more to the traditional Iron Age round house than to Roman building methods.

By the end of the fifth century Clovis had brought much of northern and western Gaul under Frankish domination, leaving the more Germanic enclaves of Burgundia and Alamania and the Ostrogothic kingdoms to control the centre and east. With the exception of Brittany, Latin was strongly entrenched, and in considerable part survived as the basis of French. In Britain German settlement had advanced rapidly across most of the romanized south-east. Here the emergence of Anglo-Saxon as the dominant language shows that the impact of germanization must have been considerable.

During this period of turmoil there was some movement among the surviving Celtic communities of the west. The process began with Irish raids across the Celtic Sea against the coastal communities of Roman Britain. The Attocotti from the Western Isles off Scotland and the Picts from north of the frontier

202 The 'Petrie Crown', named after the collector George Petrie, is a fragmentary bronze head piece found somewhere in Ireland. The elegant decoration is a fine example of Irish insular La Tène art, probably dating to the first or second century AD. National Museum of Ireland, Dublin.

joined in, and there is a suggestion, in the contemporary historical record, that these northern and western raiders worked together with Germans from across the North Sea in what was called the Barbarian Conspiracy of AD 367. Whether the raids were concerted or fortuitous in their timing, they had a devastating effect on the Roman province. The Irish, Attocotti, and Picts were probably Celtic peoples, although some linguists claim to be able to detect a pre-Indo-European element in the Pictish language. The reason for the raids are unrecorded, but it is likely that simple opportunism and the prevailing atmosphere of 'folk wandering' that characterized the period played an important part.

The continuous pressure of the Irish on the western coasts of Britain, which began as raids in the late third century AD, led, a century later, to the establishment of permanent colonial settlements. In south-west Wales, in Pembrokeshire and the Gower, the Déisi carved out enclaves; in the Lleyn Peninsula of north-west Wales, more Irish settlers established themselves; while in the western coastal region of what is now Scotland the Scotti, from northern Ireland, took control of a territory which eventually became part of the kingdom of Dál Riata extending to both sides of the Celtic Sea. These Irish settlers brought with them their own distinct dialects of the Celtic language.

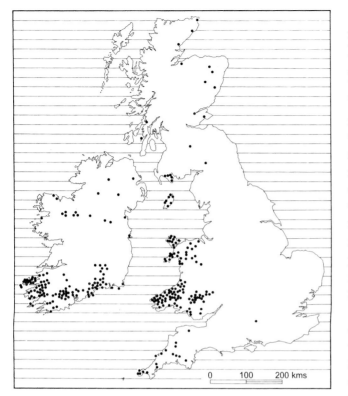

203 The distribution of
Ogham and early Christian
inscribed stones in Britain
reflects the penetration of
Irish settlers in the fourth
and fifth centuries AD.

Another folk movement took place from south Wales and south-western Britain southwards across the Channel to Armorica (which thereafter can be called by its more familiar name—Brittany). The movement may have begun in the fourth century with the use of British troops in the defence of Roman Gaul against barbarian attack, but by the mid-fifth century it had taken on the character of a folk movement. Although the bulk of the migrant population probably came from Cornwall and Devon, the communities of south Wales played a significant part in providing the leadership. There may also have been an Irish element joining the restless movements.

The leaders came from the local élites. Some were evidently *peregrini*, or spiritual leaders, many of whom took solace in the remote islands off the Breton coast or deep in the Breton forests. Others were probably younger sons seeking new lands for themselves and their followers. Their personalities and adventures contributed to the rich store of saints' lives composed four or five centuries after the event from surviving scraps of oral tradition. The reason behind the migration of the western Britons was presented by Gildas in simplistic terms. For him the prime cause was pressure from the Saxon advance from the east. While this may have contributed to the exodus, the Irish expansion into Wales and the south-west, internal population increases, and the new sense of freedom and adventure born as the constraints of Roman government crumbled are all likely to have played a part.

The complexities inherent in the study of the early British settlement in Armorica are considerable, and many issues remain the source of energetic debate. The peninsula was divided into three territories, Dumnonia (Dom-nonée), Cornovia (Cornouaille), and Broërec. The first two may have taken their names from the tribes of south-western Britain who settled the coastal regions: the third was carved out by the Breton chieftain Waroc, who advanced into the Vannetais, where Gallo-Roman culture still remained strong.

In attempting to trace the early settlement much has been made of place-name evidence. The concentration of names containing Plou, Lan, and Tré in northern and western Armorica has long been argued to reflect the settlements of the Britons. A very high percentage of the Plou names are compounded with male personal names, either saints or laymen, and of those which can be

264

identified most have a British origin. Recent work has, however, suggested that some of the Plou-plus-common-name places may date to the pre-migration period. The second set of significant names are those ending in the suffix -*ac*. These concentrate in the south-east of Armorica, particularly in the Morbihan. They were believed to represent the survival of Gallo-Roman place names ending in -*acum*, but since it has been shown that this is a modification of the Gaulish -*acos* and that these names are only rarely compounded with Latin prefixes, it is now argued that the -*ac* names may well reflect the survival of the Gaulish language.

The whole question of the Breton language is equally subject to lively debate. It is widely accepted that there are four main dialects. Three, covering Cornouaille, Léon, and Trégor, are similar and are referred to as the Kerneu of Léon and Trégor (KLT). The fourth, in the Vannetais, is significantly different. This pattern has interesting similarities to the place-name distributions mentioned above. Two diverging hypotheses are offered. The traditional view, championed by Joseph Loth and Kenneth Jackson, argues that Old Breton developed from the same Primitive Brittonic roots as Cornish and Welsh, which persisted in south-western Britain at the time of the migrations and that the Breton dialects developed only after the eleventh century. If so, then the Breton language was a form of Celtic reintroduced from Britain. The alternative view, that developed by Chanoine Falc'hun, argues that Breton derives substantially from indigenous pre-Roman Celtic. He suggests that the two principal dialect groups reflect a pre-Caesarian division, the Vannetais thus deriving from the language spoken by the Veneti while KLT was the dialect of

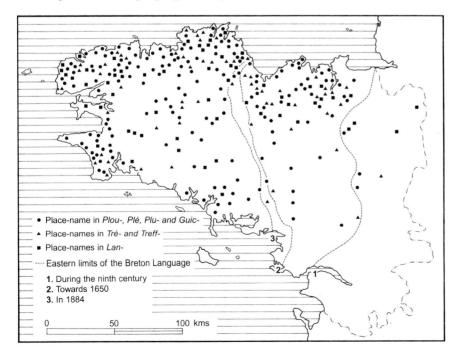

204 Map of early place names in Brittany, showing the extent of the Celtic language in the fourth–sixth centuries AD.

• Place-name in *Plou-, Plé, Plu- and Guic-*
▲ Place-names in *Tré- and Treff-*
■ Place-names in *Lan-*
---- Eastern limits of the Breton Language
  1. During the ninth century
  2. Towards 1650
  3. In 1884

0   50   100 kms

the Osismi and Coriosolites. Falc'hun accepts, however, the contribution of British Celtic in strengthening the Celtic spoken in the north and west.

These issues will remain at the centre of scholarly debate for some time to come. There is nothing, however, inherently unlikely in the survival of Celtic in Armorica from pre-Roman times, but the close relationship between Armorica and south-western Britain throughout the Late Iron Age and Roman period may well have been sufficient to have maintained a degree of parallel development in the languages of the two peninsulas during the millennium before the British migration.

A population movement still further south into Galicia in north-western Iberia is implied by the fifth-century writer Orosius, who refers to the Galician city of Brigantia, which had, he claimed, a direct relationship with Ireland. The Irish contact is further reflected in the presence of the Celtic monastery of Santa Maria de Bretoña near Mondoñedo, which was included in the episcopate of Britoña. To what extent these links along the Atlantic sea-ways reflect a substantial movement of population or simply the influx of a small religious élite it is difficult to say.

The Celtic Communities of the Middle Ages and After

The Celtic communities of the Atlantic zone survived in different degrees of isolation throughout the early Middle Ages. The Viking attacks which began in the eighth century ravaged coastal areas of Scotland, Ireland, Cornwall, and Brittany, and in Scotland and the eastern parts of Ireland settlement followed, introducing a strong Scandinavian element into local culture. A little later the westward advance of the Norman élite established a firm hold on Wales and large tracts of Ireland. In Brittany following the Viking onslaught many of the characteristics of the Carolingian system survived, and the duchy, which eventually came into existence, became increasingly part of the greater continuum of Francia.

The complex politics of the Middle Ages brought the Celtic populations of the west into direct contact with the rising power of the mongrel élites of England and France, while the spread of Christianity in its many guises introduced new value systems with new role models, mythologies, and symbolisms. Inevitably the Celtic cultures of the west suffered some dilution, but the isolation of their lands at the far extremities of the civilized world allowed much of the indigenous pattern of life to continue behind the thin Anglo-Norman façade. The vibrant epics and folk tales of Ireland and, to a lesser extent, Wales survived, albeit modified by Christianized redactors, while in Scotland, Cornwall, and Brittany, though little of literary merit has come down to us, the scraps of folk tales and legends that do survive are a reminder of what there once was. In the Law Tracts of Ireland and Wales we glimpse Celtic society in all its intricacies.

The growing imperialism of France and England during the eighteenth century, with its deliberate attempts to impose metropolitan values and rule on all the distant peripheries, began to erase the already-weakened Celtic cultures, but in doing so created a new spirit of resistance. The Celtic past, in all its manifestations, took on a new importance as a symbol of unity. It was in this mood of ethnic struggle that the Celtic revival, which we briefly reviewed in Chapter 1, had its genesis. To what extent the Celticism of the Atlantic façade is a survival or a revival is a matter for anthropologists to debate. What is not in doubt, as anyone familiar with Galicia, Brittany, Ireland, or Wales will well know, is the very strong emotional appeal which the idea of sharing a common Celtic heritage has. Perhaps the only real definition of a Celt, now as in the past, is that a Celt is a person who believes him or herself to be Celtic.

14
Retrospect

S<small>INCE</small> the early eighteenth century the quest for the Celts has become a consuming passion for an increasing number of historians, linguists, folklorists, art historians, and archaeologists. Inevitably, this intensity of effort and enthusiasm has spilled over into the public's understanding of the past, in part informing it but at the same time introducing imperfectly understood concepts which are sometimes used to underpin vague notions of ethnicity and, occasionally, to excuse extremes of political behaviour. This woolly, fey, and sometimes dangerous 'Celtic fringe' has brought the word 'Celt' into disrepute in some academic circles, and understandably so, but it would be as well to remind ourselves that the concept of 'Celticness' exists and has existed only through the interpretations which observers have chosen to put upon it, whether they be Polybius or Yeats—for both of whom the Celts were real.

In this book we have chosen to take a broad view. For us the Celts comprise a large number of ethnic groups who occupied much of central and western Europe in the first millennium BC and spoke a series of related dialects which linguists define as 'Celtic'. Some of these groups moved into east Europe to settle. They were rapidly assimilated. Over much of the rest of the Continent 'Celticness' eventually disappeared in the turmoil and reformation of the first half of the first millennium AD and only in the extreme western fringes did the language, and with it the memory of the Celtic heritage, survive.

Over such a vast tract of land and period of time there was, inevitably, much variation. Tribes trekked far and wide and polities came and went. To what extent the different entities regarded themselves as having a common heritage we can only speculate. The huge hordes that moved eastwards in the third century must have felt themselves to be part of a single people and so too did the disparate tribes called upon by Vercingetorix to send troops to Alesia to oppose the Romans. That contacts were maintained over considerable distances is suggested by historical anecdotes referring to political links between the Galatians in Asia Minor and the inhabitants of the area around Massalia, but whether any of this meant that individual lineages felt that they belonged to a shared international 'Celticness' will always remain in doubt.

The two most commonly used methods of defining Celts—language and La Tène material culture and art—both present problems in that they represent very different cultural attributes. Celtic languages appear to have been spoken over wide, if discontinuous, areas of western Europe by the sixth century BC, while the material manifestations of La Tène culture reflect the emergence, expansion, and subsequent evolution of one cultural complex for a brief period of three or four centuries. Whilst these two aspects of Celticness overlap in time and space, they are by no means coterminous.

To characterize the social and economic dynamics of western Europe in the first millennium BC it is necessary to understand something of the basic structures which provide a constant framework throughout. At its simplest we may distinguish three broad geographical zones: an Atlantic zone, a Rhine–Danube zone, and a west Mediterranean zone, each with its own internal systems of interaction and each interacting with the others. The Atlantic zone, stretching from Andalucía to the west coast of Scotland, was bound by the sea, which provided comparative ease of communication between adjacent territories and over longer distances. Besides this its greatest attribute was its metal-rich geo-

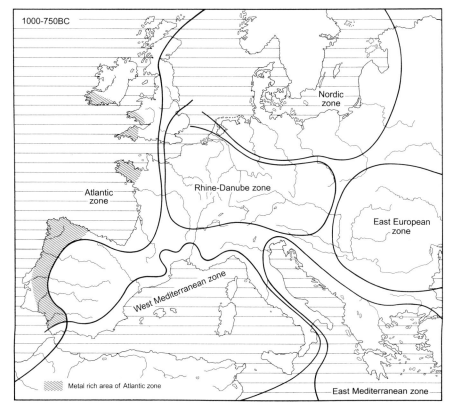

205 Europe in the Late Bronze Age, showing the major socio-cultural zones into which the Late Bronze Age communities can be arranged.

logy. Galicia, Armorica, south-west Britain, south Wales, and southern Ireland between them offered, and no doubt provided, huge quantities of copper, tin, silver, and gold to the polities of central and Mediterranean Europe. The Rhine–Danube zone was particularly favoured as the principal route nexus of Peninsular Europe, where the river systems of the Rhine, Danube, Seine, and Rhône came together. The zone sat astride the east–west routes from the Atlantic zone to eastern Europe and beyond as well as the north–south routes between the Mediterranean and the northern Europe–Baltic (or Nordic) zone. The west Mediterranean constituted the third system. The sea provided the means of communication along the entire littoral zone from Italy to Andalucía and between the many islands from Sicily to the Balearics.

The different pace of social and economic interaction between these three zones provided the dynamics which underlay the emergence and expansion of Celtic societies. But before exploring this in a little more detail we should remind ourselves that Peninsular Europe, which is our prime concern, was in contact with other major socio-cultural complexes: the Nordic zone, the east European zone, and the east Mediterranean zone. During the first millennium the Celtic-speaking peoples of the west interacted with these distant zones in different ways, at different times, and in differing degrees of intensity. It was during the Late Bronze Age, roughly 1300–750 BC, that the Celtic language developed its recognizable characteristics in western Europe. By 600 BC Celtic was spoken in Iberia, Ireland, and around the Italian Lakes, and it is reasonable to suppose that it was also in use over much, but not all, of the intervening area. Where and when Celtic emerged as a language distinct from other Indo-European tongues is still a matter of much debate, but the general consensus of linguists—that the origin lay within the Rhine–Danube zone late in the second or early in the first millennium—is perfectly consistent with the archaeological evidence. Indeed it could be argued that the re-formations underway in the different zones of Europe in the Late Bronze Age, the intensification of production and exchange, the apparent population growth, and the greater stability in the settlement pattern provided optimum conditions for the crystallizing-out of the major European language groups.

If the origins of the Celtic language lay within the Rhine–Danube zone, then when and by what mechanism did it spread to the Atlantic zone? There is little in the archaeological record to suggest migration or even the spread of a dominant military élite, but what is apparent is a rapid increase in the production and movement of bronze and a change in the socio-religious systems with a new emphasis on propitiating the chthonic deities. It is quite possible that increasing demands for metals led to a much greater mobility among those with pyrotechnical skills and that with this élite came new systems of religious beliefs. In such a context it is easy to see how the Celtic language could have spread both as a lingua franca and as the language of a technico-religious caste. While such a hypothesis is difficult to prove, it has the benefit of being, at least, plausible.

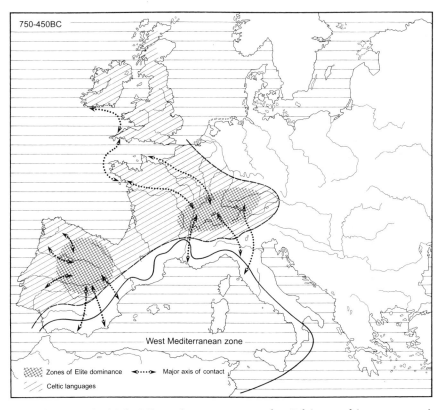

750-450BC

West Mediterranean zone

Zones of Elite dominance ◁····▷ Major axis of contact

Celtic languages

206 Europe in the Hallstatt period. By this stage the Celtic languages were spoken over much of western Europe and two major zones of innovation were developing in Iberia and west central Europe. Both were in active contact with the west Mediterranean zone and with the metal-rich Atlantic zone.

In the period which followed, *c.*750–450 BC, the Celtic-speaking communities of the west developed increasingly close contacts with the Mediterranean zone. In two core areas, the West Hallstatt region of the Rhine–Danube zone and the Meseta of Iberia, distinctive élites emerged. The West Hallstatt chieftains adopted selected behaviour patterns, and the luxury goods which supported them, from the Etruscan and Greek communities of the northern littoral of the Mediterranean, while the Celtiberian élite of north central Spain embraced a range of traits learned from the complex Iberian culture developing at this time in south-eastern Spain under the influence of Greek, Etruscan, and Phoenician contacts.

These two innovating core zones benefited, by virtue of their position, from contact with the Mediterranean world, and, while it is inappropriate to argue that their development was *caused* by Mediterranean influence, it was certainly facilitated by ease of access to Mediterranean markets. Beyond both 'cores' there existed broad peripheries extending westwards to the Atlantic, through which, no doubt, commodities such as metals flowed eastwards, while luxury goods like horses and weapon sets will have been used for reciprocal exchanges. One way of viewing these two innovating cores is to see them as benefiting from their favoured locations between the metal-rich Atlantic zone and the metal-demanding Mediterranean. This level of generalization is a helpful simplification, but it should not be allowed to obscure the complexity of the dynamics involved or to suggest too close a similarity between the Celtiberian or West Hallstatt communities, since both existed largely in isolation from each other.

It may well have been during this period that divergence in language became apparent. Celtiberian retained much of its earlier structure, while in the West Hallstatt zone it seems likely that developments began which were to lead to Brythonic or 'P-Celtic'.

The next major phase began in *c.*450 and lasted until about 200 BC. In west central Europe this saw the emergence of a new élite, around the northern and western fringes of the West Hallstatt chiefdom zone—an élite which can be characterized by the distinctive La Tène material culture. After a brief period of development the traditional social system which had been slowly evolving for more than 500 years collapsed. The suddenness of this and the massive social upheaval which ensued make the events of the late fifth century BC a classic example of systems-collapse. The causes are difficult to untangle but may in part have been the social instability inherent in the élite system exacerbated by population increase and reorientations within the Mediterranean economy.

What followed was an outpouring of populations into the Mediterranean zone and the east European zone. The expansion was temporarily halted in the Balkans by the power of Macedonia, but, following the death of Alexander in 323 BC, and the political instability which followed, Celtic-speaking peoples thrust eastwards, establishing themselves in the Middle Danube (the Scor-

207 Europe in the Early and Middle La Tène period. It was during this time that populations from the élite zones began to expand into peripheral areas away from the territories in which Celtic languages had been spoken for some centuries.

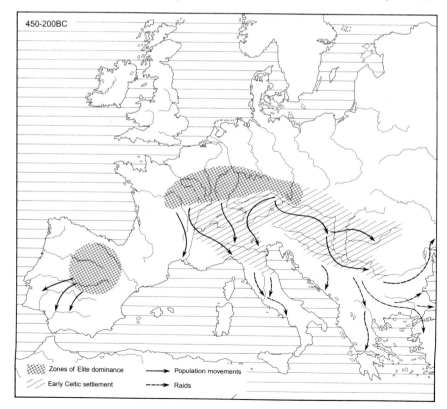

450-200BC

Zones of Elite dominance
Early Celtic settlement
Population movements
Raids

disci), on the eastern shores of the Black Sea (the kingdom of Tylis), in Asia Minor (the Galatians), and probably in Moldova. Elsewhere within this broad zone Celts settled among existing populations or served as mercenaries wherever they could find employment. The numbers involved are difficult to estimate but must have run into hundreds of thousands.

To what extent there was an equivalent expansion westwards is unclear. There is nothing in the archaeological record to suggest any significant disruption. Indeed it could be argued that communities of the western periphery up to the Atlantic coast and beyond were saved from predatory attack because they had long been bound in networks of reciprocal exchange with the élite-dominated zone. Whether or not this was so, it is abundantly clear that the main thrust of the migratory moves was to the south and east.

The situation in Iberia is less clear but that there was some expansion to the south and west is borne out both by the classical sources and by the distribution of tribal names.

The migrations were largely at an end by 200 BC. This was the moment at which Rome, freed from the threat of Carthage by her hard-won victories during the Second Punic War, entered into a more expansive mode. Military involvement in Iberia led to the gradual subjugation of the Celtiberians, while increasing intensity in trade with the Transalpine Celts introduced a new range of opportunities and the catalyst for change. Here the energies, which previously had been dissipated in aggression, were turned to more productive pursuits, and the social display of luxuries acquired through trade, in cycles of conspicuous consumption, replaced the desire for prowess gained in the successful accomplishment of a raid. In this way the Celtic tribes began to be transformed into urban-based states where gifts, dues, and other exchanges were articulated through the exchange of coins.

The transformation of the Celtic world was gradual and uneven. In the century and a half from 200 to 50 BC, the communities closest to the Roman frontiers had changed dramatically, but at this point local developments were overtaken by Germanic pressures from the Nordic zone, Dacian and Sarmatian pressures from the east European zone, and a rapid escalation in the Roman desire for empire. In a brief sixty years the Celtic communities of continental Europe were completely overrun and within the century much of the south of Britain had been absorbed as well.

Only the insular Celtic-speaking communities of the far west remained free. Those of Cornwall, Wales, and northern Britain were loosely controlled within the frontiers of the empire: beyond in the Highlands and Islands of Scotland and in Ireland they lay beyond the reach of Rome and when, in the late third to fifth century, Roman control weakened, there was a limited resurgence with small populations moving east and south along the Atlantic sea-ways. The survival of the language, laws, and traditions of these Atlantic fringe Celtic communities and the revival that began in the eighteenth century are part of a different but no less fascinating story.

208 Europe in the Late La Tène period. This period saw the Celtic communities under increasing pressures particularly from the Romans but also to a lesser extent from Dacians and Germans. By AD 400 Celtic languages survived only in the Atlantic zone.

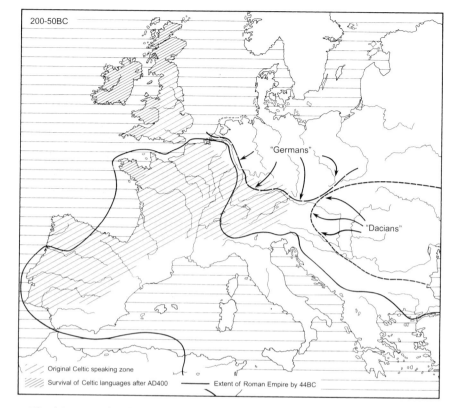

200-50BC

"Germans"

"Dacians"

Original Celtic speaking zone
Survival of Celtic languages after AD400 — Extent of Roman Empire by 44BC

The history of Celtic-speaking communities in Europe covers nearly two millennia. The process began in the formative period c.1300–750 BC, when most of Europe underwent a dramatic transformation. Then followed the emergence of early chiefdoms, 750–450, as the increasing rhythms of the Mediterranean economy began to impinge. The systems-collapse and diaspora of 450–200 created a warrior society which was to provide the classical world with its stereotype of the 'northern barbarian' and the archaeologist with a material culture and art which could be called 'Celtic'. Thereafter, in the final phase, the Mediterranean-based culture of the Romans spread its influence northwards, first through traders, then through the army, and finally, and more devastatingly, through provincial administrators, until only a few insular communities, long isolated from the developments in continental Europe, were left clinging to a precarious freedom along the Atlantic fringes.

Sufficient has been said in this brief retrospect to remind us that Celtic-speaking peoples have had a long and complex history: their diversity in social and cultural terms is beyond dispute. Yet the stereotype which, for a variety of reasons, their literate contemporaries created of them echoes across the ages. These visions have provided, and no doubt will continue to provide, metaphors for later generations. The 'Celt' is a powerful and emotive image which pervades our culture, and it is entirely proper that we should spend time attempting to understand it.

A Guide to Further Reading

The quantity of literature on the subject of the Celts is enormous and to guide those wishing to go deeper into the subject is not easy. In the section to follow we offer, first, a series of books written for the general reader, which, in many cases, are attractively illustrated. Then follows a list of more specialist works published since about 1970. Together, in some 200 individual papers, they provide a fair coverage of the detailed research currently being undertaken. These volumes should be approached only by those of resilient disposition.

Thereafter some guidance is given as to the most significant general reading on a chapter-by-chapter basis. Wherever possible English works have been chosen, but, where nothing suitable exists, French, German, and Spanish sources have been suggested. Most of the works cited have extensive bibliographies which will help the enthusiast to begin detailed research on virtually any Celtic topic. It is a pursuit which can fill many lifetimes.

General Books

Among books offering overviews of the ancient Celts, the two classic texts are T. G. E. Powell, *The Celts* (London, 1958, and subsequent editions), and Jan Filip, *Celtic Civilization and its Heritage* (first published in Czech in 1960 with the first English edition appearing in Prague in 1962). Though elderly, both texts are well worth reading for the mastery and style of their authors. Three books, focusing more on the historical Celts but still offering a broad sweeping approach, can be recommended: Nora Chadwick, *The Celts* (Harmondsworth, 1971); Myles Dillon and Nora Chadwick, *The Celtic Realms* (London, 1967); and Alwyn and Brinley Rees, *Celtic Heritage: Ancient Traditions in Ireland and Wales* (London, 1961).

More recent general works include a massive tome *The Celts*, edited by Sabatino Moscati and others, and published in 1991 in Milan to accompany a comprehensive exhibition entitled 'The Celts, the Origins of Europe' which was held in Venice. The volume includes a large number of papers on sites or themes, written by scholars with a first-hand research knowledge of the subject area, and illustrated with photographs of incomparable quality, mostly in colour. Though physically unwieldy and unindexed, *The Celts* presents a brilliant kaleidoscope of Celtic achievement. A second large composite volume, *The Celtic World*, edited by Miranda Aldhouse Green (London, 1995), presents a valuable collection of thematic papers reflecting research. More general single-authored books which can be recommended because of their carefully integrated texts and illustrations are: Paul-Marie Duval, *Les Celtes* (Paris, 1977); *The Celts of the West*, text by Venceslas Kruta with brilliant photographs by Werner Forman (London, 1985); Barry Cunliffe, *The Celtic World* (London, 1979); Simon James, *Exploring the World of the Celts* (London, 1993); Christiane Eluère, *The Celts: First Masters of Europe* (first English edition: London, 1993); and *Celts: Europe's People of Iron*, a Time-Life

Book (Alexandria, Va., 1994). Of these the most useful as an up-to-date and comprehensive introduction is Simon James's book.

More Specialist Works

An increasing number of edited compilations of specialist papers, often emanating from conferences or colloquia and designed mainly for the specialist reader, are being published. These contain work of varying degrees of usefulness usually concerned with research in progress. Among those which offer a selection of interesting papers are T. C. Champion and J. V. S. Megaw (eds.), *Settlement and Society: Aspects of West European Prehistory in the First Millennium BC* (Leicester, 1985); K. Kristiansen and J. Jensen (eds.), *Europe in the First Millennium BC* (Sheffield, 1994); J. D. Hill and C. G. Cumberpatch (eds.), *Different Iron Ages: Studies on the Iron Age in Temperate Europe* (Oxford, 1995); and B. Arnold and D. B. Gibson (eds.), *Celtic Chiefdom, Celtic State* (Cambridge, 1995).

In addition to these volumes, which could reasonably claim to have a European-wide scope, there are a number of more regionally based compilations which may be cited as important reference works for the specialist. These include: Catalogue: Steyr 1980, *Die Hallstattkultur; Frühform europäischer Einheit* (Steyr, 1980); Symposium: Steyr 1980, *Die Hallstattkultur* (Steyr, 1980); E. Jerem (ed.), *Hallstatt Kolloquium Veszprem 1984* (Budapest, 1986); L. Pauli (ed.), *Die Kelten in Mitteleuropa: Salzburger Landesausstellung im Keltenmuseum Hallein Österreich* (Salzburg, 1980); K. Bittel, W. Kimmig, and S. Schiek, *Die Kelten in Baden-Württemberg* (Stuttgart, 1981); Catalogue: Ljubljana, *KEΛTOI: Kelti in njihovi sobobniki na ozemljn Jugoslavije* (Ljubljana, 1983); J.-W. Neugebauer, *Die Kelten im Osten Österreichs* (St Pölten/Vienna, 1992). J. Fitz, *The Celts in Central Europe* (Székesfehérvár, 1975); Paul-Marie Duval and Venceslas Kruta (eds.), *Les Mouvements celtiques du Ve au Ier siècle avant notre ère* (Paris, 1979); P. Drda and A. Rybová, *Les Celtes de Bohême* (Paris, 1995); M. Szabó, *Les Celtes de l'est* (Paris, 1992); Paul-Marie Duval and Venceslas Kruta, *L'Habitat et la nécropole à l'âge du fer en Europe occidentale et centrale* (Paris, 1975); Memoires de la Société archéologique champenoise, *L'Âge du fer en France septentrionale* (Reims, 1981); J. Collis, A. Duval, and R. Pèrichon, *Le Deuxième Âge du fer en Auvergne et en Forez* (Sheffield/St Etienne, 1983); A. Cahen-Delhaye, A. Duval, G. Leman-Delerive, and P. Leman, *Les Celtes en Belgique et dans le nord de la France* (Villeneuve d'Ascq, 1984); Revue Archéologie de l'Ouest, *Les Gaulois d'Armorique* (Rennes, 1990); Revue Archéologie de l'Ouest, *Les Celtes en Normandie* (Rennes, 1993); M. Almagro-Gorbea and G. Ruiz Zapatero, *Los Celtas: Hispania y Europa* (Madrid, 1993); and *Aquitania*, vol. 12, *L'Age du fer en Europe sud-occidentale* (Toulouse, 1994).

Chapter 1. Visions of the Celts

The most challenging work on the whole question of validity of the concept of 'Celtic' is M. Chapman, *The Celts: The Construction of a Myth* (New York, 1992). It deserves careful reading as an essential preliminary. Other writers have been quick to espouse a politically correct disdain for the use of 'Celt' though usually without Chapman's depth of scholarship.

The Graeco-Roman vision of the Celts is admirably summed up in *Celts and the Classical World* by H. D. Rankin (London, 1987). The principal classical texts are usefully gathered in translation in John T. Koch with John Carey (eds.), *The Celtic Heroic*

Age: Literary Sources for Ancient Celtic Europe and Early Ireland and Wales (Malden, Mass., 1995). The seminal scholarly discussion of the works of the classical historian Poseidonius with the full classical texts in translation is J. J. Tierney, 'The Celtic Ethnography of Poseidonius', *Proceedings of the Royal Irish Academy*, 60 (1960), 1892–46. A source worthy of study, and fascinating to read, is Julius Caesar's *Commentaries on the Gallic War*, of which there are many good modern translations (e.g. that of A. and P. Wiseman: London, 1980). As the war reminiscences of an old soldier and politician, they must be treated with critical attention, but they contain much relevant detail. A helpful discussion of Caesar as a source for the Celts is a paper by Daphne Nash, 'Reconstructing Poseidonios's Celtic Ethnography; Some Considerations', *Britannia*, 7 (1976), 111–26.

The reawakening of the post-medieval world to the Celts and the emergence of Celtomania is part of the history of archaeology which is treated with great panache by Stuart Piggott, *William Stukeley* (1st edn., Oxford, 1950), *The Druids* (London, 1968) and *Ancient Britons and the Antiquarian Imagination* (London, 1989).

The contribution of archaeology to the early years of Celtic studies is a theme too massive to document here, but two period pieces well worthy of attention are Napoleon III, *Histoire de Jules César* (Paris, 1865), and Mortimer Wheeler, *Maiden Castle, Dorset* (London, 1943). In both cases the authors show how carefully planned excavations and fieldwork can be used to enliven, and sometimes to create, historical narrative.

Chapter 2. The Reality of the Celts

The questions posed by the origins and development of Celtic language are extremely complex and much of the literature is impenetrable to all but the most skilled scholar. Two recent books, Colin Renfrew, *Archaeology and Language* (London, 1987), and J. P. Mallory, *In Search of the Indo-Europeans* (London, 1989), present the problems (from very different viewpoints) in clear uncluttered prose and offer valuable starting-points. A helpful overview is offered by D. Greene, 'The Celtic Languages', in J. Raftery (ed.), *The Celts* (Cork, 1967). Thereafter things become difficult! Among the more scholarly works are J. Whatmough, *A Study of the Dialects of Ancient Gaul* (Ann Arbor, 1970); D. E. Evans, *Gaulish Personal Names* (Oxford, 1967); and A. Tovar, *Sprachen und Inschriften: Studien zum Mykenischen Lateinischen und Hispanokeltischen* (Amsterdam, 1973). The complexities of the problems are also well exposed in three review papers: K. H. Schmidt, 'On the Celtic Languages of Continental Europe', *Bulletin of the Board of Celtic Studies*, 28 (1979), 189–205; D. E. Evans, 'Celts and Germans', ibid., 29 (1981), 230–55; and D. E. Evans, 'The Labyrinth of Continental Celtic', *Proceedings of the British Academy*, 65 (1978), 497–538.

The insular tradition of vernacular literature is an immense and specialist subject. The two central original sources are the Irish epic, the *Táin Bó Cuailnge*, available as *The Táin* in elegant translation by Thomas Kinsella (Oxford, 1969) and the Welsh epic, *The Mabinogion*, trans. Jeffrey Gantz (Harmondsworth, 1976), which includes a helpful introduction. The most accessible introduction to the complexities of the Irish literature is Myles Dillon, *Early Irish Literature* (Chicago, 1948), which is usefully augmented by Gerald Murphy, *The Ossianic Lore and Romantic Tales of Medieval Ireland* (Dublin, 1955). The classic attempt to use the Irish literature to present a picture of Iron Age society is Kenneth Jackson, *The Oldest Irish Tradition* (Cambridge, 1964). Jackson's stimulating, but oversimple, interpretation has been challenged in two important papers by J.

P. Mallory, 'The Sword in the Ulster Cycle', in B. Scott (ed.), *Studies on Early Ireland* (Belfast, 1981), 99–114, and 'Silver in the Ulster Cycle of Tales', *Proceedings of the Seventh International Congress of Celtic Studies* (Oxford, 1986), 31–78. The subject of the war chariot as depicted in the Irish literature provides a fascinating insight into the problems posed by using the texts. Three papers can be particularly recommended: D. Greene, 'The Chariot as Described in Irish Literature', in Charles Thomas (ed.), *The Iron Age in the Irish Sea Province* (London, 1972), 59–73; Peter Harbison, 'The Old Irish "Chariot"', *Antiquity*, 45 (1971), 171–7; and the relevant sections of Stuart Piggott's wide-ranging book *The Earliest Wheeled Transport* (London, 1983), in particular pp. 195–238. For the law tracts, Fergus Kelly, *A Guide to Early Irish Law* (Dublin, 1988), is an excellent introduction.

The contribution of archaeology has been immense and the major texts will be referred to in the pages that follow. A number of the classic works have been mentioned in the main text and need not be repeated here. The subject of Celtic art will be considered more fully under Chapter 6.

Chapter 3. Barbarian Europe and the Mediterranean: 1300–500 BC

As a general background to this chapter the relevant chapters of Barry Cunliffe (ed.), *The Oxford Illustrated Prehistory of Europe* (Oxford, 1994), will be useful.

The subject of the early chiefdoms has excited much discussion in recent years following the publication of an inspiring paper by Susan Frankenstein and Mike Rowlands, 'The Internal Structure and Regional Context of Early Iron Age Society in South-Western Germany', *Bulletin of the Institute of Archaeology, London*, 15 (1978), 73–112. A different approach with much background material is presented by Wolfgang Kimmig, 'Die griechische Kolonisation im westlichen Mittelmeergebiet und ihre Wirkung auf die Landschaften des westlichen Mitteleuropa', *Jahrbuch des Römisch-Germanischen Zentralmuseums Mainz* (1983), 5–78. A less detailed treatment of the same material is given in Barry Cunliffe, *Greeks, Romans and Barbarians: Spheres of Interaction* (London, 1988). Other works of significance discussing this general subject area include Peter Wells, *Culture Contact and Culture Change* (Cambridge, 1980); Patrice Brun, *Princes et princesses de la Celtique: Le Premier Age du fer (850–450 av. J-C)* (Paris, 1987); *Les Princes celtes et La Méditerranée* (Recontres de l'École du Louvre; Paris, 1988), and Chris Pare, 'Fürstensitze, Celts and the Mediterranean World: Developments in West Hallstatt Culture in the 6th and 5th Centuries BC', *Proceedings of the Prehistoric Society*, 57 (1991), 183–202.

In addition to these discussions there are a large number of publications dealing with individual sites: full bibliographies will be found in the books listed above. For one of the most recent discoveries of a chieftain's burial, Jörg Biel's well-illustrated book, *Der Keltenfürst von Hochdorf* (Stuttgart, 1985), provides a spectacular insight. The most important of the settlements to be excavated, the Heuneburg, is usefully summarized in a guide book by Wolfgang Kimmig, *Die Heuneburg an der oberen Donau* (Stuttgart, 1983).

Chapter 4. The Migrations: 400–200 BC

The classical sources, which provide the main 'historical' account of the migrations, are conveniently brought together and discussed by H. D. Rankin in *Celts and the Classical World* (London, 1987). Two other general discussions—Ludwig Pauli, 'Early Celtic

Society: Two Centuries of Wealth and Turmoil in Central Europe', and Daphne Nash, 'Celtic Territorial Expansion and the Mediterranean World', both in T. C. Champion and J. V. S. Megaw (eds.), *Settlement and Society* (Leicester, 1985)—add significantly to the debate. For more specific regional studies, Venceslas Kruta's 'Les Boïens de Cispadane: Essai de paléoethnographie celtique', *Études celtiques*, 17 (1980), 7–32, and the same author's 'Les Sénons de l'Adriatique d'après l'archéologie (prolégomènes)', *Études celtiques*, 18 (1981), 7–38, present a range of evidence from the Po Valley. The proceedings of a conference, Paul-Marie Duval and Venceslas Kruta (eds.), *Les Mouvements celtiques du Ve au Ier siècle avant notre ère* (Paris, 1979) contains sixteen individual papers, together covering much of Europe. For the Middle Danube region, Jovan Todorović, *Skordisci* (Novi Sad, 1974), provides a detailed coverage, while Miklós Szabó, *The Celtic Heritage in Hungary* (Budapest, 1971), offers a general assessment of Transdanubia and the Great Hungarian Plain. Evidence for Celtic culture in Poland is discussed in detail by Z. Woźniak, *Osadnictwo celtyckie w Polsce* (with an English summary) (Wrocław, 1970). Evidence for Celtic movements further east is explored in three detailed papers: Michail Treister, 'The Celts in the North Pontic Area: A Reassessment', *Antiquity*, 67 (1993), 789–804; M. B. Shchukin, 'The Celts in Eastern Europe', *Oxford Journal of Archaeology*, 14 (1995), 201–27; and M. B. Shchukin *et al.*, 'Two Finds Belonging to La Tène and Roman Periods from the Moldavian Republic', *Oxford Journal of Archaeology*, 12 (1993), 67–75. References to Celtic movements and settlement in Asia Minor will be given under Chapter 9. The intriguing question of reflux movements from east to west is examined in a detailed study by Venceslas Kruta, 'Les Celtes des Gaules d'après l'archéologie', in K. H. Schmidt (ed.), *Geschichte und Kultur der Kelten* (Heidelberg, 1986), 33–51. The classic Celtic folk movement, that of the Helvetii, is described in first-hand detail by Julius Caesar in the first book of his *Commentaries on the Gallic War*.

Chapter 5. Warfare and Society

The nature of Celtic warfare and social systems can be gleaned from various of the classical texts usefully discussed in Chapters 4–6 of H. D. Rankin, *Celts and the Classical World* (London, 1987). A succinct account of the archaeological evidence for warfare is offered in W. F. and J. N. G. Ritchie, *Celtic Warriors* (Princes Risborough, 1985). The sword is given thorough treatment by Radomir Pleiner in *The Celtic Sword* (Oxford, 1993). For shields and spears, see A. Rapin, 'Boucliers et lances', in J.-L. Brunaux and A. Rapin, *Gournay II* (Paris, 1988). Works on chariots have already been mentioned in the bibliography for Chapter 2, to which should be added Peter Harbison, 'The Chariot of Celtic Funerary Tradition', *Fundberichte aus Hessen*, 1 (1969), 34–58, and Ian Stead, 'The Celtic Chariot', *Antiquity*, 39 (1965), 259–65. The most ambitious attempt at reconstructing social systems is Carol Crumley, *Celtic Social Structure: The Generation of Archaeologically Testable Hypotheses from Literary Evidence* (Michigan, 1974). Daphne Nash, 'Territory and State Formation in Central Gaul', in D. Greene *et al.* (eds.), *Social Organization and Settlement* (Oxford, 1978), 455–75, remains a classic account of the changes in Gaulish society as Roman influence increased.

Chapter 6. The Arts of the Migration Period

The subject of Celtic art has been dealt with extensively in a number of general books. The classic text is Paul Jacobsthal, *Early Celtic Art* (Oxford, 1944), which has set the scene for everything to follow, but the most up-to-date and helpful text, copiously illustrated, is Ruth and Vincent Megaw, *Celtic Art* (London, 1989), which is now the essential starting-point; the volume also has an extensive bibliography arranged thematically. Other broadly based studies of value include: Nancy Sanders' elegant and emotive chapter in her *Prehistoric Art in Ancient Europe* (2nd edn., Harmondsworth, 1985); Paul-Marie Duval, *Les Celts* (Paris, 1977); Paul-Marie Duval and Christopher Hawkes (eds.), *Celtic Art in Ancient Europe: Five Protohistoric Centuries* (London, 1976); Paul-Marie Duval and Venceslas Kruta (eds.), *L'Art celtique de la période d'expansion: IVe and IIIe siècles* (Geneva and Paris, 1982). A number of excellent regional surveys exist, among which may be listed: Miklós Szabó and Eva Petres, *A Keleti Kelta Müvészet— Eastern Celtic Art* (text largely in English) (Székesfehérvár, 1974); *L'Art celtique en Gaule: Collections des musées de Province* (Ministère de la Culture; Paris, 1983); Alain Duval, *L'Art celtique de la Gaule* (Paris, 1989); Ian Stead, *Celtic Art in Britain before the Roman Conquest* (London, 1985); Vincent and Ruth Megaw, *Early Celtic Art in Britain and Ireland* (Princes Risborough, 1986); Morna MacGregor, *Early Celtic Art in North Britain* (Leicester, 1976); H. N. Savory, *Early Iron Age Art in Wales* (Cardiff, 1968); and Barry Raftery, *A Catalogue of Irish Iron Age Antiquities* (Marburg, 1983), and *La Tène in Ireland: Problems of Origins and Chronology* (Marburg, 1984). Ceramic art is seldom dealt with as a theme, but a number of specialist papers on painted pottery will be found in *La Céramique peinte celtique dans son contexte Européen* (Reims, 1991), while Frank Schwappach provides accounts of stamp-decorated pottery in *On the Chronology of the Eastern Early La Tène Pottery* (Bad Bramstedt, 1979) and in two papers, 'Die stempelverzierte Latène-Keramik aus den Gräbern von Braubach', *Bonner Jahrbuch*, 77 (1977), 119–83, and 'Frühkeltischen Ornament zwischen Marne, Rhein und Moldau', *Bonner Jahrbuch*, 73 (1973), 53–111. For Celtic coins, the best overview is D. F. Allen, *The Coins of the Ancient Celts* (Edinburgh, 1980).

Chapter 7. Iberia and the Celtiberians

The question of the Celtiberian language is most simply dealt with by A. Tovar in *The Ancient Languages of Spain and Portugal* (New York, 1961). A more detailed treatment will be found in his *Sprachen und Inschriften: Studien zum Mykenischen, Lateinischen und Hispanokeltischen* (Amsterdam, 1973). The standard works on the Iron Age of Iberia and the 'Celtic' problem are: E. Sangmeister, 'Die Kelten in Spanien', *Madrider Mitteilungen*, 1 (1960), 75–100; W. Schüle, *Die Meseta-Kulturen der Iberischen Halbinsel* (Berlin, 1969), and M. Lenerz-de Wilde, *Iberia Celtica* (Stuttgart, 1991). For a Spanish view of their archaeology, Martín Almagro-Gorbea and Gonzalo Ruiz Zapatero (eds.), *Los Celtas: Hispania y Europa* (Madrid, 1993), has much to offer, most notably the papers by: Martín Almagro-Gorbea, 'Los Celtas en la Península Ibérica: Origen y personalidad cultural' (pp. 121–74); Luis A. García Morena, 'Organizacíon sociopolítica de los Celtas en la Península Ibérica' (pp. 327–56); Janier de Hoz, 'Testimonios lingüisticos relativos al problema céltico en la Península Ibérica' (pp. 357–408); and Francisco Marco Simón, 'La religiosidad en la Céltica hispana' (pp. 477–512). Barry Cunliffe and Simon Keay (eds.), *Social Complexity and the Development of Towns in Iberia: From the Copper Age to the Second Century AD* (London, 1995), contains several papers of relevance, including: Martín Almagro-Gorbea, 'From Hillforts to *Oppida* in "Celtic" Iberia' (pp. 175– 208); Gonzalo Ruiz Zapatero and Jesús R. Alvarez-Sanchís, 'Las Cogotas: Oppida and the roots of Urbanism in the Spanish Meseta' (pp. 209–36), and Armando

Coelho Ferreira da Silva, 'Portuguese castros: The Evolution of the Habitat and the Proto-Urbanization Process' (pp. 263–90). Three detailed regional studies of a specialist nature can be recommended: Martín Almagro-Gorbea and Ana Mª Martín, *Castros y Oppida en Extremadura* (Marid, 1995); Lusis Berrocal-Rangel, *Los pueblos Celticos del Suroeste de la Península Iberica* (Madrid, 1992); and Armando Coelho Ferreira da Silva, *A Cultura Castreja no noroeste de Portugal* (Paços de Ferreira, 1986).

Chapter 8. The Communities of the Atlantic Façade

The question of the origins and development of the Celtic languages in the West is of particular interest. Some general references have been given in the bibliography for Chapter 2. More specific to this chapter are two important papers by John T. Koch, 'Gallo-Brittonic vs Insular Celtic', in G. Le Mena and J.-Y. Le Moing, *Bretagne et pays celtique-langues, histoire, civilization* (Saint-Brieuc/Rennes, 1992), 471–95, and 'Ériu, Alba, and Letha: When was a Language Ancestral to Gaelic First Spoken in Ireland?', *Emania*, 9 (1991), 17–27. This same volume of *Emania* contains a number of other papers directly relevant to the Iron Age culture of Ireland. For an up-to-date review of Ireland, Barry Raftery, *Pagan Celtic Ireland: The Enigma of the Irish Iron Age* (London, 1994), is of incomparable value. For Brittany, P.-R. Giot, J. Briard, and L. Pape offer an overview of the Armorican Iron Age in *Protohistoire de la Bretagne* (2nd edn. Rennes, 1995), which can be augmented by reference to a number of specialist papers in *Les Gaulois d'Armorique* (*Revue Archéologique de l'Ouest*, supp. 3; Rennes, 1990). Still the best account of the fortifications of Armorica and Normandy and their historical context is R. E. M. Wheeler and K. M. Richardson, *Hillforts of Northern France* (Oxford, 1957). The question of emigration from Britain to Brittany is well covered in Nora Chadwick, *Early Brittany* (Cardiff, 1969), the same author's 'Colonization of Brittany from Celtic Britain', *Proceedings of the British Academy*, 51 (1965), 235–99, and P.-R. Giot and L. Fleuriot, 'Early Brittany', *Antiquity*, 51 (1977), 106–16. For more recent views about the origins of the Breton language the works of Chanoine Falc'hun are challenging, in particular his *Perspectives nouvelles sur l'histoire de la langue bretonne* (Paris, 1981). The Atlantic sea-ways have generated a considerable literature, but the principal issues (fully referenced) are summed up in three papers: Barry Cunliffe, 'Britain, the Veneti and Beyond', *Oxford Journal of Archaeology*, 1 (1982), 39–68; Sean McGrail, 'Cross-Channel Seamanship and Navigation in the Late First Millennium BC', ibid., 2 (1983), 299–337; and C. F. C. Hawkes, 'Ictis Disentangled and the British Tin Trade', ibid., 3 (1984), 211–33. For the Iron Age of Britain, Barry Cunliffe, *Iron Age Communities of Britain* (3rd edn., London, 1991), provides an overview; for northern Gaul, Nico Roymans, *Tribal Societies in Northern Gaul: An Anthropological Perspective* (Amsterdam, 1990), is comprehensive. For south-west France, two specialist monographs provide up-to-date detail: Richard Boudet, *L'Age du fer récent dans la partie méridionale de l'estuaire Girondin* (Périgueux, 1987), and Jean-Pierre Mohen, *L'Age du fer en Aquitaine* (Paris, 1980).

Chapter 9. The Communities of the Eastern Fringes

As background reading to the horse-riding peoples of the Pontic region, E. D. Philips, *The Royal Hordes: Nomad Peoples of the Steppes* (London, 1965), provides a wide-ranging introduction, while Renate Rolle, *The World of the Scythians* (English edn., London, 1989), offers a more detailed account of one of the major ethnic groups. References have already been given to Celts in the Pontic region under Chapter 4. The Celtic settlement in Asia Minor was presented from a historical view by W. M. Ramsey in his *A Historical Commentary on St Paul's Epistle to the Galatians* (London, 1900). The most recent scholarly account is Stephen Mitchell, *Anatolia: Land, Men and Gods in Asia Minor*, i. *The Celts in Anatolia and the Impact of Roman Rule* (Oxford, 1993). More detailed assessments of the fortifications are given in Stephen Mitchell, 'Blucium and Peium: The Galatian forts of King Deiotarus', *Anatolian Studies*, 24 (1974), 61–75. Distribution of Celtic artefacts are considered by A. Müller-Karpe, 'Neue galatische funde aus Anatolien', *Istanbuler Mitteilungen*, 38 (1988), 189–99. The monuments depicting Celts set up at Pergamum are discussed by E. Künzl, *Die Kelten des Epigonos von Pergamon* (Würzburg, 1971); R. Wennig, *Die Galateranatheme Attalus I. Ein Untersuchung zum Bestand und der Nachwirkung Pergamenischer Skulptur* (Berlin, 1978); and Lise Hannestad, 'Greeks and Celts: The Creation of a Myth', in P. Bilde *et al.* (eds.), *Centre and Periphery in the Hellenistic World* (Aarhus, 1993), 15–38.

Chapter 10. Religious Systems

There is a fascinating literature on Celtic religious systems. Three books stand out both for their content and their literary merit: Marie-Louise Sjoestedt, *Gods and Heroes of the Celts* (English edn., repr. Dublin, 1994); Proinsias MacCana, *Celtic Mythology* (rev. edn., Feltham, 1983); and Stuart Piggott, *The Druids* (London, 1968). Others covering the subject broadly include J. De Vries, *Keltische Religion* (Stuttgart, 1961); E. Thévenot, *Divinités et sanctuaires de la Gaule* (Paris, 1968); P.-M. Duval, *Les Dieux de la Gaule* (Paris, 1976); J.-L. Brunaux, *The Celtic Gauls: Gods, Rites and Sanctuaries* (English edn., London, 1988); Miranda Green, *The Gods of the Celts* (Gloucester, 1986); and Claude Sterckx, *Elements de cosmogonie celtique* (Brussels, 1986). The significance of animals in religion and in propitiatory burials is considered in Miranda Green, *Animals in Celtic Life and Myth* (London, 1992); Patrice Méniel, *Les Sacrifices d'animaux chez les Gaulois* (Paris, 1992), and Barry Cunliffe, 'Pits, Preconceptions and Propitiation in the British Iron Age', *Oxford Journal of Archaeology*, 11 (1992), 69–83. On festivals and the measurement of time, see Màire MacNeill, *The Festival of Lughnasa* (Oxford, 1962), and Garrett Olmsted, *The Gaulish Calendar* (Bonn, 1992). A general overview of religious locations is provided by Stuart Piggott, 'Nemeton, temenos, bothros, Sanctuaries of the Ancient Celts', *Academia nazionale dei Lincei*, 375 (1978), 37–54. The most informative publications of the temple sites excavated in recent years, are: J.-L. Brunaux *et al.*, *Gournay I. Les fouilles sur le sanctuaire et l'oppidum (1975–1984)* (Amiens, 1985) and J.-L. Brunaux and A. Rapin, *Gournay II. Boucliers et lances: Dépôts et trophées* (Paris, 1988); Ann Woodward and Peter Leach, *The Uley Shrines: Excavation of a Ritual Complex on West Hill, Uley, Gloucestershire: 1977–9* (London, 1993); and W. F. Grimes and J. Close-Brooks, 'The Excavation of Caesar's Camp, Heathrow, Harmondsworth, Middlesex, 1944', *Proceedings of the Prehistoric Society*, 59 (1993), 303–60. A classic example of a ritual deposit of weapons in a bog is Llyn Cerrig Bach: Cyril Fox, *A Find of the Early Iron Age from Llyn Cerrig Bach, Anglesey* (Cardiff, 1946). For a recent study of a bog burial, see I. M. Stead *et al.*, *Lindow Man: The Body in the Bog* (London, 1986).

Chapter 11. The Developed Celtic World

An introduction to the complex interactions between the Roman world and the Celtic north is provided in Barry Cunliffe, *Greeks, Romans and Barbarians: Spheres of*

Interaction (London, 1988). The importance of wine in the developing trading systems is considered in detail in Andre Tchernia, *Le Vin de l'Italie romaine* (Rome, 1986), and Fanette Laubenheimer, *Le Temps des amphores en Gaule* (Paris, 1990). The background to the early romanization of southern Gaul is given in Charles Ebel, *Transalpine Gaul: The Emergence of a Roman Province* (Leiden, 1976). The social changes in Gaulish society at this time are examined by Daphne Nash in 'Territory and State Formation in Central Gaul', D. Greene, C. Haselgrove, and M. Spriggs (eds.), *Social Organization and Settlement* (Oxford, 1978), 455–75. The complex history of relations between Rome and the kingdom of Noricum are described by Géza Alföldy in *Noricum* (London, 1974). The archaeology and protohistory of the Dacians is much less accessible, but brief treatments exist in E. Condurachi, *Romania* (London, 1967), and D. Berciu, *Daco-Romania* (Geneva, 1978). A more detailed study of social interactions is to be found in I. Glodariu, *Dacian Trade with the Hellenistic and Roman World* (Oxford, 1976). For a very broad overview of the protohistory of east Europe, see M. Shchukin, *Rome and the Barbarians in Central and Eastern Europe* (Oxford, 1989). The study of *oppida* has inspired a considerable literature. A readable, simplified account is provided by F. Audouze and O. Buchsenschutz, *Towns, Villages and Countryside of Celtic Europe, from the beginnings of the 2nd millennium to the end of the 1st century BC* (English edn., London, 1991). Other useful detailed studies include J. Collis, *Oppida: Earliest Towns North of the Alps* (Sheffield, 1984); O. H. Frey, *Die Bedeutung der Gallia Cisalpina für die Entstehung der Oppida-Kultur. Studien zu Siedlungsfragen der Latènezeit* (Marburg, 1984); O. Buchsenschutz, *Structures d'habitats et fortifications de l'Age du fer en France septentrionale* (Paris, 1984); and various specialist papers in Barry Cunliffe and R. T. Rowley (eds.), *Oppida: The Beginnings of Urbanization in Barbarian Europe* (Oxford, 1976). The most extensive excavation of an *oppidum* is that of Manching in southern Germany, published in a highly detailed multi-volume monograph series of which the first sets the scene: W. Krämer and F. Schubert, *Die Ausgrabungen in Manching 1955–1961. Einführung und Fundstellen-übersicht, Die Ausgrabungen in Manching 1* (Wiesbaden, 1970). There has been much theorizing about the origins and meaning of *oppida*. One of the more thoughtful of the recent considerations is Greg Woolf's paper 'Rethinking the Oppida', *Oxford Journal of Archaeology*, 12 (1993), 223–4.

Chapter 12. The Celts in Retreat

A number of excellent background histories exist dealing with the early stages of Roman contact and conquest. For Iberia: L. A. Curchin, *Roman Spain: Conquest and Assimilation* (London, 1991); S. J. Keay, *Roman Spain* (London, 1988); and J. Alarcão, *Portugal Romano* (Lisbon, 1974). For Gaul: J. F. Drinkwater, *Roman Gaul* (Beckenham, 1983); A. King, *Roman Gaul and Germany* (London, 1990); A. L. F. Rivet, *Gallia Narbonensis* (London, 1988); and E. M. Wightman, *Gallica Belgica* (London, 1985). Caesar's conquest of Gaul is dealt with in fine critical detail by C. Goudineau in *César et la Gaule* (Paris, 1990). For Britain: S. S. Frere, *Britannia: A History of Roman Britain* (3rd edn., London, 1987); and M. Millett, *The Romanization of Britain* (Cambridge, 1990). For the Rhine–Danube area: C. M. Wells, *The German Policy of Augustus* (Oxford, 1972); G. Alföldy, *Noricum* (London, 1974); and A. Mócsy, *Pannonia and Upper Moesia* (London, 1974). Together these easily accessible sources provide a full background to the main events using both historical and archaeological sources. Each provides bibliographies introducing the huge specialist literature.

Chapter 13. Celtic Survival

The best introduction to the survival of Celtic peoples and institutions is Nora Chadwick, *The Celts* (Harmondsworth, 1971), Myles Dillon and Nora Chadwick, *The Celtic Realms* (London, 1967), and Alwyn and Birley Rees, *Celtic Heritage: Ancient Traditions in Ireland and Wales* (London, 1961). For the most part these works deal with Ireland, Wales, and Scotland. For Brittany the most accessible sources are Nora Chadwick, *Early Brittany* (Cardiff, 1969); L. Fleuriot, *Les Origines de la Bretagne* (Paris, 1982); and A. Chédeville and H. Guillotel, *La Bretagne des saints et des rois V^e–Xe siècles* (Rennes, 1984). A taste of the quality of the surviving literary tradition is given by K. H. Jackson in *A Celtic Miscellany* (rev. edn., Harmondsworth, 1971).

Chronological Tables

Table 1

The history of the Celts
and related events

			Mediterranean		Italy
600 BC	c.600		Foundation of Massalia		
	c.560		Foundation of Alalia on Corsica		
	c.535		Battle of Alalia		
	c.530–520		Foundation of Spina and Adria		
	525		Etruscans at war with Cumae	c.508	End of Etruscan domination of Rome
500 BC					
	474		Etruscans beaten at Cumae		
	415–413		Athenian expedition against Syracuse		
400 BC				c.400	Celts invade Po Valley
				391	Celts at Clusium
				390/6	Battle of Allia: Celts take Rome
	335–327		Alexander conquers from Thrace to India	334	Rome signs peace treaty with Senones
	323		Death of Alexander		
300 BC				295	Celts defeated at Sentium
				285–282	Roman victory over Senones
	264–241		First Punic War	232	Roman settlement in territory of Senones
				225	Celtic force routed at Telamon
				224	Rome campaigns against Boii
	218–202		Second Punic War	222	Rome attacks Insubres
	206		The capture of Cádiz by the Romans	197	Cenomani sue for peace
200 BC				191	Rome defeats Boii
	149–146		Third Punic War		
	c.123		Romans found the Provincia		
	102		Defeat of Teutones at Aix-en-Provence		
	101		Defeat of Cimbri at Vercelli		
100 BC					
AD 100					

	Balkans and Greece		Asia Minor and the East		Western and Central Europe
380	Celts raid Illyria				
369–368	Celtic mercenaries in Greece				
335	Celts meet Alexander at the Danube				
325	Death of Alexander	323	Celtic embassy visits Alexander at Babylon		
298	Celts invade Thrace: defeated at Mt Haemus	278	Celts arrive in Asia Minor		
279	Celts sack Delphi	275	Victory of Antioch I over Galatae		
278–277	Celts migrate to Asia Minor	274	Celts in army of Ptolemy I in Egypt		
227	Celts at Gallipoli	c.250–240	Celts raid Aegean coastal towns of Asia Minor		
212	End of Celtic kingdom of Tylis	233–232	War between Attalus I and Galatae		
		218	Celts in service of Attalus II		
		217	Celts in battle of Raphia		
		190	Celts at battle of Magnesia		
		189	Romans beat Galatians at Olympus		
		167	Galatian attacks on Pergamene territory		
				c.123	Romans annex Gallia Narbonensis
114–113	Scordisci defeat C. Cato			122–121	Domitius Ahenobarbus routs Allobroges and Arverni
				113–101	Migration of Cimbri and Teutones
				106	Revolt of Volcae and Tectosages. Romans annex Tolosa (Toulouse)
		88	Mithridates IV slaughters Galatian leaders	58–51	Caesar campaigns in Gaul, Britain, and Germany
				44	Julius Caesar and Burebista assassinated
				27	Octavian becomes emperor
				15	Tiberius and Drusus in eastern Alps
				13–9	Tiberius in southern Pannonia. Illyricum becomes a province
				7	Victory monument at La Turbie
				AD 20	Revolt of Florus and Sacrovir
				43	Claudius invades Britain
				60	Rebellion of Boudica
				84	Battle of Mons Graupius

Table 2 Principal classical sources writing about the Celts

late 6th century BC	Hecataeus	Quoted by Avienus and Strabo
5th century BC	Herodotus	*Hist.* 2.33
429–347 BC	Plato	*Laws* 1.637d–e
384–322 BC	Aristotle	*Politics* 2.6.6
c.405–330 BC	Ephorus	Quoted in Strabo, *Geog.* 4.4.6
4th century BC	Ptolemy I	Quoted in Strabo, *Geog.* 7.3.8
c.378–305 BC	Theopompus	Quoted in Athenaeus, *Deipnosophistae* 10.443b–c
276 BC–c.196 BC	Eratosthenes	Quoted by Strabo
3rd century BC	Phylarchus	Quoted in Athenaeus, *Deipnosophistae* 4.105d–f
c.204–122 BC	Polybius	*Hist.* 2.14–33
c.135–c.50 BC	Poseidonius	Quoted by Athenaeus, Strabo and Diodorus Siculus
106–43 BC	Cicero	*De Divinatione* 1.41.90
100–44 BC	Julius Caesar	*De Bello Gallico, passim,* but especially 6.11–20
wrote c.60–30 BC	Diodorus Siculus	Quoting Poseidonius, *Hist.* 5.22–32
c.64 BC–AD 21	Strabo	Probably largely quoting Poseidonius, *Geog.* 4.1.13; 4.4.1–6; 7.2; 12.5.1
59 BC–AD 17	Livy	*Hist.* 5.33–48; 10.28; 23.24
wrote AD 37–50	Pomponius Mela	*De Sita Orbis* 3.2.18–19
AD 39–65	Lucan	*Pharsalia* 1.450–58
AD 23–79	Pliny	*Nat. hist.* 16.24; 24.103–4; 29.52; 30.13
c.AD 55–120	Tacitus	*Agricola, passim*
		Hist. 3.45; 5.54
		Annals 12.40; 14.30; 32, 35
late 2nd century AD	Pausanius	*Periegesis*
AD 155–230+	Dio Cassius	*Hist.* 62
3rd century AD	Arrianus Flavinus	*Anabasis of Alexander* 1.4.6–5.2
3rd century AD	Athenaeus	Quoting Poseidonius, *Deipnosophistae* 4.36–40; 6.49
c.AD 330–395	Ammianus Marcellinus	*Hist.* 15.9.4 and 8

Table 3 A concordance of frequently used archaeological terminology in western and central Europe, 1300 BC to the Roman era

		Central Europe	Switzerland	North France	Britain Roman Conquest	Art Styles
0	Roman	D3		Roman Conquest		
		D2			Late Iron Age	Late strict style
100		La Tène D1	La Tène III	Final La Tène		
		C2	IIb			
200	La Tène	La Tène C1	La Tène IIa	Middle La Tène	Middle Iron Age	Plastic style and sword style
300		B2	Ic	III		
		La Tène B1	Ib	II		Vegetal style
400		La Tène A	La Tène Ia	Early La Tène I	Early Iron Age	Early strict style
		D3	Hallstatt II	Hallstatt IIb		
500	Hallstatt	D2		Hallstatt IIa		
		Hallstatt D1				
600					Early Iron Age/ Llyn Fawr	
700		Hallstatt C	Hallstatt I	Hallstatt I		
		B3			Ewart Park/ Carps Tongue	
800					Ewart Park/ Blackmore	
900		B2				
		Hallstatt B1			Wilburton	
1000						
		A2			Penard II	
1100						
		Hallstatt A1			Penard I	
1200						
		Bronze D				
1300						

(left margin: La Tène / Hallstatt / Urnfield period (Late Bronze Age))

Map Section

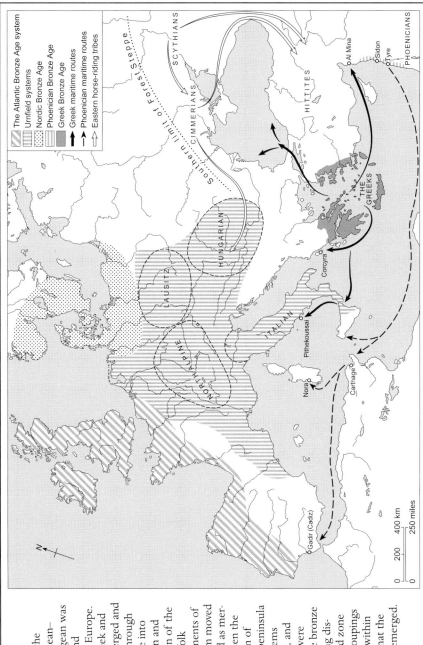

1. Europe, 1300–700 BC

The period that followed the breakdown of the Mycenaean–Minoan culture of the Aegean was a time of massive social and economic reformations in Europe. In the Mediterranean, Greek and Phoenician city-states emerged and extended their influence through colonies and ports-of-trade into the western Mediterranean and the Black Sea. In the region of the Pontic Steppe large-scale folk movements displaced segments of population, some of whom moved into Asia Minor to be used as mercenaries in conflicts between the Assyrians and the kingdom of Urartu. On the European peninsula three distinct cultural systems emerged: Atlantic, Nordic, and Urnfield. Copper and tin were extensively mined to make bronze which was traded over long distances. Within the Urnfield zone several distinct cultural groupings can be recognized. It was within the north Alpine culture that the Celtic language probably emerged.

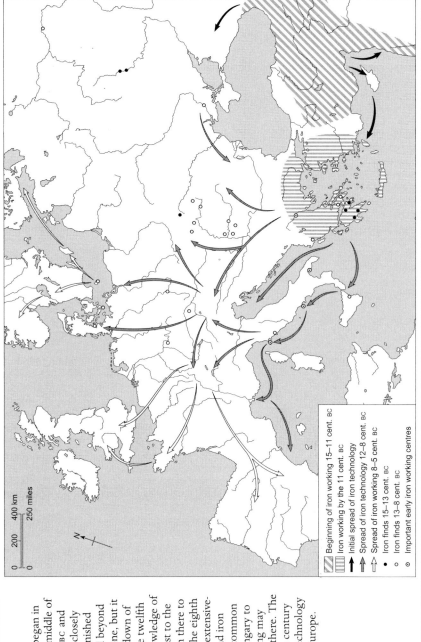

2. The spread of iron

The extraction of iron began in Asia Minor around the middle of the second millennium BC and was, for a long while, a closely guarded secret. A few finished objects were distributed beyond this early production zone, but it was not until the breakdown of the Hittite empire in the twelfth century BC that the knowledge of iron working spread, first to the Aegean region and from there to the rest of Europe. By the eighth century iron was being extensively worked in Etruria, and iron objects are sufficiently common in graves in eastern Hungary to suggest that iron working may have been in operation there. The latter part of the eighth century saw the spread of the technology to most of the rest of Europe.

0   200   400 km
0   250 miles

N

Beginning of iron working 15–11 cent. BC

Iron working by the 11 cent. BC

Initial spread of iron technology

Spread of iron technology 12–8 cent. BC

Spread of iron working 8–5 cent. BC

• Iron finds 15–13 cent. BC

○ Iron finds 13–8 cent. BC

◎ Important early iron working centres

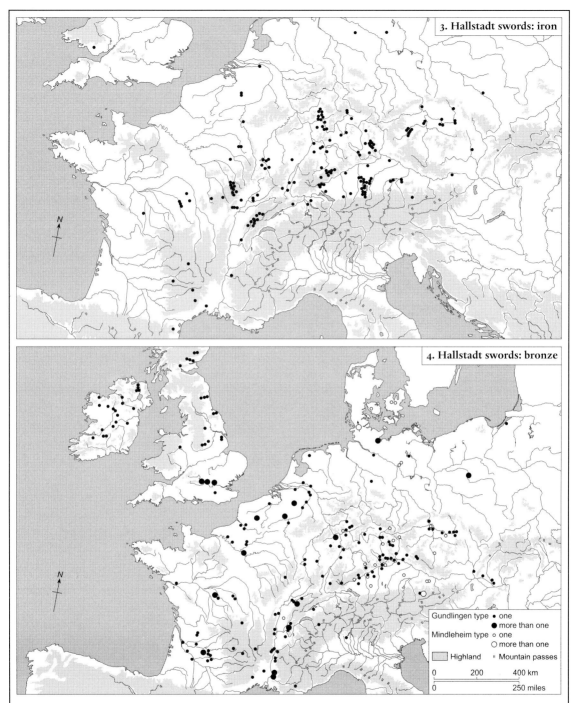

3 & 4. The distribution of long swords of iron and bronze in the seventh century BC

The Hallstatt C long sword evolved in middle Europe as the culmination of a long tradition of manufacturing. The most common type was the bronze Gundlingen sword, which was widely distributed and formed the model for local schools of swordsmiths to copy. The more elaborate bronze Mindleheim type had a more restricted distribution. Iron versions of the Hallstatt C sword developed in the late eighth and seventh centuries in this core region but spread quite widely through exchange. Possession of a sword was a symbol of warrior status.

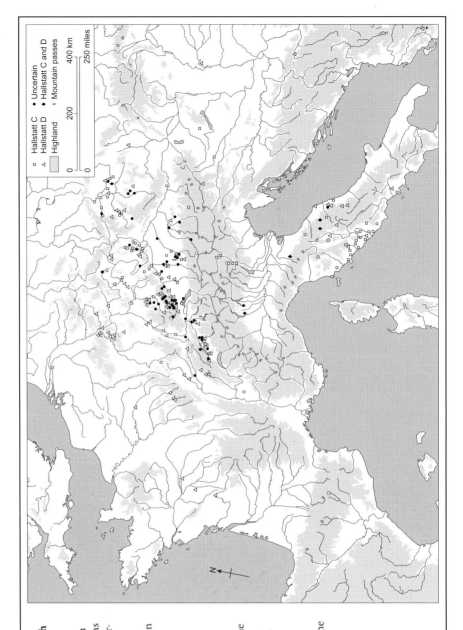

5. Wagon graves of the seventh and sixth centuries BC

In the Hallstatt C and D periods the élite of the middle European zone adopted the burial wagon as a symbol of status. The dead person was taken to the grave on a funerary vehicle which was buried with him or her, usually in a timber-lined pit beneath a barrow. The earliest burials of this kind occur in a comparatively restricted zone extending from southern Germany to Bohemia. The idea of the funerary cart goes back to the beginning of the late Bronze Age in the area, but influences from the east or from the Etruscan region may have encouraged the development of the fashion. In the Hallstatt D period the centre of the élite zone moved west and the concept of vehicle burial was more widely adopted.

In the map legend:
- Hallstatt C
- Hallstatt D
- Highland
- Uncertain
- Hallstatt C and D
- Mountain passes

0   200   400 km
0   250 miles

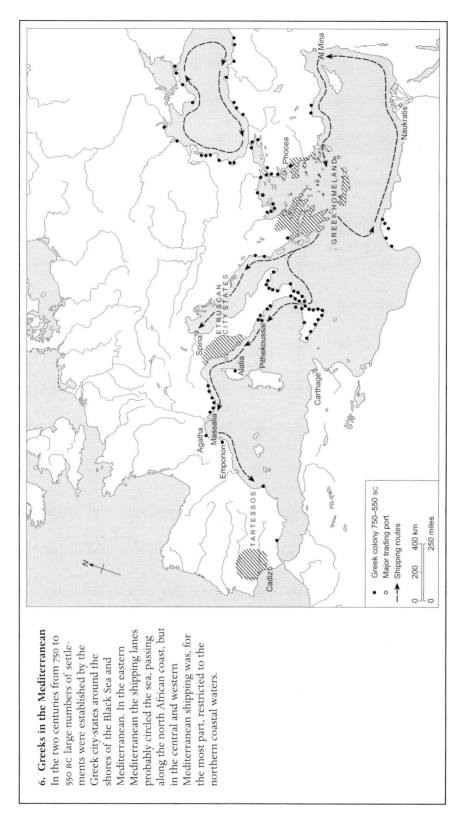

6. Greeks in the Mediterranean

In the two centuries from 750 to 550 BC large numbers of settlements were established by the Greek city-states around the shores of the Black Sea and Mediterranean. In the eastern Mediterranean the shipping lanes probably circled the sea, passing along the north African coast, but in the central and western Mediterranean shipping was, for the most part, restricted to the northern coastal waters.

Al Mina

Naukratis

Phocea

GREEK HOMELAND

ETRUSCAN CITY-STATES

Spina

Alalia

Pithekoussai

Agatha

Massalia

Carthage

Emporion

TARTESSOS

Cadiz

- Greek colony 750–550 BC
- o Major trading port
- Shipping routes

0   200   400 km
0   250 miles

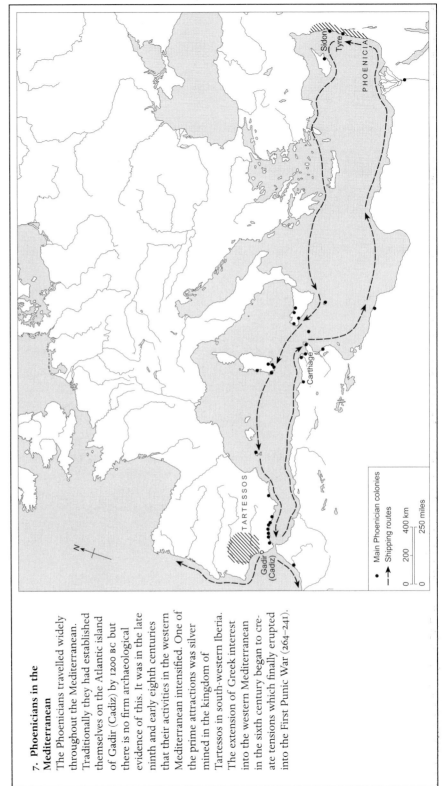

7. Phoenicians in the Mediterranean

The Phoenicians travelled widely throughout the Mediterranean. Traditionally they had established themselves on the Atlantic island of Gadir (Cadiz) by 1200 BC but there is no firm archaeological evidence of this. It was in the late ninth and early eighth centuries that their activities in the western Mediterranean intensified. One of the prime attractions was silver mined in the kingdom of Tartessos in south-western Iberia. The extension of Greek interest into the western Mediterranean in the sixth century began to create tensions which finally erupted into the First Punic War (264–241).

8. Etruscans in the Mediterranean

The Etruscan coastal cities were heavily involved in trade in the north-western Mediterranean, as the distribution of their characteristic black Bucchero pottery indicates. The development of Greek interests around the shores of southern France began to conflict with the traditional Etruscan zone particularly after c.540 BC. Etruscan attempts to develop a sphere of interest in southern Italy were rapidly halted by the growing power of the cities of Magna Grecia. Partly as a result of these constraints the Etruscans began to extend through the Apennines into the Po valley.

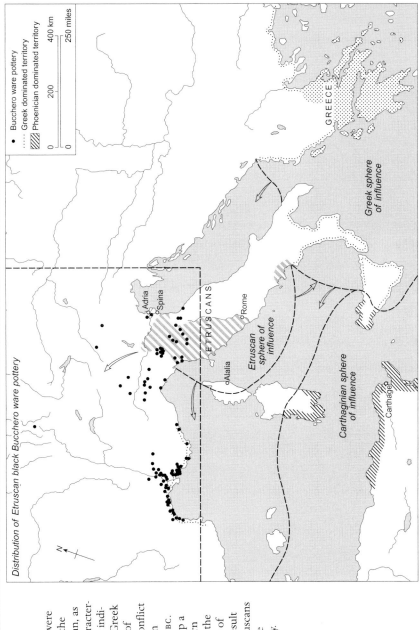

Distribution of Etruscan black Bucchero ware pottery

- Bucchero ware pottery
- Greek dominated territory
- Phoenician dominated territory

0   200   400 km
0   250 miles

GREECE

Greek sphere of influence

Adria
Spina

ETRUSCANS

Rome

Alalia

Etruscan sphere of influence

Carthaginian sphere of influence

Carthage

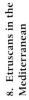

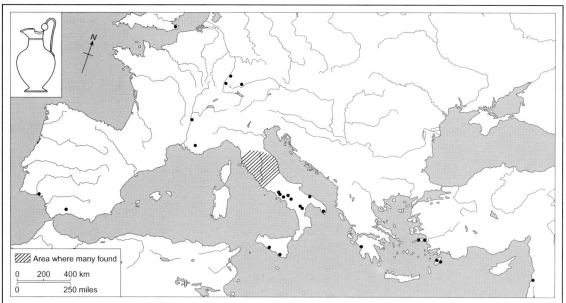

9. Rhodian flagons

Rhodian flagons, which were probably made in Greek workshops in southern Italy, were used for pouring wine. In the first half of the sixth century BC a number of them were used, possibly as gifts, in the trading relationships that were beginning to develop between the western Greek colonies and native communities in southern Spain and western central Europe.

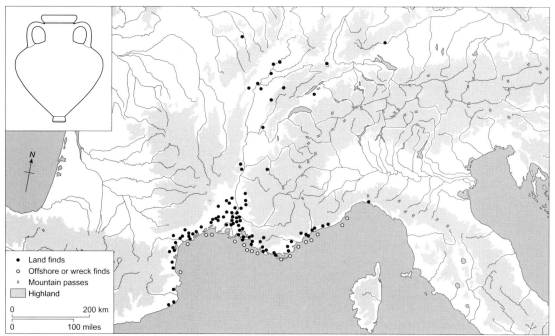

10. Massilliot wine amphorae

Wine manufactured in the Greek coastal zone of southern France was transported in distinctive amphorae. The distribution of sherds of sixth century BC amphorae in western central Europe indicates the zone receiving wine as a luxury product.

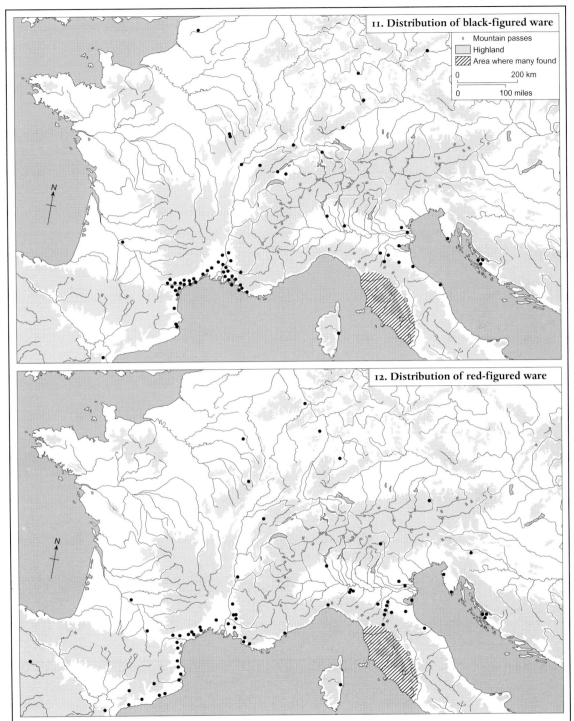

11 & 12. Attic black- and red-figured pottery

Greek pottery was traded extensively in the western Mediterranean. Two more distinctive types are the Attic black- and red-figured wares. Black-figured wares date broadly to the latter part of the sixth century BC, while red-figured wares were common in the fifth century. Their distribution in western central Europe reflects the 'chieftain' zone.

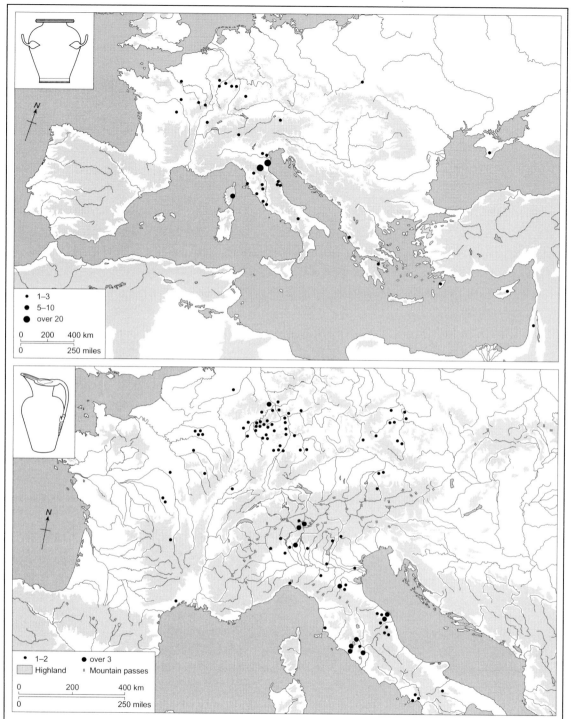

13 & 14. Etruscan bronze stamnoi and beaked flagons

Two distinctive Etruscan products are the bronze beaked flagon and the stamnos. Both were traded into western central Europe and are found in aristocratic burials mostly dating to the early La Tène period. The great concentration in the Rhine–Moselle area suggests that the Etruscans had established a special relationship with the élite of this region.

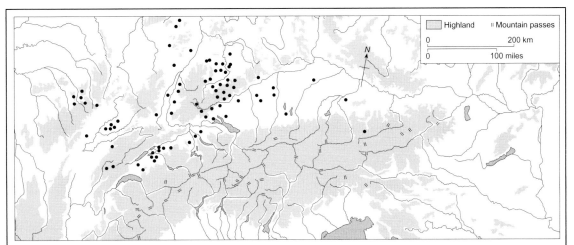

15. Gold

Gold was frequently found in the élite burials of western central Europe in the Hallstatt period. The distribution of gold provides an indication of the extent of the élite zone.

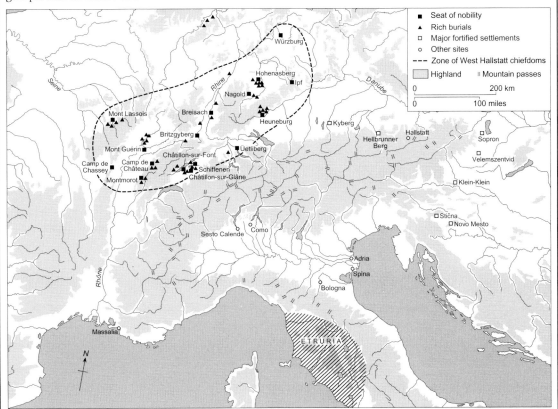

16. Centres of power

It is possible to recognize centres of power in western central Europe that existed during the late Hallstatt period (c.600–480 BC). These were invariably focused on strongly fortified hilltops in the vicinity of which rich burials usually clustered. During this period there was some fluctuation in the power of these 'seats of nobility' suggesting active, sometimes aggressive, competition. In the eastern Alpine region, while hillforts were built and maintained, there is no evidence of comparably rich burials or of arrays of Mediterranean luxury goods or of gold used in burial contexts.

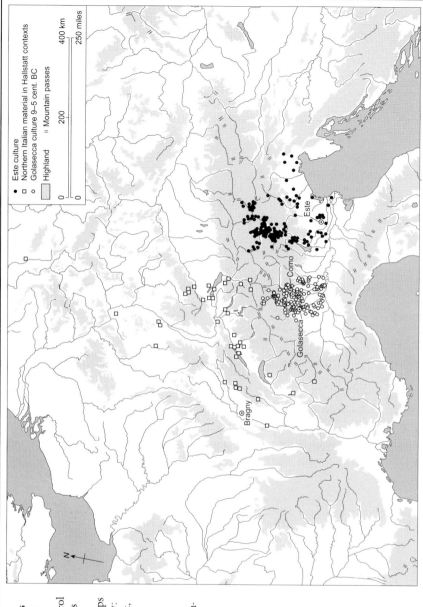

17. Golasecca and Este cultures
The communities who occupied the southern flank of the Alps were in a prime position to control the routes between the Etruscans and the Celtic zone of western central Europe. Two major groups can be identified archaeologically: the Golasecca culture in the west, and the Este culture in the east. The distribution of small objects of northern Italian manufacture north of the Alps indicates the principal focus of the trading contacts.

• Este culture
▫ Northern Italian material in Hallstatt contexts
○ Golasecca culture 9–5 cent. BC
▨ Highland   ‖ Mountain passes

0   200   400 km
0   250 miles

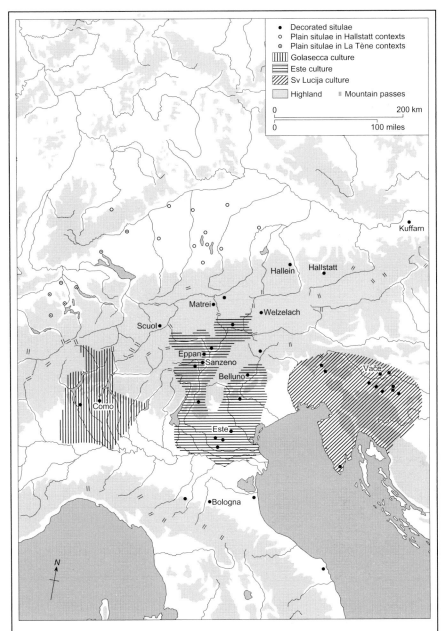

18. Bronze situlae

Bronze situlae (buckets) were extensively used for feasting and in burials. Many of those made in northern Italy and Slovenia were elaborately decorated with figured scenes.

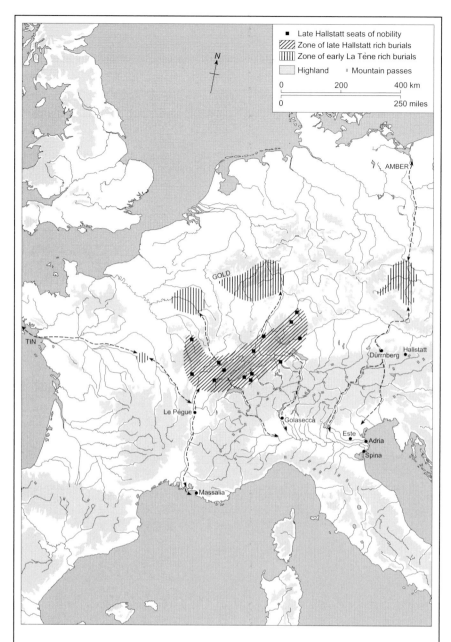

19. Europe in the fifth century BC
In the late Hallstatt period a zone of chiefdoms existed stretching across the northern Alpine zone from Burgundy to southern Germany. This zone was in contact with the Mediterranean principally along the Rhône route and through the Alpine passes. By the middle of the fifth century four separate regions around the northern fringes of the old Hallstatt zone had begun to develop rich innovating chiefdoms. Here, particularly in the Marne and Moselle regions, a new art style, characterizing the early La Tène culture, began to emerge.

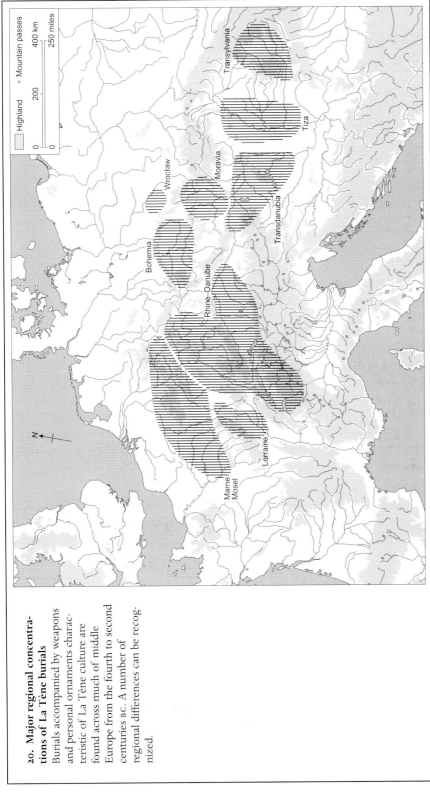

20. Major regional concentrations of La Tène burials
Burials accompanied by weapons and personal ornaments characteristic of La Tène culture are found across much of middle Europe from the fourth to second centuries BC. A number of regional differences can be recognized.

Highland " Mountain passes

0 200 400 km
0 250 miles

Transylvania

Tiza

Wrocław

Moravia

Bohemia

Transdanubia

Rhine–Danube

Lorraine

Marne
Mosel

N

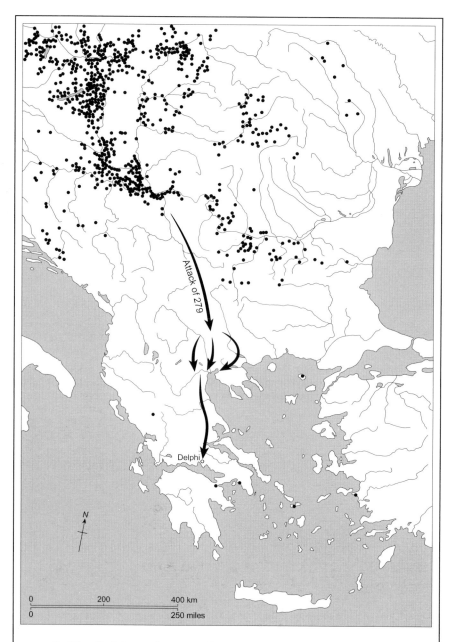

21. La Tène finds in south-eastern Europe
By the beginning of the third century BC the La Tène culture had spread to the
middle and lower Danube valley, with a particular concentration in the middle
Danube and Sava region. It was probably from here that, in 279, the attack on
Delphi was launched. In spite of the size of the raiding force and the disruption
which it caused to the Greek states, it is unrecognizable in the archaeological evidence. The map, showing finds of La Tène material, vividly makes the point that
major historical events need leave no archaeological trace.

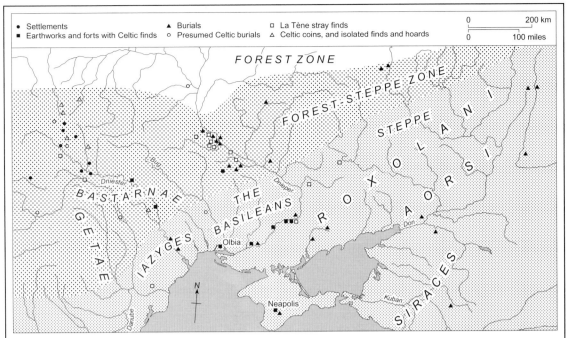

22. Celtic finds in the northern Pontic Steppe

In the latter part of the first millennium BC the Pontic Steppe was an area with a complex mix of populations among whom there was much mobility. The quantity of La Tène material found, particularly in the west of this region, suggests that some Celtic groups may have moved to settle in Moldova and to raid and serve as mercenaries over a wider area.

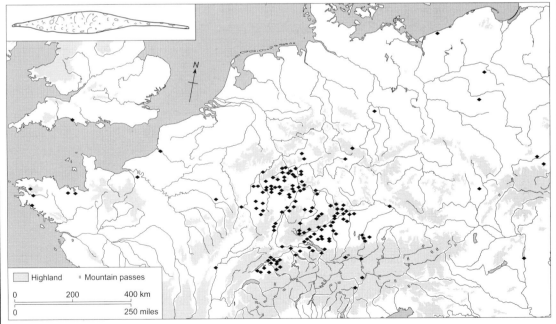

23. Double pyramidal ingots of iron

The production of iron intensified during the second and first centuries BC. Iron was made into ingots of various kinds (of which the double pyramidal form is one) for trade and exchange. By drawing out the ends of the bar into thin rods the smith was physically demonstrating the quality of the iron since impurities would cause visible cracking.

307

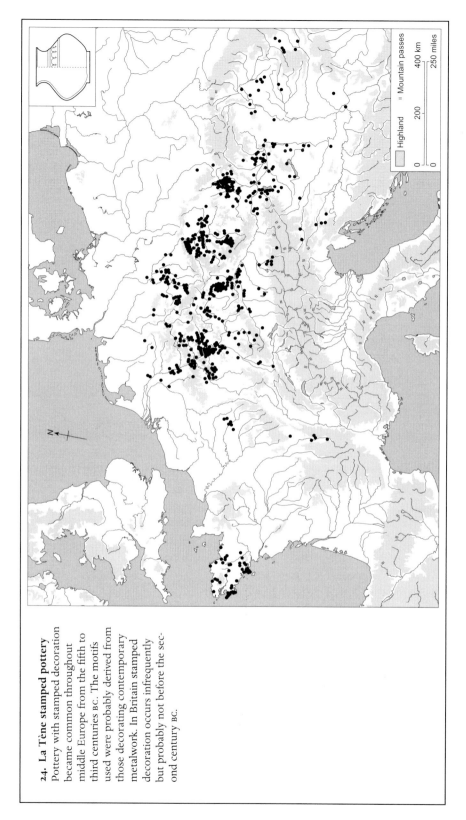

24. La Tène stamped pottery
Pottery with stamped decoration became common throughout middle Europe from the fifth to third centuries BC. The motifs used were probably derived from those decorating contemporary metalwork. In Britain stamped decoration occurs infrequently but probably not before the second century BC.

Highland

■ = Mountain passes

0   200   400 km

0   250 miles

25. Vehicle burials of the middle and late La Tène period
Two-wheeled vehicles pulled by a pair of horses were popular in much of the Celtic world. Lightly constructed versions served as war chariots, others were used in the funerary ritual though only in certain rather restricted areas as the map shows.

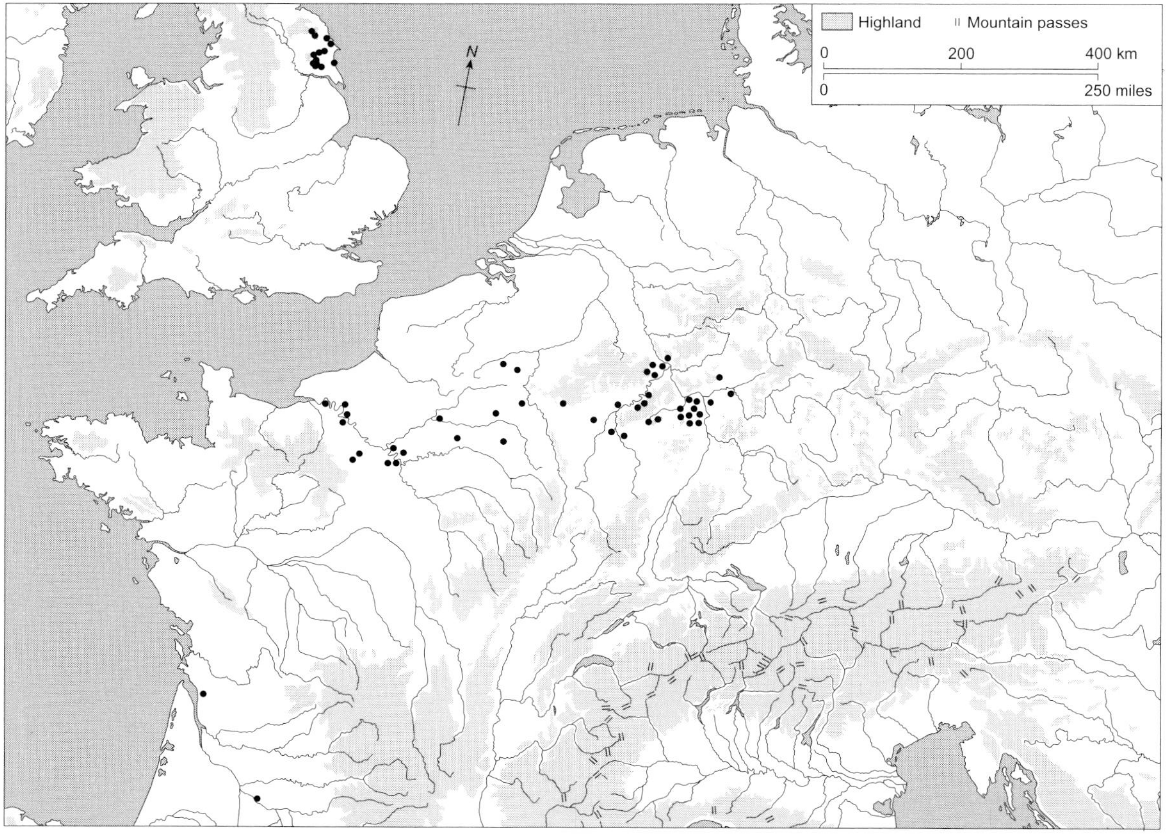

Highland

‖ Mountain passes

0   200   400 km

0   250 miles

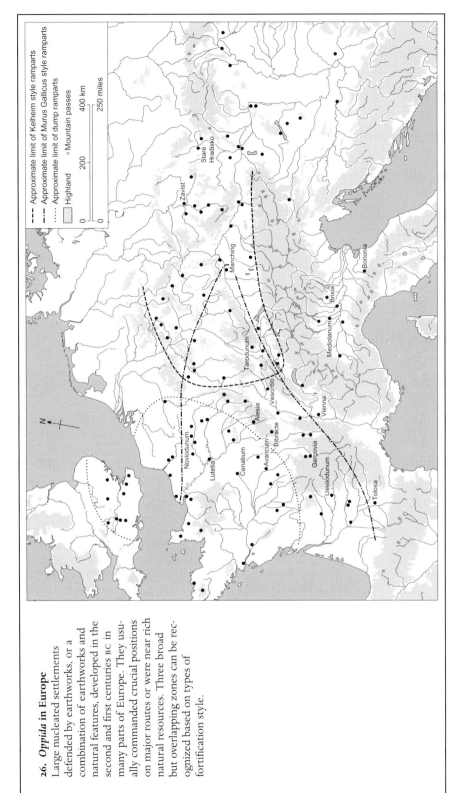

26. Oppida in Europe

Large nucleated settlements defended by earthworks, or a combination of earthworks and natural features, developed in the second and first centuries BC in many parts of Europe. They usually commanded crucial positions on major routes or were near rich natural resources. Three broad but overlapping zones can be recognized based on types of fortification style.

Approximate limit of Kelheim style ramparts

Approximate limit of Murus Gallicus style ramparts

Approximate limit of dump ramparts

Highland   " Mountain passes

0   200   400 km

0   250 miles

N

Staré Hradisko
Závist
Manching
Tarodunum
Vesontio
Alesia
Bibracte
Avaricum
Cenabum
Noviodunum
Lutetia
Gergovia
Vienna
Uxellodunum
Tolosa
Brixia
Mediolanum
Bononia

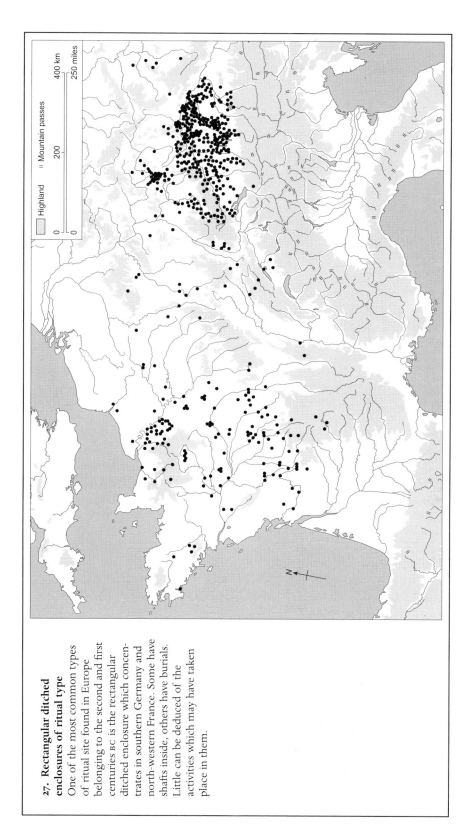

27. Rectangular ditched enclosures of ritual type
One of the most common types of ritual site found in Europe belonging to the second and first centuries BC is the rectangular ditched enclosure which concentrates in southern Germany and north-western France. Some have shafts inside, others have burials. Little can be deduced of the activities which may have taken place in them.

Highland ‖ Mountain passes

0   200   400 km

0   250 miles

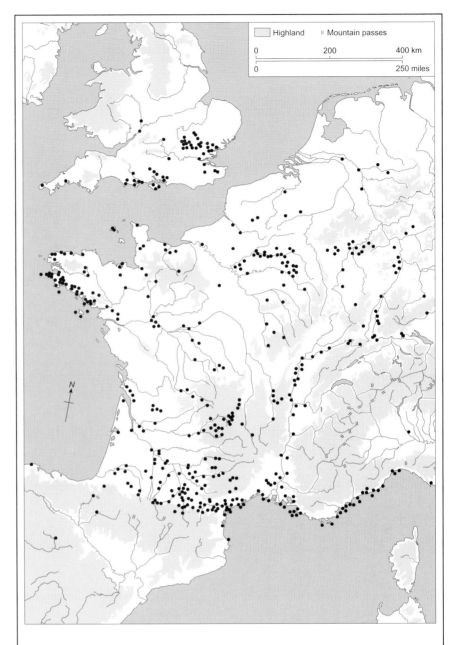

28. Dressel 1 amphorae
Amphorae were commonly used to transport wine. After the middle of the second century BC there developed an extensive trade in wine between the producers of northern Italy and the distributors along the southern coast of France who dealt with the Gauls further inland. Two characteristic types of amphorae mapped here, Dressel types 1A and 1B, emphasize the major trade routes in operation between c.150 BC and AD 10. The importance of rivers and the Atlantic are clearly apparent.

29. The movements of the Cimbri and Teutones

The migration of two northern tribes, the Cimbri and the Teutones, caused much disruption in Europe between c.114 and 101 BC. Travelling so far and over such a long period, it is highly likely that the migrating groups gathered followers as they progressed. After beating Roman armies on several occasions, they were eventually defeated by Marius in 102 and 101, removing what was widely perceived to be a serious threat to Rome itself.

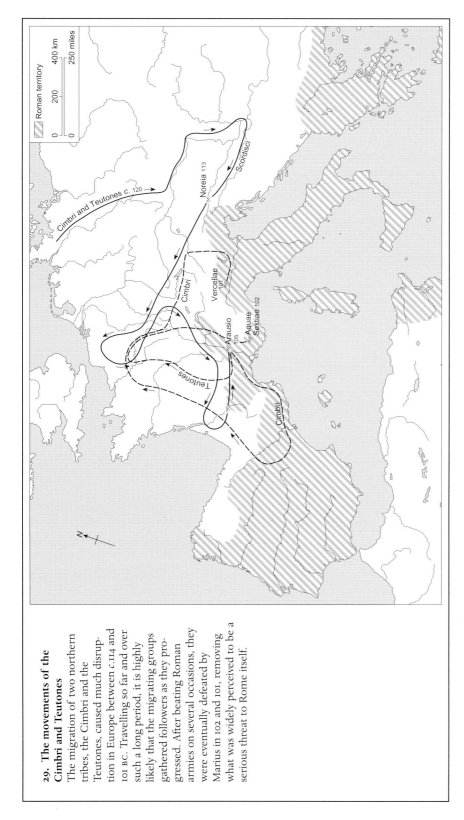

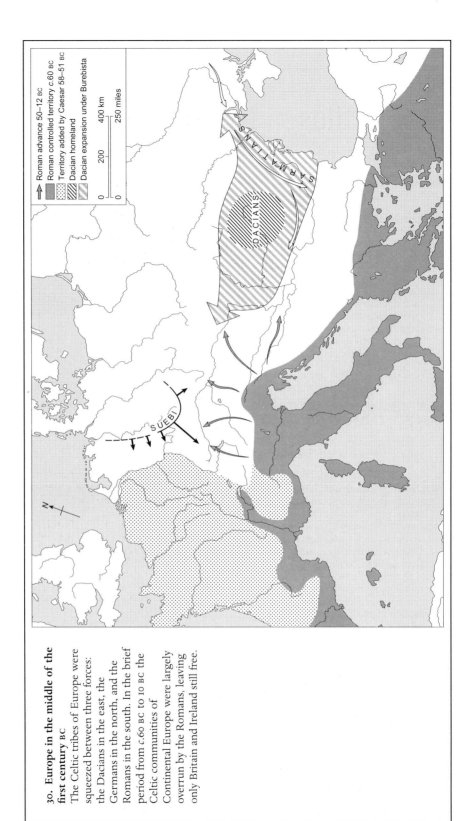

30. Europe in the middle of the first century BC

The Celtic tribes of Europe were squeezed between three forces: the Dacians in the east, the Germans in the north, and the Romans in the south. In the brief period from c.60 BC to 10 BC the Celtic communities of Continental Europe were largely overrun by the Romans, leaving only Britain and Ireland still free.

Roman advance 50–12 BC
Roman controlled territory c.60 BC
Territory added by Caesar 58–51 BC
Dacian homeland
Dacian expansion under Burebista

0   200   400 km
0   250 miles

SARMATIANS

DACIANS

SUEBI

N

Illustration Sources

The editor and publishers wish to thank the following who have kindly given permission to reproduce the illustrations on the following pages:

2 Museo Nazionale, Rome/Alinari
3 Staatliche Museen Antikensammlung Preussischer Kulturbesitz, Berlin
5 John Speed, *Historie* (1611)
6 Raphael Holinshed, *Chronicles* (1578)
7 William Stukeley, *Stonehenge* (1740)
8 Musée d'Alesia, Société des Sciences Historiques et Naturelles de Sémur-en-Auxois/E. Rabeisen
9 Mansell Collection
10 Agence Roger-Viollet
11 Napoleon III, *Historie de Jules César* (1865)
12 Napoleon III, *Historie de Jules César* (1865)
13 Musée des Antiquités Nationales, Saint-Germain-en-Laye/Lauros-Giraudon
14 A. Forestier, *The Glastonbury Lake Village* (1911)/Somerset Local History Library, Taunton Castle Museum
15 Musée Calvet, Avignon
16 Museo Gregoriano Vaticano, Rome
18 Museo Civico Arqueologico Giovio, Como/Soprintendenza Archeologica di Milano
19 Prähistorische Abteilung der Naturhistorisches Museum, Wien
21 Society of Antiquaries, London
22 Prähistorische Abteilung der Naturhistorisches Museum, Wien
23 Paul Vouga, *La Tène* (1923)
24 Paul Vouga, *La Tène* (1923)
25 Paul Vouga, *La Tène* (1923)
27 J. Filip, *Keltové ve střední Europě* (1956)
28 Léon Morel, *Album de la Campagne Souterraine ... dans la Marne* (1898)/Bibliotèque d'Art et d'Archéologie, Fondation Jaques Doucet, Paris
29 Peabody Museum, Harvard University
33 Everhard-Karls-Universät, Tübingen; Institut für Ur- und Frühgeschichte
35 Everhard-Karls-Universät, Tübingen; Institut für Ur- und Frühgeschichte/Fischer
36 Historisches Museum, Berne/S. Rebsamen
38 Landesdenkmalampt Badem-Württemberg, Stuttgart
39 Everhard-Karls-Universät, Tübingen; Institut für Ur- und Frühgeschichte
40 Everhard-Karls-Universät, Tübingen; Institut für Ur- und Frühgeschichte
42 Everhard-Karls-Universät, Tübingen; Institut für Ur- und Frühgeschichte
43 Luftbildarchiv A. Brugger/Schnepf, Stuttgart
45 Stuart Piggott, *Ancient Europe* (1984); courtesy of Edinburgh University Press
46 J. Biel, *Der Keltenfürst von Hochdorf* (Stuttgart)
47 J. Biel, *Der Keltenfürst von Hochdorf* (Stuttgart)
48 Württembergisches Landesmuseum, Stuttgart/Landesdenkmalampt Baden-Württemberg; Archäeologisches Denkmalpflege, Stuttgart
49 Württembergisches Landesmuseum, Stuttgart
50 Württembergisches Landesmuseum, Stuttgart
51 Württembergisches Landesmuseum, Stuttgart/Landesdenkmalampt Baden-Württemberg; Archäeologisches Denkmalpflege, Stuttgart
52 Württembergisches Landesmuseum, Stuttgart/Landesdenkmalampt Baden-Württemberg; Archäeologisches Denkmalpflege, Stuttgart
54 Museo Civico Arqueologico, Bologna
59 Magyar Nemzeti Múzeum, Budapest
60 Musée de Saint-Raymond, Toulouse/J. Rouge
61 Magyar Nemzeti Múzeum, Budapest
63 British Museum
65 Mortimer Wheeler, *Maiden Castle* (1943), Pl.CIV A/Society of Antiquaries/RCHM/National Monuments Record, Crown©
66 RCHM/National Monuments Record Air Photographs, Crown©
67 Mortimer Wheeler, *Maiden Castle* (1943)
68 Giraudon
69 Nationalmuseet, Copenhagen
70 National Museum of Ireland, Dublin
71 British Museum
72 (*above*) Museul National de Istorie a Romäniei, Bucharest
72 (*below*) British Museum/Werner

Forman Archive
73 Nationalmuseet, Copenhagen
74 Biblioteque Nationale, Paris
75 Ashmolean Museum, Oxford
78 Nationalmuseet Copenhagen
79 Musée Cantonal d'Archéologie, Neuchâtel, Switzerland
80 British Museum
81 British Museum/Werner Forman Archive
82 Musée des Jacobins, Morlaix
83 Musée des Antiquités Nationales, Saint-Germain-en-Laye/RMN Paris
85 National Museum of Ireland, Dublin/Werner Forman Archive
86 Museum Carolino Augusteum, Salzburg
87 Bernisches Historisches Museum, Berne
88 British Museum
89 *The Gauls: Celtic Antiquities from France* (British Museum Pubs.), fig. 4
90 Historisches Museum der Pfalz, Speyer
91 Schweizerisches Landesmuseum, Zurich
93 Bibliotèque Nationale, Paris
96 Württembergisches Landesmuseum, Stuttgart/Landesdenkmalampt Baden-Württemberg, Archäeologisches Denkmalpflege, Stuttgart
97 Rheinisches Landesmuseum, Bonn
98 Landesbildstelle Württemberg, Stuttgart
100 Württembergisches Landesmuseum, Stuttgart/Landesdenkmalampt Baden-Württemberg, Archäeologisches Denkmalpflege, Stuttgart
102 Musée des Antiquités Nationales, Saint-Germain-en-Laye/RMN Paris
103 Musée des Antiquités Nationales, Saint-Germain-en-Laye/RMN Paris
104 Institute of Archaeology, Oxford
105 Institute of Archaeology, Oxford
109 Museu Nacional de Arqueologia e Etnologia, Lisbon/Arquivo Nacional de Fotografia
110 Dr G. R. Zapatero
112 Museu Nacional de Arqueologia e Etnologia, Lisbon/Arquivo Nacional de Fotografia
114 Museo Arqueológico Nacional, Madrid
115 Museo de Prehistórico de Valencia
116 Museo Municipal de Córdoba
117 Museo Arqueológico Nacional, Madrid
119 Museo Municipal de Córdoba
120 National Museum of Ireland, Dublin
121 British Museum
129 Musée Nationale d'Archéologie, Saint-Germain-en-Laye/Werner Forman Archive
130 University of Cambridge Collection of Air Photographs
132 Werner Forman Archive
134 Wisbech & Fenland Museum, Cambridgeshire

135 Ashmolean Museum, Oxford
136 British Museum
137 National Museum of Scotland, Edinburgh
138 University of Cambridge Collection of Air Photographs
140 Prof. Dr Armando Coelho Ferreira da Silva, University of Porto, Portugal
141 Vladimir Vitanov Agency USA
144 Narodnija Archeologičeski Museg, Sofia
146 Ashmolean Museum, Oxford
147 Dr Stephen Mitchell, University of Swansea, Wales
148 Service des Antiquités, Cairo; courtesy of Prof. Stuart Piggott/Edinburgh University Press
149 British Museum
150 Roman Baths Museum, Bath
151 Musée de la Civilisation Gallo-Romaine, Lyon/Christian Thoc
152 Musée de la Civilisation Gallo-Romaine, Lyons/Christian Thoc
153 British Museum
154 Prof. Barry Cunliffe
156 Rheinisches Landesmuseum, Bonn
157 Prof. Barry Cunliffe
158 Musée Archéologique de Dijon/Erich Lessing
159 Musée d'Archéologie et d'Histoire, Geneva
160 Bayerisches Landesamt für Denkmalpflege, Munich/Otto Braasch, archiv no: 8134/006, 23 Dec 1984
162 Landesdenkmalampt Baden-Württemberg, Archäeologisches Denkmalpflege, Stuttgart
163 Musée d'Archéologie Mediterranéenne, Marseilles/Piero Baguzzi
164 Musée d'Archéologie Mediterranéenne, Marseilles
165 Musée des Antiquités Nationales, Saint-Germain-en-Laye/RMN
169 Cambridge University Collection of Air Photographs
170 Cambridge University Collection of Air Photographs
174 Prof. Barry Cunliffe
177 Musée de Saint-Raymond, Toulouse
179 Dr René Goguey, Talant
181 Römisch-Germanische Kommission; courtesy: Prähistorische Staatssamm-lung, Munich/Franz Schubert
185 Society of Antiquaries, London
190 Museo Farnese, Rome/Alinari
193 Agence Roger Viollet
194 Dr René Goguey, Talant
201 English Heritage/Skyscan
202 National Museum of Ireland, Dublin

Picture research by Sara Waterson

Index

The page numbers of black and white illustrations are given in *italic*; colour plates are indicated by the number of the page opposite in *italic*, followed by (Pl).

see also France
Geneva 199, *200*, 236
Genthe, Hermann 36
Germanic tribes 221–3, 237–8, *238*, 242, 250, 261–2, 263
Germany:
 and Hallstatt culture 52–64
 and La Tène culture 63–5
 Rhineland 75, 79
 sacred sites 200, *201*
 sculpture 126, *127*
 see also Kelheim; Manching; Waldalgesheim
Glastonbury *17*, 130
goddesses 26, 185–7, 199, 255
 triple 187, *187*
gods 184–8
 offerings to 155, 194–7
 shape-shifting 184
Goidelic, *see* Q-Celtic
Golasecca culture 51, 62, 65, 66, 70–2
gold 113, 134, 135, 149, 150, 165, 221
 buffer-headed torcs 121
 coinage 131
 as gauge of wealth 73
 in Hallstatt burials 57
 hoards 195–6, *196*
 Moselle art 117
 see also Erstfeld rings; metals; Snettisham gold
'Golden Age' 8
Gorsedd 12
Goulvars 156
Gournay-sur-Aronde 202, *204*, 261
Grächwil 53, *53*
Graeco-Roman historians 1–10, 20, 68–9, 91–3
 on Iberia 136–7
 see also individual writers
Grafenbühl burial 63, 64
graphite 228
Great Hungarian Plain 47, 48, 78–9, 80, 86, 170, 250
Greece:
 800–650 BC 44–6
 650–450 BC 48–9, 50, 51
 and Asia Minor 171, 172
 Celtic invasion of 5, 7, 81–2
 and Celtic migrations 80–2
 'Dark Ages' 40
 and eastern Europe 168, 169, 170, 171
 and Iberia 134, 135
 Persian Wars 50
 and raids 88
 see also Aegean region
groves 197–8
Gundestrup cauldron 98, 99, *103*, 125

Hallstatt:
 excavations 28, *28*, 29, 31, 32, 35, 36 (Pl.)
Hallstatt culture 37, 43, 45, 78, 271, *271*
 chronological divisions 32, 33, 51–2
 'C' 47–8, *64*, 150–1
 'D' 151
 'D1' 52–3, 64
 'D2–3' 53–64, *64*, 65, 66
 decline 66–7
Hannibal 104, 212
Hawkes, Christopher 17
Hawkes, Jacquetta 19
Hayling Island 204, 205, *205*, 259, 261
head, importance of 127–8, 209–10
 see also art, head motifs
Heathrow ambulatory 205, *205*
Hecataeus of Miletus 3
Heidelberg head 126, *127*
Heidengraben 229
Helden disc 125
helmets *85* (Pl.), *98*, 98, 112, 117, *149* (Pl.)
 jockey-cap 119–21
Helvetii 89–90, 223, 224, 228, 231
Hengistbury Head 219–20, 229
Heracles 4
Herodotus 3, 42, 49, 91, 155
 on Iberia 136
 on Scythians 170
Heuneburg 53, *54*, 55, 57, 61, 63
Hieronymus of Cardia 81, 91
Hildebrant, Hans 32
hill-forts 44, 164
 British 162–3, *164*, 165
 Hallstatt 56, 57, 61, 63–4
 Iberian 165–6
 see also Danebury; Heuneburg; Maiden Castle
Himilco 150
Hirschlanden 63, *63*, 126
Histoire de Jules César 13, *14*, 15
Hittites 40
Hjortspring 96, *97*, 195, 199
Hochdorf 57, *59*, *60–1*, 62, 63
Hohenasperg 63–4
Hohmichele burial *52*, 53
Holinshed, Raphael 11
Holzgerlingen statue 126, *127*
Holzhausen 200
Homer 40, 41, 169
horse cultures 41–2, 44, 45, 47–8, 78–9, 123, 170, 250
 see also Hallstatt culture
hospitality 73, 107, 137
hostages 108
Hounslow helmets *85* (Pl.)

Hubert, Henri 36
Hungary 43, 47
 art 119, 121–2, 123, *123*, 129
 see also Great Hungarian Plain
Hyperboreans 184

Iapodes 221, 237, 249
Iberia 3, 4, 9, 16, 46, 133–44
 archaeology 140–2
 background 133–6
 Bronze Age 149, *150*
 contemporary sources 136–7
 early Celts 139–40
 expansion of culture 142–3
 Irish settlers in 266
 language/place-names 16, 21, 24, 134, *137*, 137–8, 139, 141, 142, 155
 north-west 165–7
 and Rome 107, 143–4, 166–7, 212, 213, 235, 249
 and trade 42, 134
 see also Numantia
Iceni 254, 255, 258
'Iernè' 3, 146
Illyria 80
Illyricum 247, 250
Imbolc 189
Indre, *see* Levroux
Indutiomarus 108
Insubres 71, 72, 77, 78, 212
Interceltic Congresses 16
International Congress of Prehistoric Anthropology and Archaeology (1871) 32
invasionist theories 16–17
Ionians 41, 45
Ipf 56
Ireland 15, 20, 104, 105, 109, 145–6
 800–200 BC 150, 151
 AD 100–500, 256–7, 260
 bronze work 114, *114*
 Clonoura shield *97*, 98
 epic narratives 25–7, 109, 257, 266
 language 22, 25, 146, 155–6
 law texts 27, 109, 266
 migrants in Iberia 266
 post-6th century isolation 154, 155–6
 raids on Britain 262, 263
 religion 185–7, 189, 192, 199
 sacred sites *205*, 205–8, 256
 settlements 159–60
 Vikings and Normans in 266
iron:
 art 115, *115*, *124*, 124–5
 from Noricum 218
 production 40
Iron Age 43